SHONEN JUMP MANGA

Shaman King

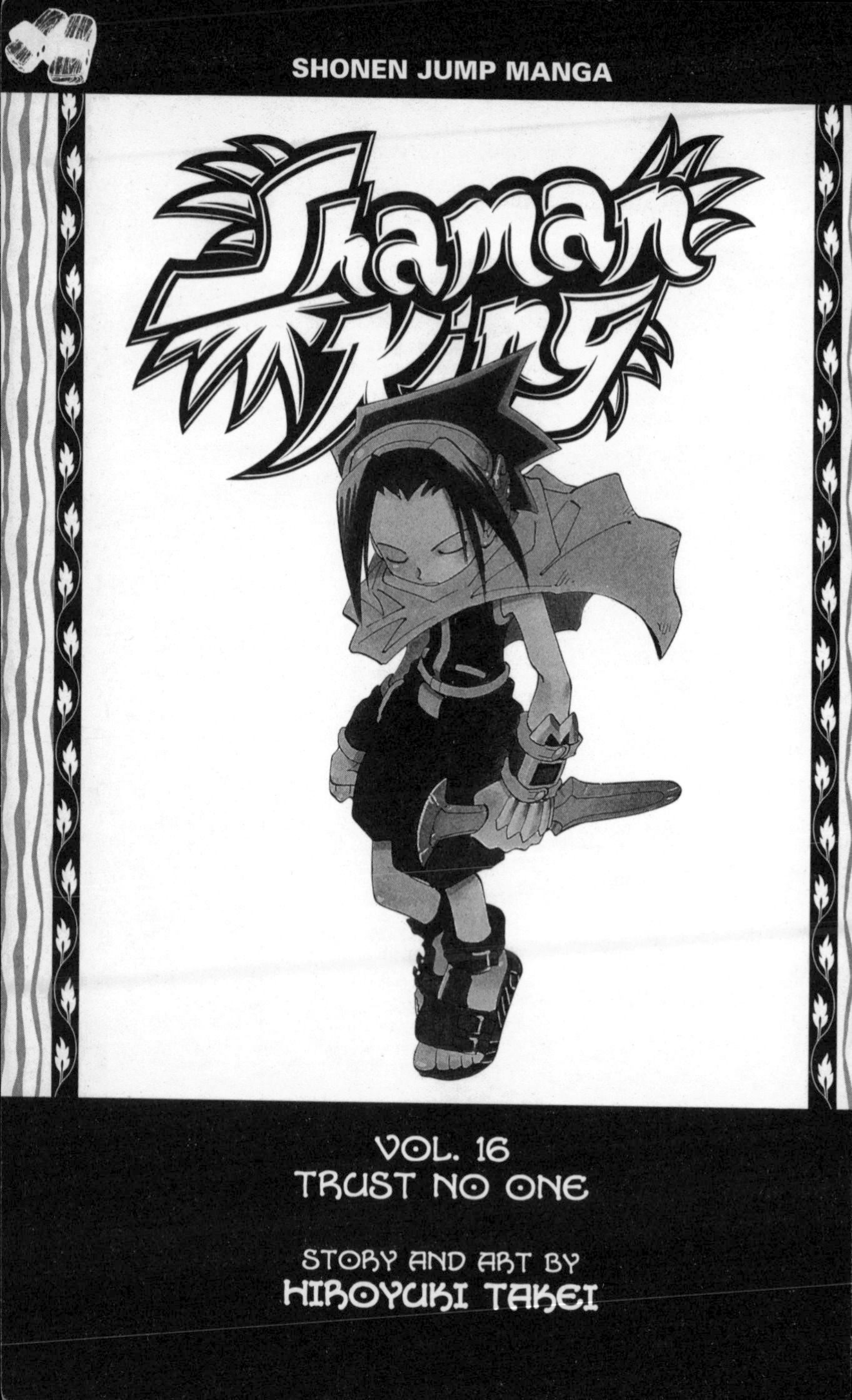

VOL. 16

TRUST NO ONE

STORY AND ART BY

HIROYUKI TAKEI

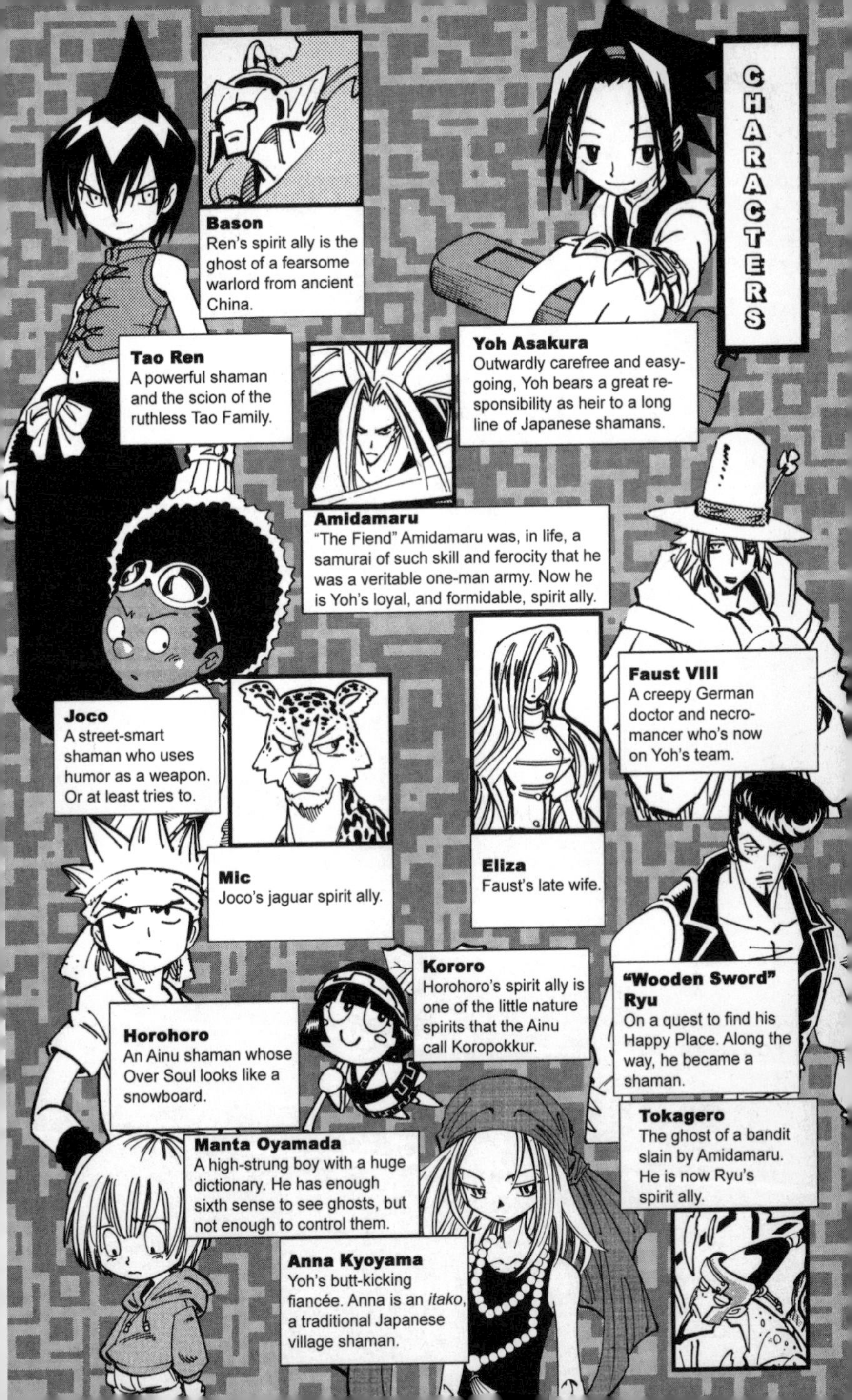
CHARACTERS
Bason
Ren's spirit ally is the ghost of a fearsome warlord from ancient China.
Yoh Asakura
Outwardly carefree and easy-going, Yoh bears a great responsibility as heir to a long line of Japanese shamans.
Tao Ren
A powerful shaman and the scion of the ruthless Tao Family.
Amidamaru
"The Fiend" Amidamaru was, in life, a samurai of such skill and ferocity that he was a veritable one-man army. Now he is Yoh's loyal, and formidable, spirit ally.
Faust VIII
A creepy German doctor and necromancer who's now on Yoh's team.
Joco
A street-smart shaman who uses humor as a weapon. Or at least tries to.
Mic
Joco's jaguar spirit ally.
Eliza
Faust's late wife.
Kororo
Horohoro's spirit ally is one of the little nature spirits that the Ainu call Koropokkur.
"Wooden Sword" Ryu
On a quest to find his Happy Place. Along the way, he became a shaman.
Horohoro
An Ainu shaman whose Over Soul looks like a snowboard.
Tokagero
The ghost of a bandit slain by Amidamaru. He is now Ryu's spirit ally.
Manta Oyamada
A high-strung boy with a huge dictionary. He has enough sixth sense to see ghosts, but not enough to control them.
Anna Kyoyama
Yoh's butt-kicking fiancée. Anna is an *itako*, a traditional Japanese village shaman.

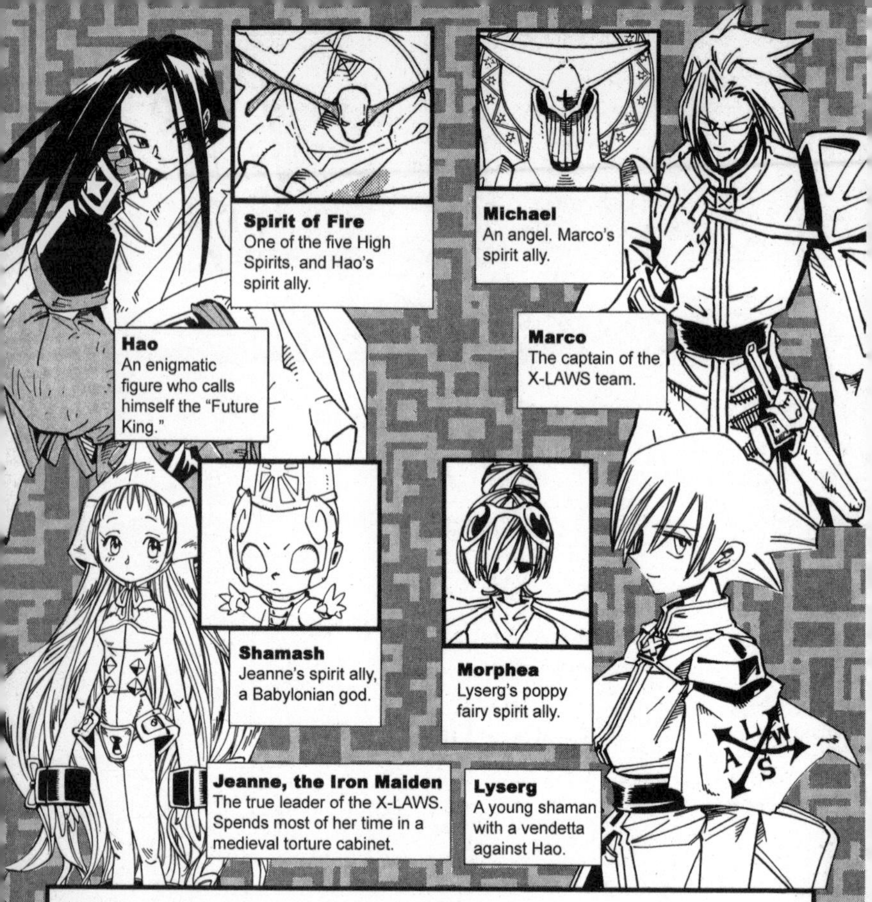
Michael
An angel. Marco's spirit ally.
Marco
The captain of the X-LAWS team.
Spirit of Fire
One of the five High Spirits, and Hao's spirit ally.
Hao
An enigmatic figure who calls himself the "Future King."
Morphea
Lyserg's poppy fairy spirit ally.
Lyserg
A young shaman with a vendetta against Hao.
Shamash
Jeanne's spirit ally, a Babylonian god.
Jeanne, the Iron Maiden
The true leader of the X-LAWS. Spends most of her time in a medieval torture cabinet.

THE STORY THUS FAR

Yoh Asakura not only sees dead people, he talks and fights with them, too. That's because Yoh is a shaman, a traditional holy man able to interact with the spirit world. Yoh is now a competitor in the Shaman Fight, a tournament held every 500 years to decide who will become the Shaman King and shape humanity's future.

The first round of the Shaman Fight is underway. With their Over Souls boosted by the Ultra Senji Ryakketsu, Yoh's team has won its first match with ease. But Hao's full powers have yet to be revealed...

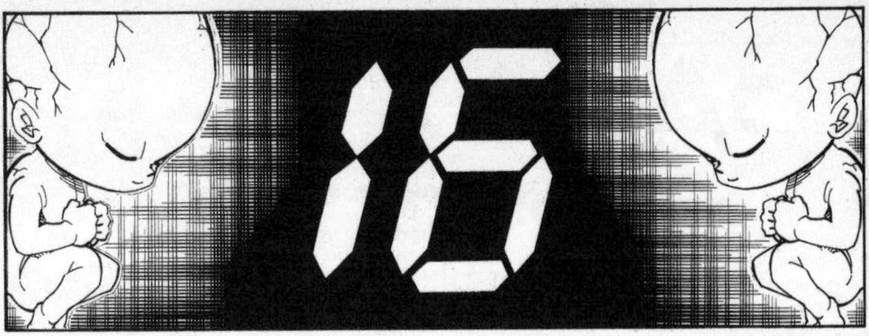
16

SHAMAN KING

VOL. 16
TRUST NO ONE

CONTENTS

Reincarnation 135: Ren's Point

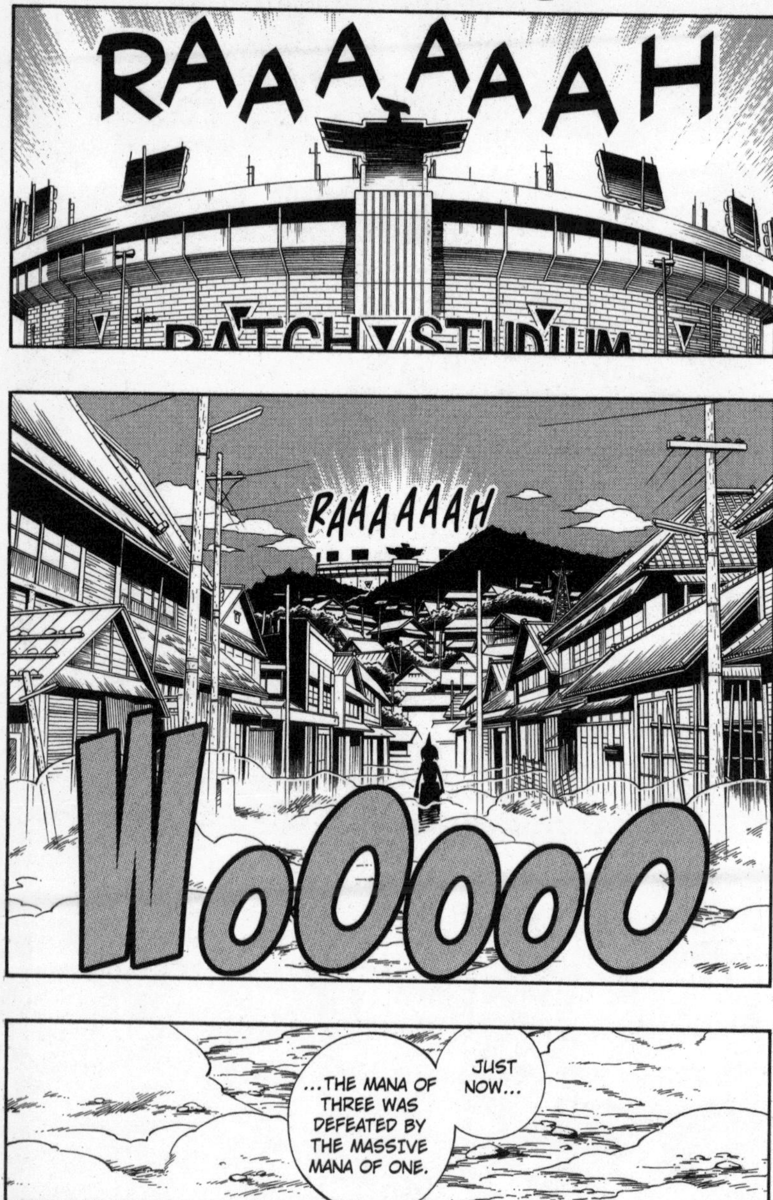
RAAAAAAH
RAAAAAAH
WOOOOO
JUST NOW...
...THE MANA OF THREE WAS DEFEATED BY THE MASSIVE MANA OF ONE.

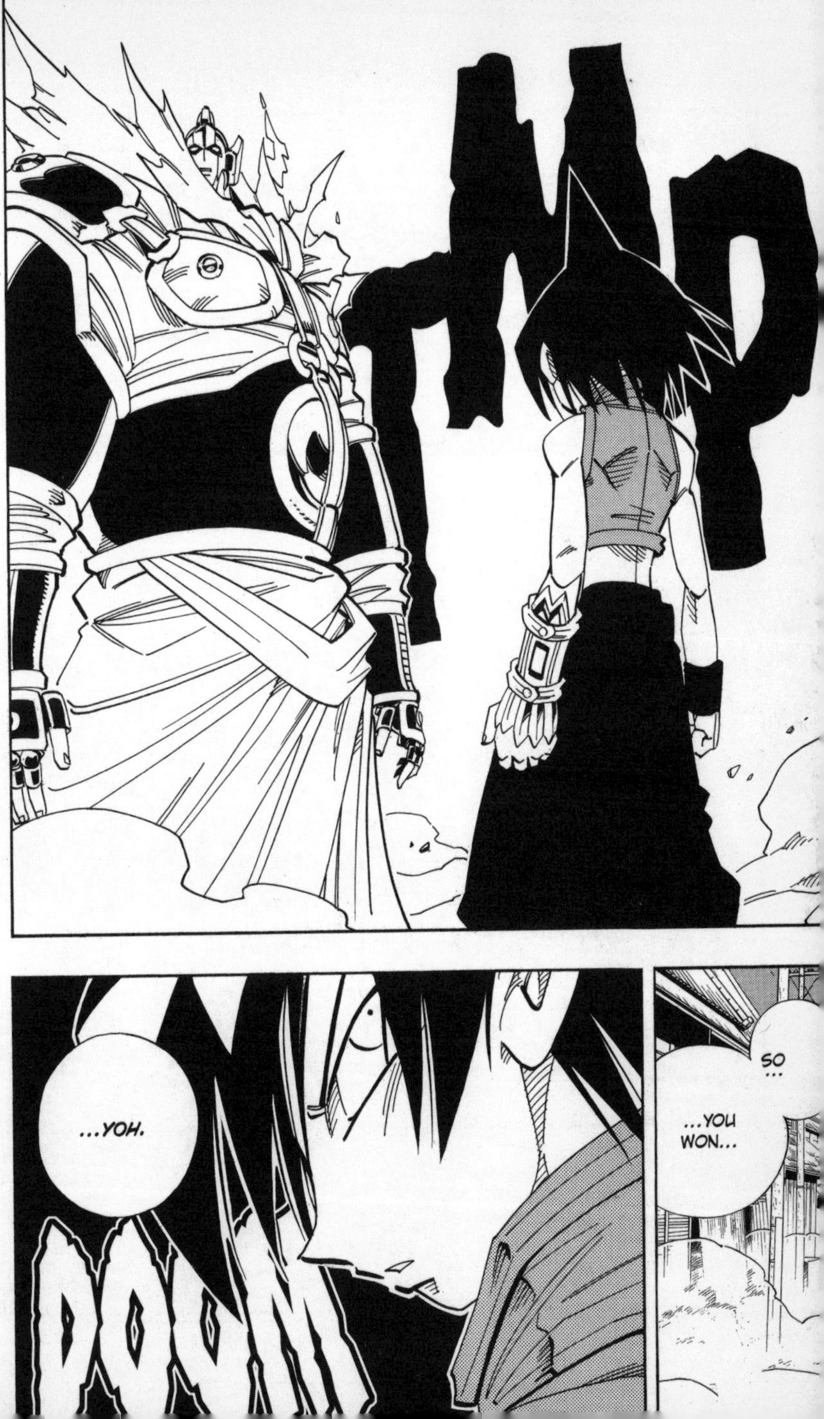
THMP
SO...
...YOU WON...
...YOH.
DOOM

Reincarnation 135: Ren's Point

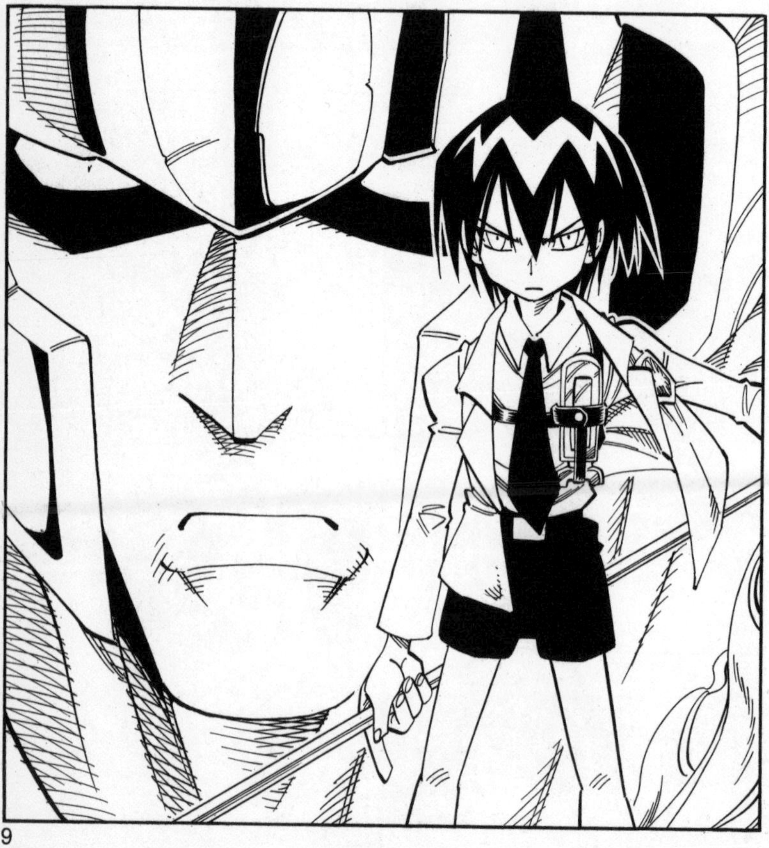

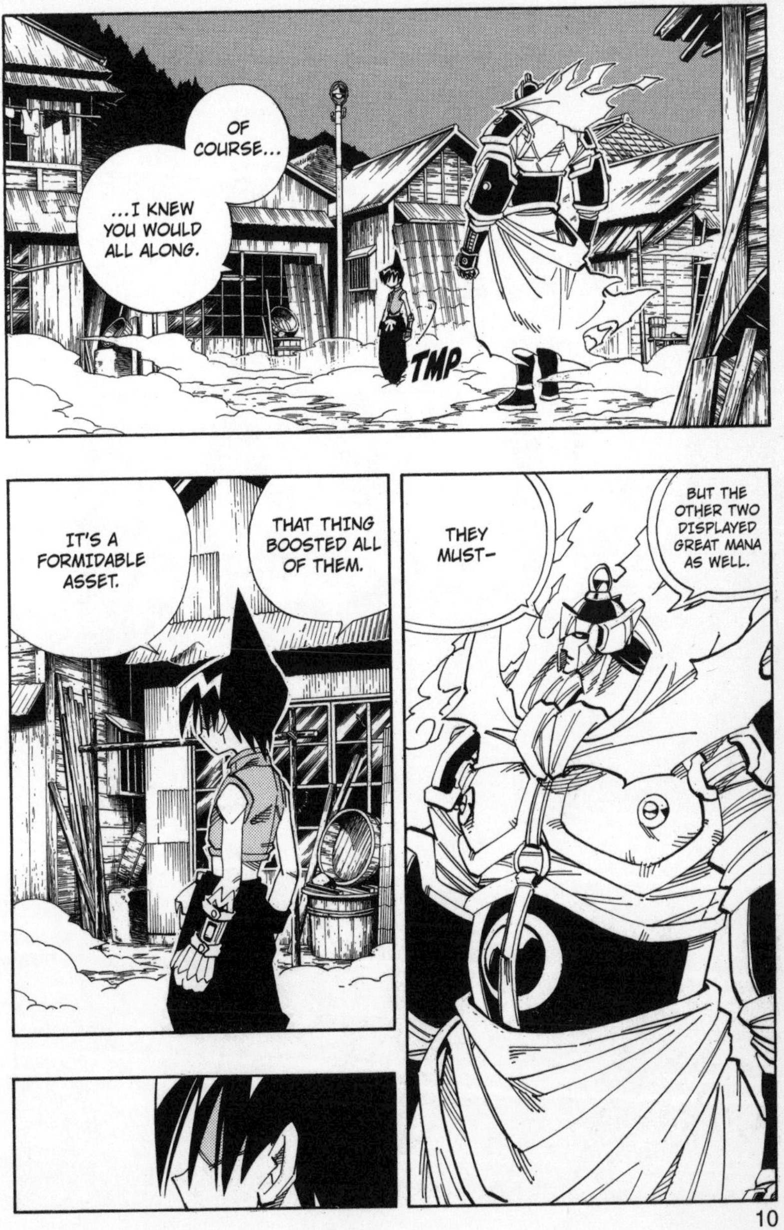
OF COURSE...
...I KNEW YOU WOULD ALL ALONG.
TMP
BUT THE OTHER TWO DISPLAYED GREAT MANA AS WELL.
THEY MUST-
THAT THING BOOSTED ALL OF THEM.
IT'S A FORMIDABLE ASSET.

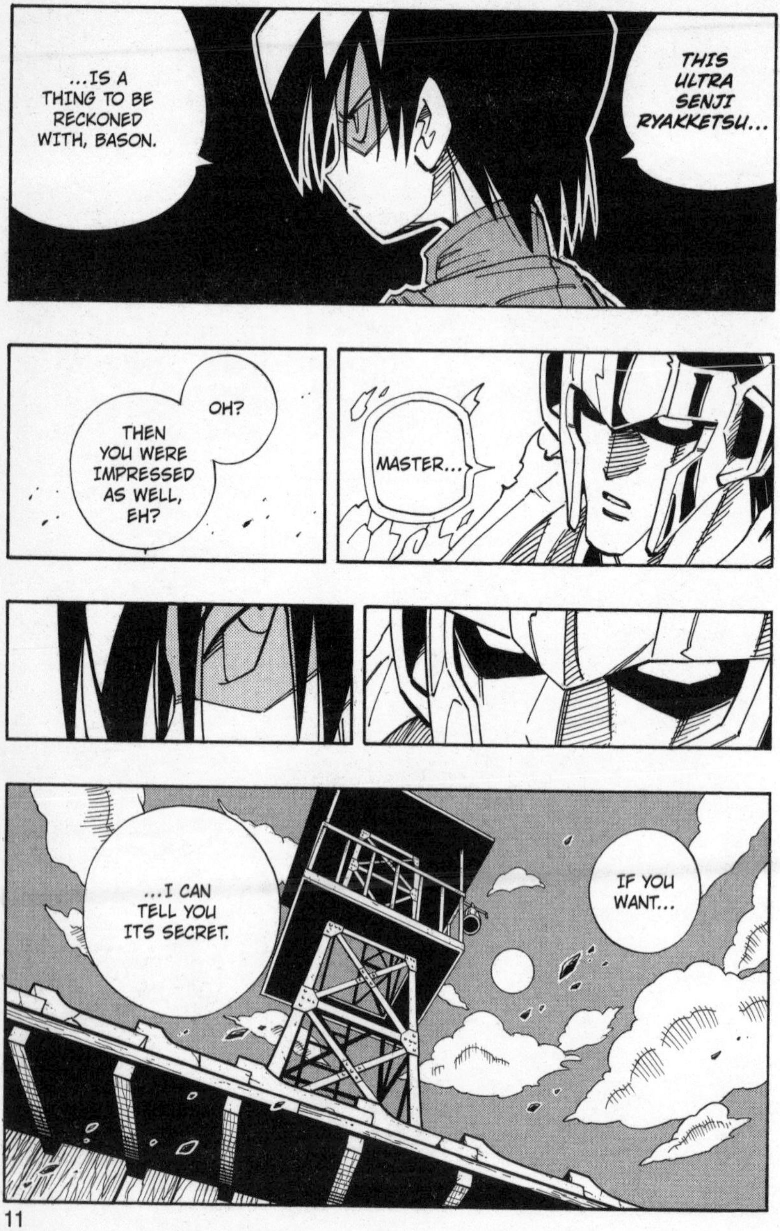
THIS ULTRA SENJI RYAKKETSU...
...IS A THING TO BE RECKONED WITH, BASON.
MASTER...
OH?
THEN YOU WERE IMPRESSED AS WELL, EH?
IF YOU WANT...
...I CAN TELL YOU ITS SECRET.

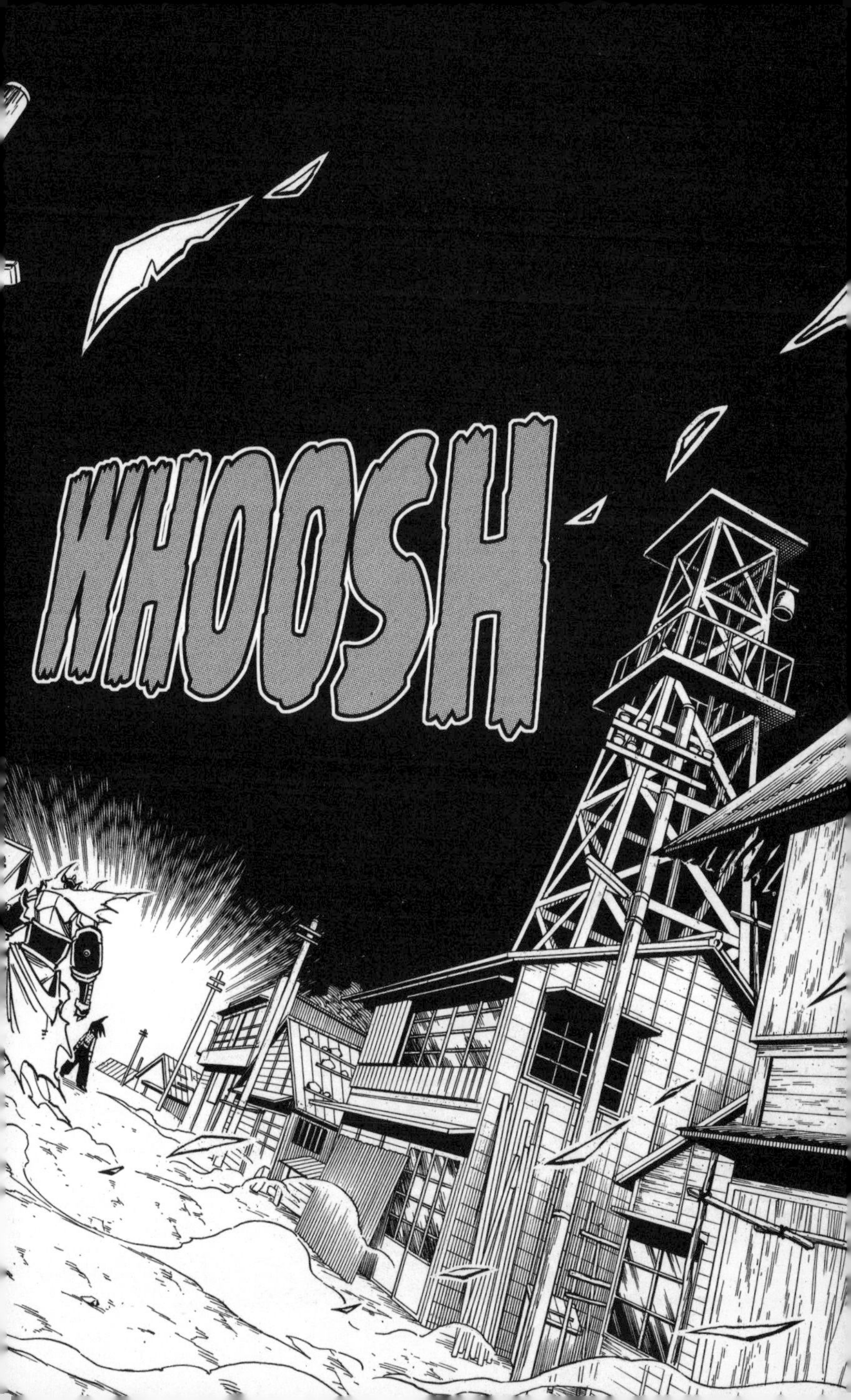
WHOOSH

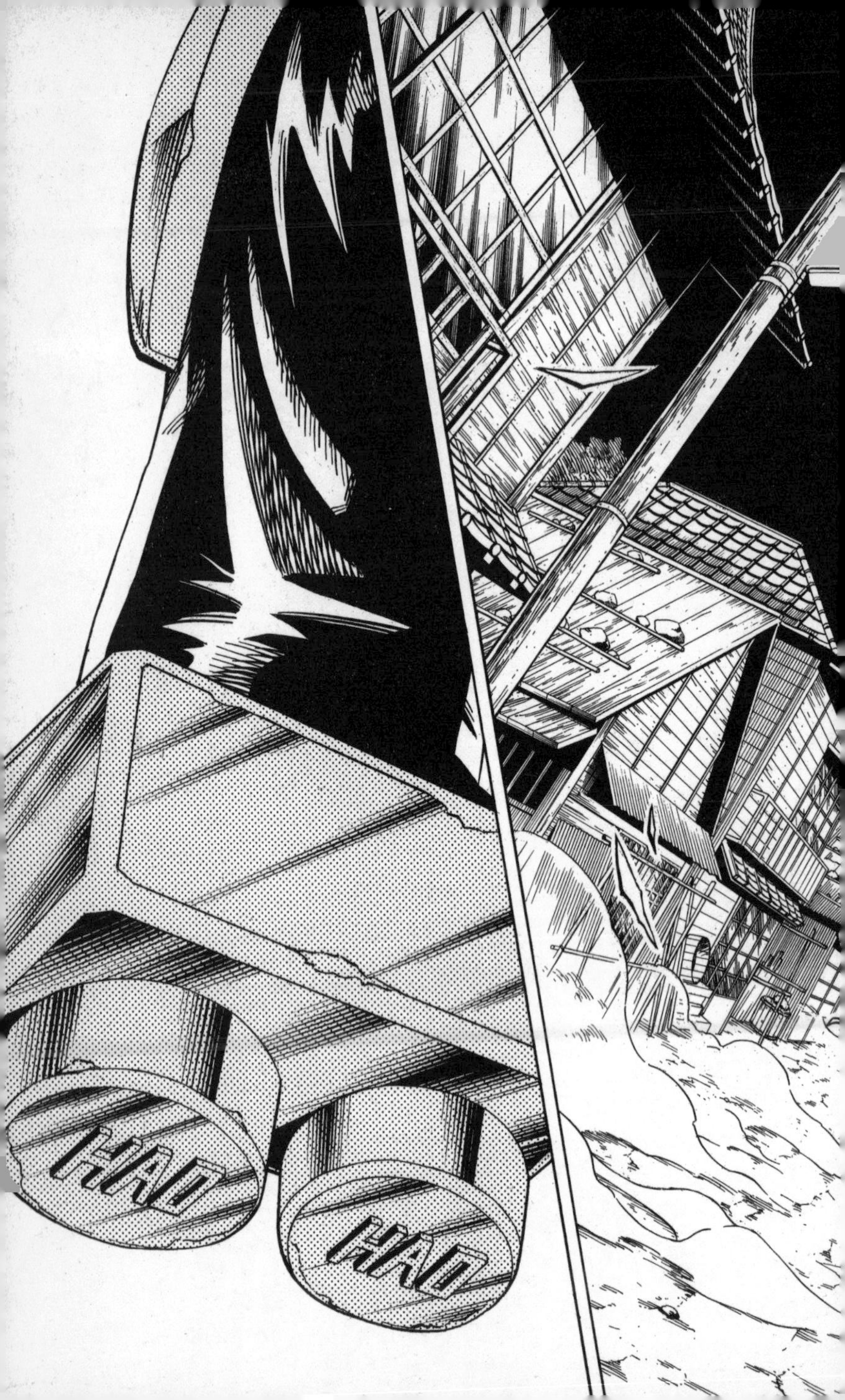
HAO
HAO

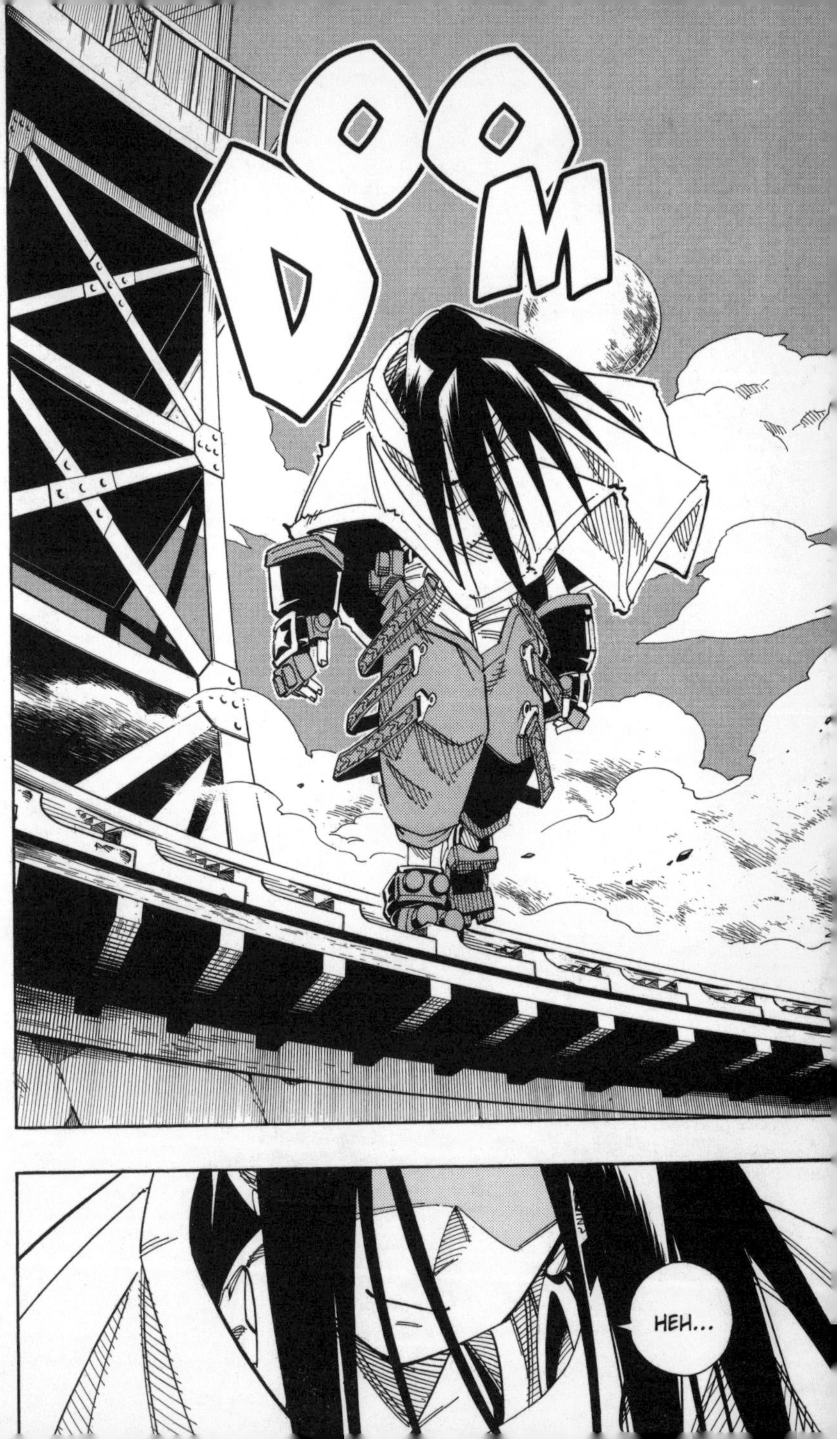
DOOM
HEH...

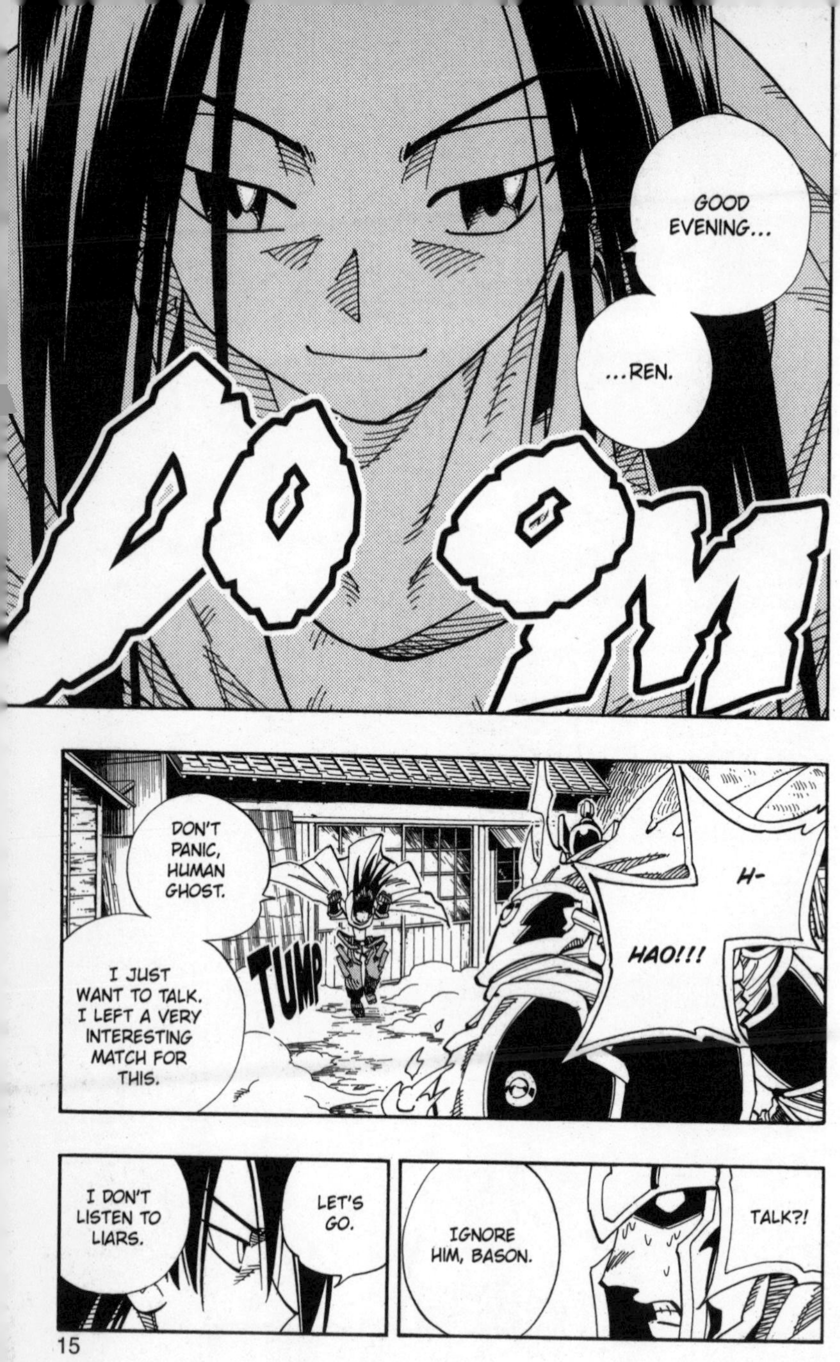
GOOD EVENING...
...REN.
DOOM
H-
HAO!!!
TUMP
DON'T PANIC, HUMAN GHOST.
I JUST WANT TO TALK. I LEFT A VERY INTERESTING MATCH FOR THIS.
TALK?!
IGNORE HIM, BASON.
LET'S GO.
I DON'T LISTEN TO LIARS.

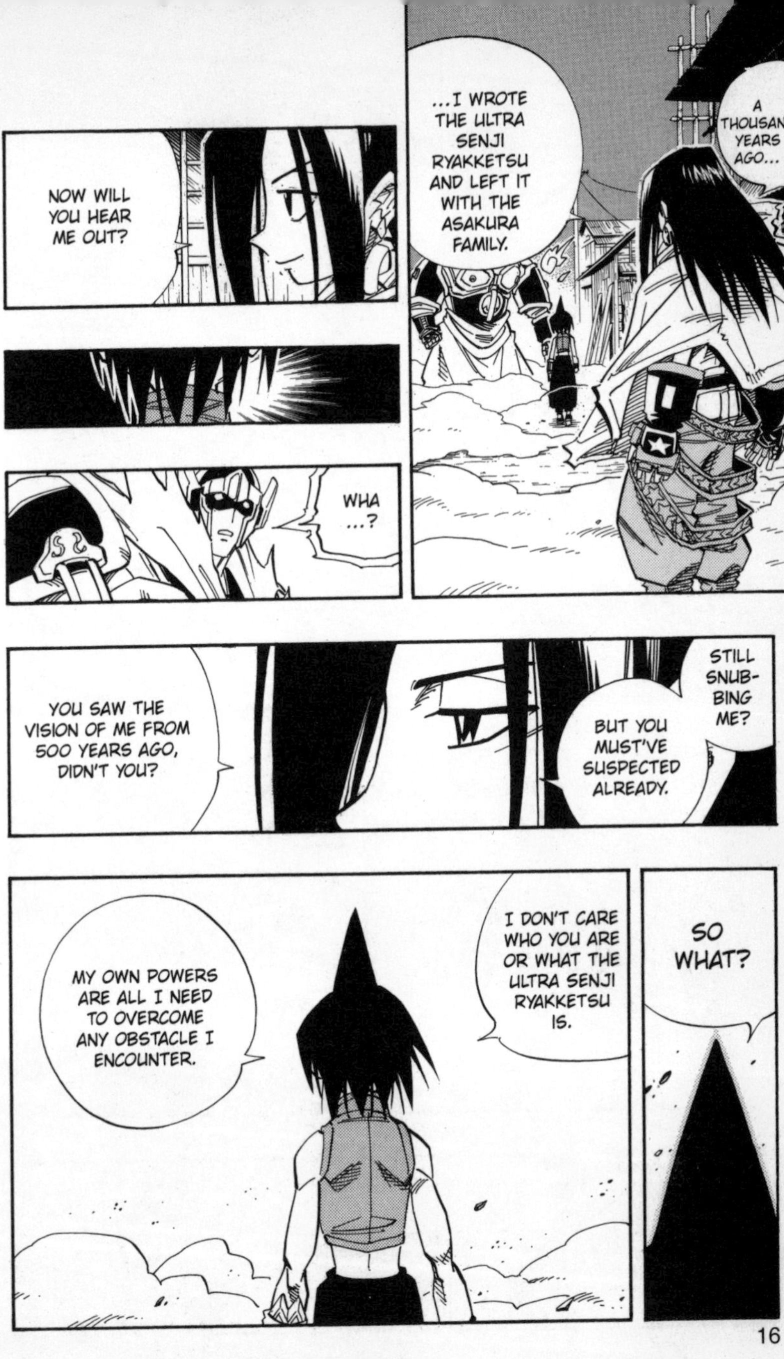
A THOUSAND YEARS AGO...
...I WROTE THE ULTRA SENJI RYAKKETSU AND LEFT IT WITH THE ASAKURA FAMILY.
NOW WILL YOU HEAR ME OUT?
WHA ...?
STILL SNUB-BING ME?
BUT YOU MUST'VE SUSPECTED ALREADY.
YOU SAW THE VISION OF ME FROM 500 YEARS AGO, DIDN'T YOU?
SO WHAT?
I DON'T CARE WHO YOU ARE OR WHAT THE ULTRA SENJI RYAKKETSU IS.
MY OWN POWERS ARE ALL I NEED TO OVERCOME ANY OBSTACLE I ENCOUNTER.

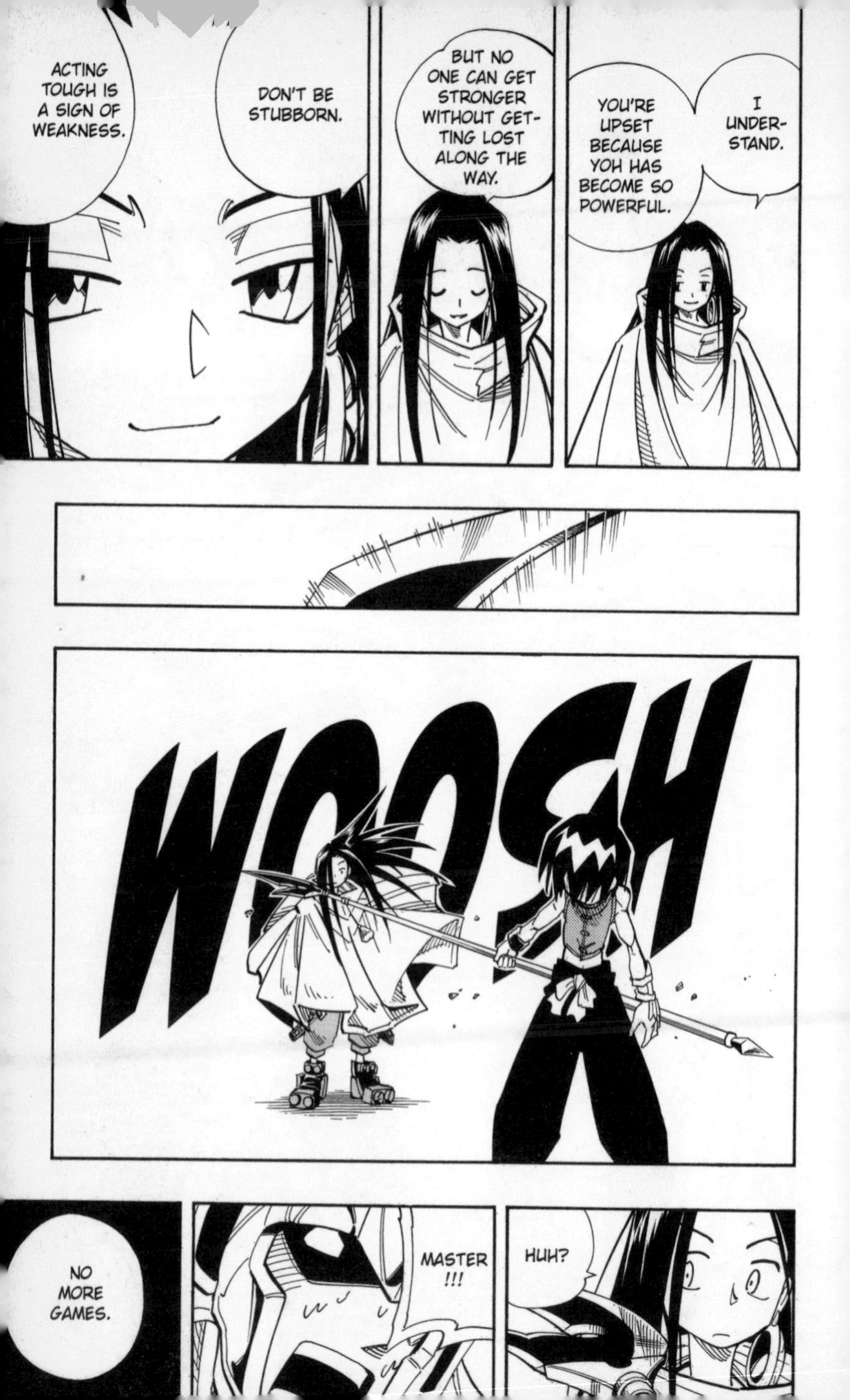
I UNDER-STAND.
YOU'RE UPSET BECAUSE YOH HAS BECOME SO POWERFUL.
BUT NO ONE CAN GET STRONGER WITHOUT GET-TING LOST ALONG THE WAY.
DON'T BE STUBBORN.
ACTING TOUGH IS A SIGN OF WEAKNESS.
WOOSH
HUH?
MASTER !!!
NO MORE GAMES.

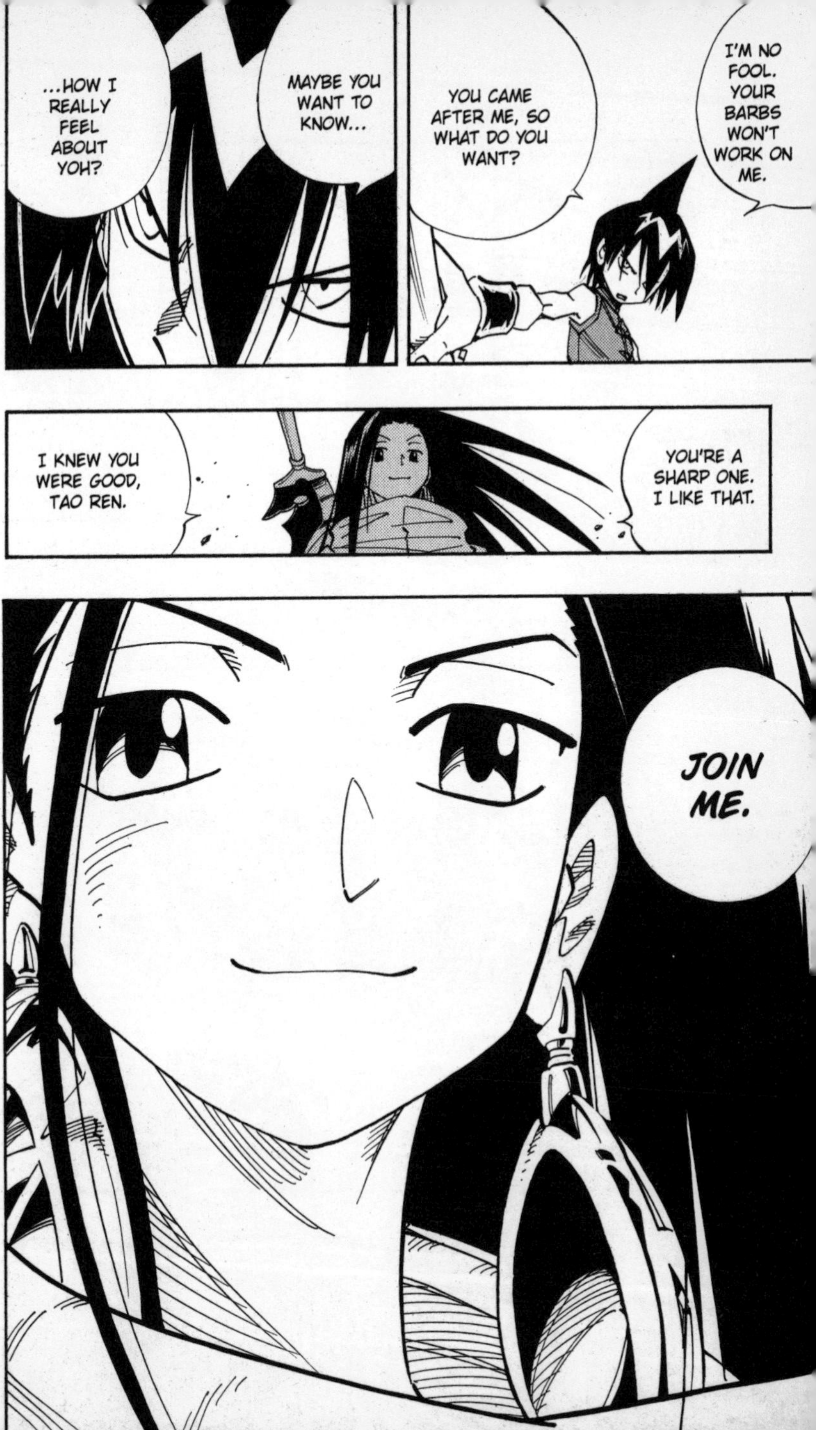
I'M NO FOOL. YOUR BARBS WON'T WORK ON ME.
YOU CAME AFTER ME, SO WHAT DO YOU WANT?
MAYBE YOU WANT TO KNOW...
...HOW I REALLY FEEL ABOUT YOH?
YOU'RE A SHARP ONE. I LIKE THAT.
I KNEW YOU WERE GOOD, TAO REN.
JOIN ME.

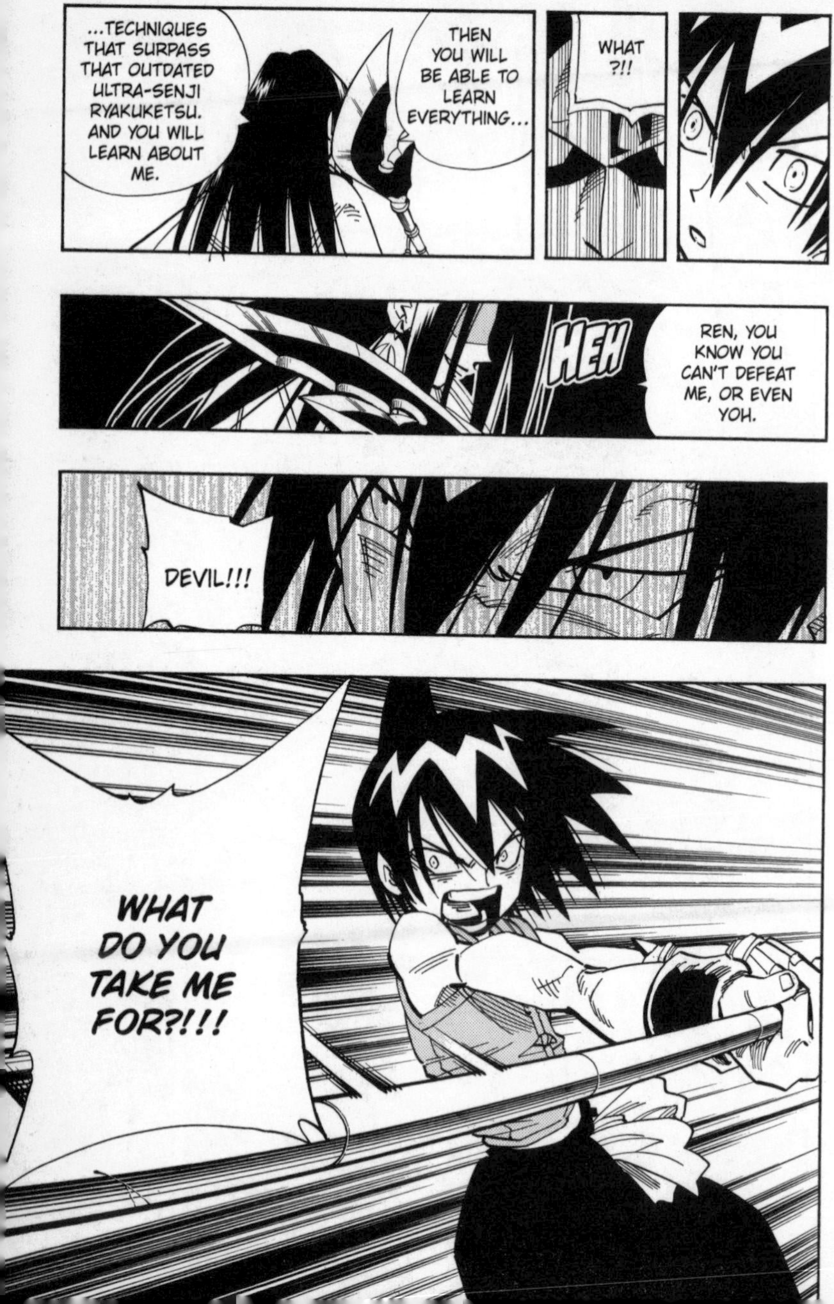

WHAT ?!!
THEN YOU WILL BE ABLE TO LEARN EVERYTHING...
...TECHNIQUES THAT SURPASS THAT OUTDATED ULTRA-SENJI RYAKUKETSU. AND YOU WILL LEARN ABOUT ME.
REN, YOU KNOW YOU CAN'T DEFEAT ME, OR EVEN YOH.
HEH
DEVIL!!!
WHAT DO YOU TAKE ME FOR?!!!

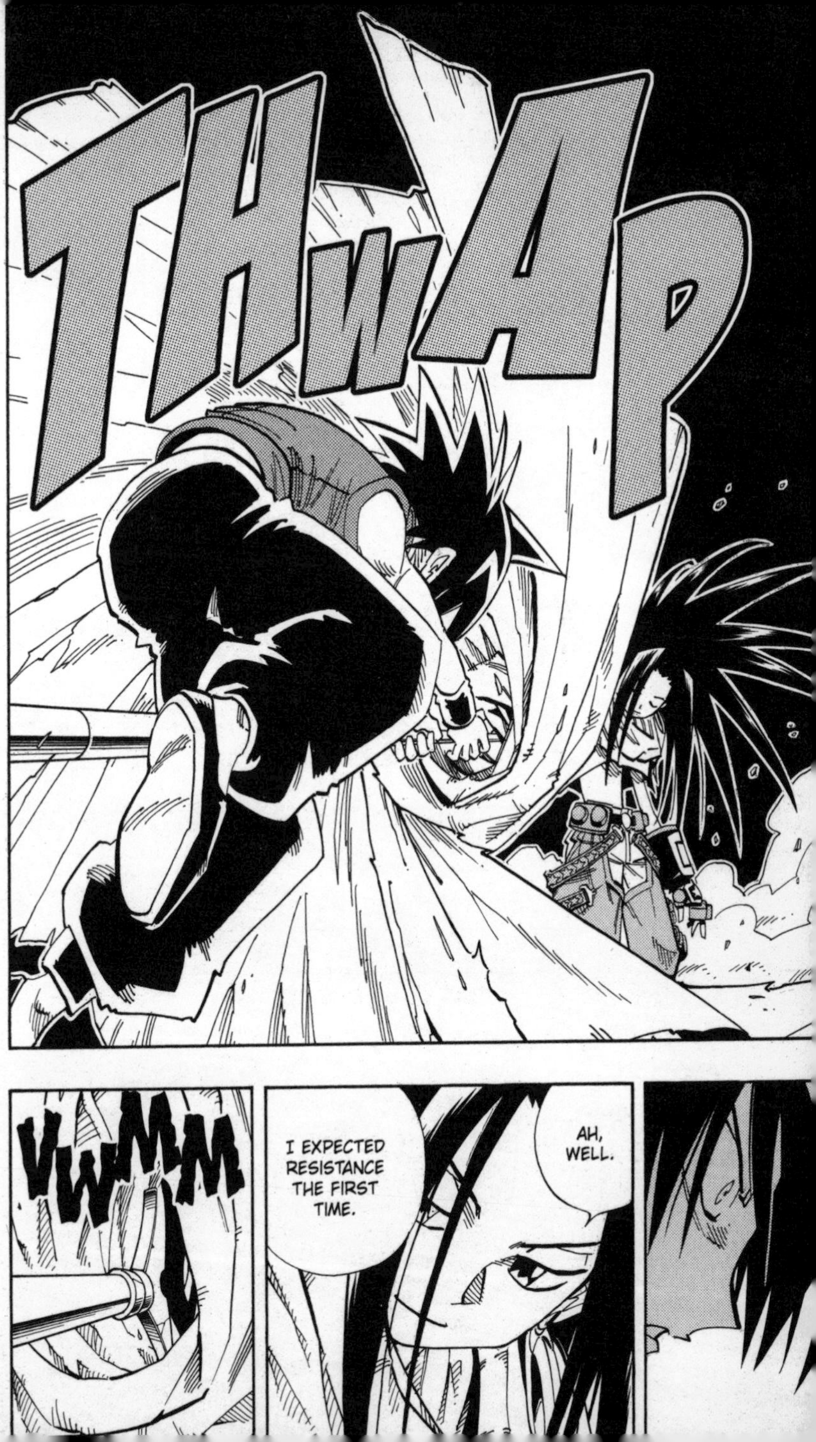
THWAP
AH, WELL.
I EXPECTED RESISTANCE THE FIRST TIME.
VWMM

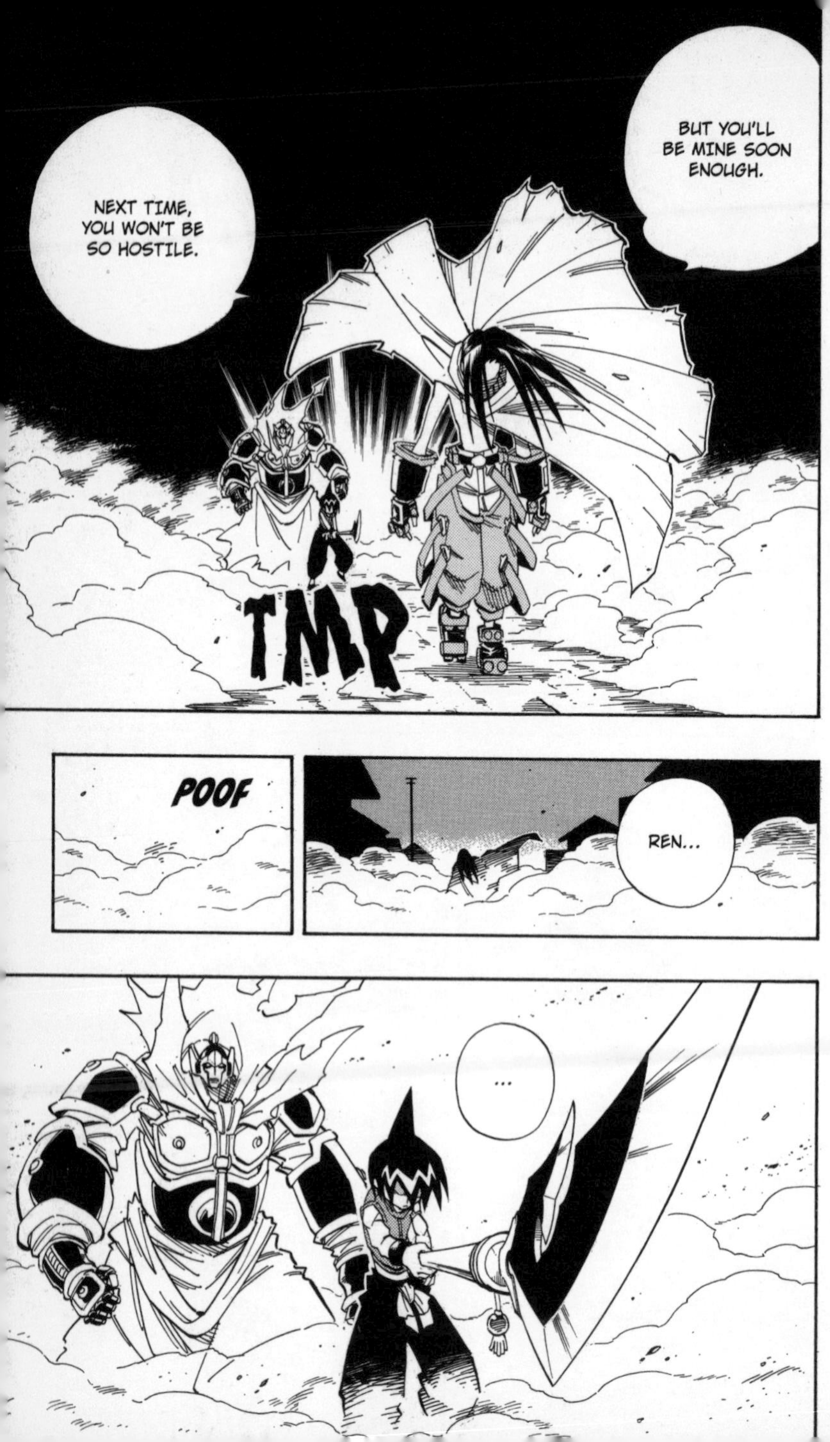
BUT YOU'LL BE MINE SOON ENOUGH.
NEXT TIME, YOU WON'T BE SO HOSTILE.
TMP
REN...
POOF
...

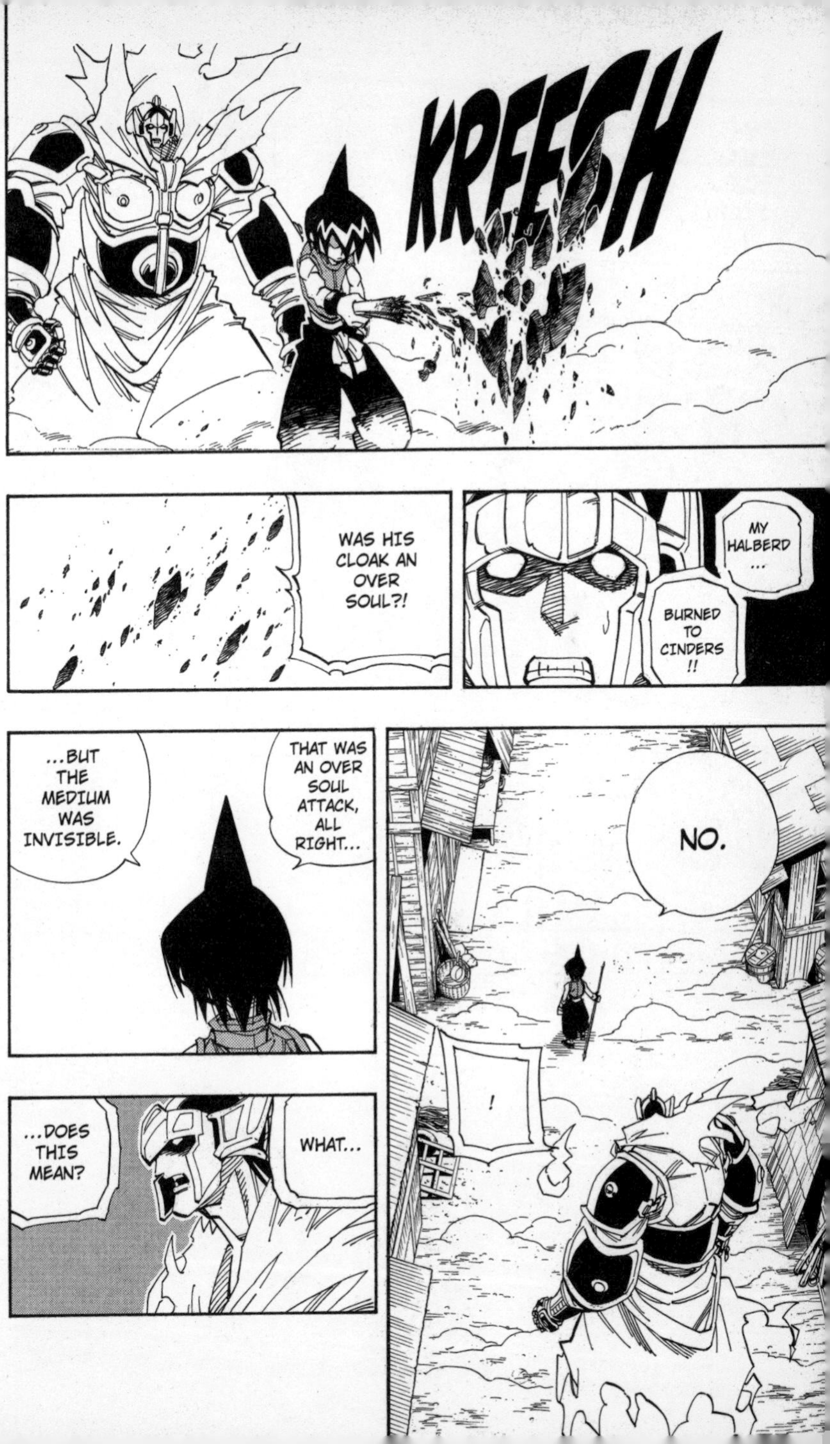
KREESH
MY HALBERD...
BURNED TO CINDERS!!
WAS HIS CLOAK AN OVER SOUL?!
NO.
!
THAT WAS AN OVER SOUL ATTACK, ALL RIGHT...
...BUT THE MEDIUM WAS INVISIBLE.
WHAT...
...DOES THIS MEAN?

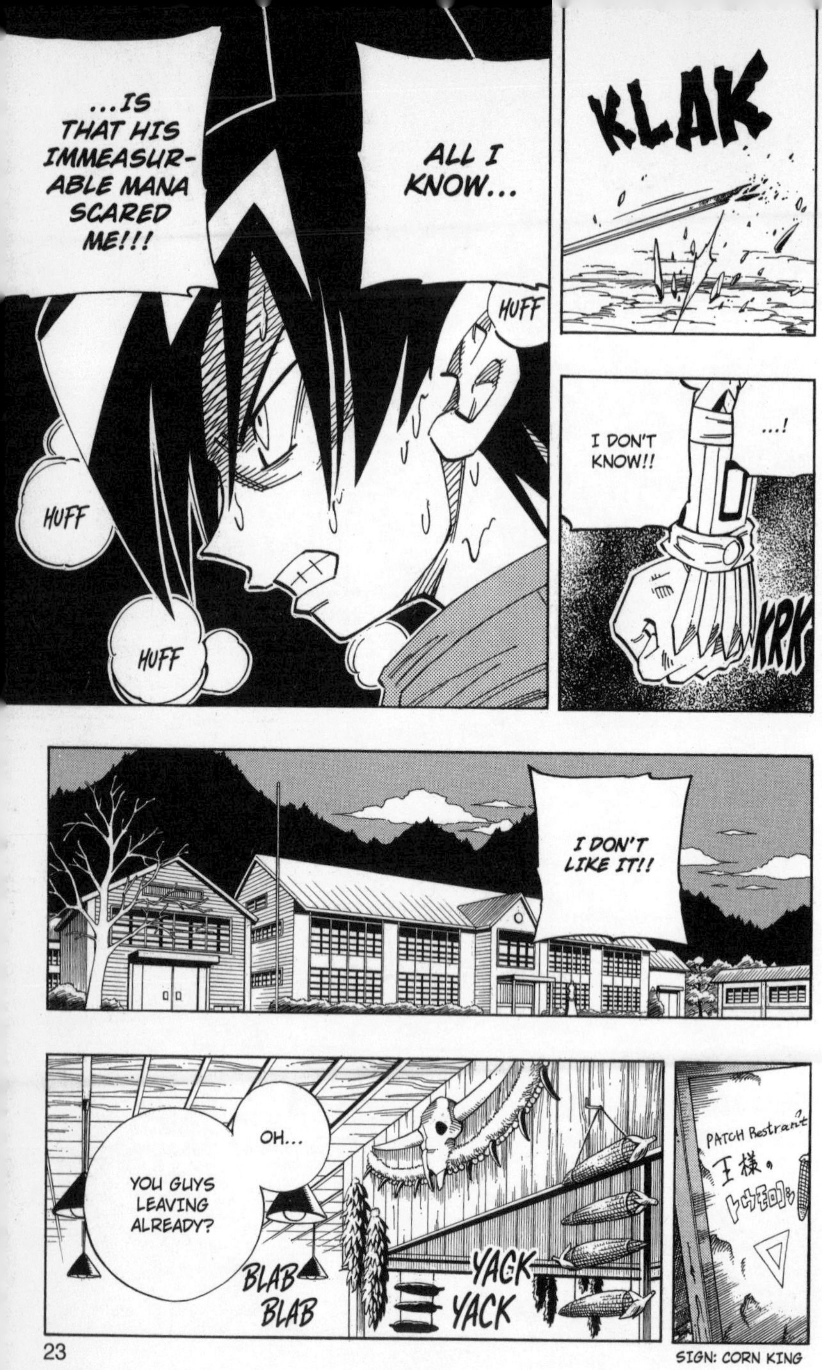
KLAK
...!
I DON'T KNOW!!
KRK
ALL I KNOW...
...IS THAT HIS IMMEASURABLE MANA SCARED ME!!!
HUFF
HUFF
HUFF
I DON'T LIKE IT!!
PATCH Restrant
王様のトウモロコシ
OH...
YOU GUYS LEAVING ALREADY?
YACK YACK
BLAB BLAB

SIGN: CORN KING

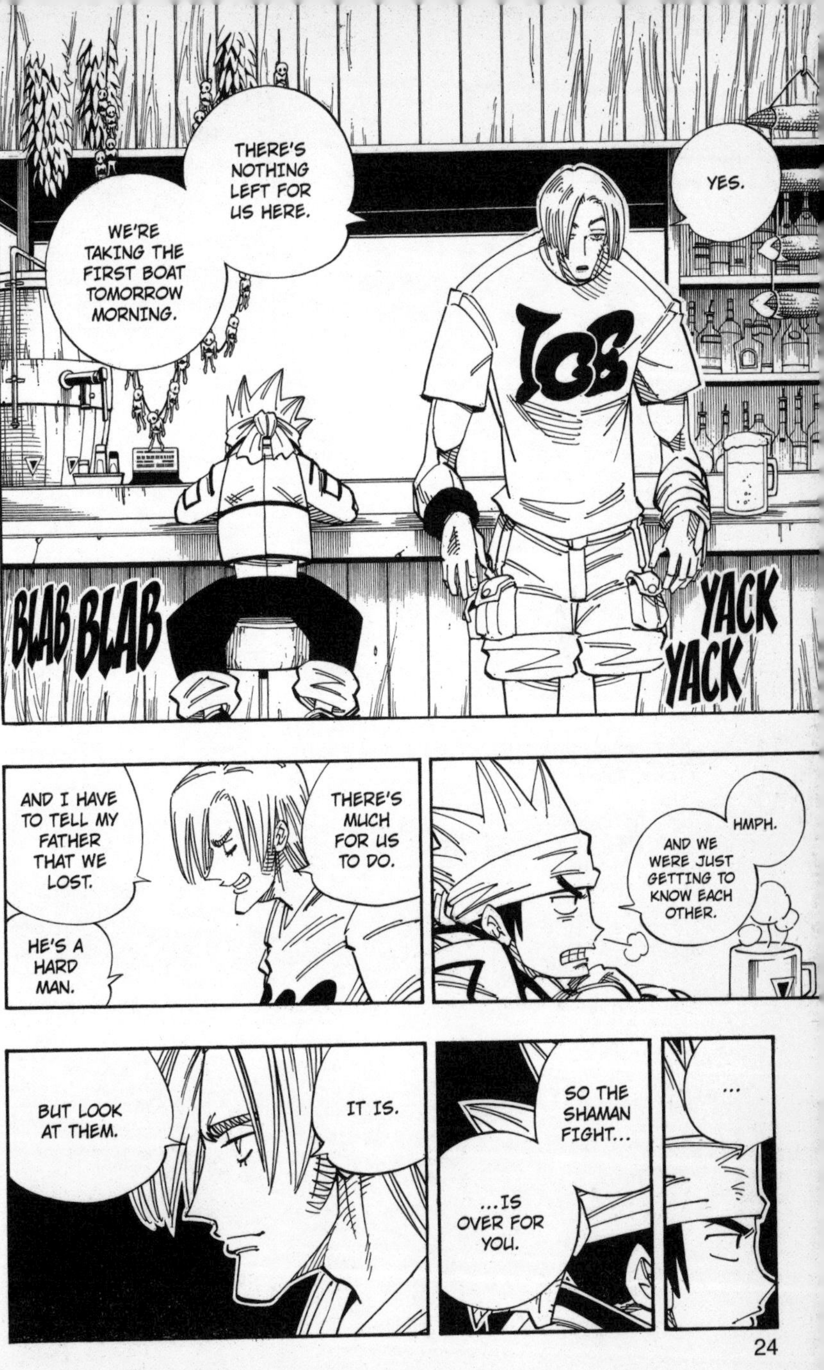
YES.
THERE'S NOTHING LEFT FOR US HERE.
WE'RE TAKING THE FIRST BOAT TOMORROW MORNING.
YACK YACK
BLAB BLAB
HMPH.
AND WE WERE JUST GETTING TO KNOW EACH OTHER.
THERE'S MUCH FOR US TO DO.
AND I HAVE TO TELL MY FATHER THAT WE LOST.
HE'S A HARD MAN.
...
SO THE SHAMAN FIGHT...
...IS OVER FOR YOU.
IT IS.
BUT LOOK AT THEM.

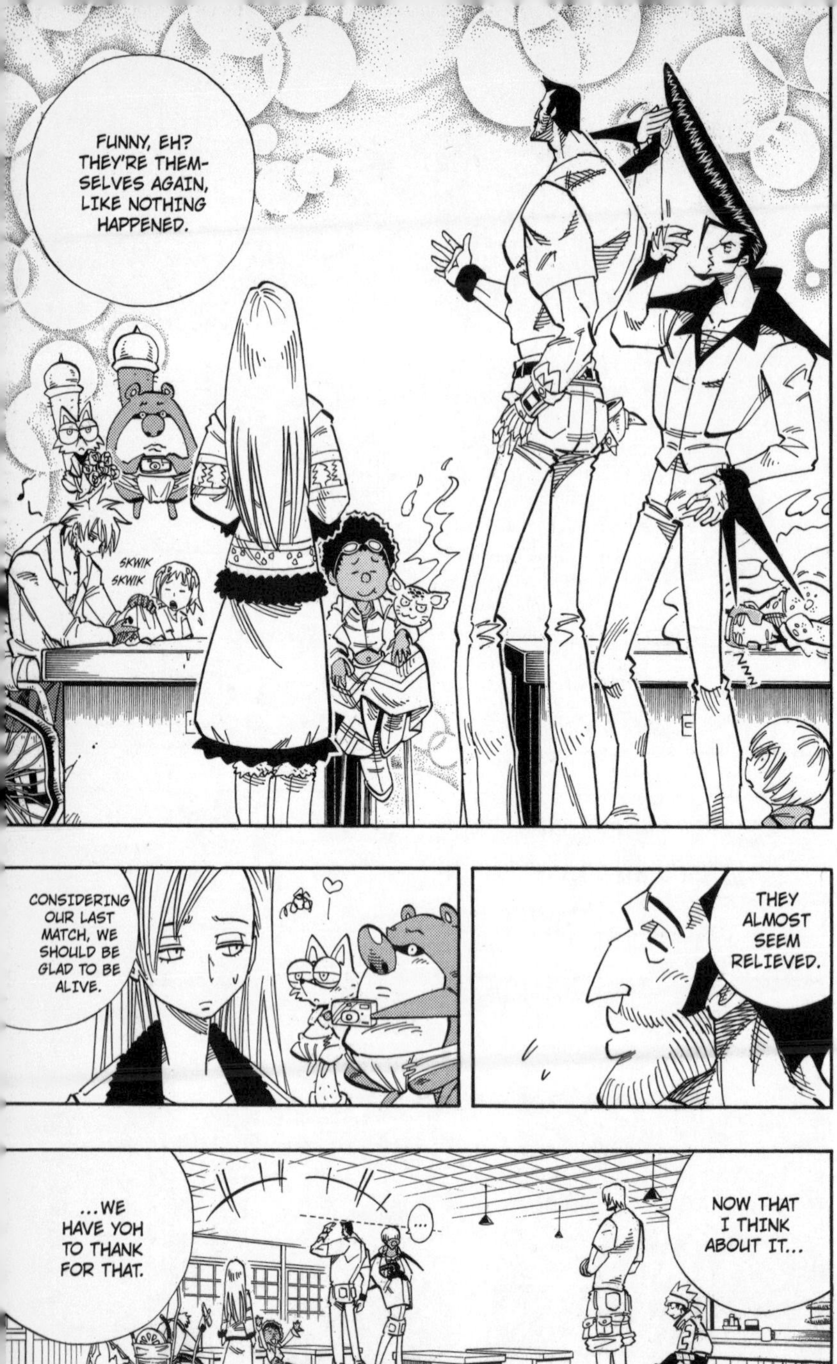
FUNNY, EH? THEY'RE THEMSELVES AGAIN, LIKE NOTHING HAPPENED.
SKWIK SKWIK
THEY ALMOST SEEM RELIEVED.
CONSIDERING OUR LAST MATCH, WE SHOULD BE GLAD TO BE ALIVE.
NOW THAT I THINK ABOUT IT...
...
...WE HAVE YOH TO THANK FOR THAT.

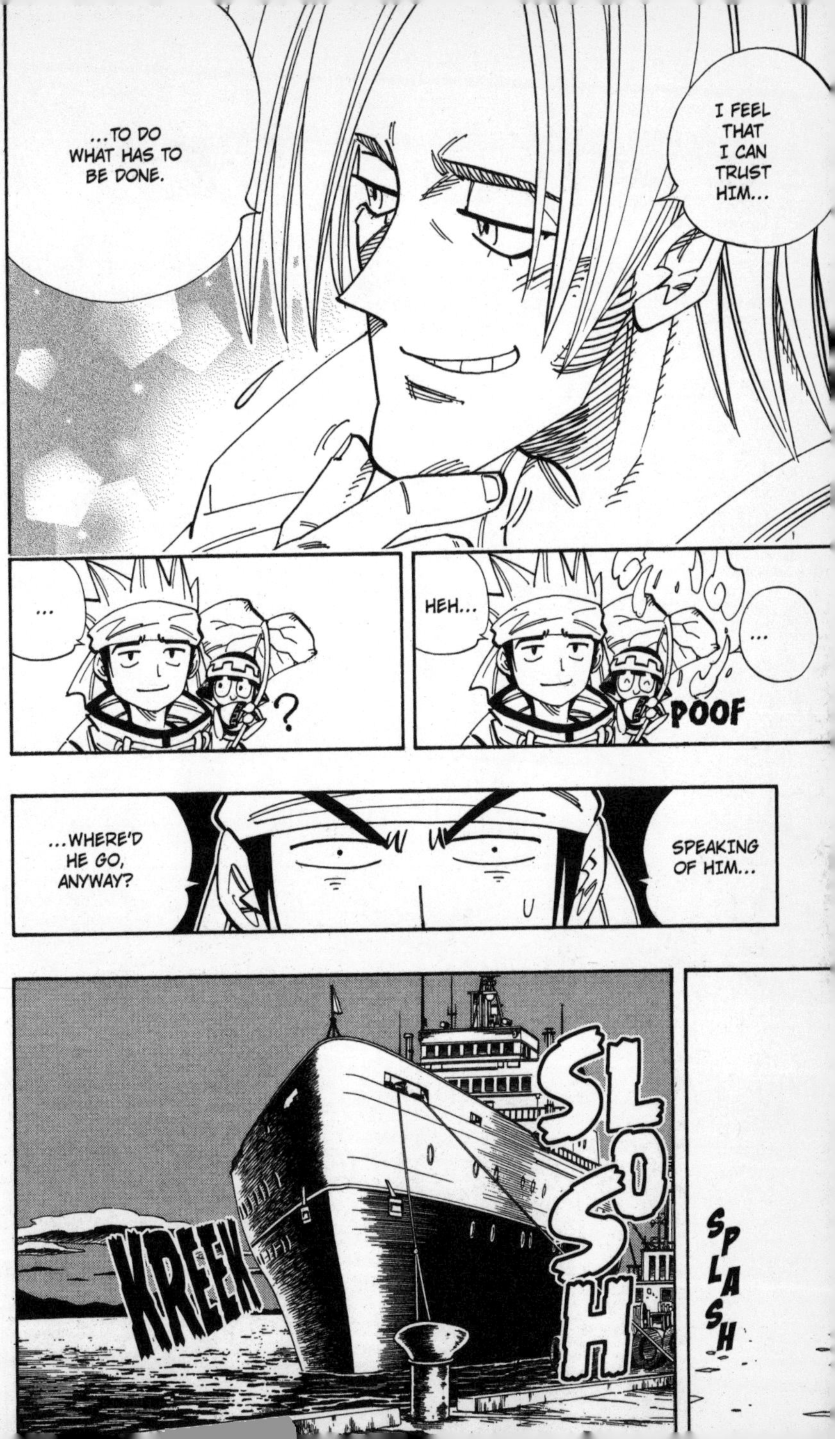
I FEEL THAT I CAN TRUST HIM...
...TO DO WHAT HAS TO BE DONE.
HEH...
...
POOF
...
?
SPEAKING OF HIM...
...WHERE'D HE GO, ANYWAY?
SPLASH
SLOSH
KREEK

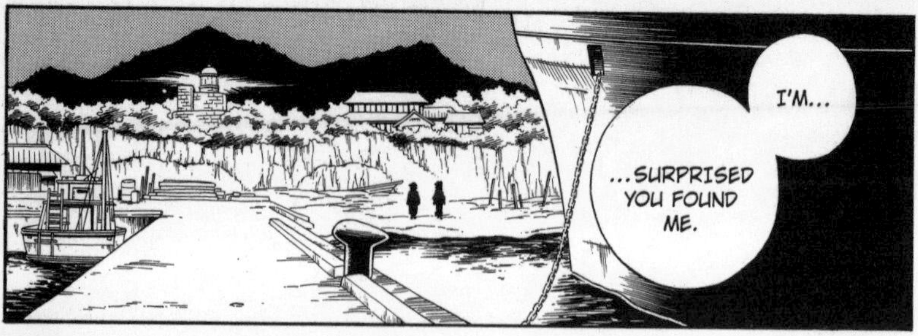
I'M...
...SURPRISED YOU FOUND ME.

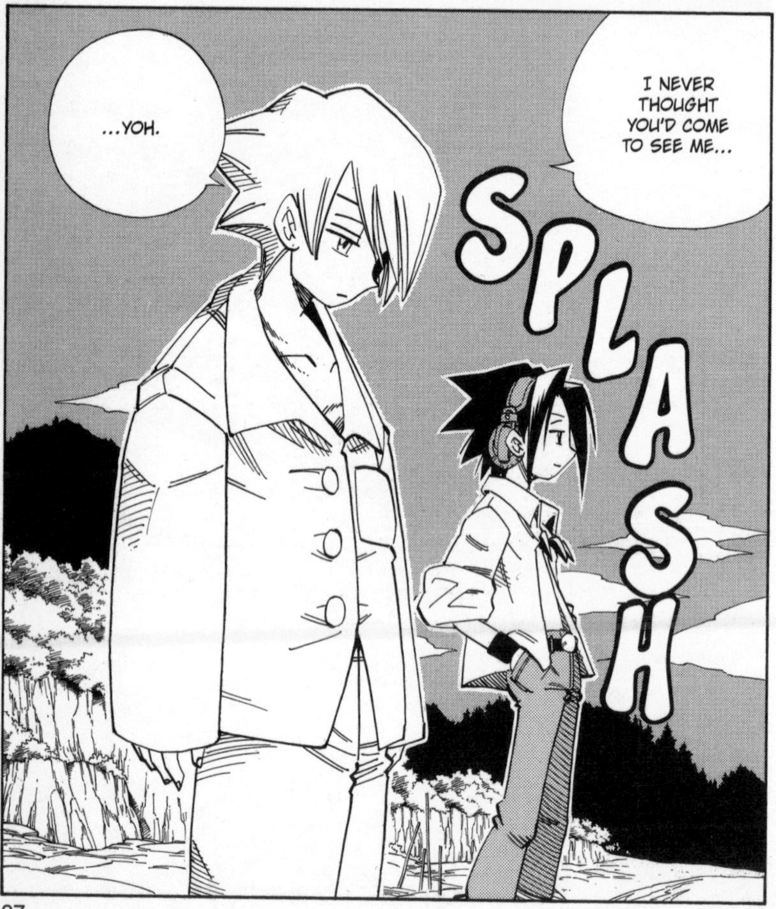
I NEVER THOUGHT YOU'D COME TO SEE ME...
SPLASH
...YOH.

SHAMAN KING ITEM FILE No.47

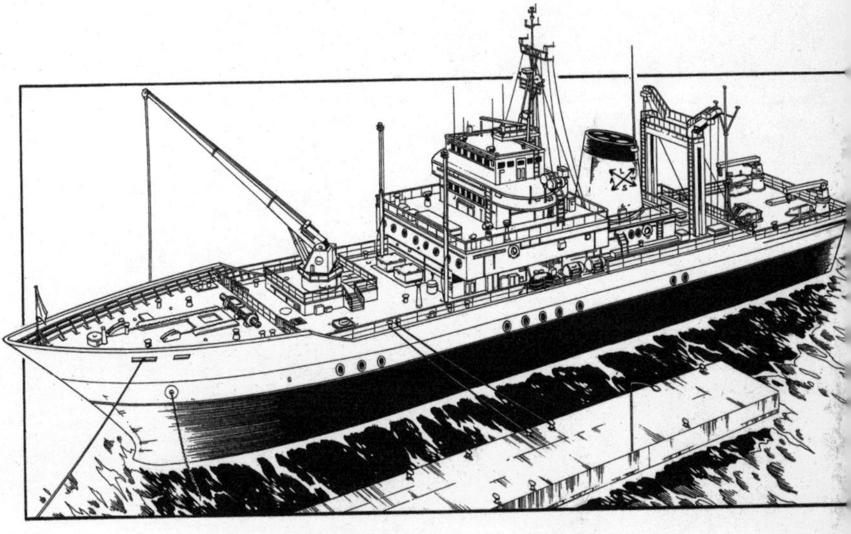

X-LAWS PRIVATE SHIP
ARK X

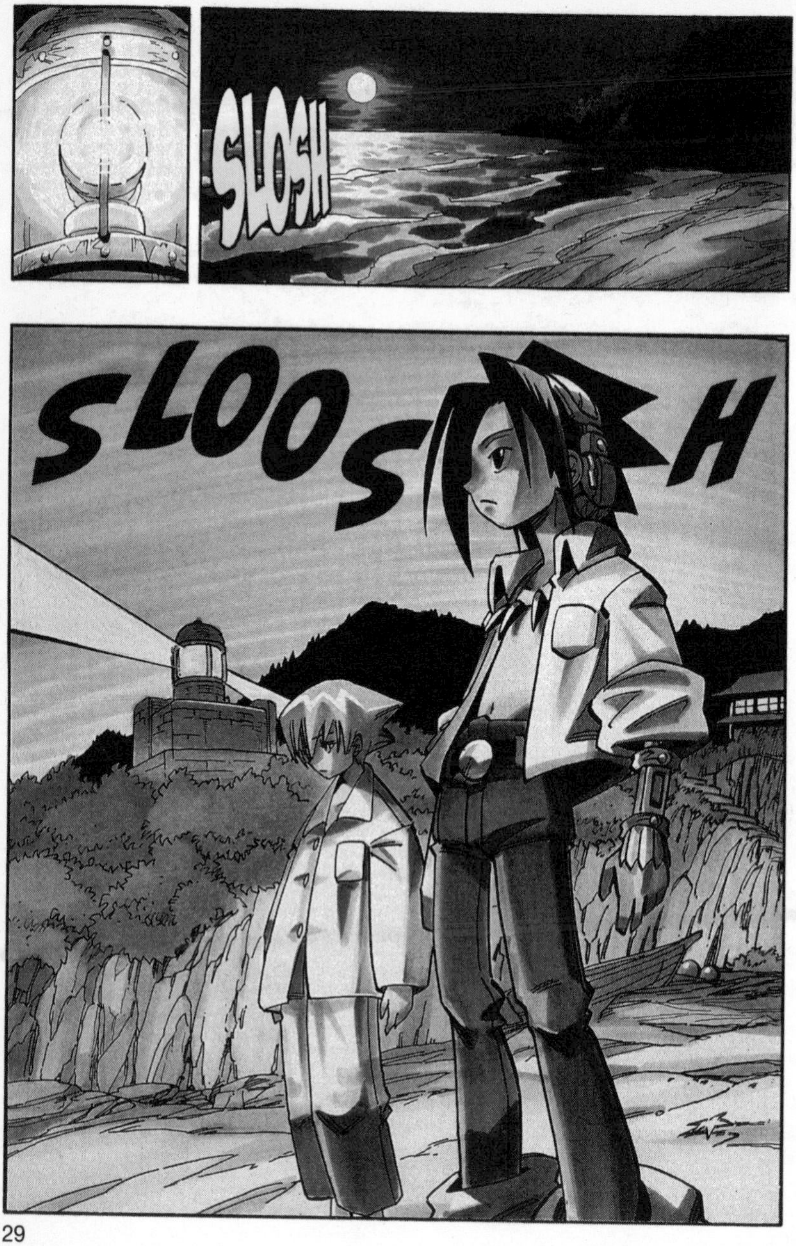
SLOSH
SLOOSH

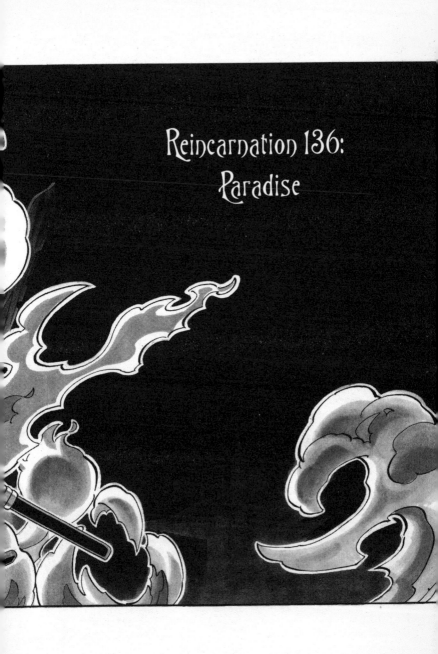

Reincarnation 136:
Paradise

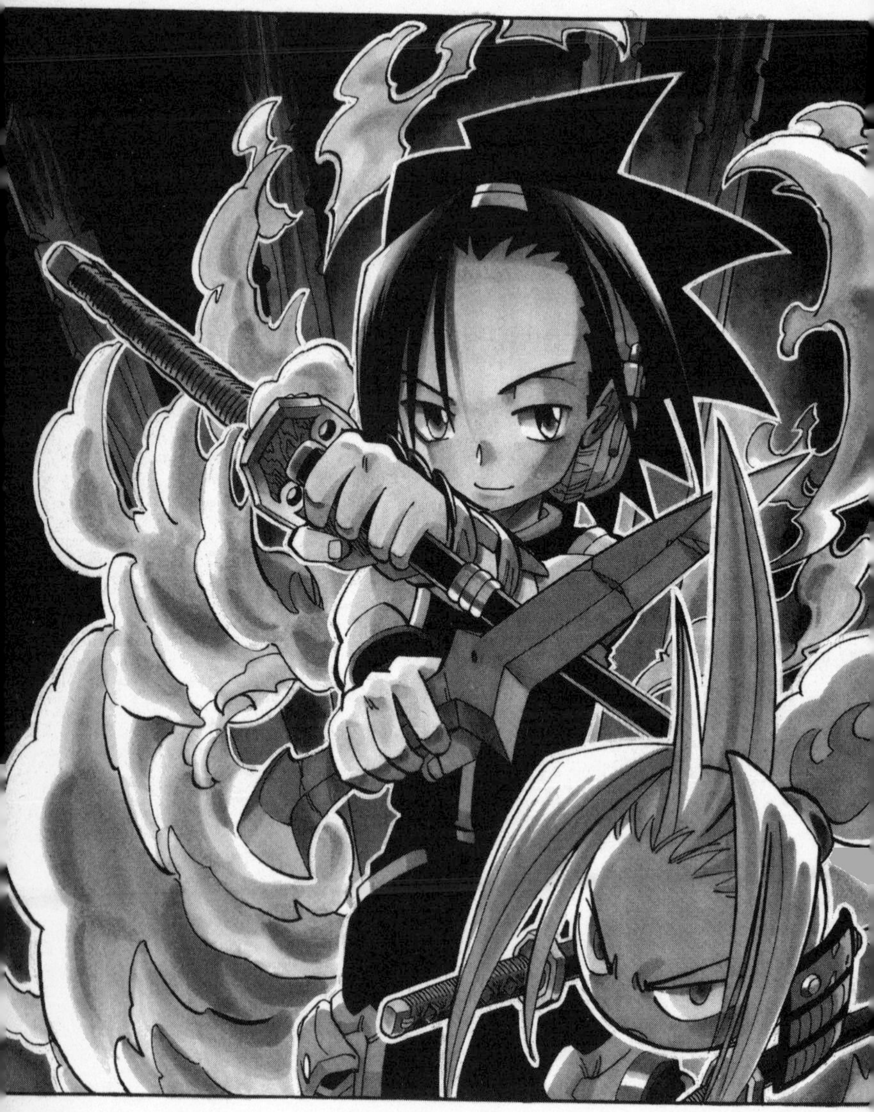

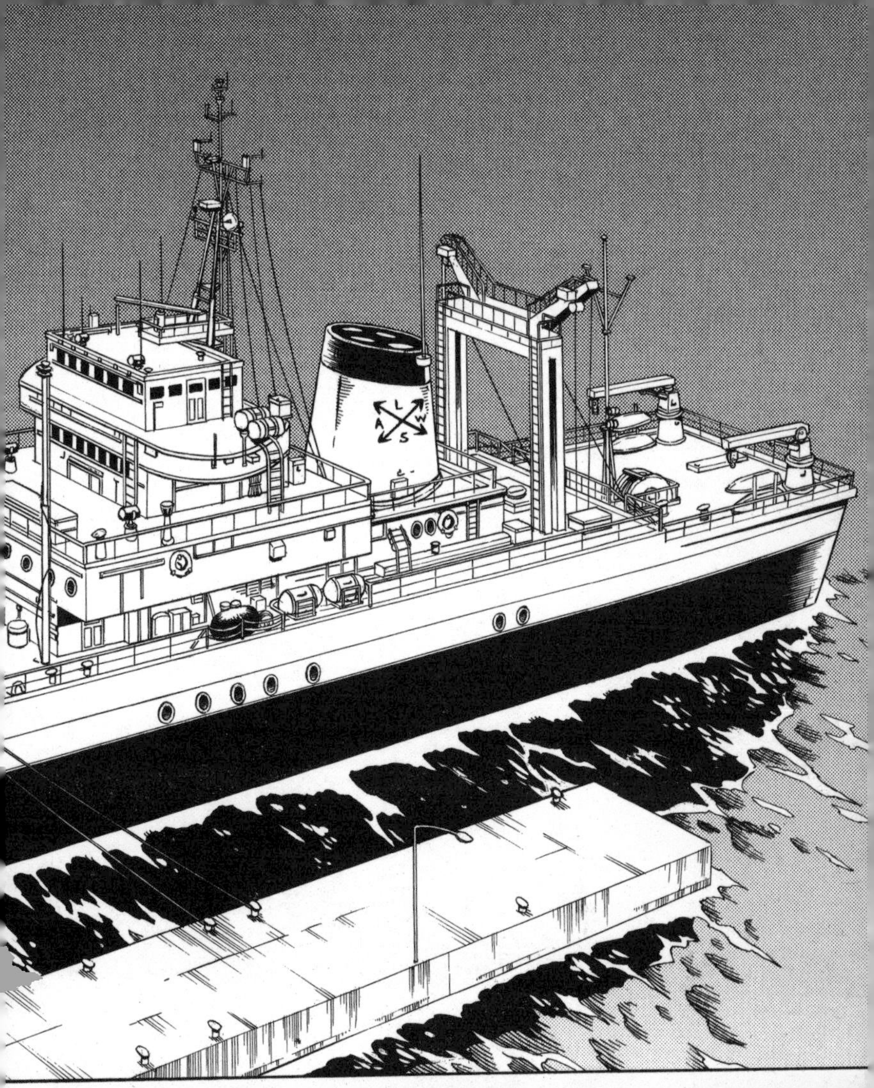

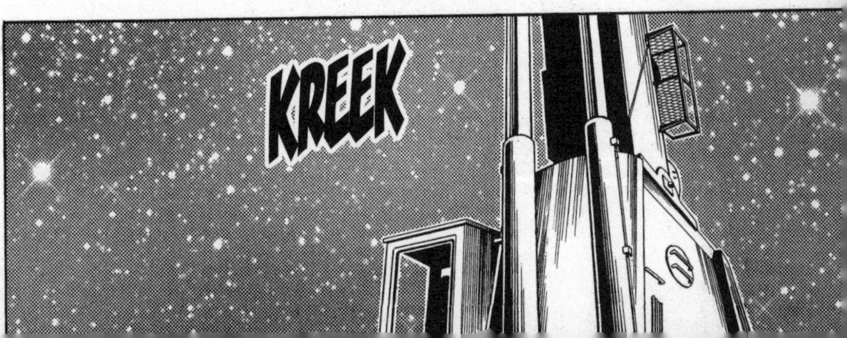
KREEK

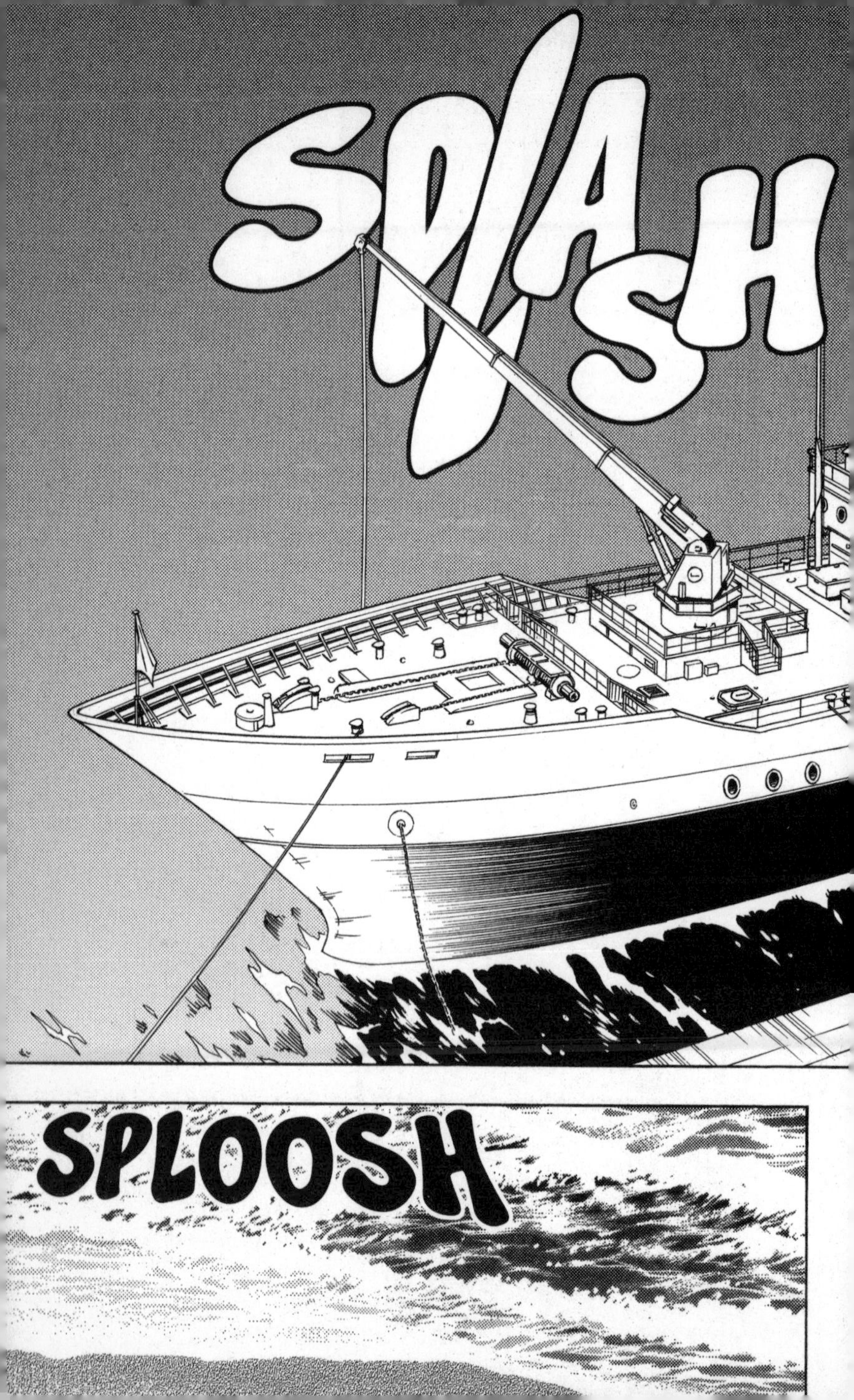
SPLASH
SPLOOSH

Shaman King

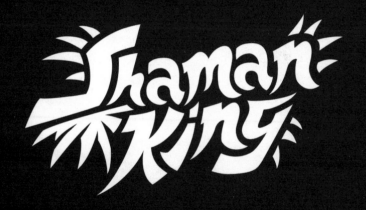

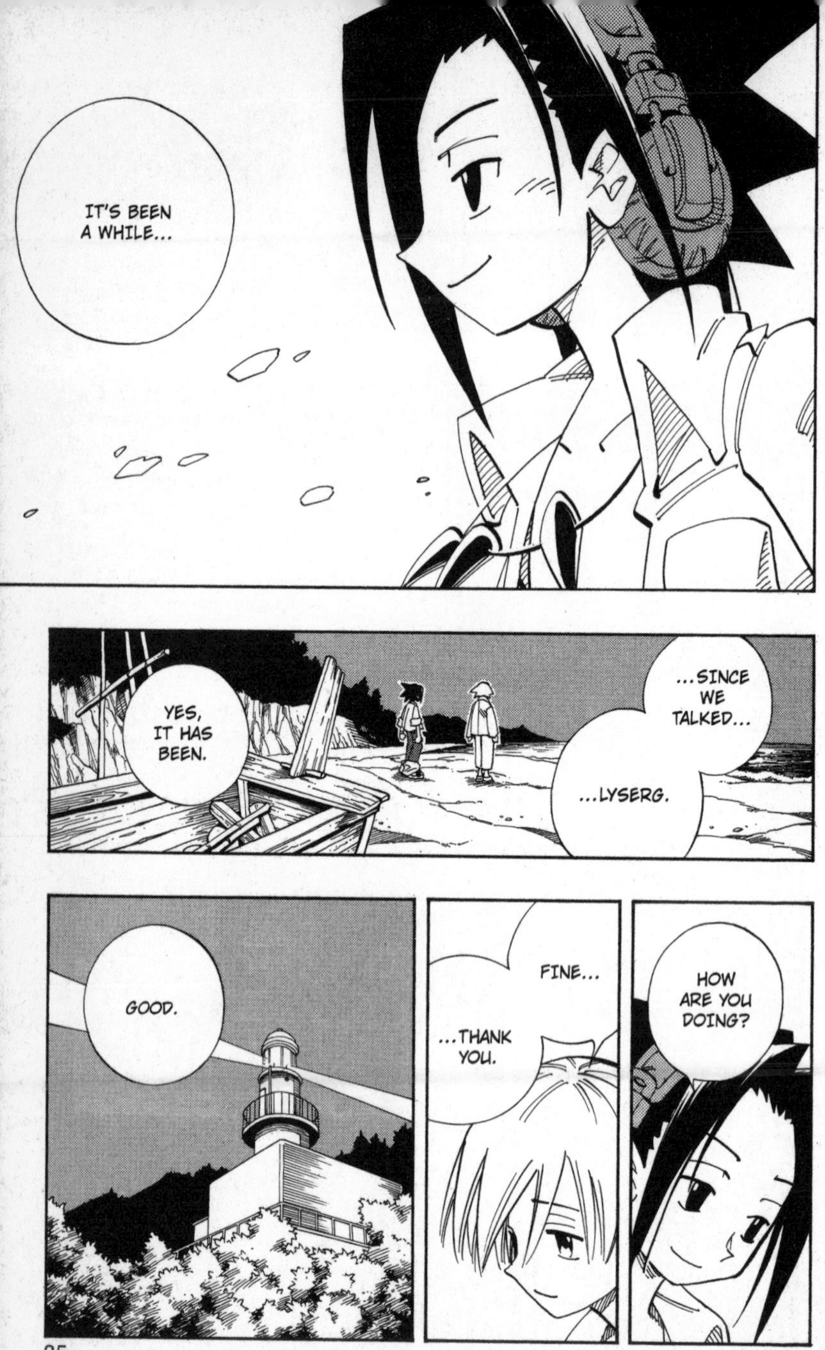
IT'S BEEN A WHILE...
...SINCE WE TALKED...
...LYSERG.
YES, IT HAS BEEN.
HOW ARE YOU DOING?
FINE...
...THANK YOU.
GOOD.

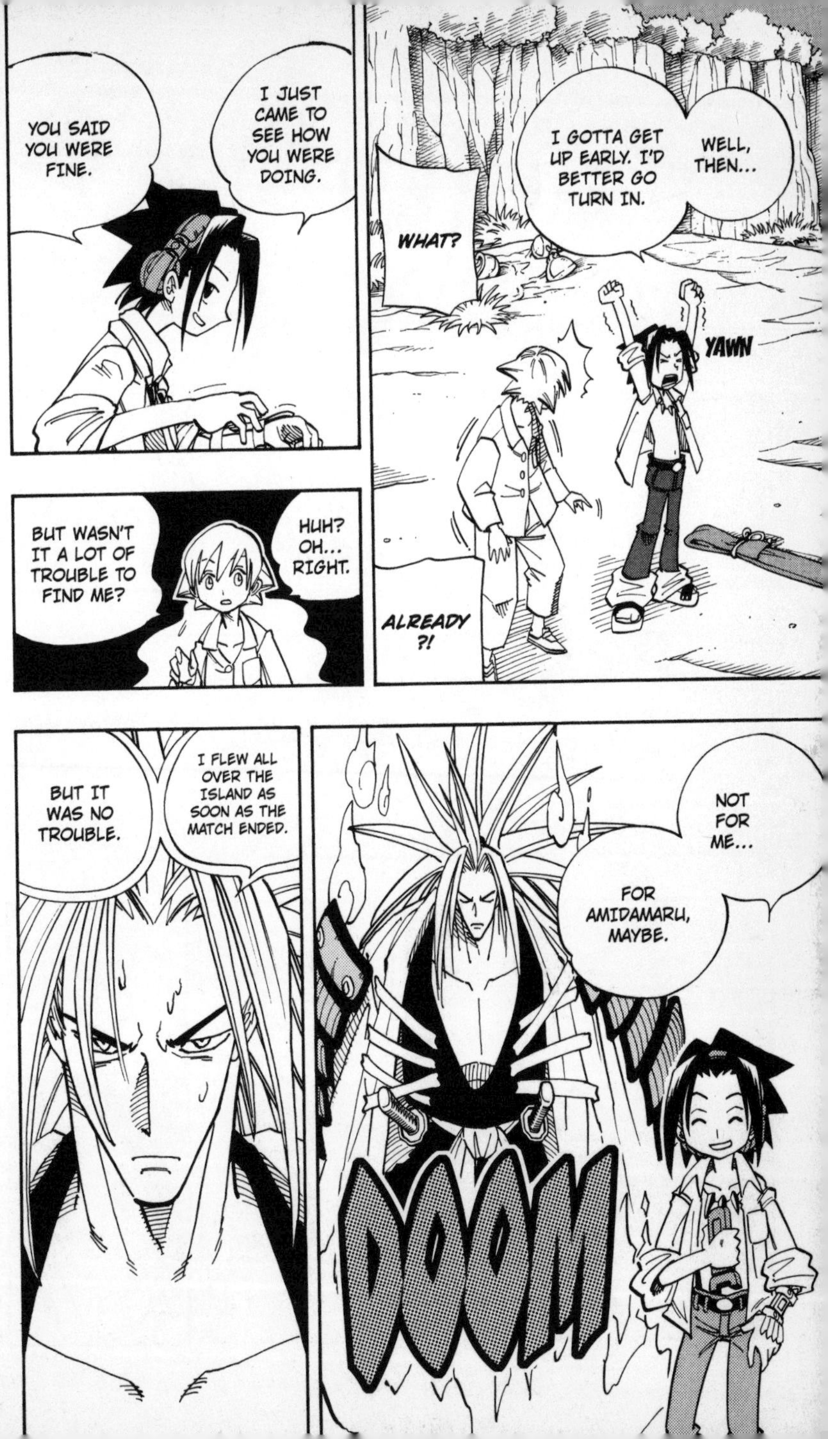
WELL, THEN...
I GOTTA GET UP EARLY. I'D BETTER GO TURN IN.
YAWN
WHAT?
ALREADY ?!
I JUST CAME TO SEE HOW YOU WERE DOING.
YOU SAID YOU WERE FINE.
HUH? OH... RIGHT.
BUT WASN'T IT A LOT OF TROUBLE TO FIND ME?
NOT FOR ME...
FOR AMIDAMARU, MAYBE.
DOOM
I FLEW ALL OVER THE ISLAND AS SOON AS THE MATCH ENDED.
BUT IT WAS NO TROUBLE.

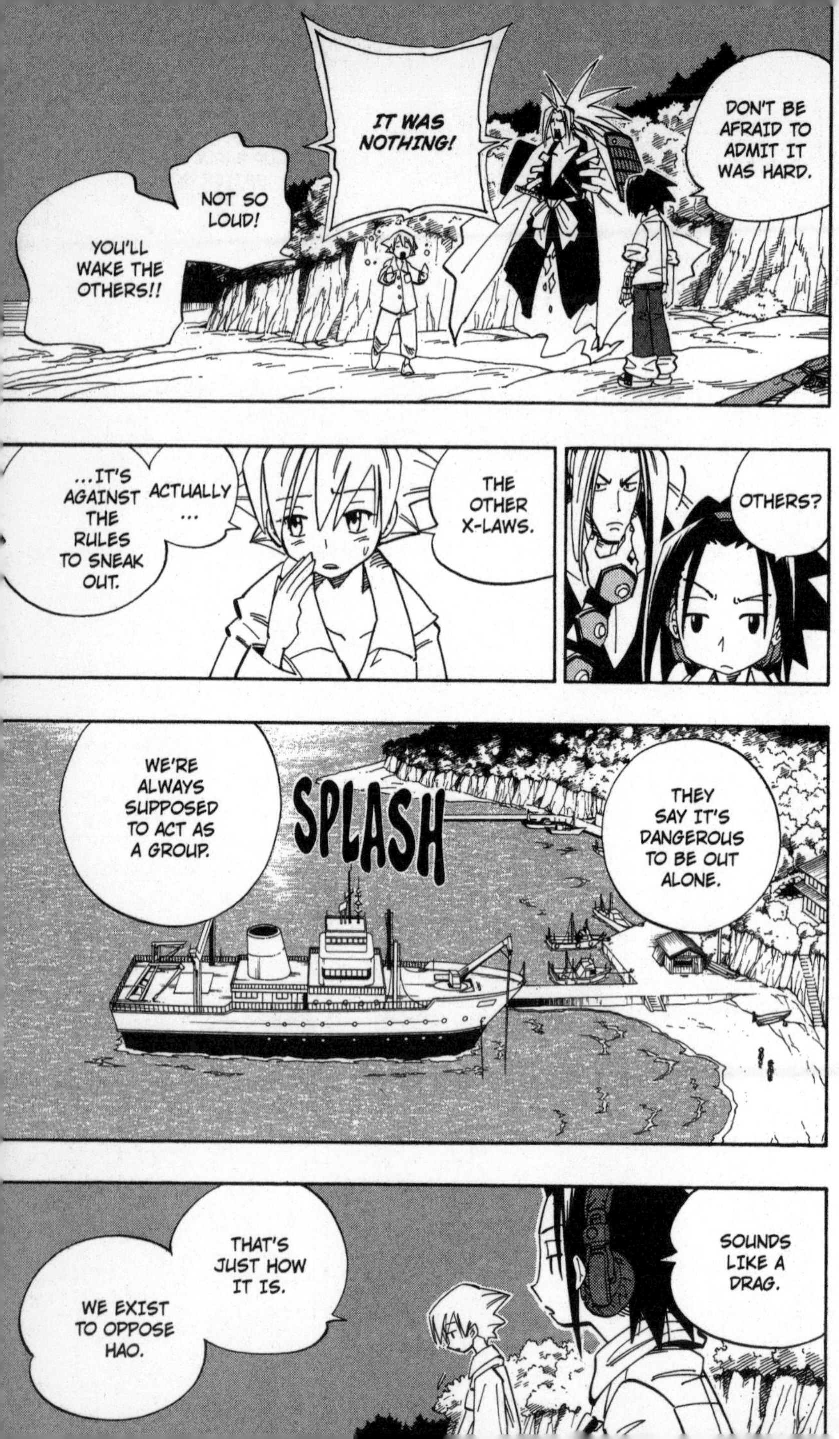
DON'T BE AFRAID TO ADMIT IT WAS HARD.
IT WAS NOTHING!
NOT SO LOUD!
YOU'LL WAKE THE OTHERS!!
OTHERS?
THE OTHER X-LAWS.
ACTUALLY ...
...IT'S AGAINST THE RULES TO SNEAK OUT.
THEY SAY IT'S DANGEROUS TO BE OUT ALONE.
SPLASH
WE'RE ALWAYS SUPPOSED TO ACT AS A GROUP.
SOUNDS LIKE A DRAG.
THAT'S JUST HOW IT IS.
WE EXIST TO OPPOSE HAO.

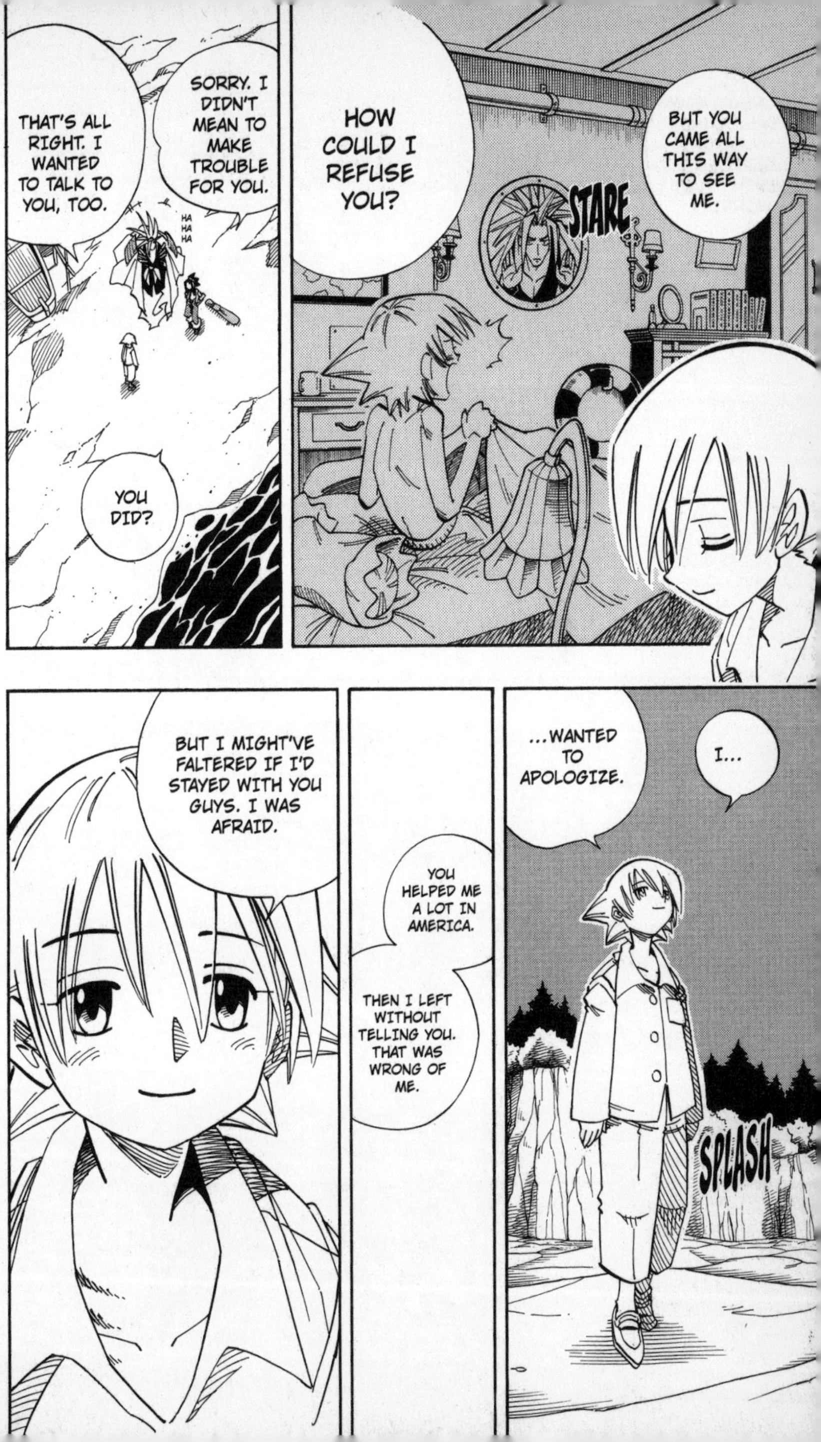
BUT YOU CAME ALL THIS WAY TO SEE ME.
HOW COULD I REFUSE YOU?
STARE
SORRY. I DIDN'T MEAN TO MAKE TROUBLE FOR YOU.
THAT'S ALL RIGHT. I WANTED TO TALK TO YOU, TOO.
HA HA HA
YOU DID?
I...
...WANTED TO APOLOGIZE.
SPLASH
YOU HELPED ME A LOT IN AMERICA.
THEN I LEFT WITHOUT TELLING YOU. THAT WAS WRONG OF ME.
BUT I MIGHT'VE FALTERED IF I'D STAYED WITH YOU GUYS. I WAS AFRAID.

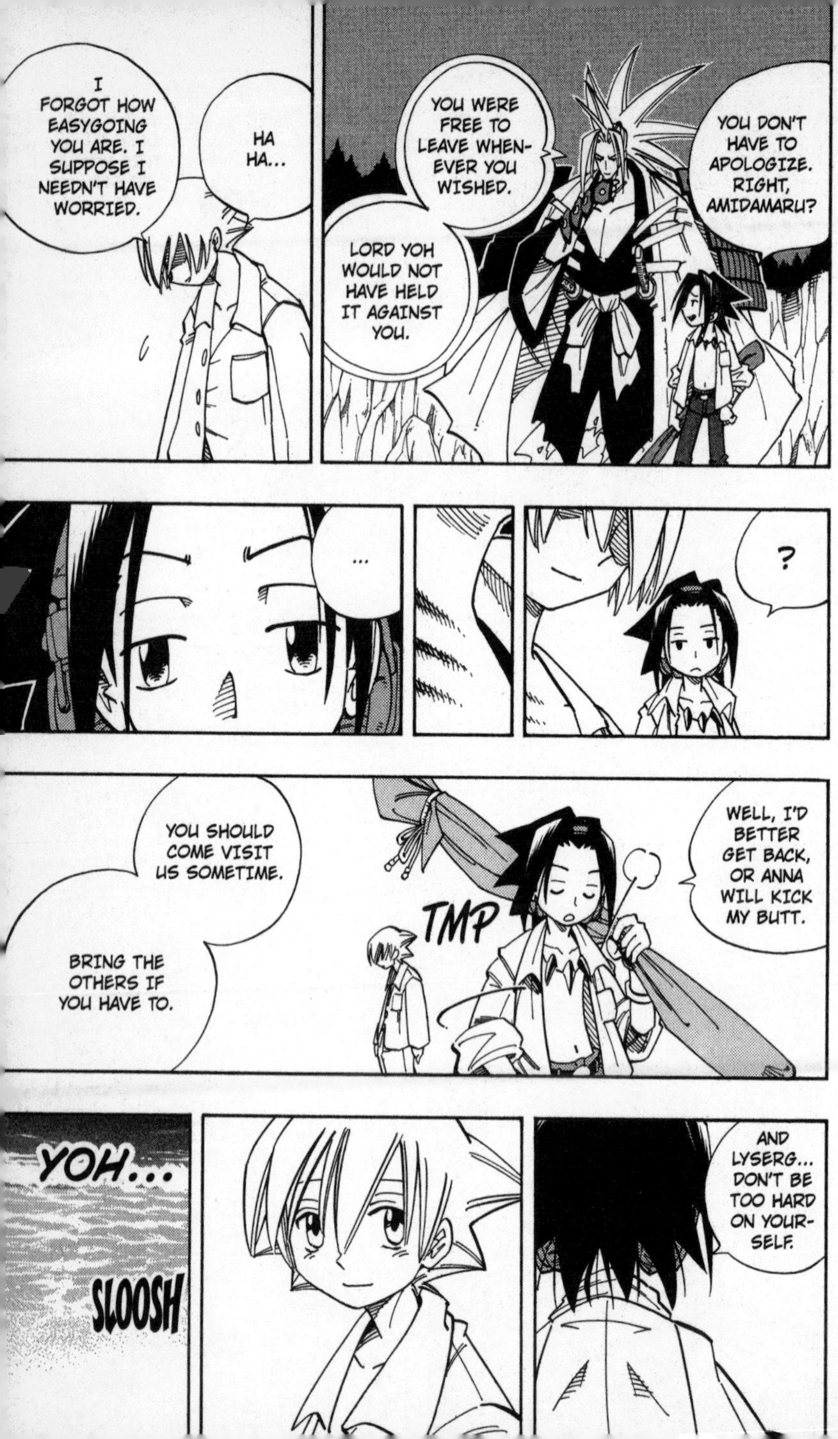
YOU DON'T HAVE TO APOLOGIZE. RIGHT, AMIDAMARU?
YOU WERE FREE TO LEAVE WHEN-EVER YOU WISHED.
LORD YOH WOULD NOT HAVE HELD IT AGAINST YOU.
HA HA...
I FORGOT HOW EASYGOING YOU ARE. I SUPPOSE I NEEDN'T HAVE WORRIED.
?
...
WELL, I'D BETTER GET BACK, OR ANNA WILL KICK MY BUTT.
TMP
YOU SHOULD COME VISIT US SOMETIME.
BRING THE OTHERS IF YOU HAVE TO.
AND LYSERG... DON'T BE TOO HARD ON YOUR-SELF.
YOH...
SLOOSH

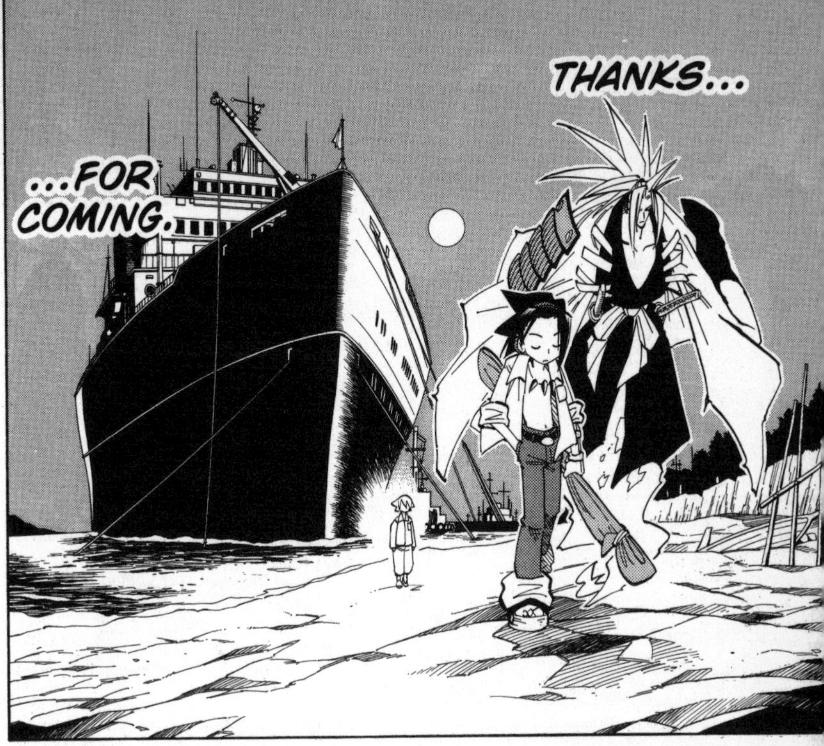
THANKS...
...FOR COMING.
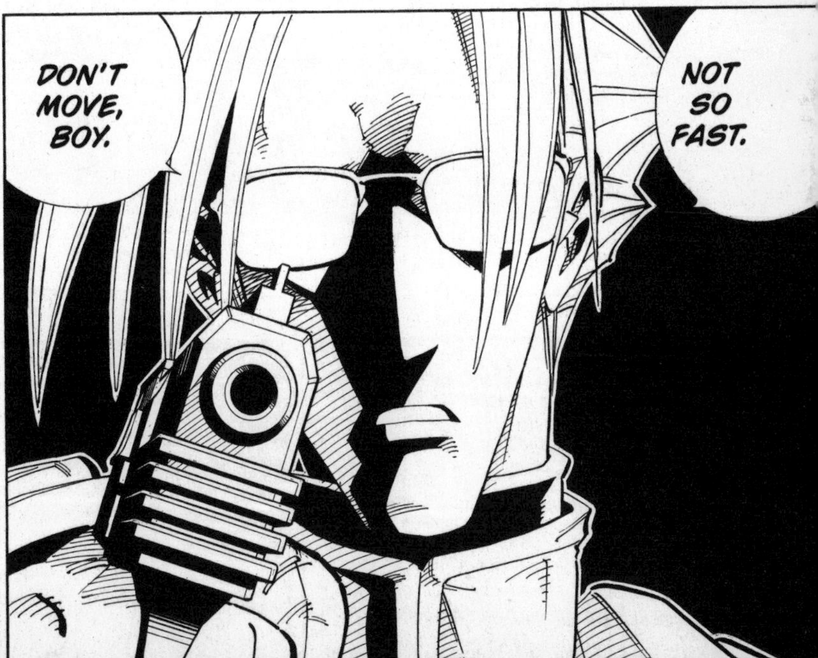
NOT SO FAST.
DON'T MOVE, BOY.

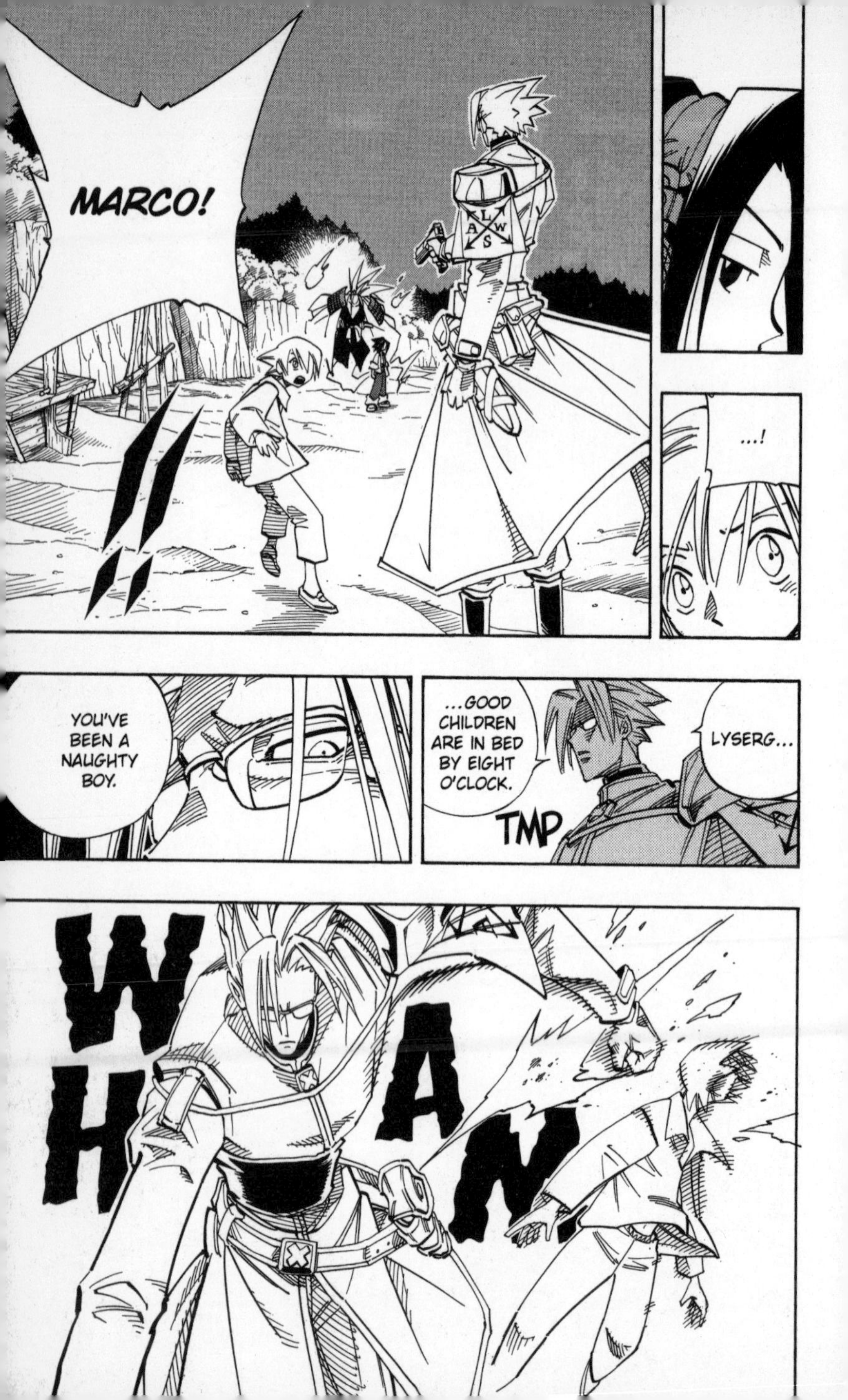
...!
MARCO!
LYSERG...
...GOOD CHILDREN ARE IN BED BY EIGHT O'CLOCK.
TMP
YOU'VE BEEN A NAUGHTY BOY.
WHAM

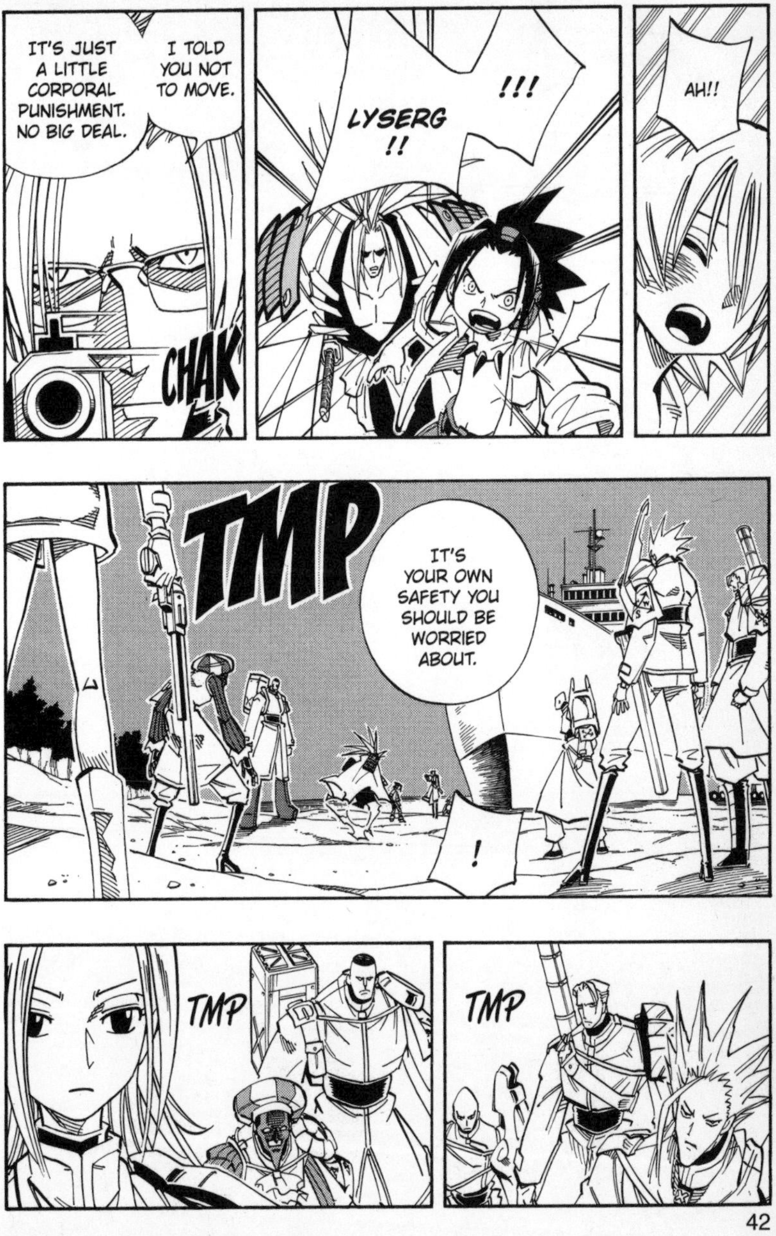
AH!!
!!!
LYSERG !!
I TOLD YOU NOT TO MOVE.
IT'S JUST A LITTLE CORPORAL PUNISHMENT. NO BIG DEAL.
CHAK
IT'S YOUR OWN SAFETY YOU SHOULD BE WORRIED ABOUT.
TMP
!
TMP
TMP

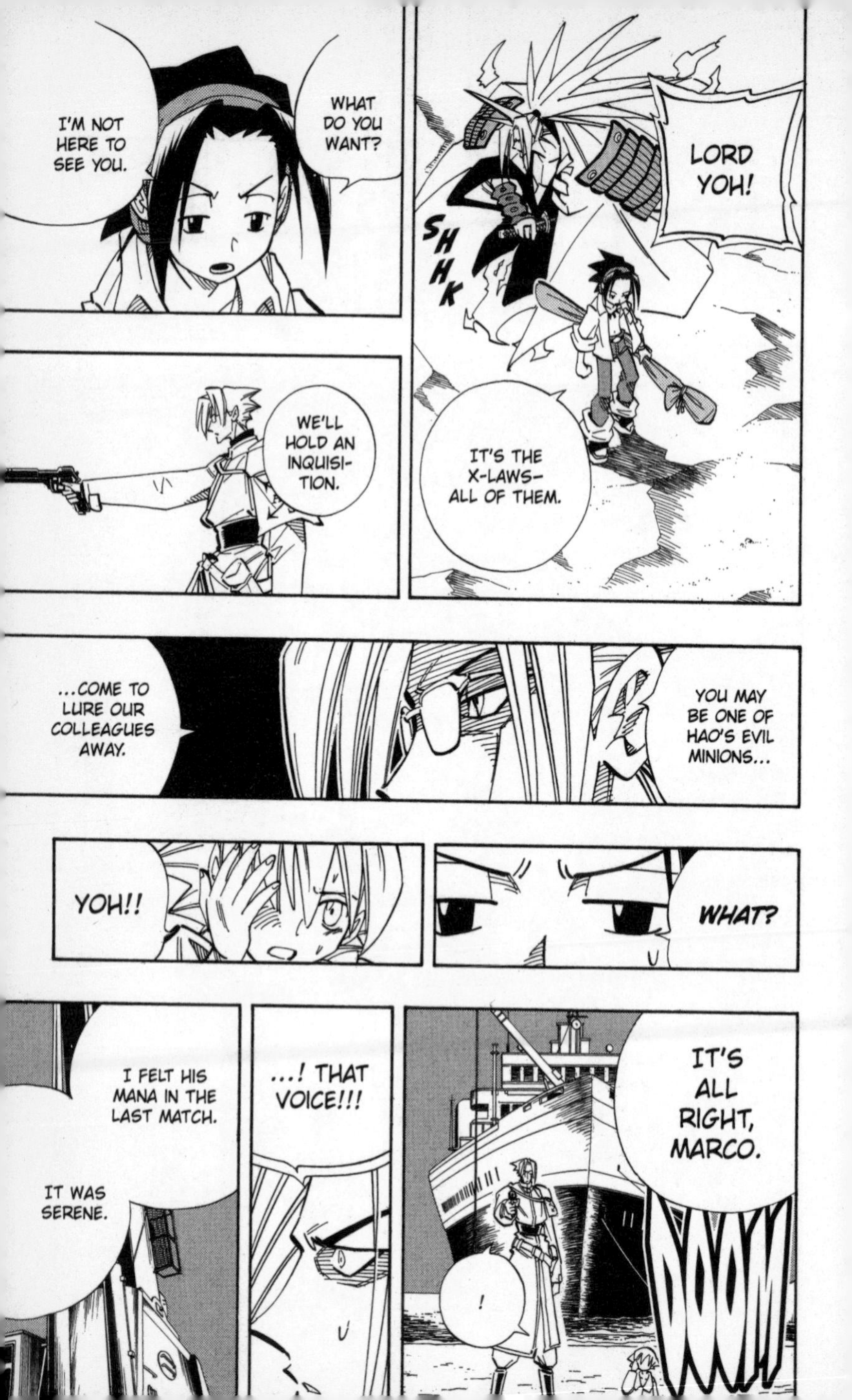
LORD YOH!
SHHK
IT'S THE X-LAWS—ALL OF THEM.
WHAT DO YOU WANT?
I'M NOT HERE TO SEE YOU.
WE'LL HOLD AN INQUISITION.
YOU MAY BE ONE OF HAO'S EVIL MINIONS...
...COME TO LURE OUR COLLEAGUES AWAY.
WHAT?
YOH!!
IT'S ALL RIGHT, MARCO.
DOOM
!
...! THAT VOICE!!!
I FELT HIS MANA IN THE LAST MATCH.
IT WAS SERENE.

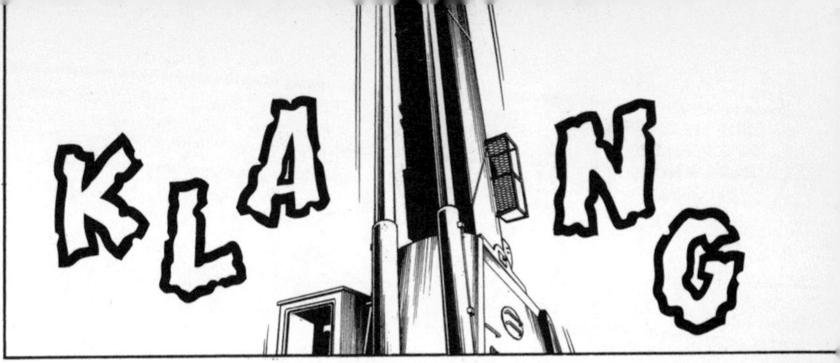
KLANG

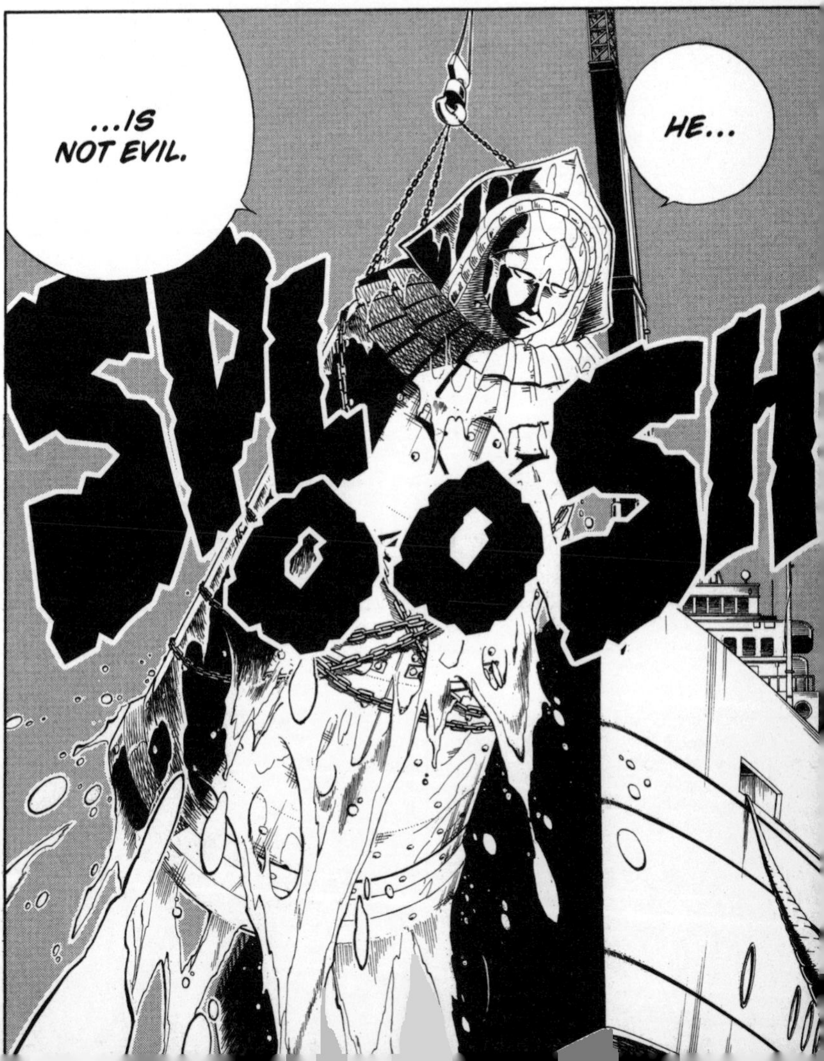
HE...
...IS NOT EVIL.
SPLOOOSH

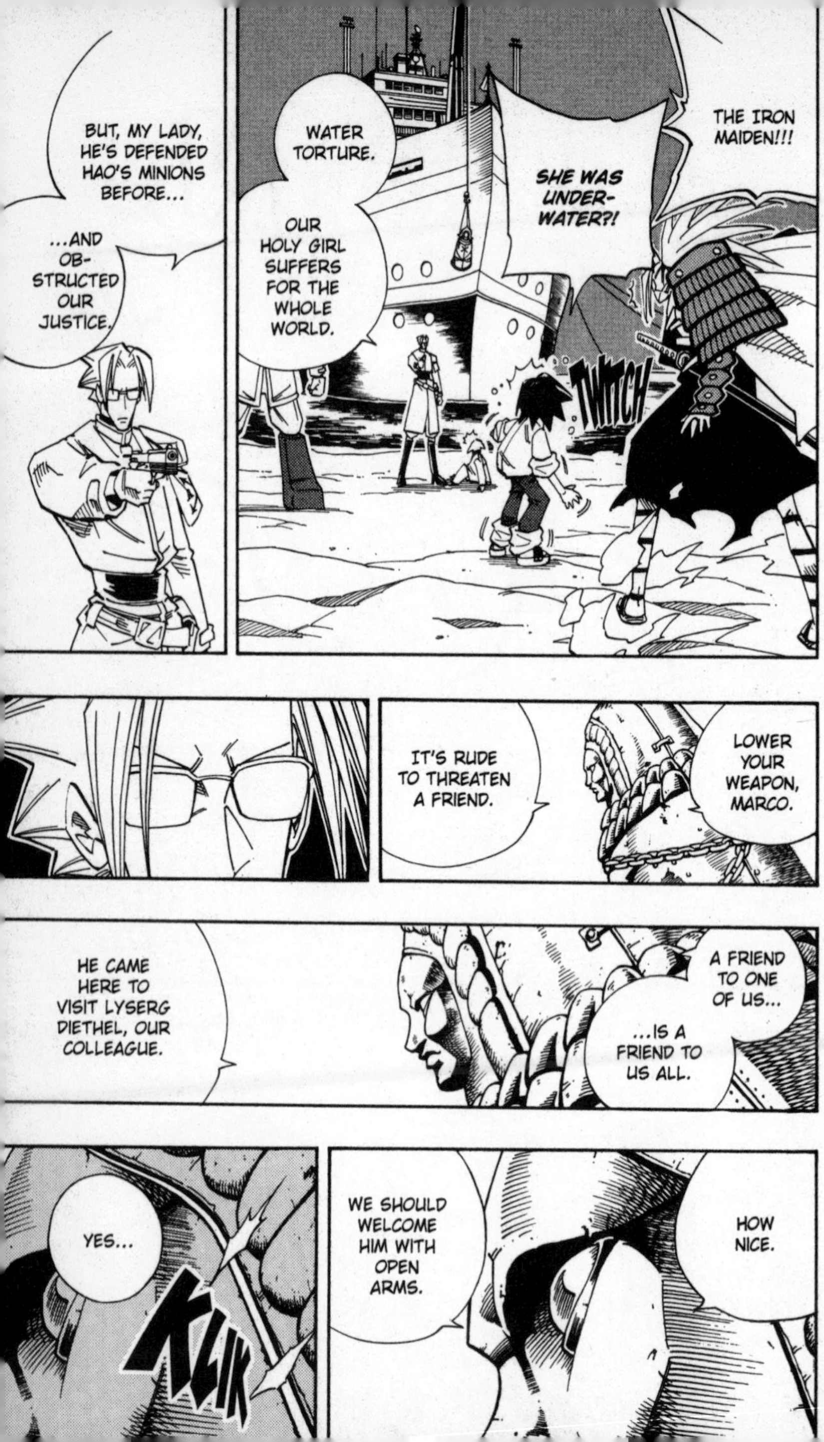
THE IRON MAIDEN!!!
SHE WAS UNDER-WATER?!
WATER TORTURE.
OUR HOLY GIRL SUFFERS FOR THE WHOLE WORLD.
TWITCH
BUT, MY LADY, HE'S DEFENDED HAO'S MINIONS BEFORE...
...AND OB-STRUCTED OUR JUSTICE.
LOWER YOUR WEAPON, MARCO.
IT'S RUDE TO THREATEN A FRIEND.
A FRIEND TO ONE OF US...
...IS A FRIEND TO US ALL.
HE CAME HERE TO VISIT LYSERG DIETHEL, OUR COLLEAGUE.
HOW NICE.
WE SHOULD WELCOME HIM WITH OPEN ARMS.
YES...
KLIK

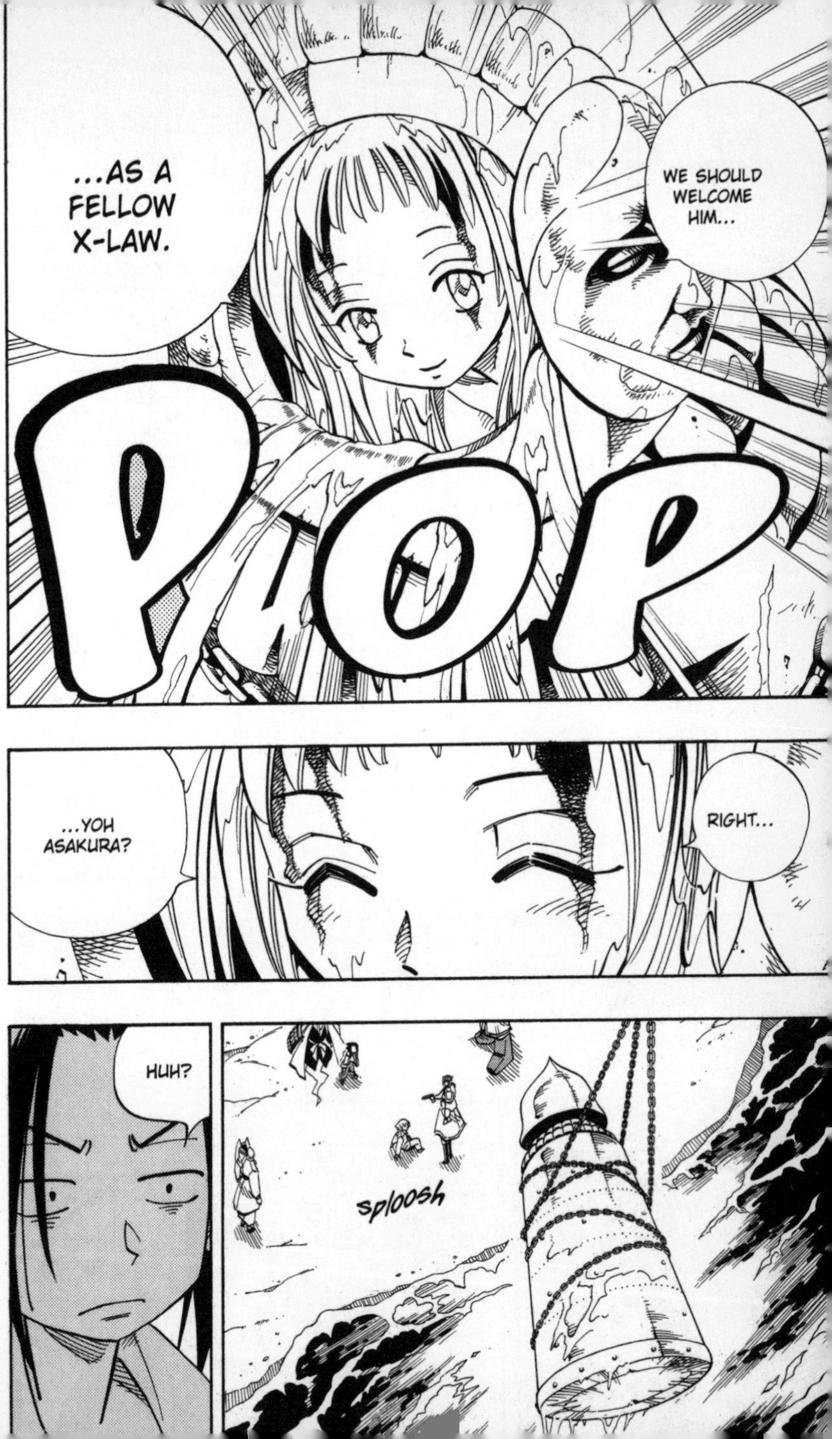
WE SHOULD WELCOME HIM...
...AS A FELLOW X-LAW.
PLOP
RIGHT...
...YOH ASAKURA?
sploosh
HUH?

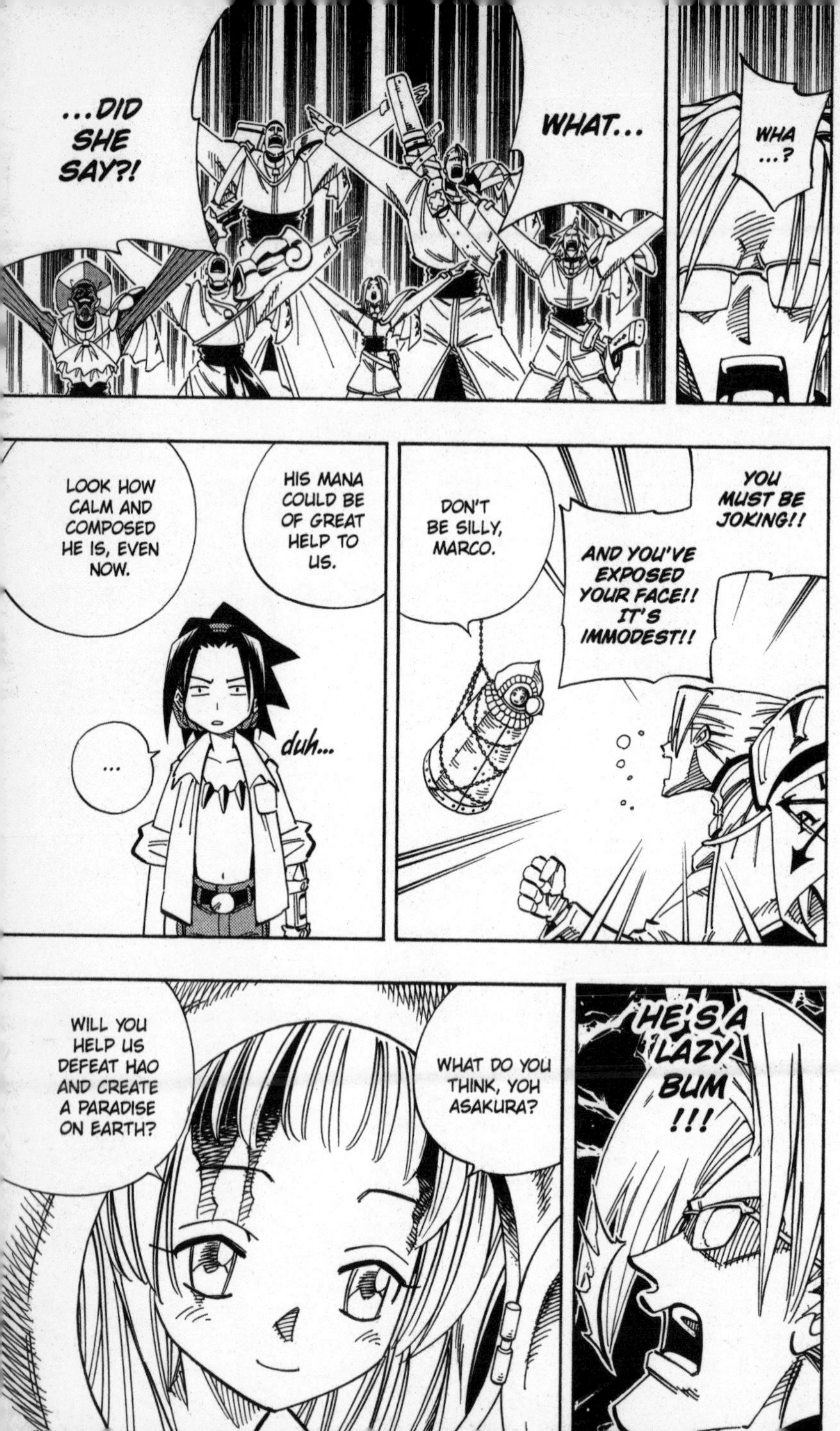
WHA ...?
WHAT...
...DID SHE SAY?!
YOU MUST BE JOKING!!
AND YOU'VE EXPOSED YOUR FACE!! IT'S IMMODEST!!
DON'T BE SILLY, MARCO.
HIS MANA COULD BE OF GREAT HELP TO US.
LOOK HOW CALM AND COMPOSED HE IS, EVEN NOW.
duh...
...
HE'S A LAZY BUM!!!
WHAT DO YOU THINK, YOH ASAKURA?
WILL YOU HELP US DEFEAT HAO AND CREATE A PARADISE ON EARTH?

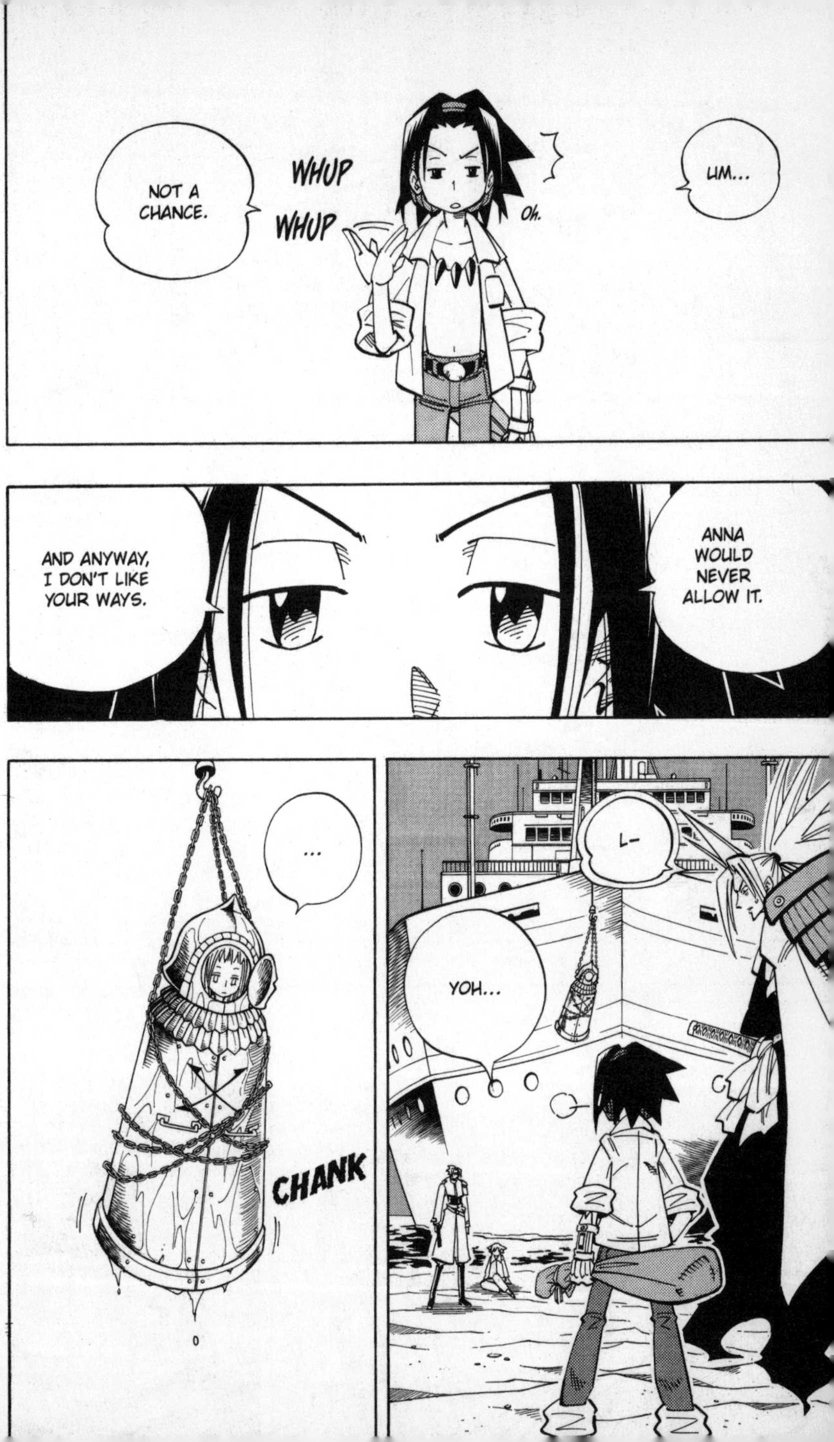
UM...
Oh.
WHUP
WHUP
NOT A CHANCE.
ANNA WOULD NEVER ALLOW IT.
AND ANYWAY, I DON'T LIKE YOUR WAYS.
L-
YOH...
...
CHANK

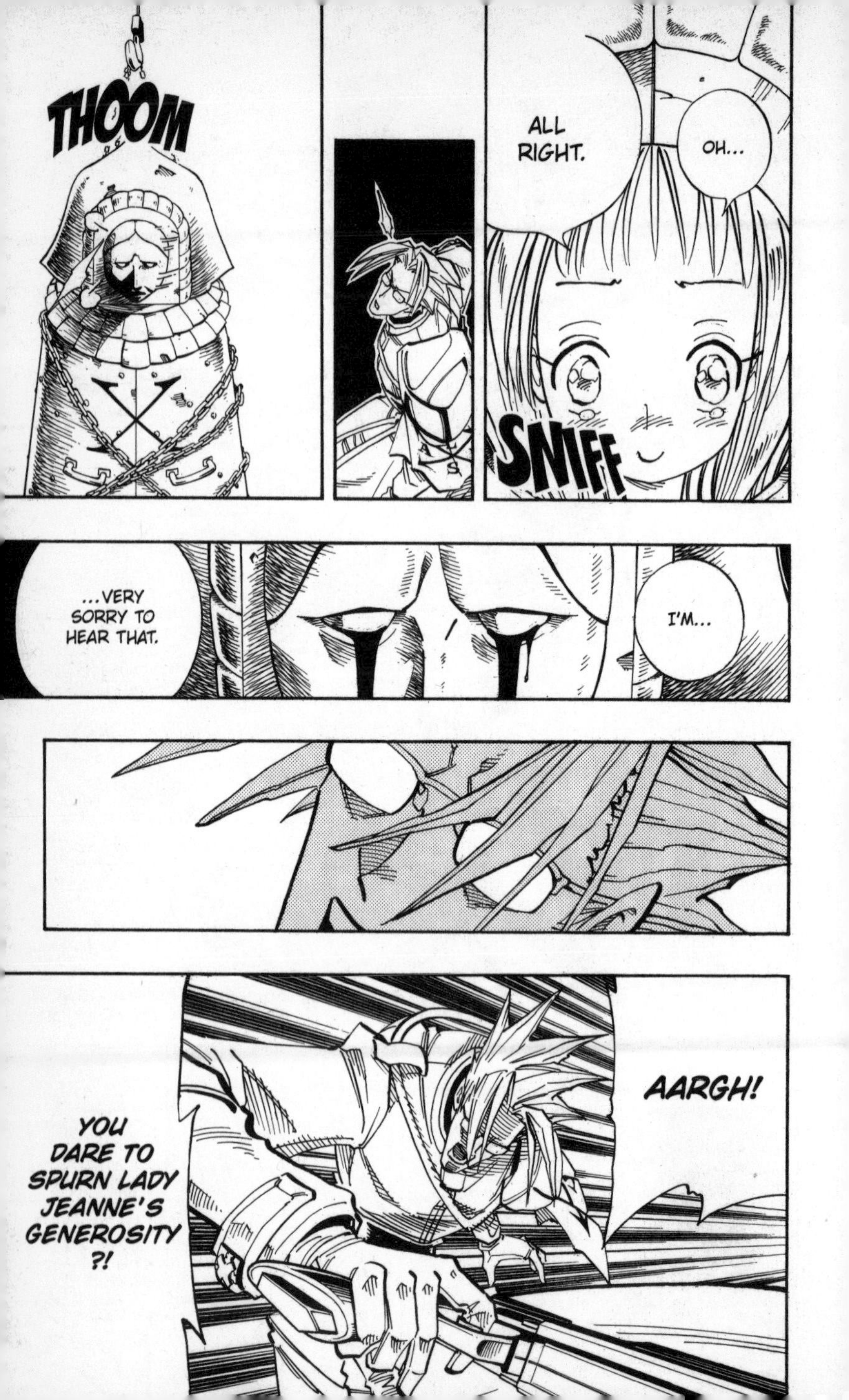
OH...
ALL RIGHT.
SNIFF
THOOM
I'M...
...VERY SORRY TO HEAR THAT.
AARGH!
YOU DARE TO SPURN LADY JEANNE'S GENEROSITY ?!

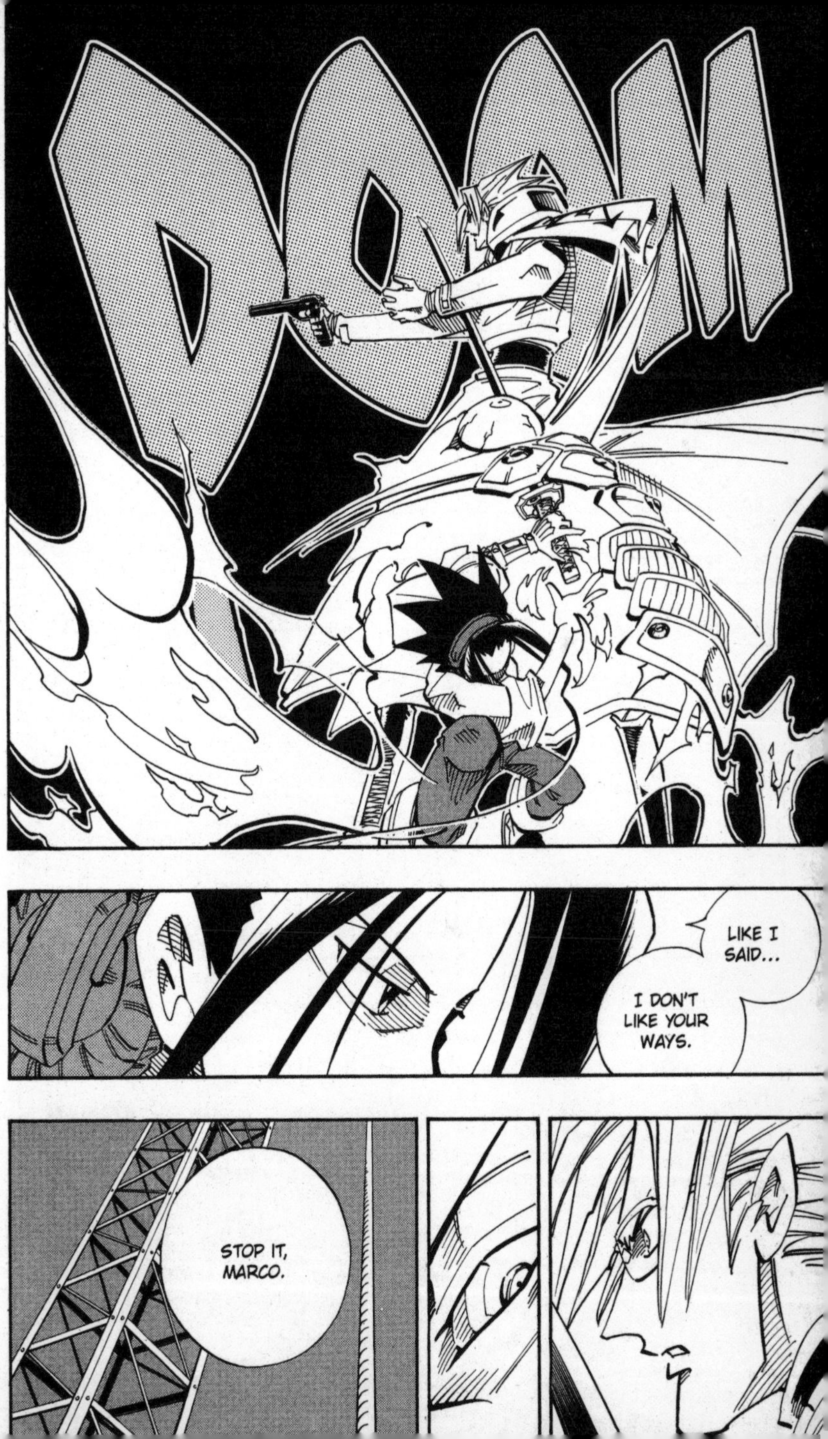
DOOM
LIKE I SAID...
I DON'T LIKE YOUR WAYS.
STOP IT, MARCO.

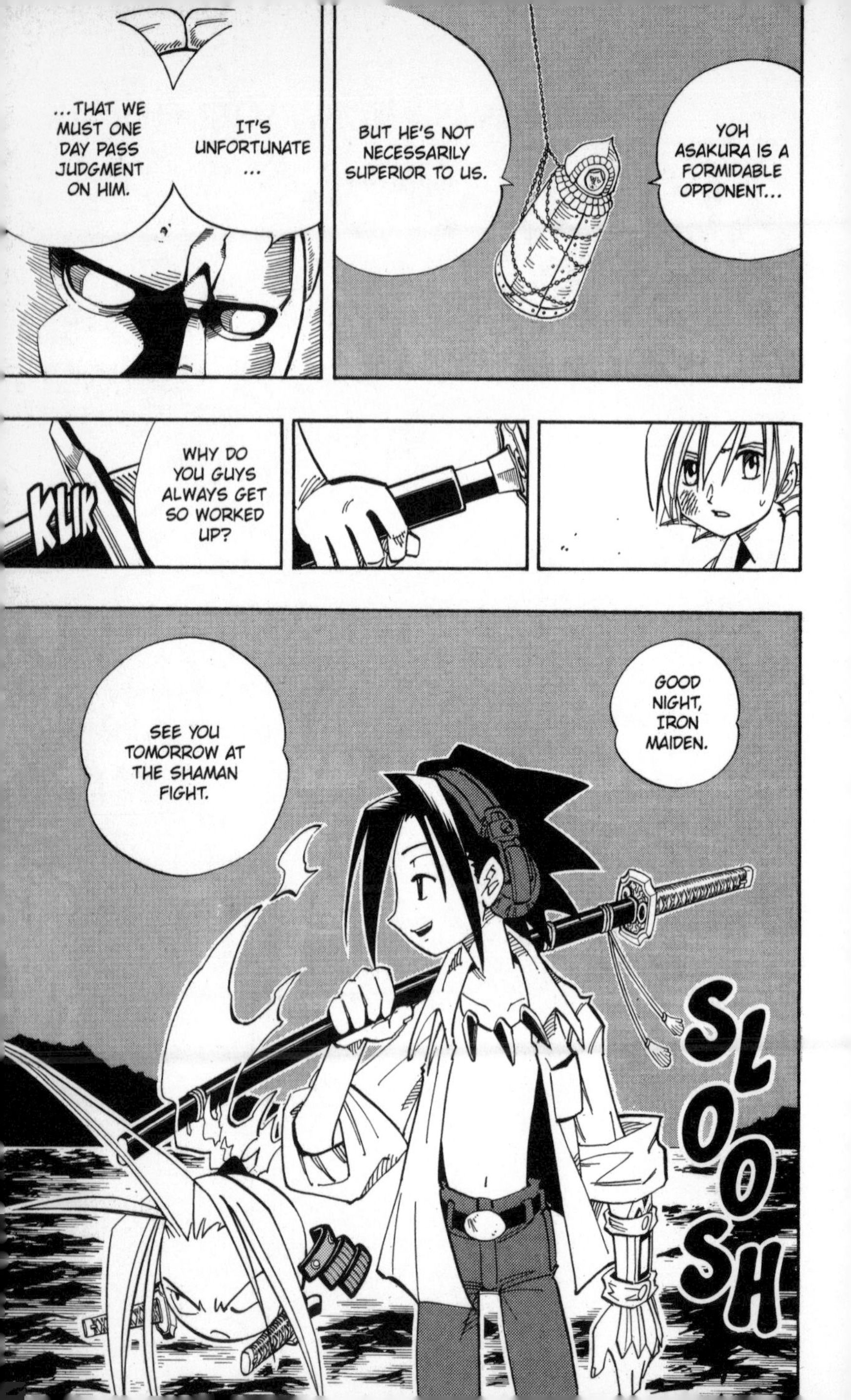
YOH ASAKURA IS A FORMIDABLE OPPONENT...
BUT HE'S NOT NECESSARILY SUPERIOR TO US.
IT'S UNFORTUNATE ...
...THAT WE MUST ONE DAY PASS JUDGMENT ON HIM.
..
WHY DO YOU GUYS ALWAYS GET SO WORKED UP?
KLIK
GOOD NIGHT, IRON MAIDEN.
SEE YOU TOMORROW AT THE SHAMAN FIGHT.
SLOOOSH

SHAMAN KING CHARACTER FILE No.79

スピリット・オブ・ファイア

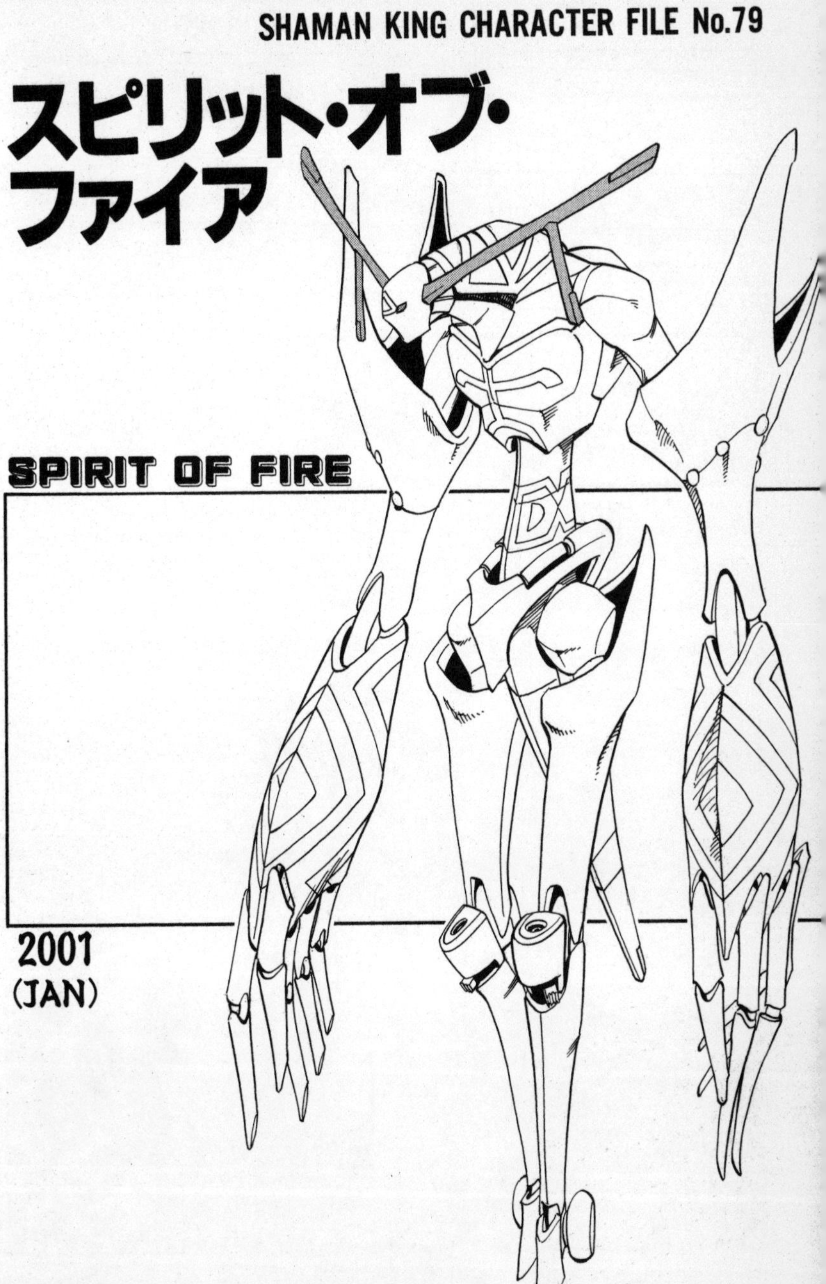

SPIRIT OF FIRE

2001
(JAN)

Reincarnation 137: Burning Angel

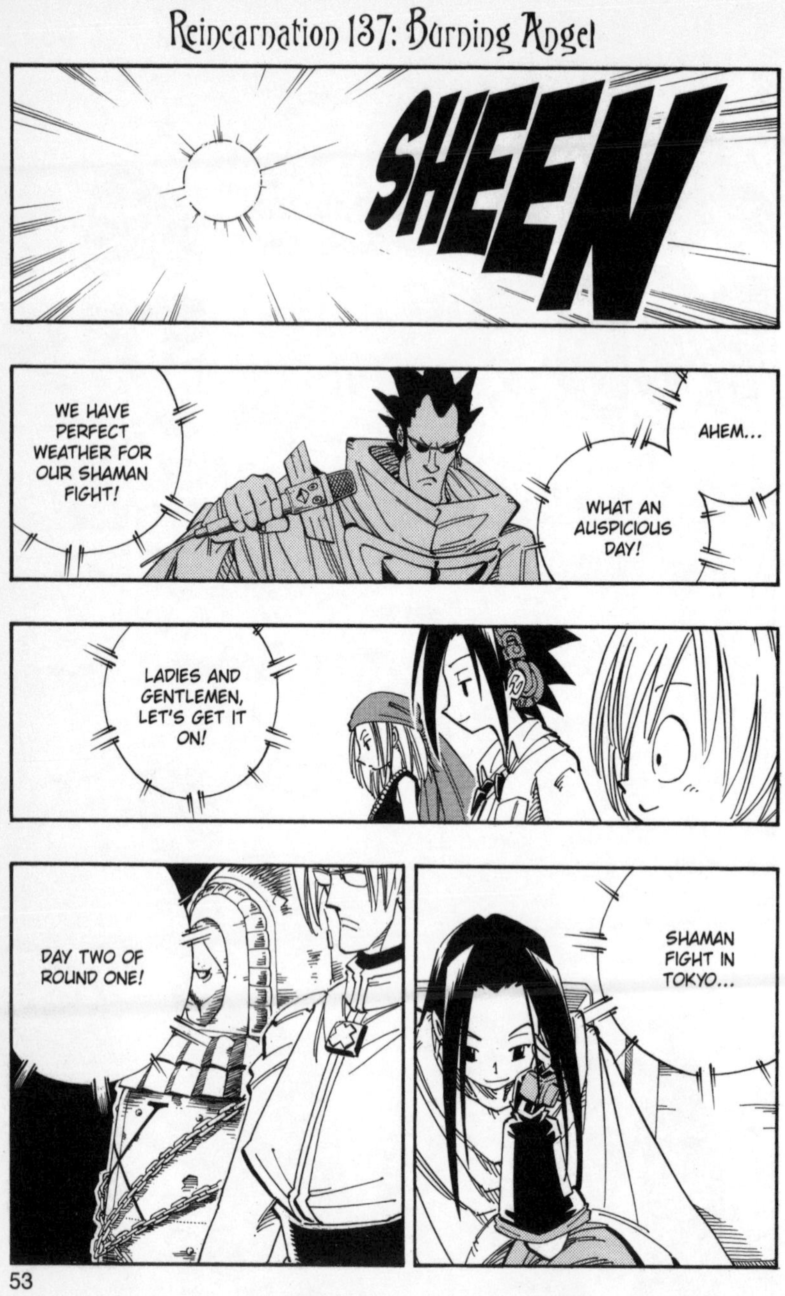
SHEEN
AHEM...
WHAT AN AUSPICIOUS DAY!
WE HAVE PERFECT WEATHER FOR OUR SHAMAN FIGHT!
LADIES AND GENTLEMEN, LET'S GET IT ON!
SHAMAN FIGHT IN TOKYO...
DAY TWO OF ROUND ONE!

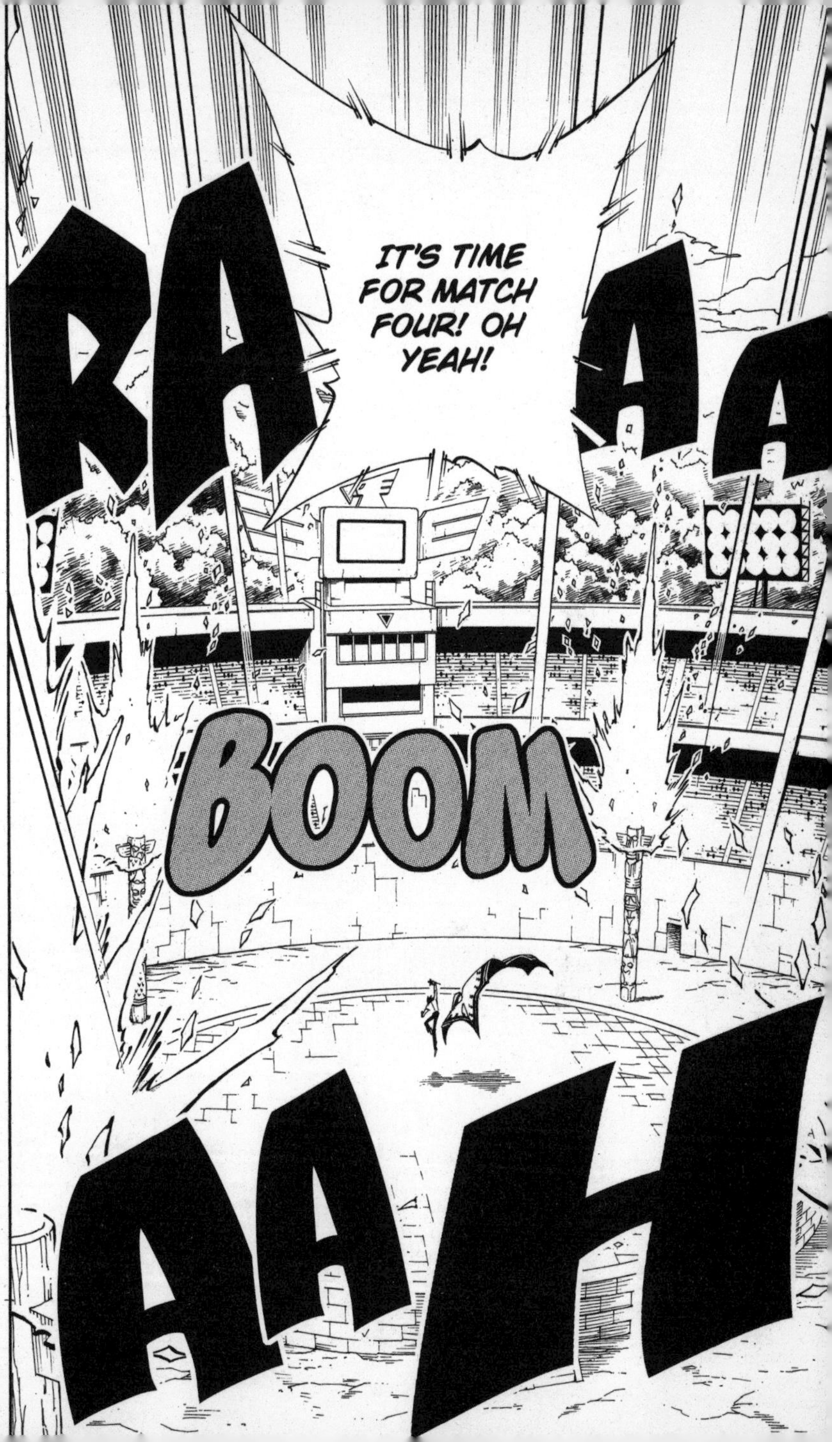
IT'S TIME FOR MATCH FOUR! OH YEAH!
BAAA
BOOM
AAH!

Reincarnation 137: Burning Angel

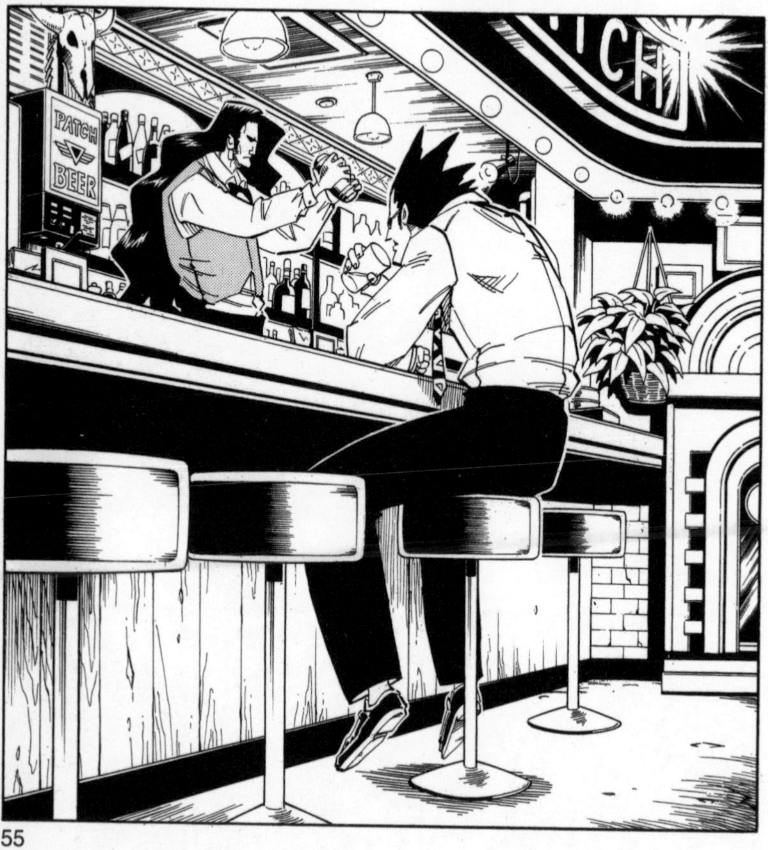
PATCH
BEER
CH

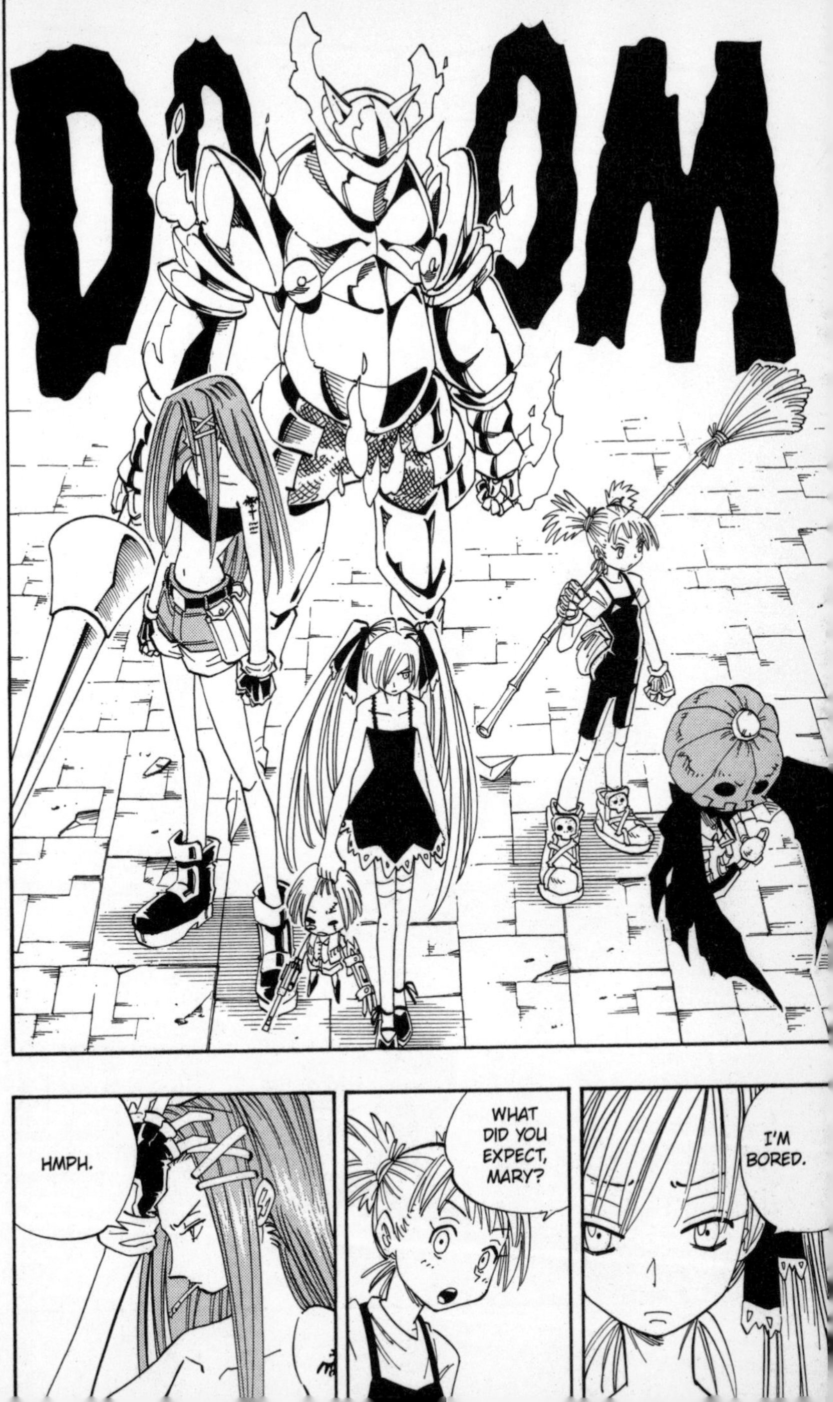
DOOM
I'M BORED.
WHAT DID YOU EXPECT, MARY?
HMPH.

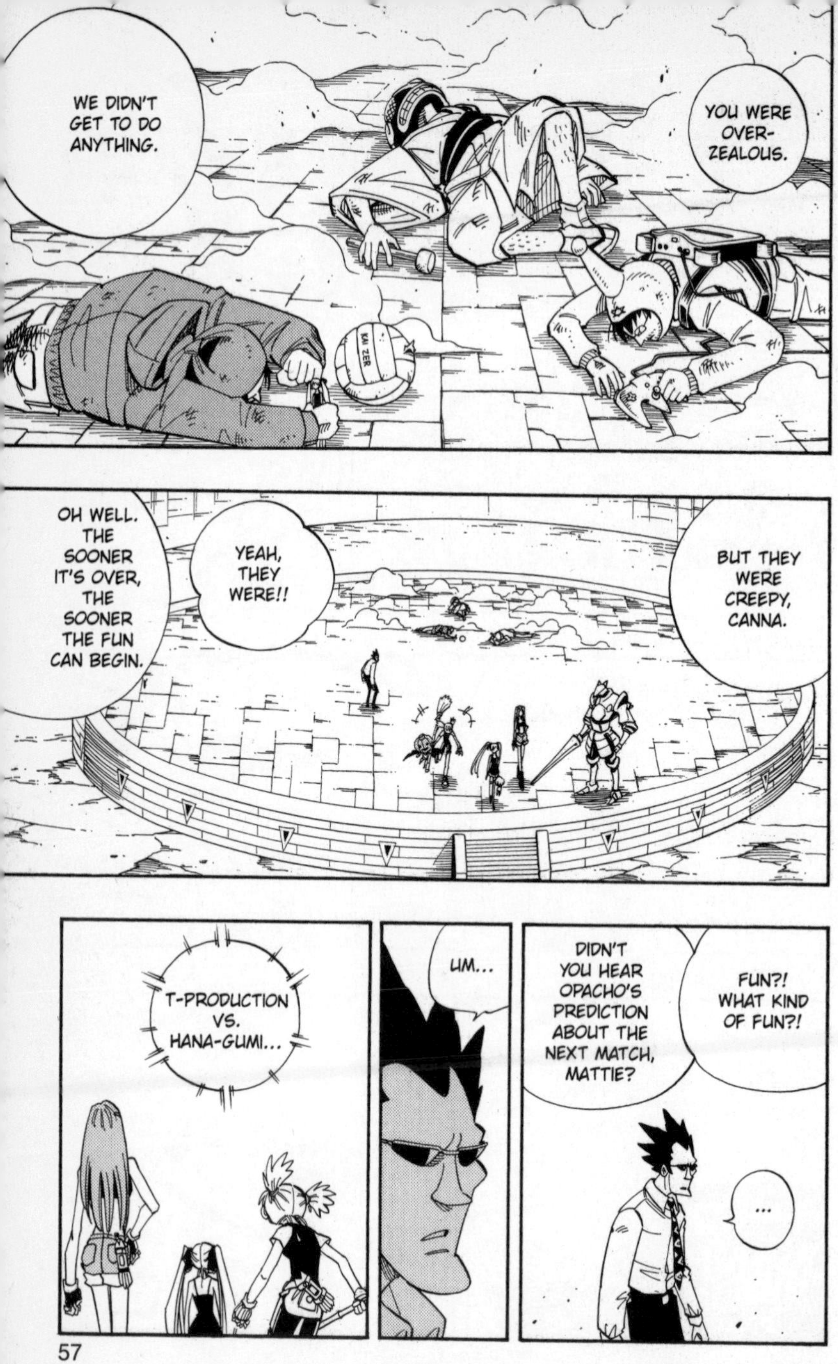
YOU WERE OVER-ZEALOUS.
WE DIDN'T GET TO DO ANYTHING.
BUT THEY WERE CREEPY, CANNA.
YEAH, THEY WERE!!
OH WELL. THE SOONER IT'S OVER, THE SOONER THE FUN CAN BEGIN.
FUN?! WHAT KIND OF FUN?!
DIDN'T YOU HEAR OPACHO'S PREDICTION ABOUT THE NEXT MATCH, MATTIE?
...
UM...
T-PRODUCTION VS. HANA-GUMI...

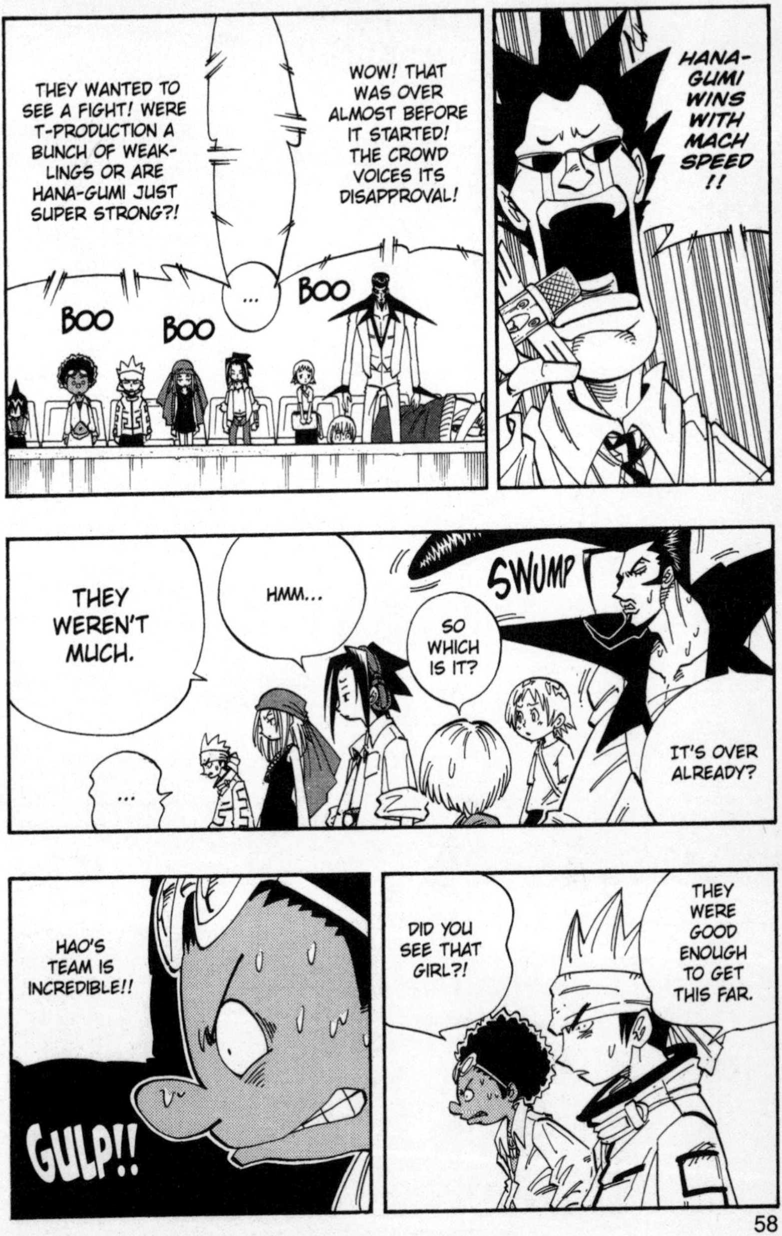
HANA-GUMI WINS WITH MACH SPEED!!
WOW! THAT WAS OVER ALMOST BEFORE IT STARTED! THE CROWD VOICES ITS DISAPPROVAL!
THEY WANTED TO SEE A FIGHT! WERE T-PRODUCTION A BUNCH OF WEAK-LINGS OR ARE HANA-GUMI JUST SUPER STRONG?!
BOO
...
BOO
BOO
SWUMP
IT'S OVER ALREADY?
SO WHICH IS IT?
HMM...
THEY WEREN'T MUCH.
...
THEY WERE GOOD ENOUGH TO GET THIS FAR.
DID YOU SEE THAT GIRL?!
HAO'S TEAM IS INCREDIBLE!!
GULP!!

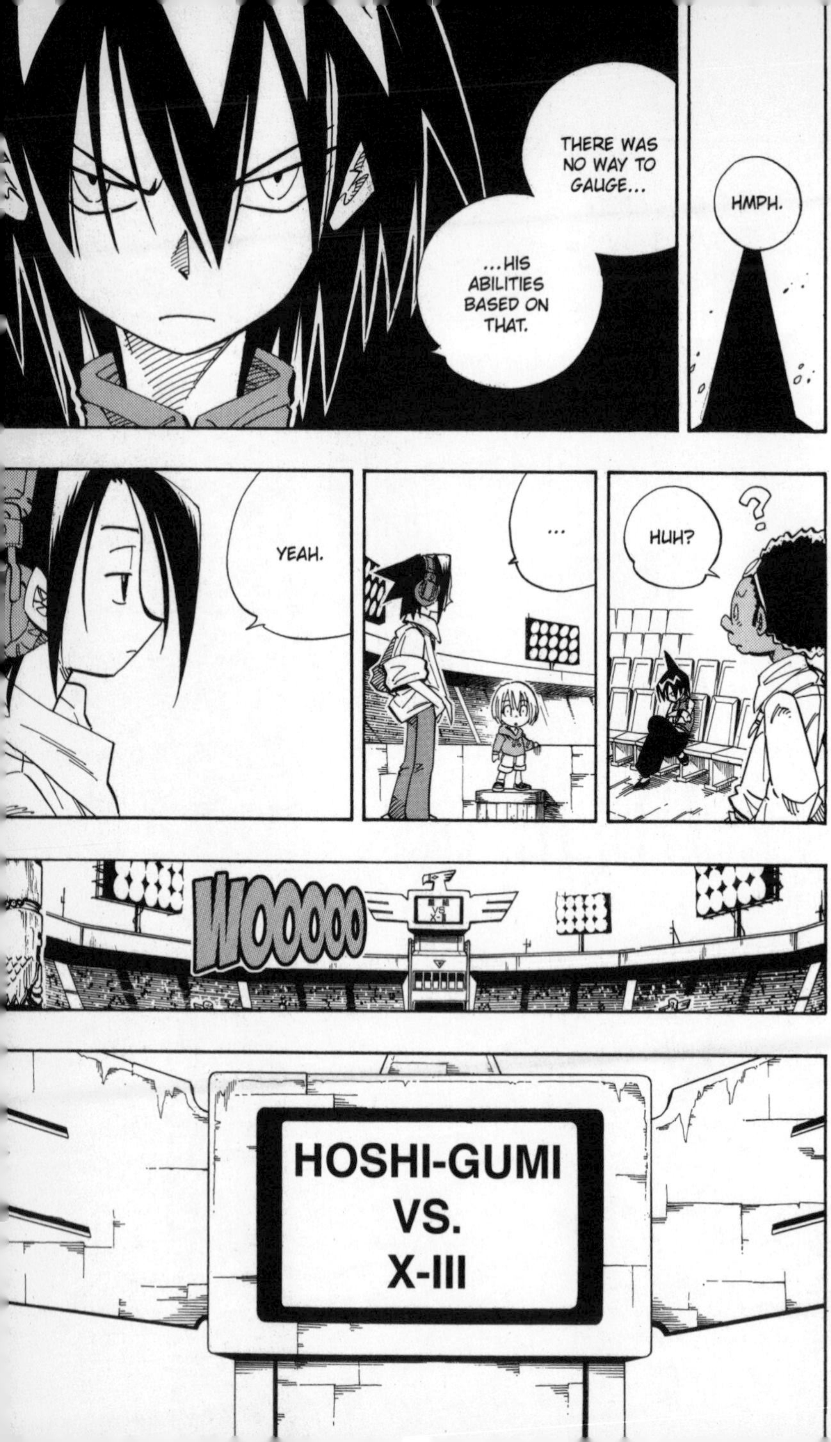
HMPH.
THERE WAS NO WAY TO GAUGE...
...HIS ABILITIES BASED ON THAT.
HUH?
...
YEAH.
WOOOOO
HOSHI-GUMI VS. X-III

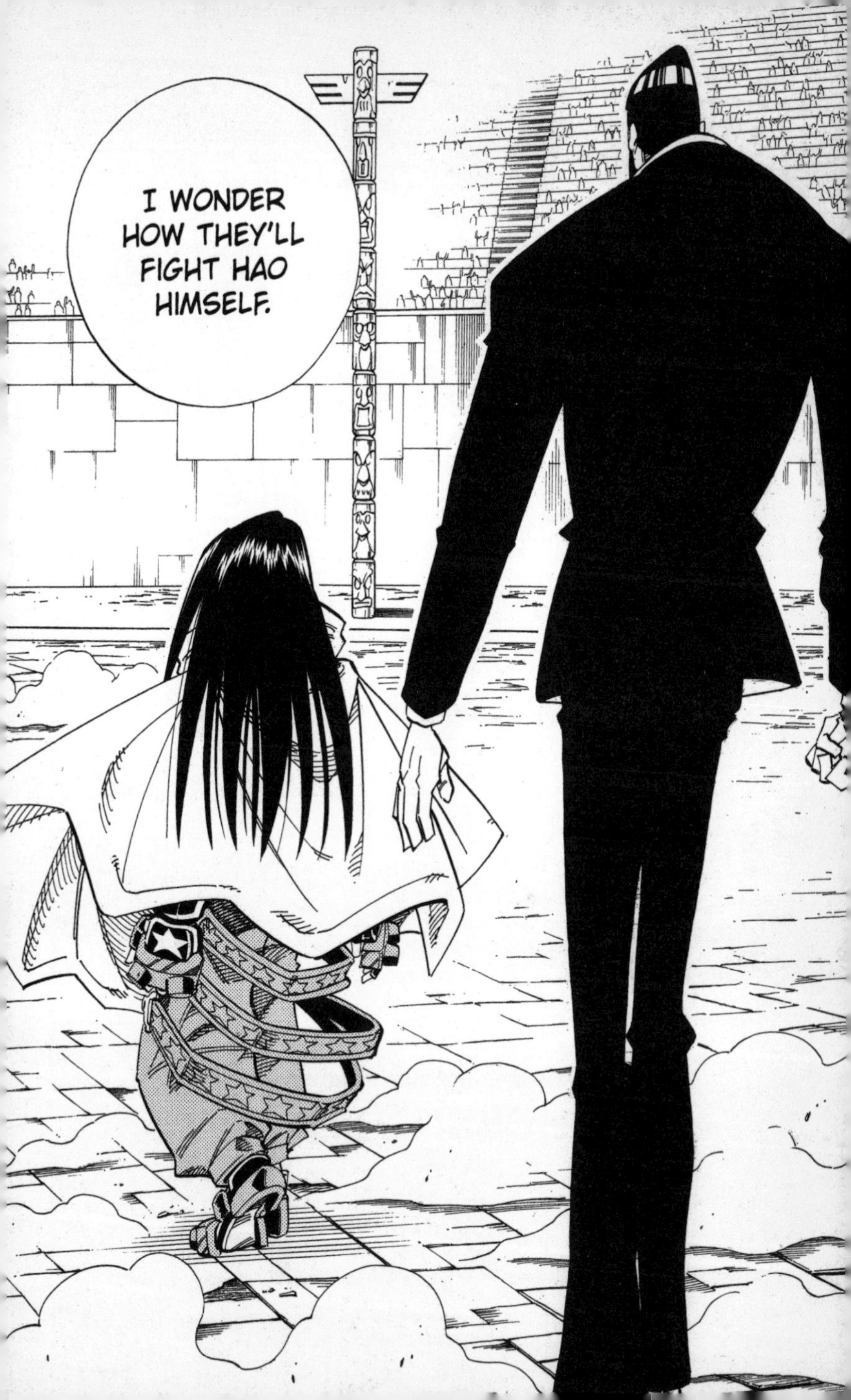
I WONDER HOW THEY'LL FIGHT HAO HIMSELF.

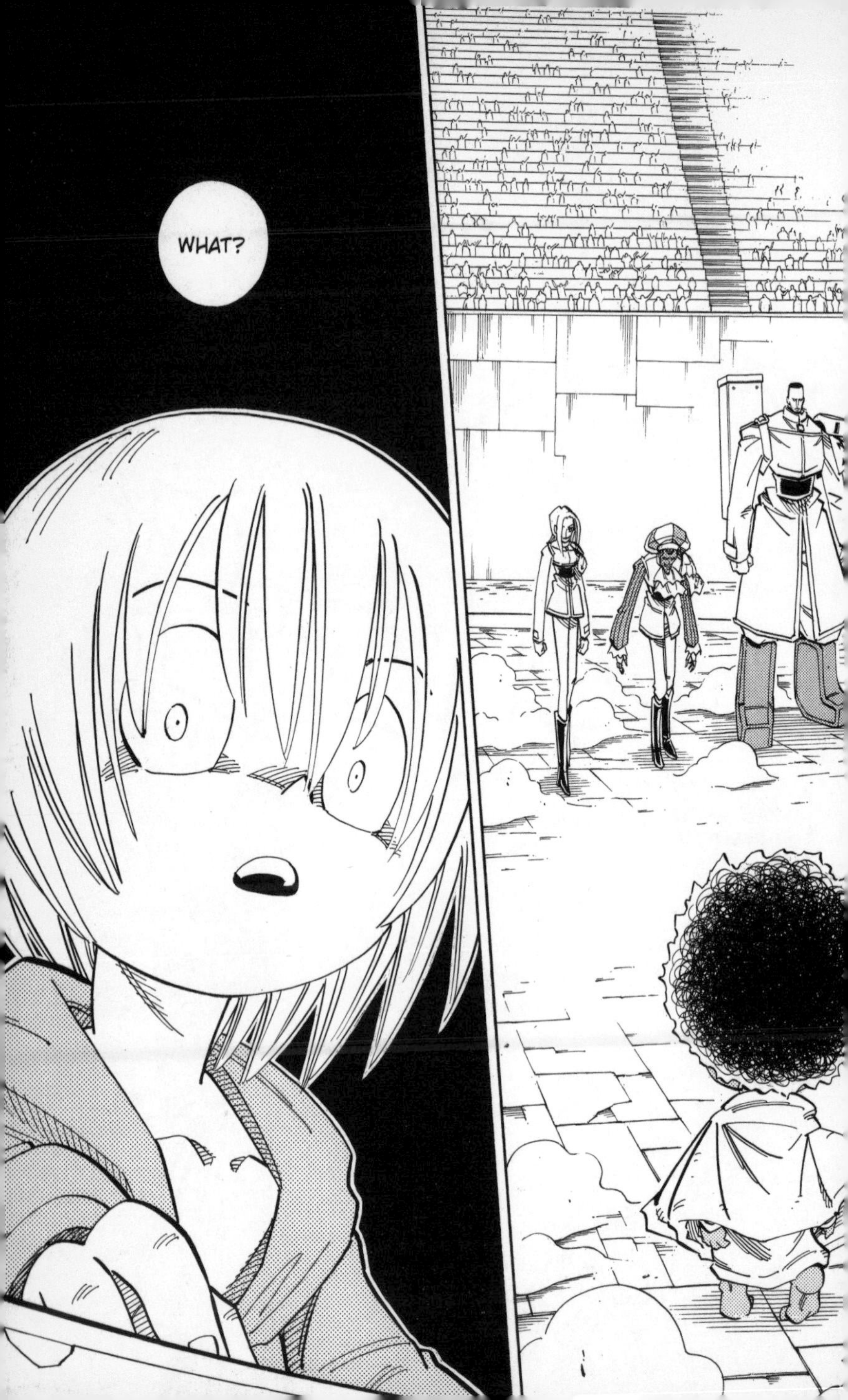
WHAT?

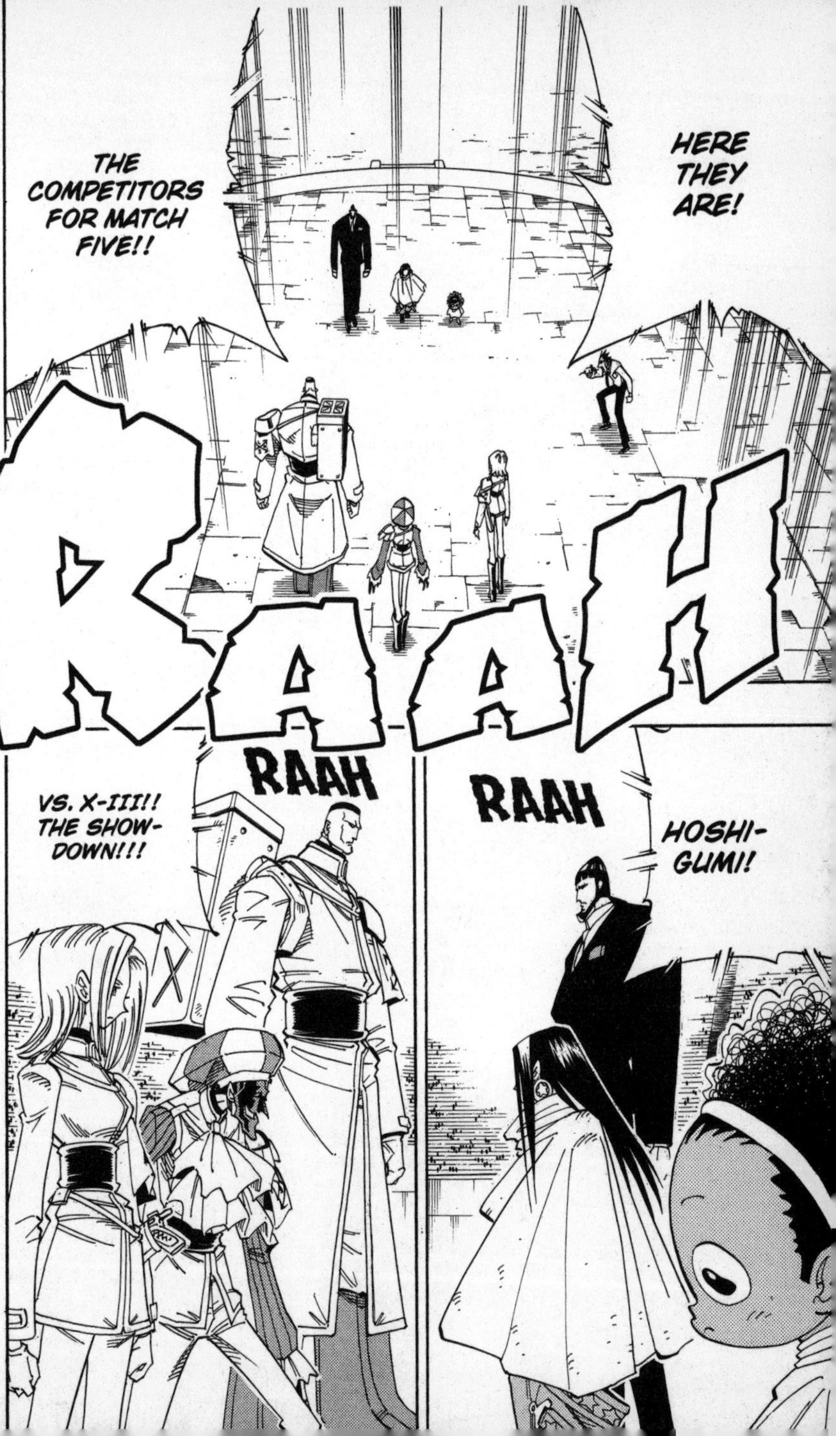
HERE THEY ARE!
THE COMPETITORS FOR MATCH FIVE!!
RAAH
RAAH
HOSHI-GUMI!
RAAH
VS. X-III!! THE SHOW-DOWN!!!

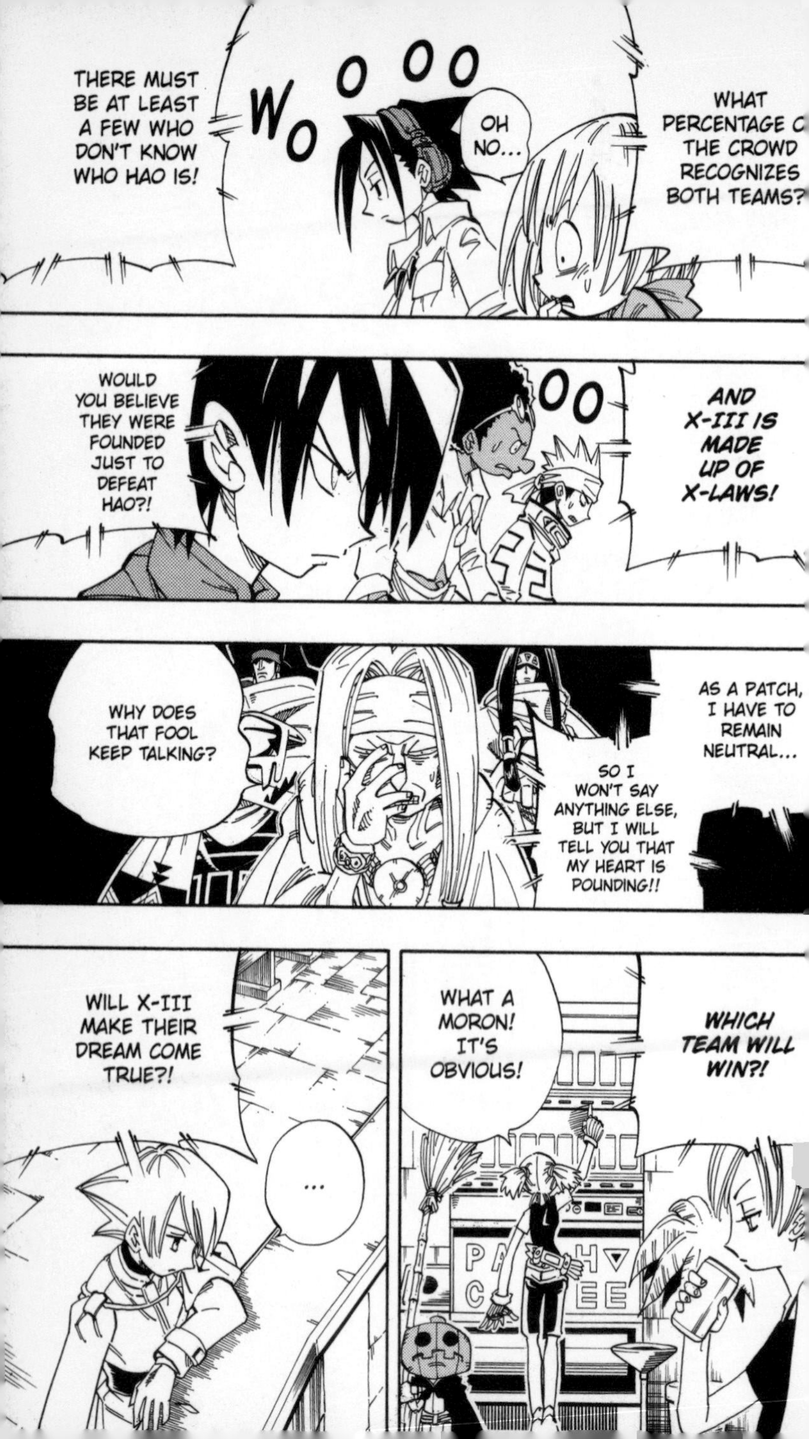
WHAT PERCENTAGE O THE CROWD RECOGNIZES BOTH TEAMS?
OH NO...
WOOOO
THERE MUST BE AT LEAST A FEW WHO DON'T KNOW WHO HAO IS!
AND X-III IS MADE UP OF X-LAWS!
OO
WOULD YOU BELIEVE THEY WERE FOUNDED JUST TO DEFEAT HAO?!
AS A PATCH, I HAVE TO REMAIN NEUTRAL...
SO I WON'T SAY ANYTHING ELSE, BUT I WILL TELL YOU THAT MY HEART IS POUNDING!!
WHY DOES THAT FOOL KEEP TALKING?
WHICH TEAM WILL WIN?!
WHAT A MORON! IT'S OBVIOUS!
WILL X-III MAKE THEIR DREAM COME TRUE?!
...

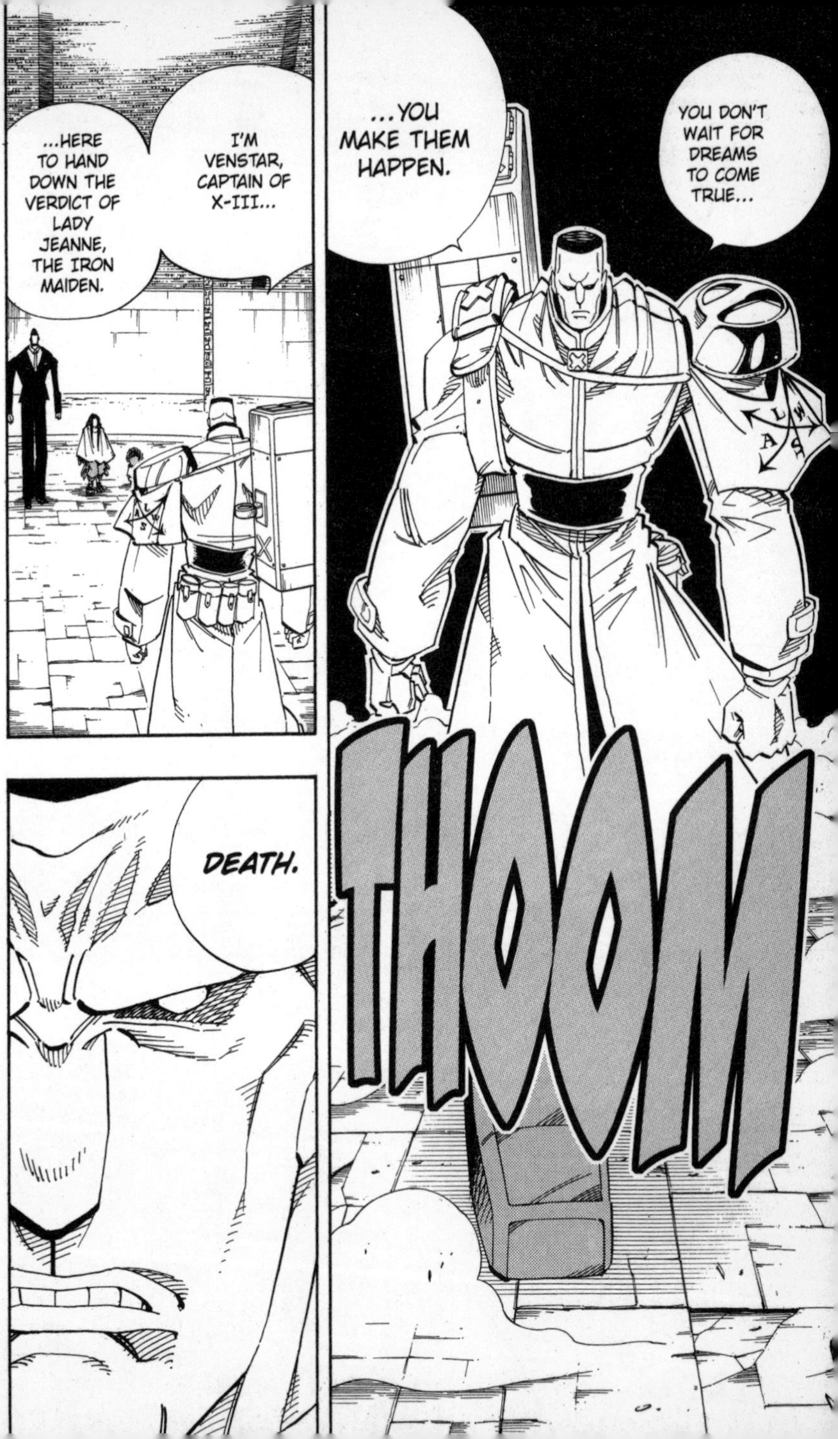
YOU DON'T WAIT FOR DREAMS TO COME TRUE...
...YOU MAKE THEM HAPPEN.
THOOM
I'M VENSTAR, CAPTAIN OF X-III...
...HERE TO HAND DOWN THE VERDICT OF LADY JEANNE, THE IRON MAIDEN.
DEATH.

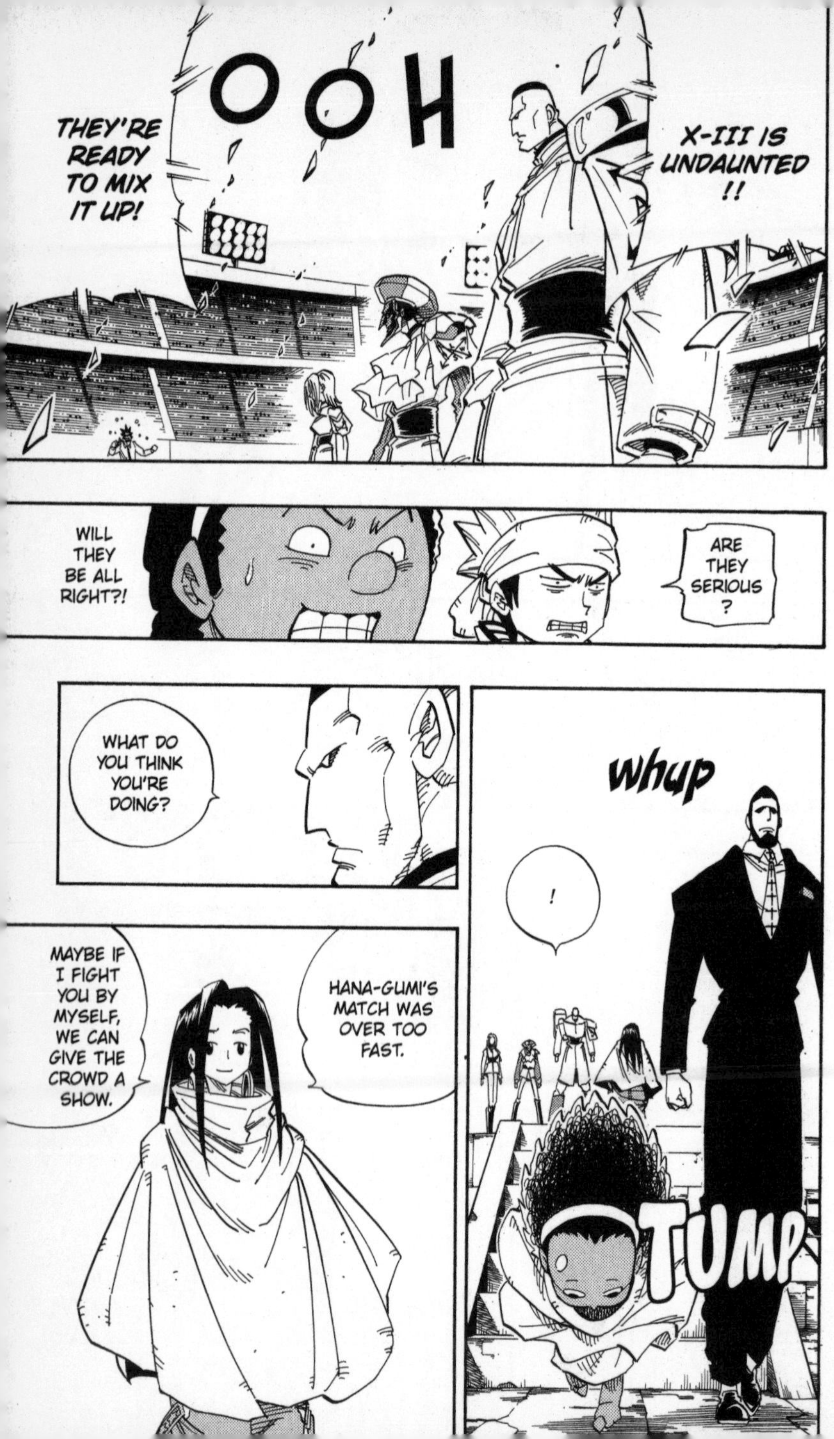
X-III IS UNDAUNTED !!
OOH
THEY'RE READY TO MIX IT UP!
ARE THEY SERIOUS ?
WILL THEY BE ALL RIGHT?!
whup
!
TUMP
WHAT DO YOU THINK YOU'RE DOING?
HANA-GUMI'S MATCH WAS OVER TOO FAST.
MAYBE IF I FIGHT YOU BY MYSELF, WE CAN GIVE THE CROWD A SHOW.

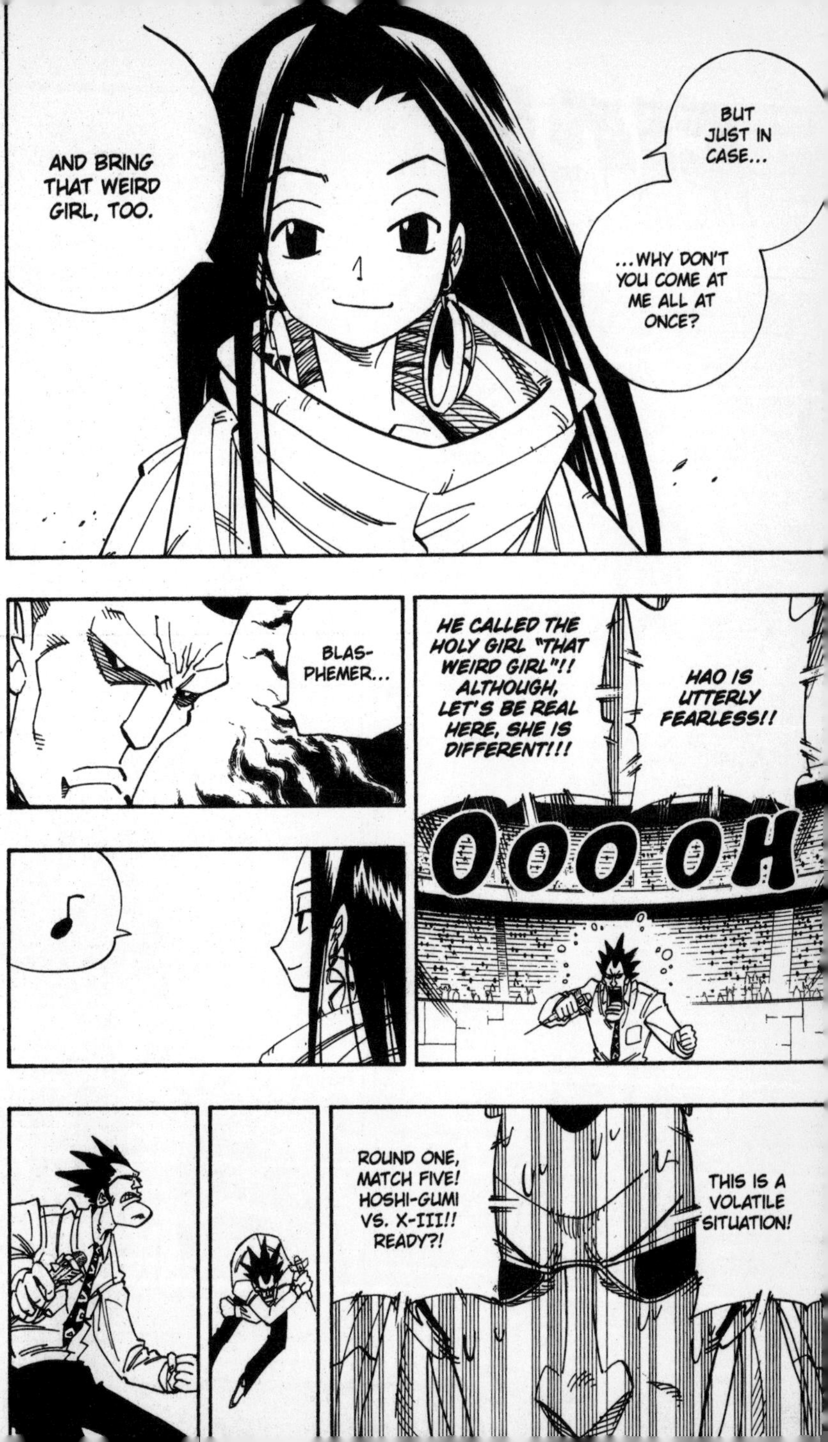
BUT JUST IN CASE...
...WHY DON'T YOU COME AT ME ALL AT ONCE?
AND BRING THAT WEIRD GIRL, TOO.
HAO IS UTTERLY FEARLESS!!
HE CALLED THE HOLY GIRL "THAT WEIRD GIRL"!! ALTHOUGH, LET'S BE REAL HERE, SHE IS DIFFERENT!!!
OOOOH
BLAS-PHEMER...
♪
THIS IS A VOLATILE SITUATION!
ROUND ONE, MATCH FIVE! HOSHI-GUMI VS. X-III!! READY?!

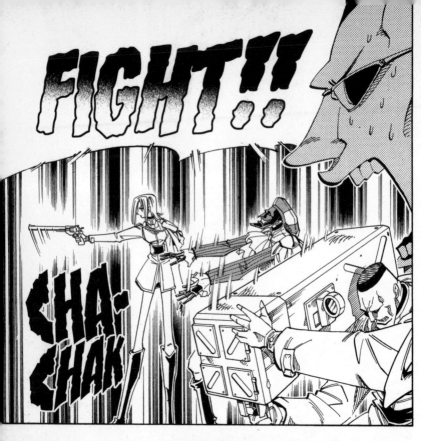

FIGHT!!

CHA-CHAK

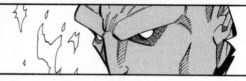

OUR HOLY ANGELS...

TAKE THIS!

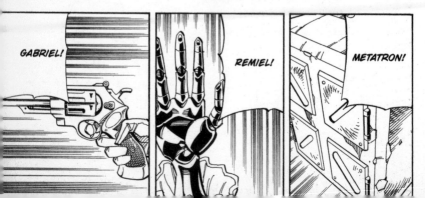

GABRIEL!

REMIEL!

METATRON!

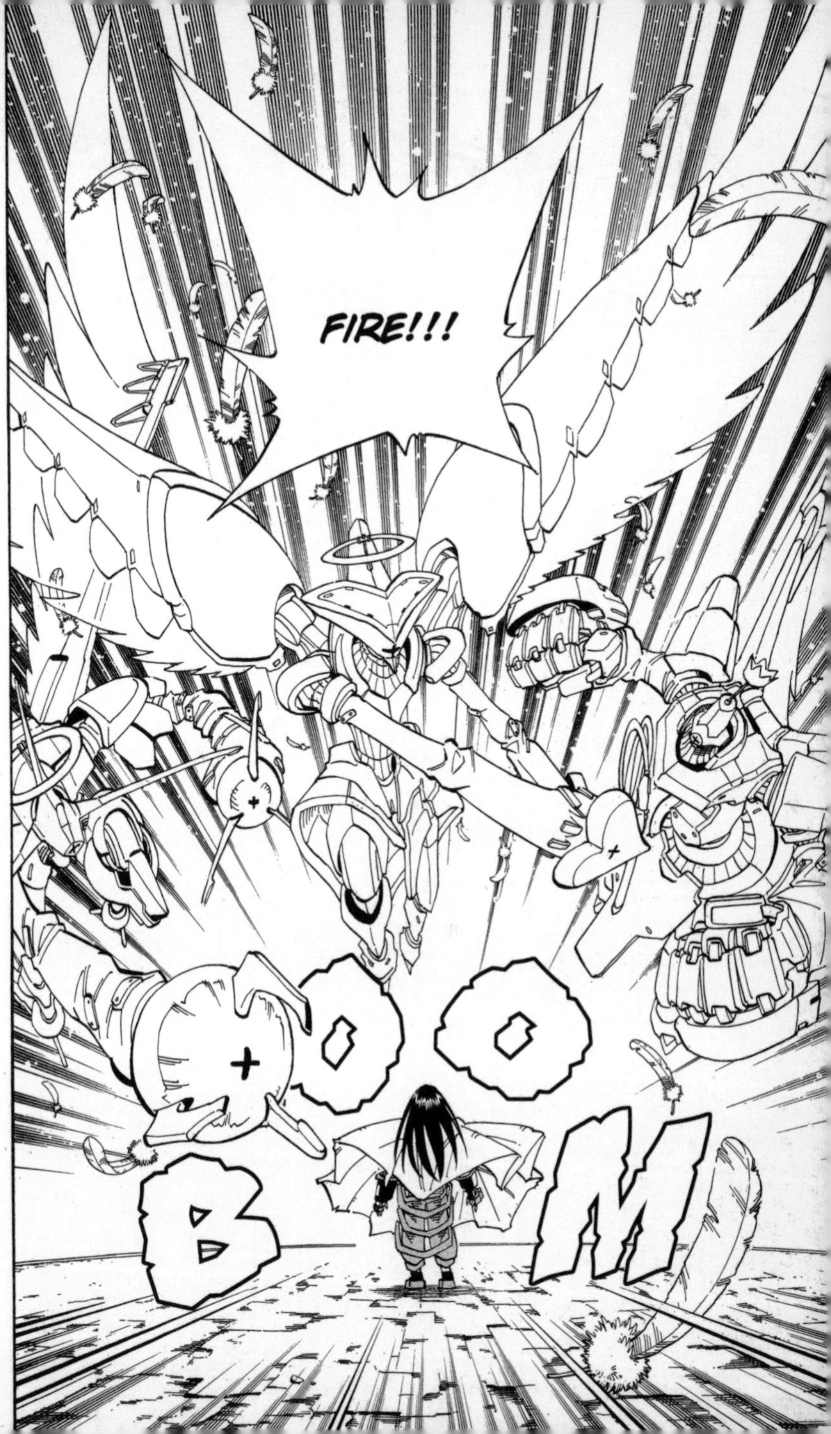
FIRE!!!
BOOOM

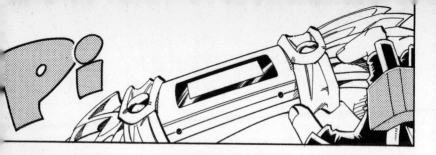

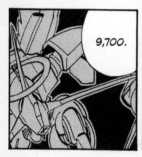

9,700.

8,300.

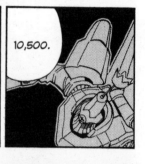

10,500.

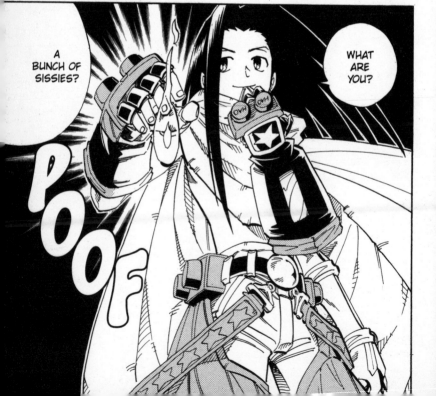

A BUNCH OF SISSIES?

WHAT ARE YOU?

POOF

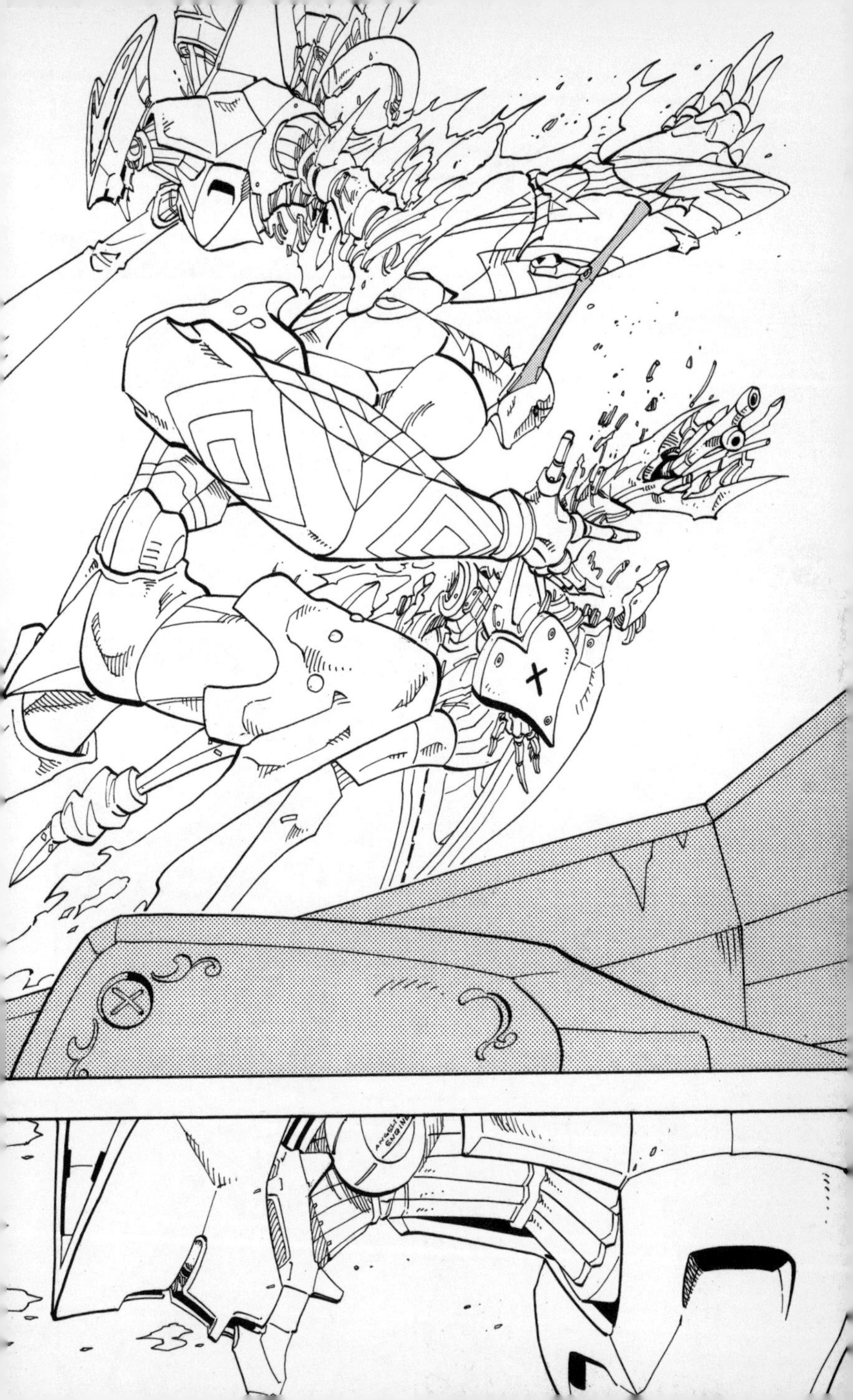

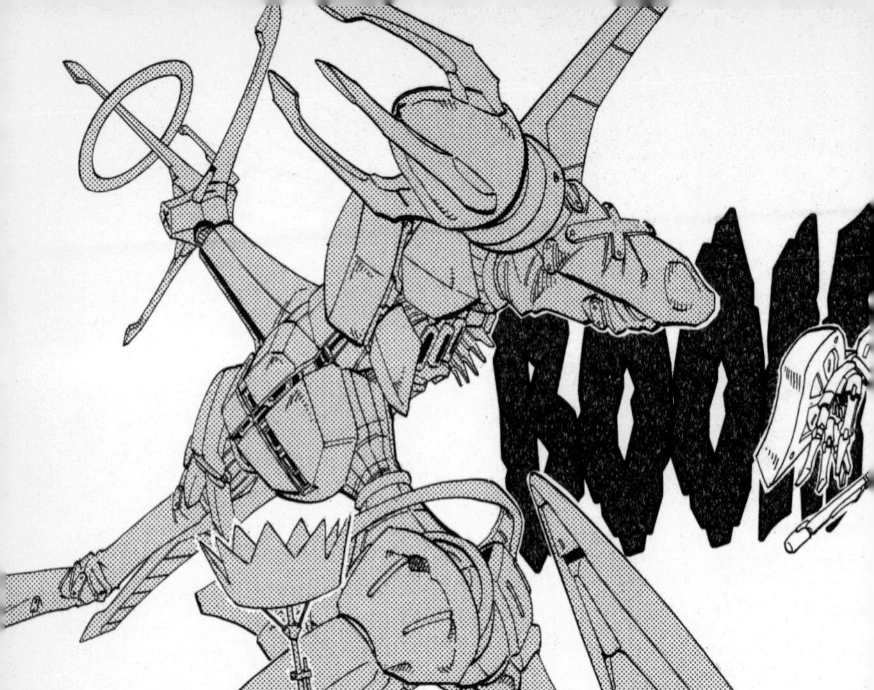

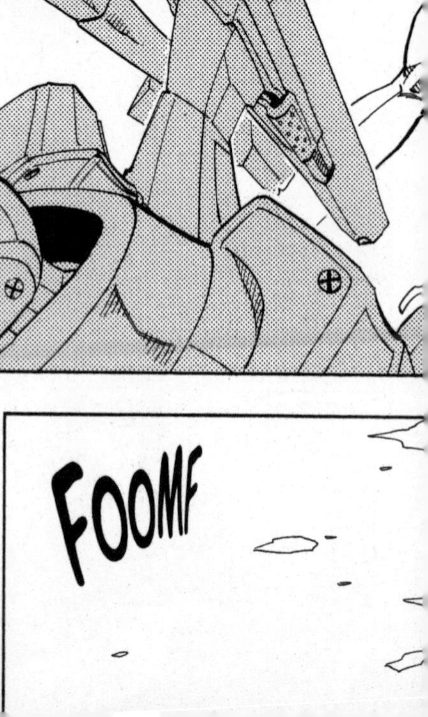
FOOMF

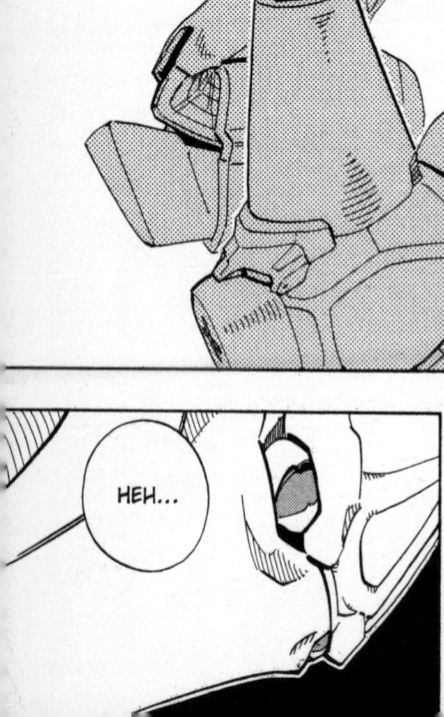
HEH...

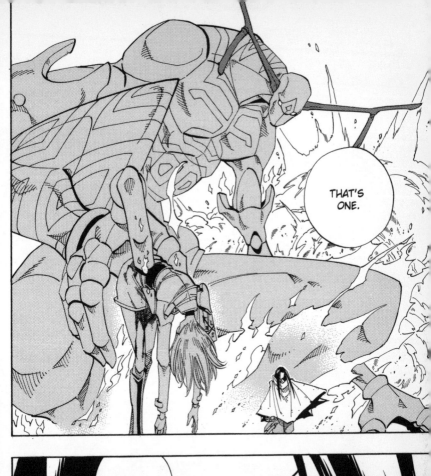

THAT'S ONE.

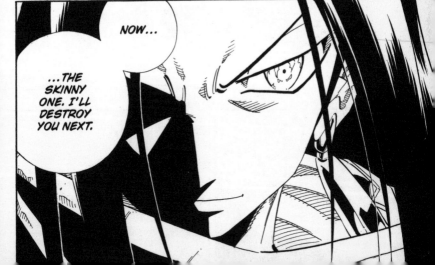

NOW...

...THE SKINNY ONE. I'LL DESTROY YOU NEXT.

Shaman King

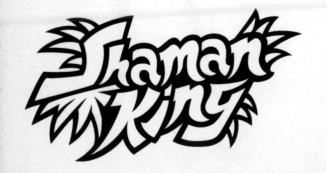

SHAMAN KING CHARACTER FILE No.80

ミイネ

MEENE

2001
(JAN)

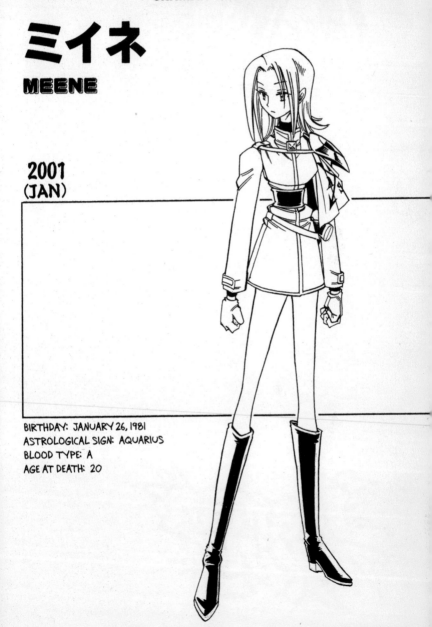

BIRTHDAY: JANUARY 26, 1981
ASTROLOGICAL SIGN: AQUARIUS
BLOOD TYPE: A
AGE AT DEATH: 20

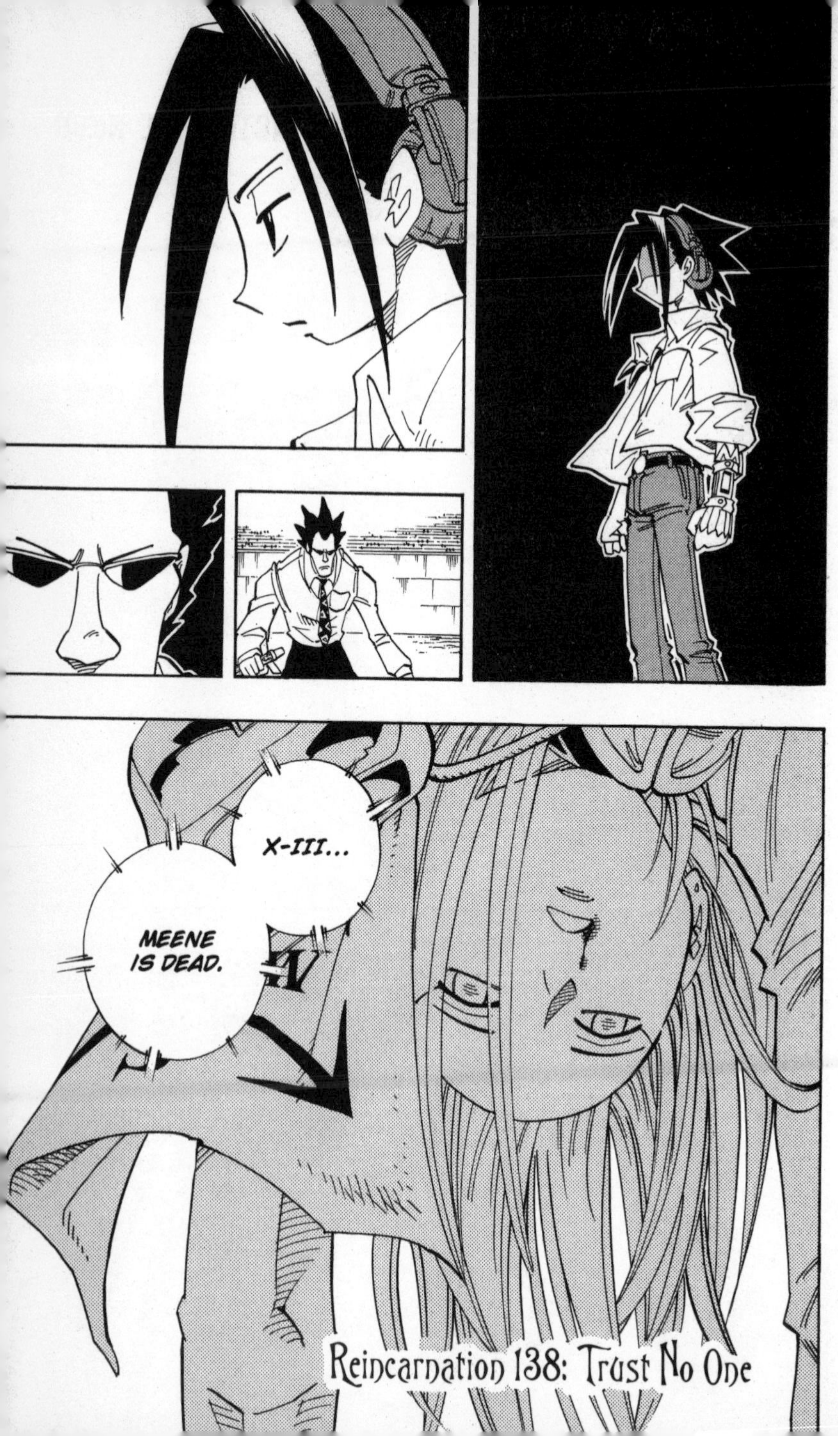
X-III...
MEENE IS DEAD.
Reincarnation 138: Trust No One

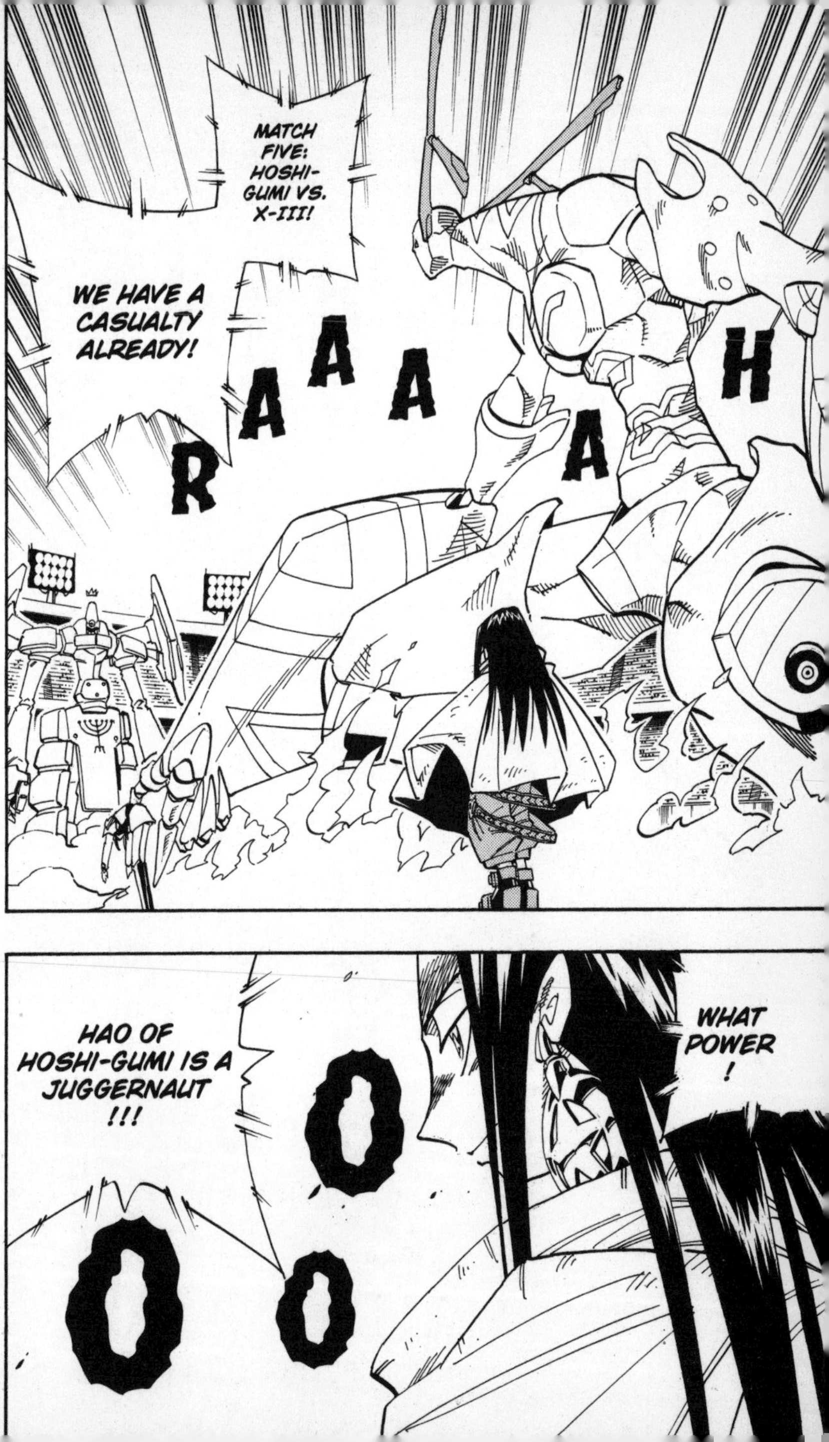
MATCH FIVE: HOSHI-GUMI VS. X-III!
WE HAVE A CASUALTY ALREADY!
RAAAAH
WHAT POWER!
HAO OF HOSHI-GUMI IS A JUGGERNAUT!!!
OOO

Reincarnation 138: Trust No One

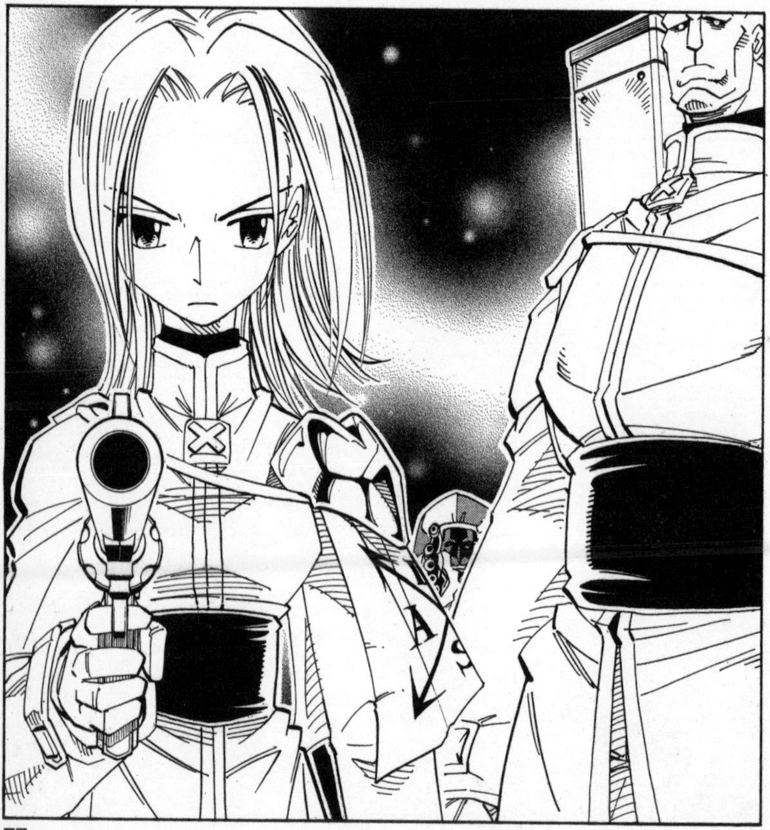

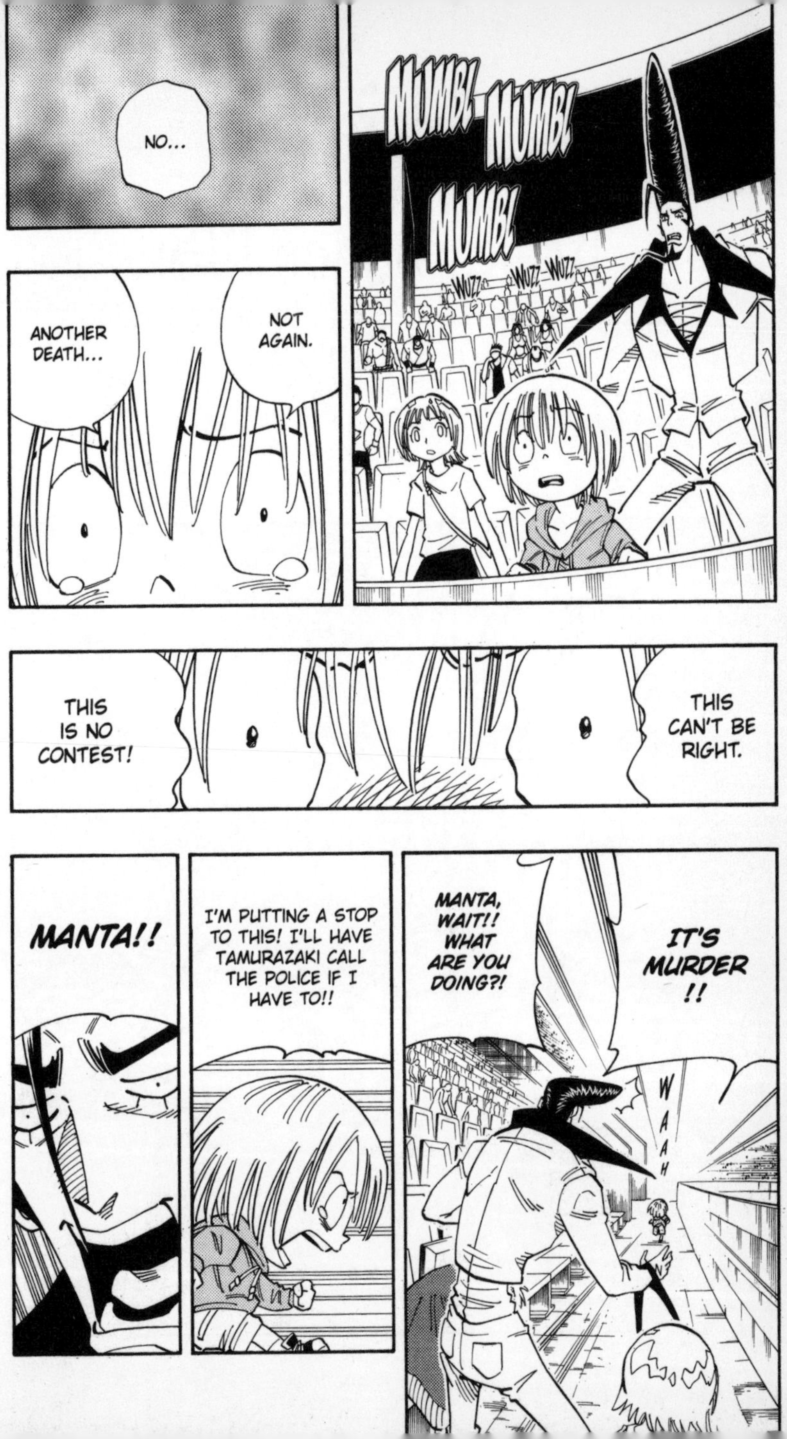
MUMBL MUMBL MUMBL
WUZZ WUZZ WUZZ
NO...
NOT AGAIN.
ANOTHER DEATH...
THIS CAN'T BE RIGHT.
THIS IS NO CONTEST!
IT'S MURDER!!
MANTA, WAIT!! WHAT ARE YOU DOING?!
WAAH
I'M PUTTING A STOP TO THIS! I'LL HAVE TAMURAZAKI CALL THE POLICE IF I HAVE TO!!
MANTA!!

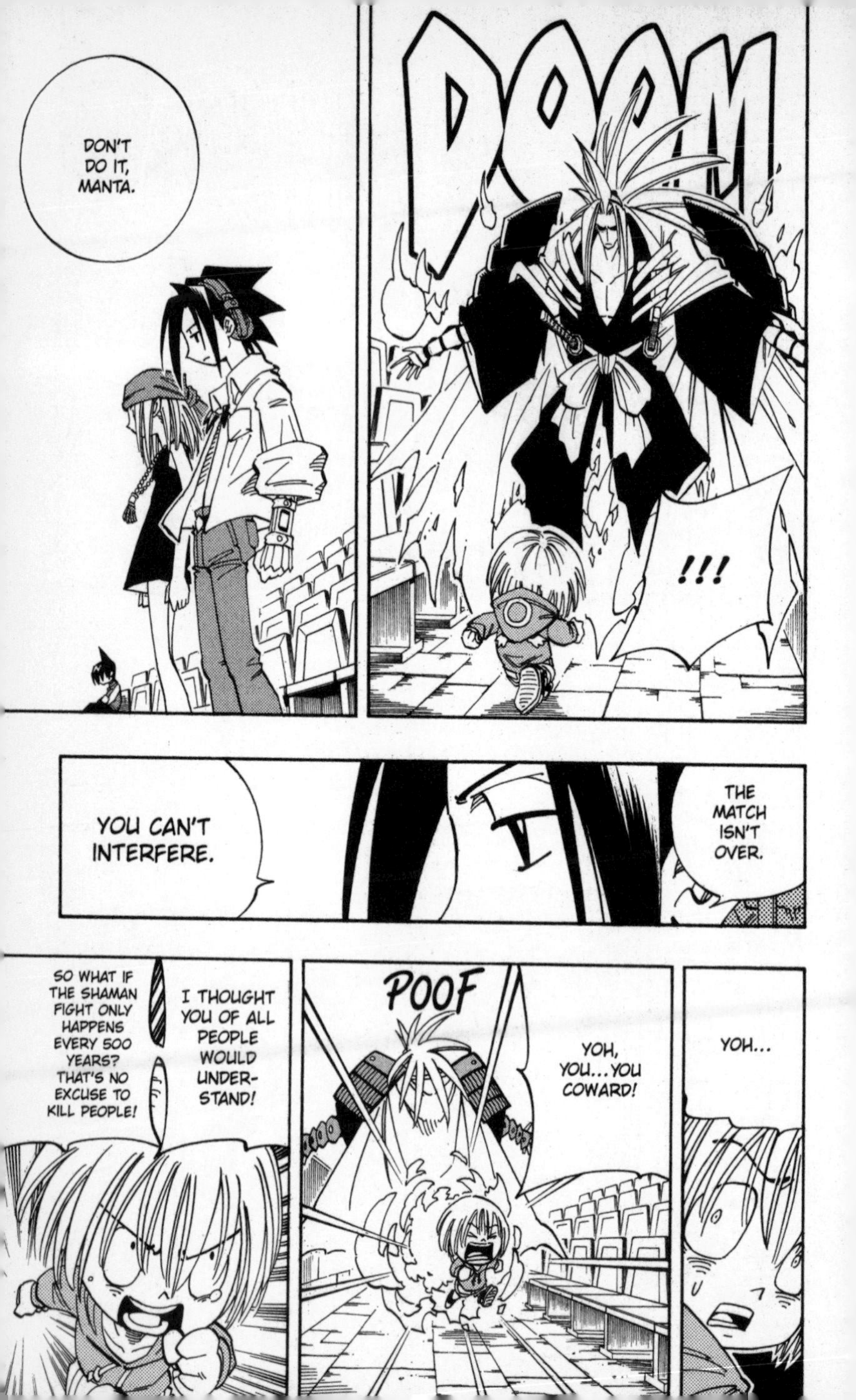
DOOM
!!!
DON'T DO IT, MANTA.
THE MATCH ISN'T OVER.
YOU CAN'T INTERFERE.
YOH...
POOF
YOH, YOU...YOU COWARD!
I THOUGHT YOU OF ALL PEOPLE WOULD UNDER-STAND!
SO WHAT IF THE SHAMAN FIGHT ONLY HAPPENS EVERY 500 YEARS? THAT'S NO EXCUSE TO KILL PEOPLE!

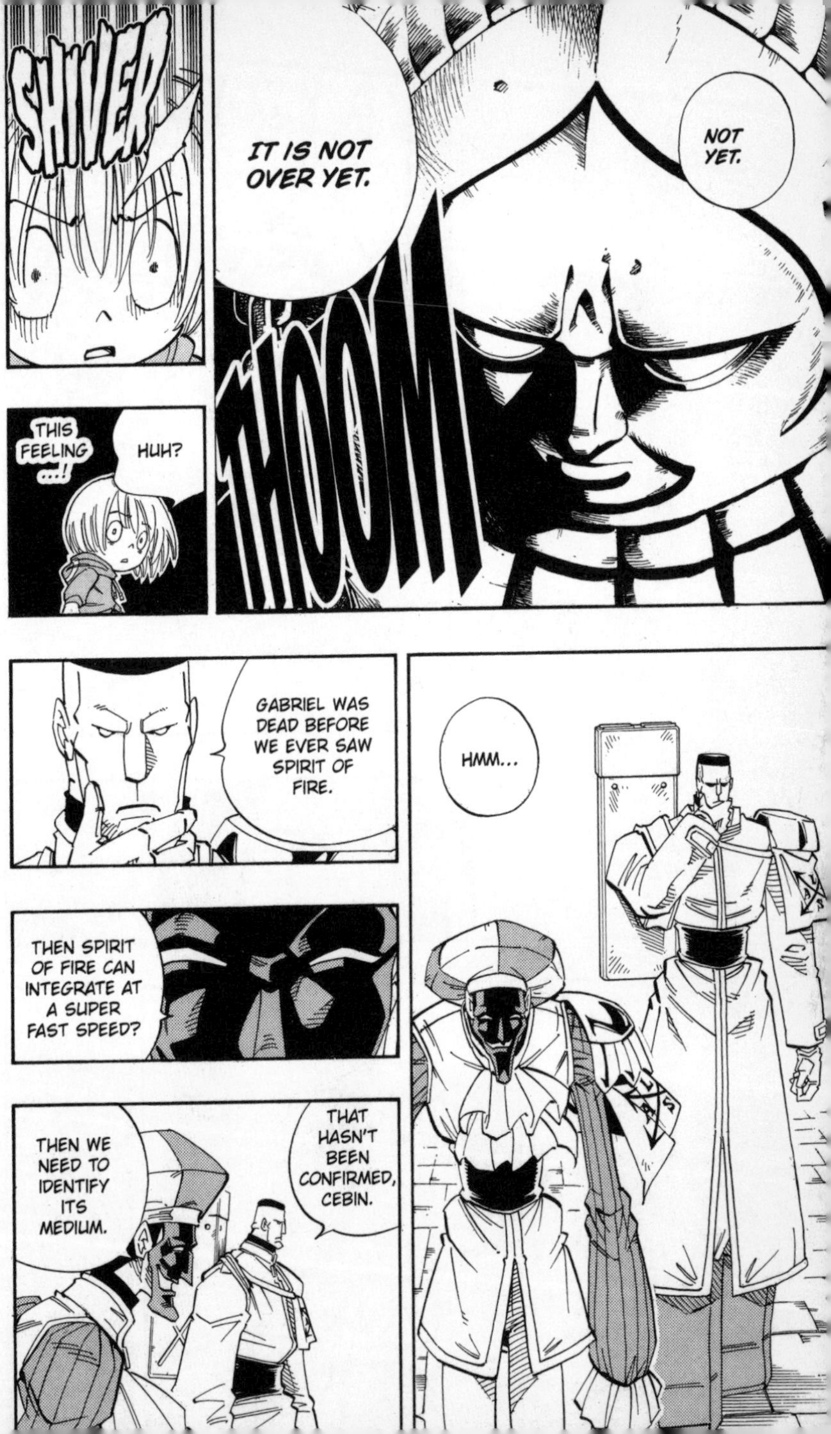
NOT YET.
IT IS NOT OVER YET.
THOOM
SHIVER
HUH?
THIS FEELING ...!
HMM...
GABRIEL WAS DEAD BEFORE WE EVER SAW SPIRIT OF FIRE.
THEN SPIRIT OF FIRE CAN INTEGRATE AT A SUPER FAST SPEED?
THAT HASN'T BEEN CONFIRMED, CEBIN.
THEN WE NEED TO IDENTIFY ITS MEDIUM.

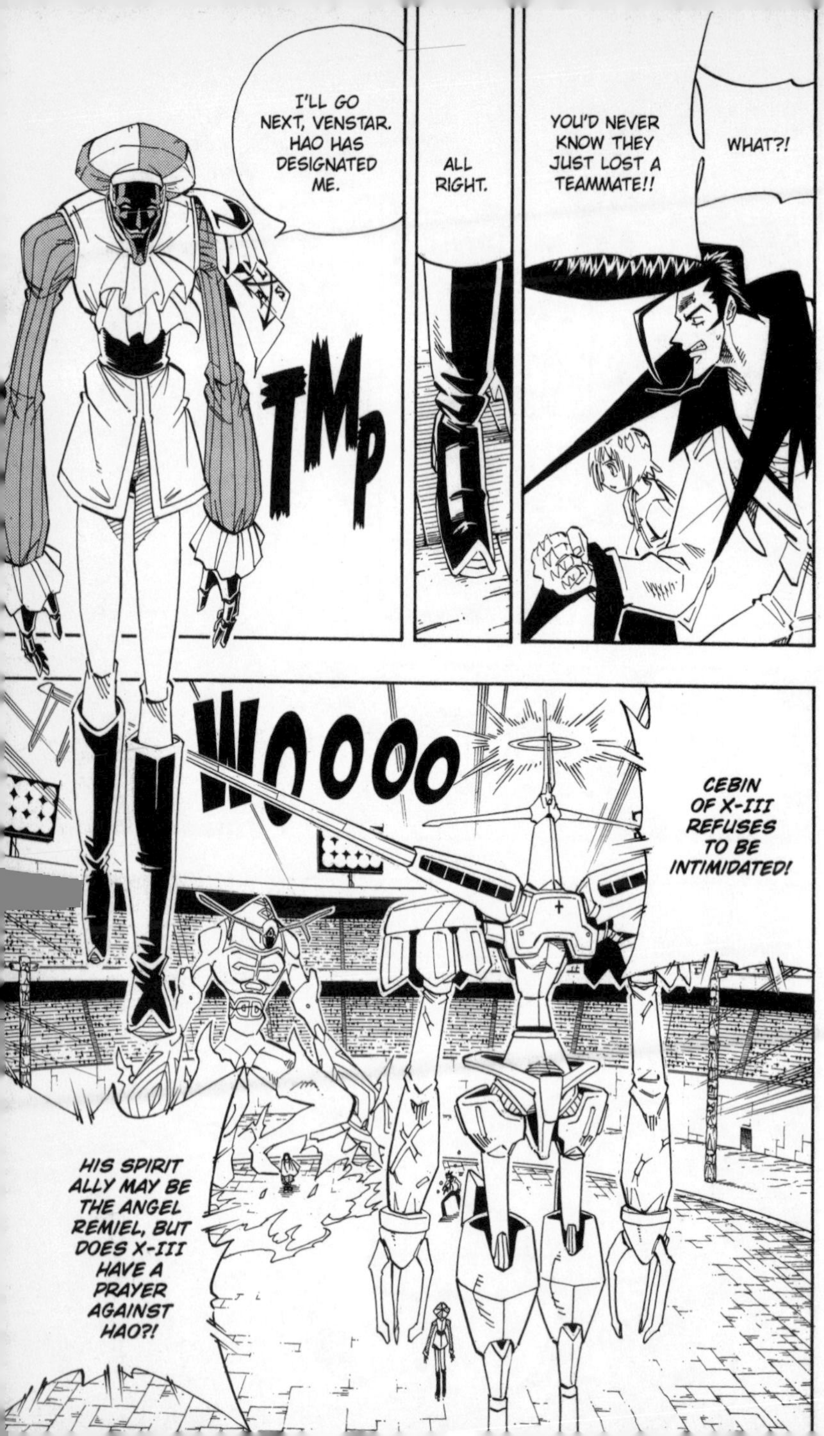
WHAT?!
YOU'D NEVER KNOW THEY JUST LOST A TEAMMATE!!
ALL RIGHT.
I'LL GO NEXT, VENSTAR. HAO HAS DESIGNATED ME.
TMP
WOOOO
CEBIN OF X-III REFUSES TO BE INTIMIDATED!
HIS SPIRIT ALLY MAY BE THE ANGEL REMIEL, BUT DOES X-III HAVE A PRAYER AGAINST HAO?!

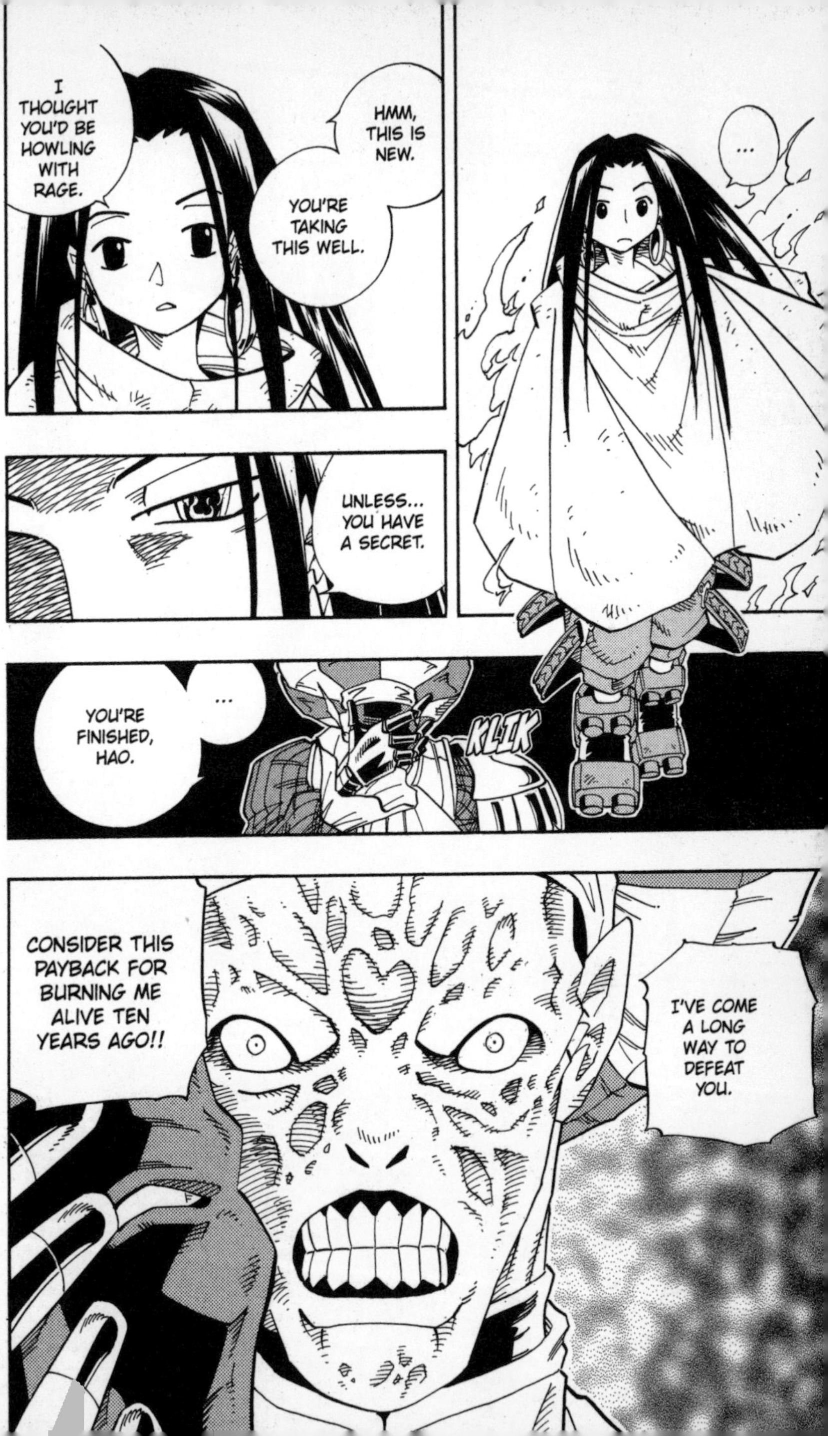
...
HMM, THIS IS NEW.
YOU'RE TAKING THIS WELL.
I THOUGHT YOU'D BE HOWLING WITH RAGE.
UNLESS... YOU HAVE A SECRET.
KLIK
...
YOU'RE FINISHED, HAO.
I'VE COME A LONG WAY TO DEFEAT YOU.
CONSIDER THIS PAYBACK FOR BURNING ME ALIVE TEN YEARS AGO!!

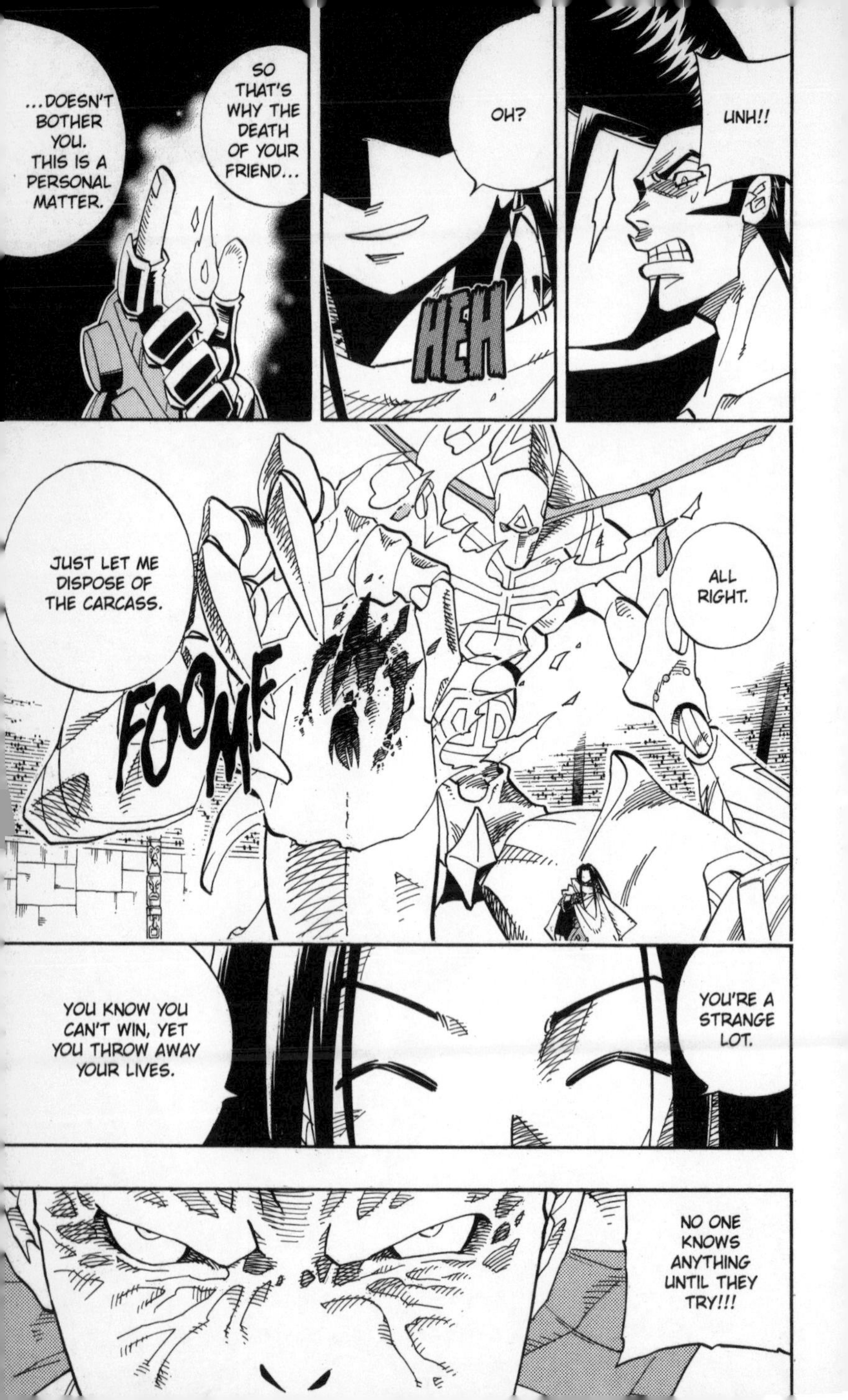
UNH!!
OH?
HEH
SO THAT'S WHY THE DEATH OF YOUR FRIEND...
...DOESN'T BOTHER YOU. THIS IS A PERSONAL MATTER.
ALL RIGHT.
JUST LET ME DISPOSE OF THE CARCASS.
FOOMF
YOU'RE A STRANGE LOT.
YOU KNOW YOU CAN'T WIN, YET YOU THROW AWAY YOUR LIVES.
NO ONE KNOWS ANYTHING UNTIL THEY TRY!!!

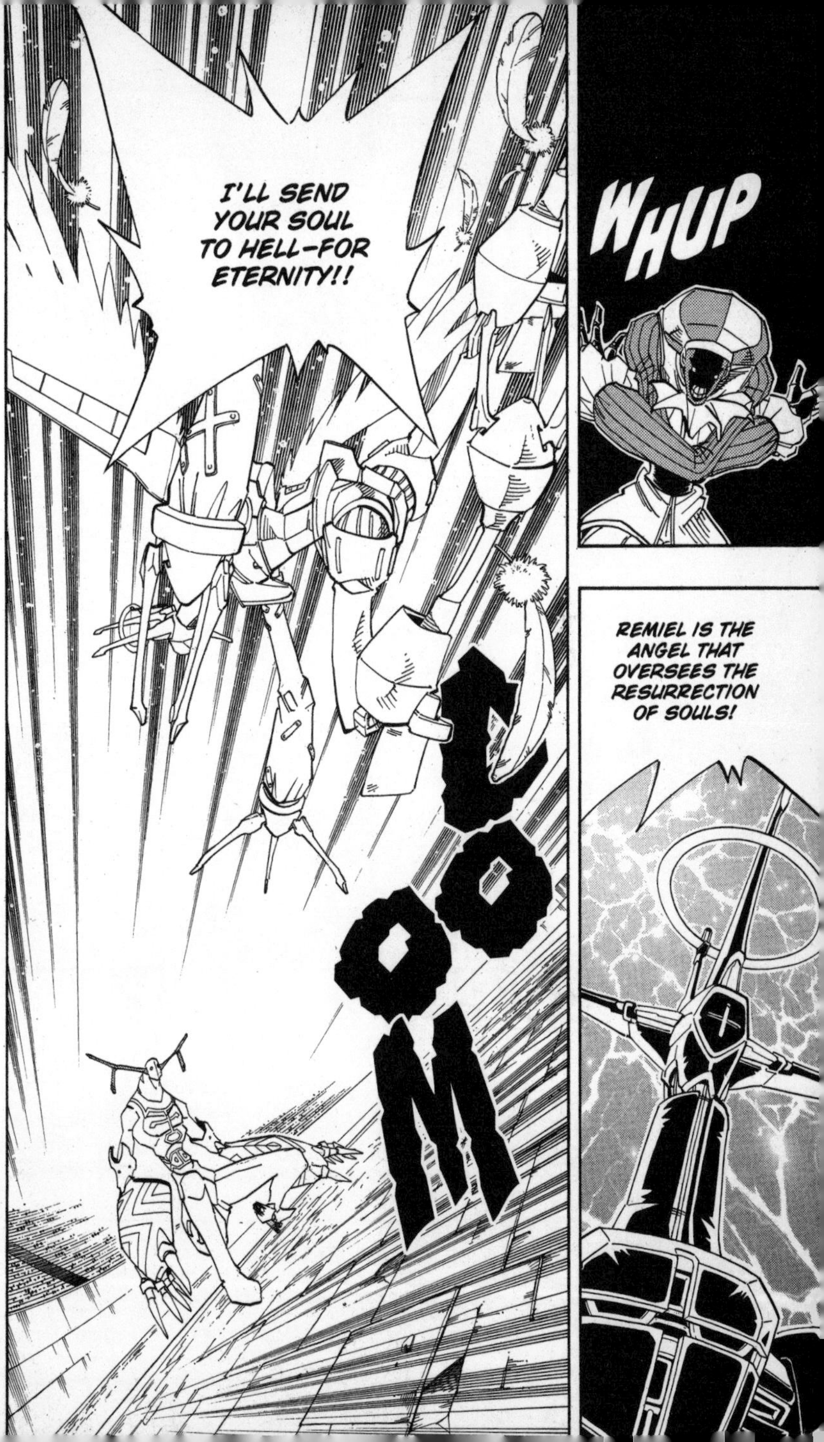
WHUP
REMIEL IS THE ANGEL THAT OVERSEES THE RESURRECTION OF SOULS!
I'LL SEND YOUR SOUL TO HELL—FOR ETERNITY!!
DOOM

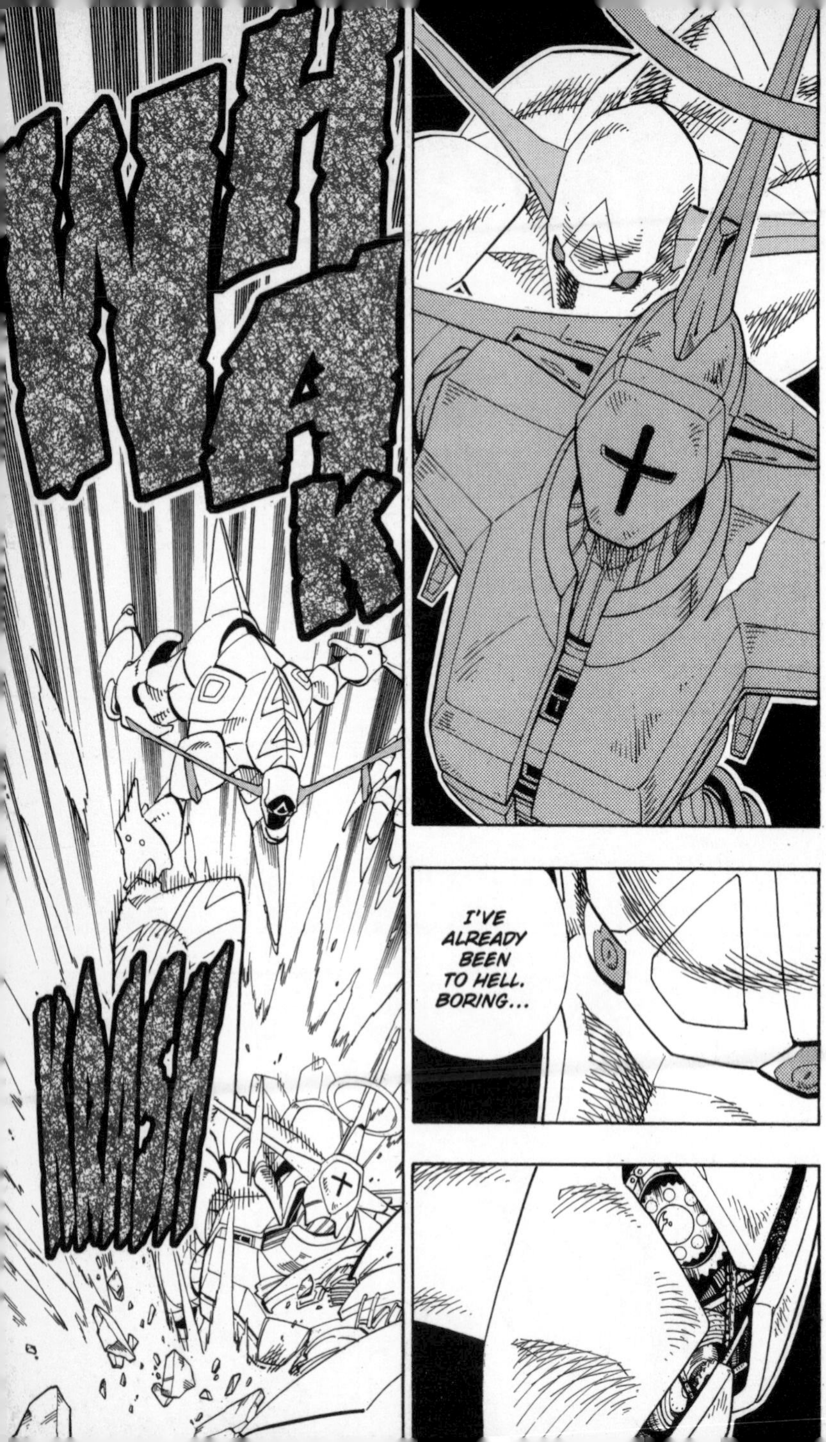
I'VE ALREADY BEEN TO HELL. BORING...
WHAK

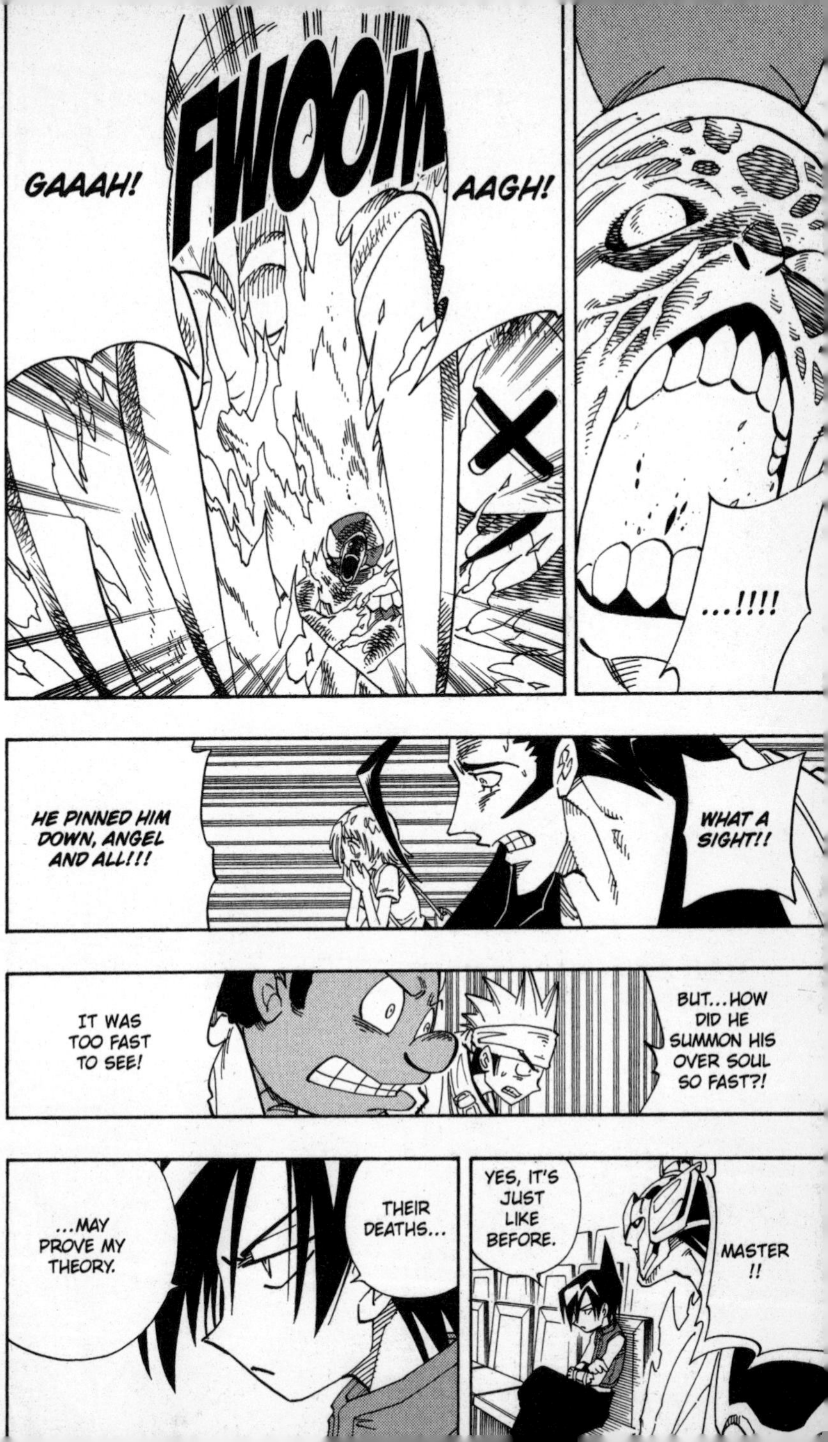
...!!!!
AAGH!
FWOOM
GAAAH!
WHAT A SIGHT!!
HE PINNED HIM DOWN, ANGEL AND ALL!!!
BUT...HOW DID HE SUMMON HIS OVER SOUL SO FAST?!
IT WAS TOO FAST TO SEE!
MASTER !!
YES, IT'S JUST LIKE BEFORE.
THEIR DEATHS...
...MAY PROVE MY THEORY.

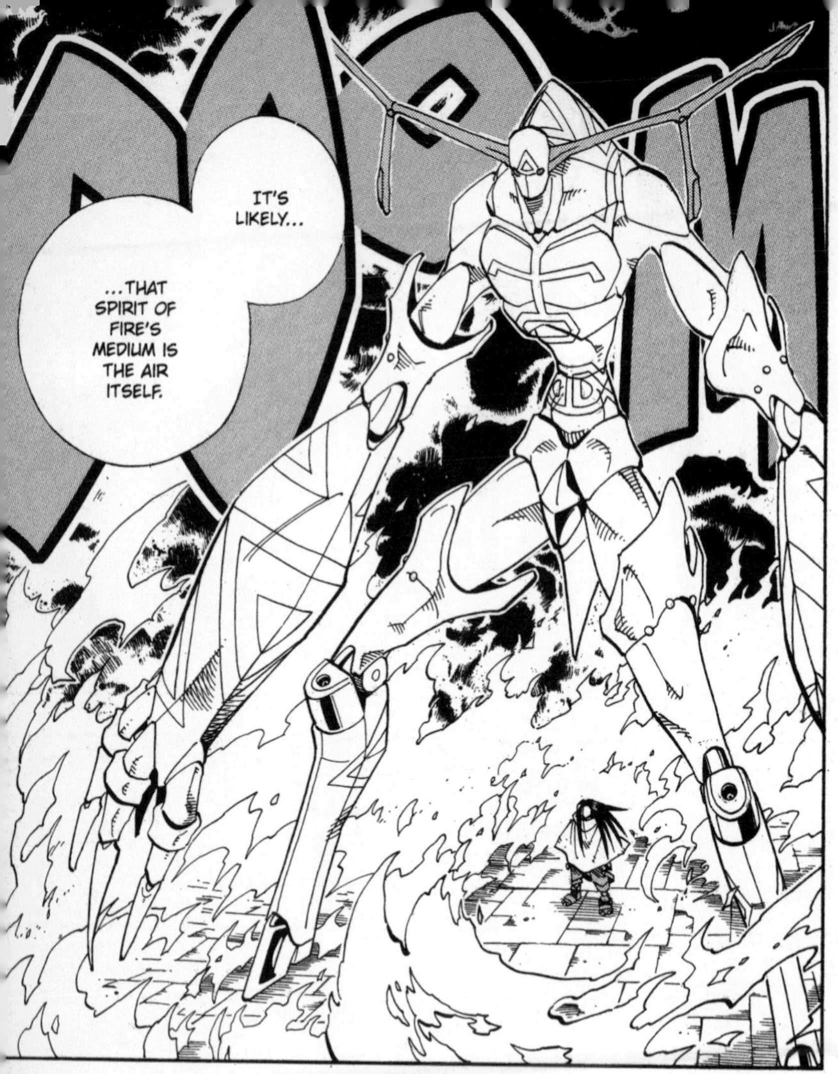
IT'S LIKELY...
...THAT SPIRIT OF FIRE'S MEDIUM IS THE AIR ITSELF.
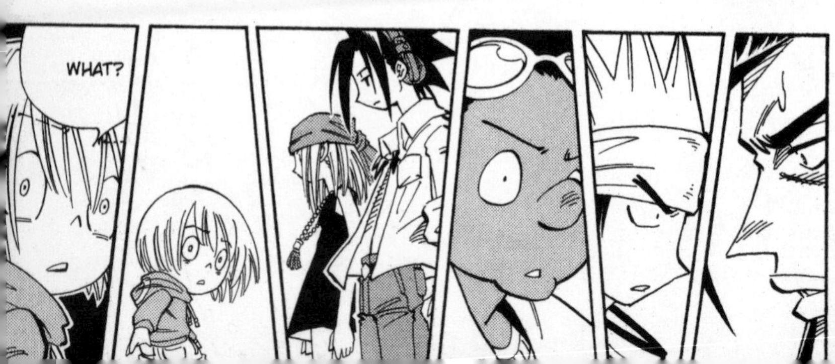
WHAT?

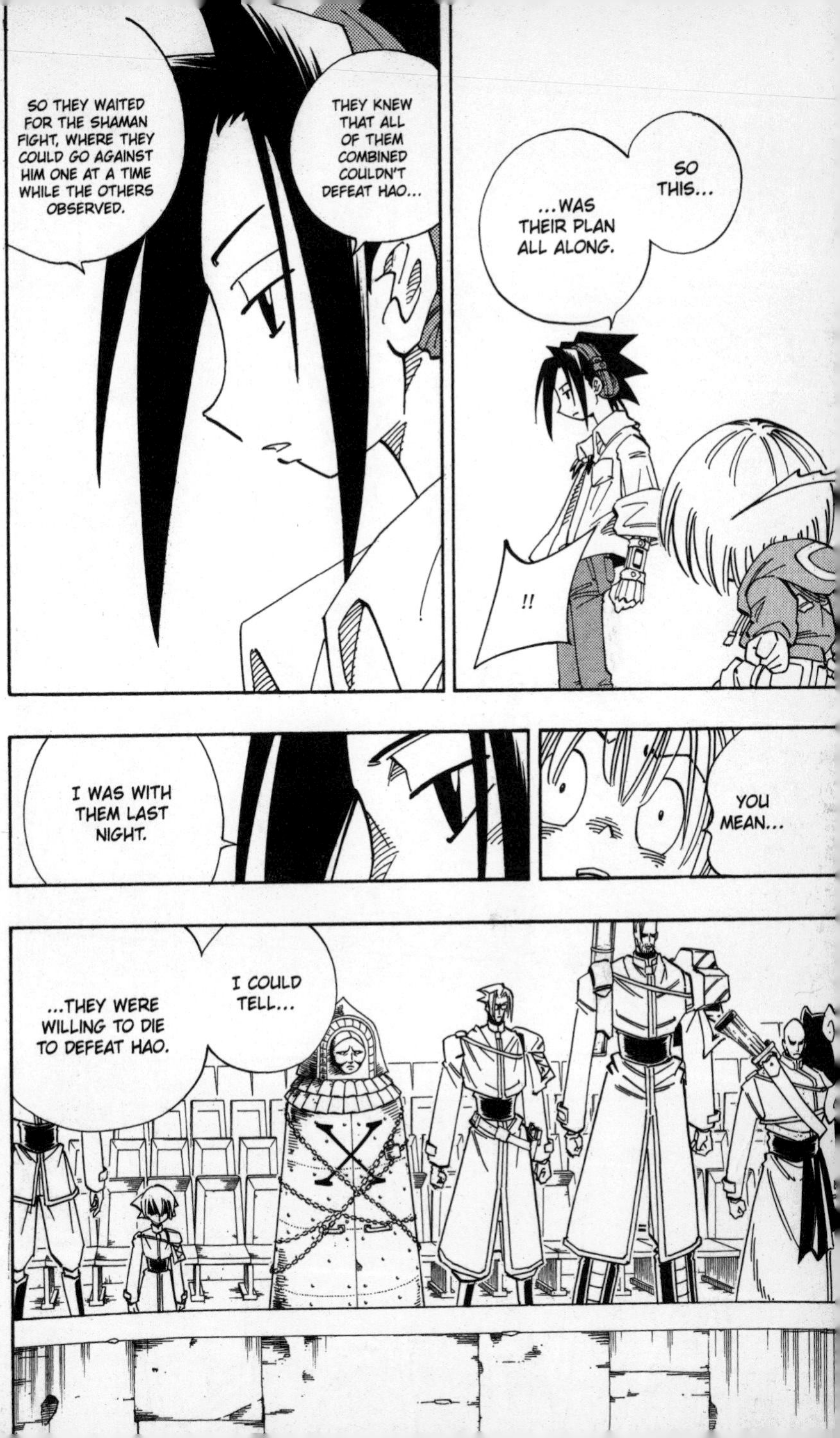
SO THIS...
...WAS THEIR PLAN ALL ALONG.
!!
THEY KNEW THAT ALL OF THEM COMBINED COULDN'T DEFEAT HAO...
SO THEY WAITED FOR THE SHAMAN FIGHT, WHERE THEY COULD GO AGAINST HIM ONE AT A TIME WHILE THE OTHERS OBSERVED.
YOU MEAN...
I WAS WITH THEM LAST NIGHT.
I COULD TELL...
...THEY WERE WILLING TO DIE TO DEFEAT HAO.

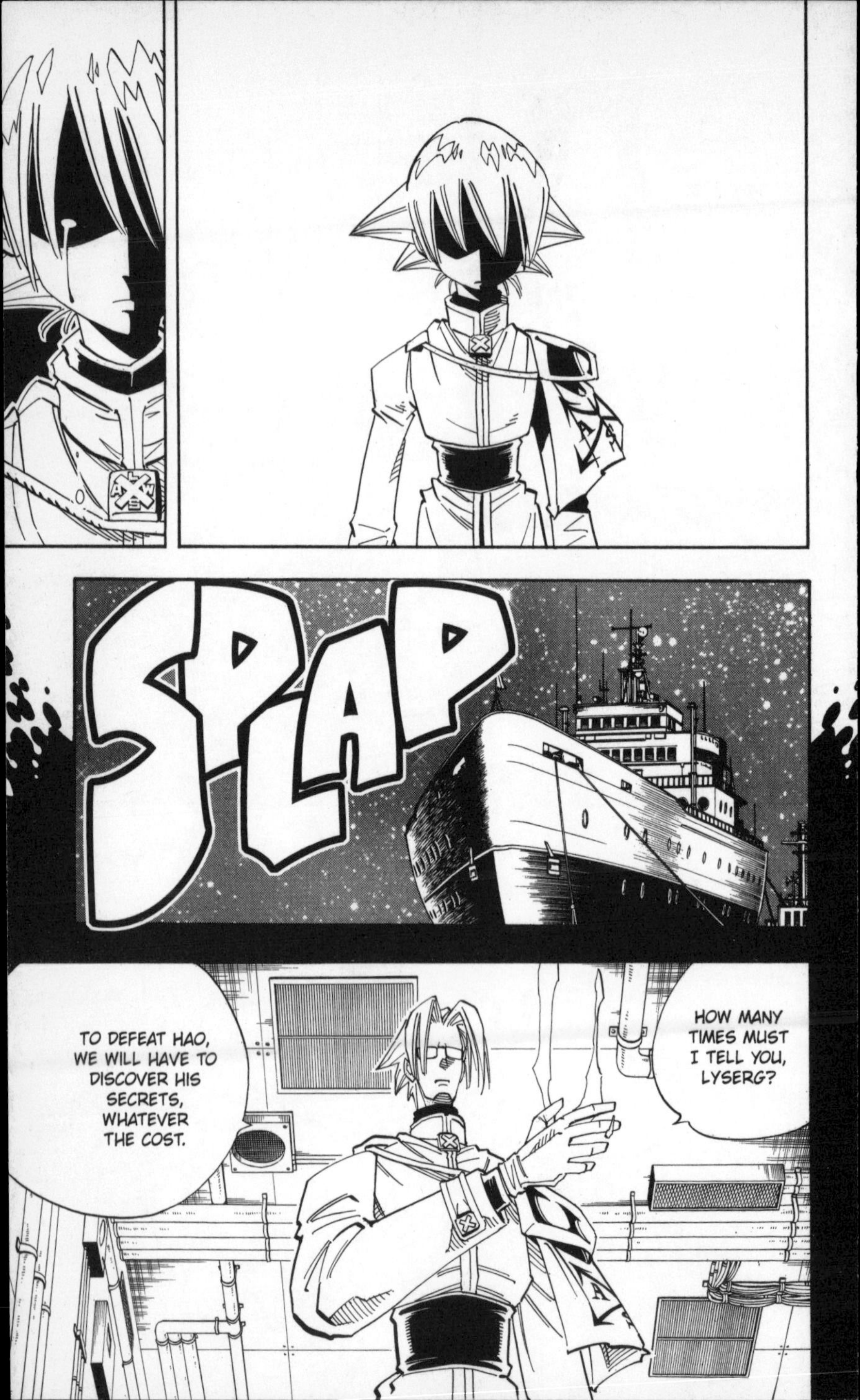
SPLAP
HOW MANY TIMES MUST I TELL YOU, LYSERG?
TO DEFEAT HAO, WE WILL HAVE TO DISCOVER HIS SECRETS, WHATEVER THE COST.

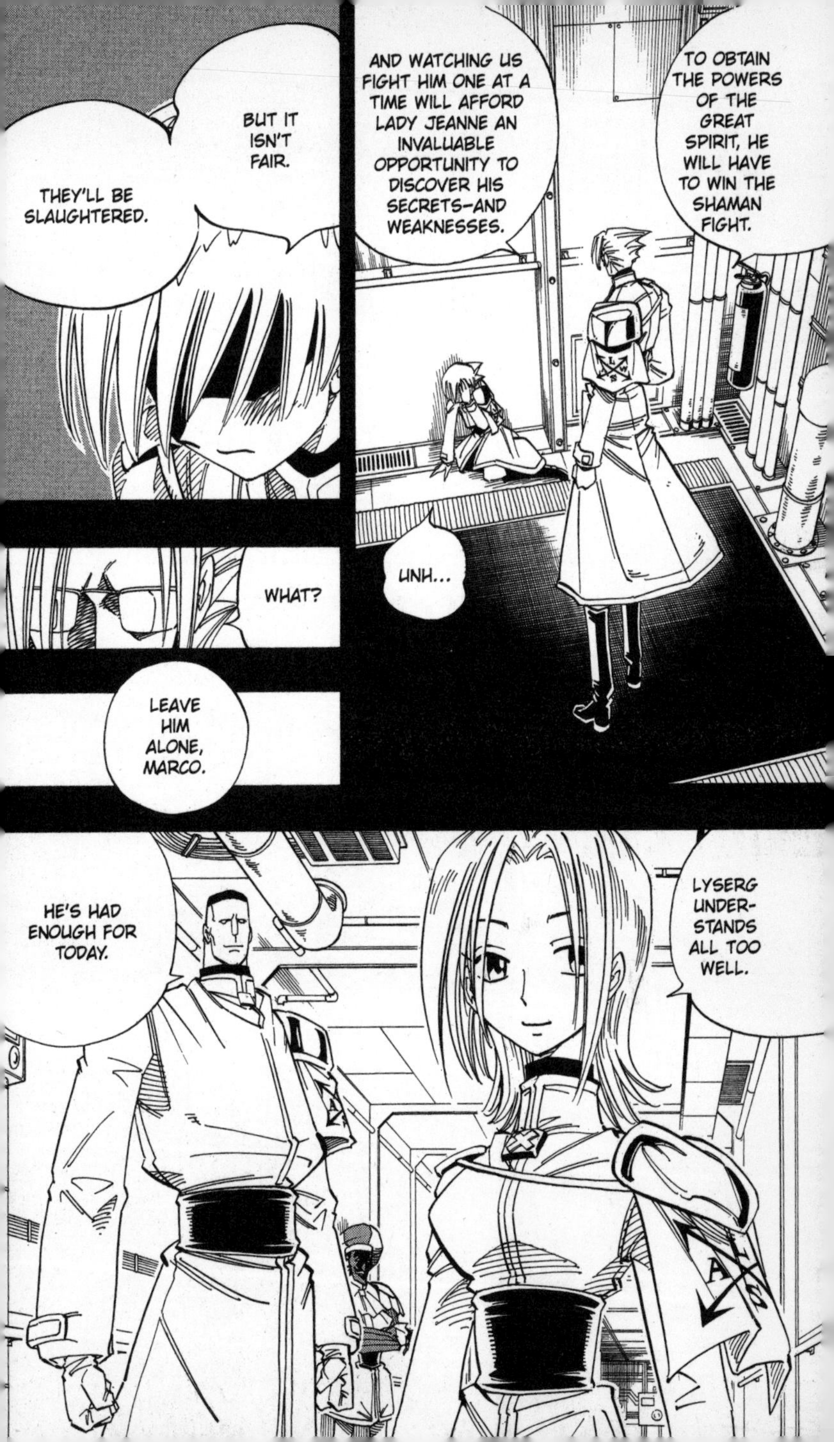
TO OBTAIN THE POWERS OF THE GREAT SPIRIT, HE WILL HAVE TO WIN THE SHAMAN FIGHT.
AND WATCHING US FIGHT HIM ONE AT A TIME WILL AFFORD LADY JEANNE AN INVALUABLE OPPORTUNITY TO DISCOVER HIS SECRETS—AND WEAKNESSES.
UNH...
BUT IT ISN'T FAIR.
THEY'LL BE SLAUGHTERED.
WHAT?
LEAVE HIM ALONE, MARCO.
LYSERG UNDER-STANDS ALL TOO WELL.
HE'S HAD ENOUGH FOR TODAY.

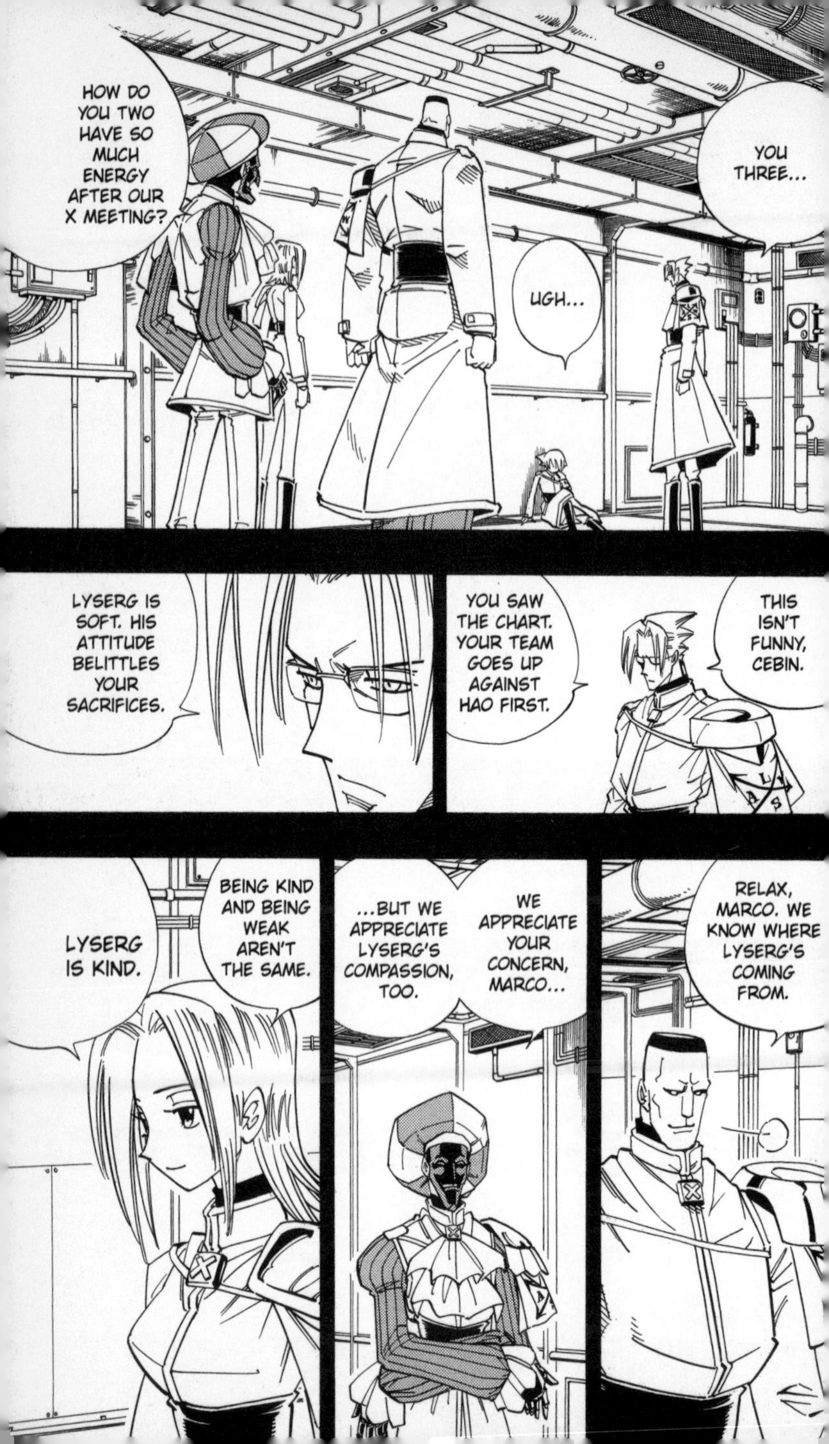
YOU THREE...
UGH...
HOW DO YOU TWO HAVE SO MUCH ENERGY AFTER OUR X MEETING?
THIS ISN'T FUNNY, CEBIN.
YOU SAW THE CHART. YOUR TEAM GOES UP AGAINST HAO FIRST.
LYSERG IS SOFT. HIS ATTITUDE BELITTLES YOUR SACRIFICES.
RELAX, MARCO. WE KNOW WHERE LYSERG'S COMING FROM.
WE APPRECIATE YOUR CONCERN, MARCO...
...BUT WE APPRECIATE LYSERG'S COMPASSION, TOO.
BEING KIND AND BEING WEAK AREN'T THE SAME.
LYSERG IS KIND.

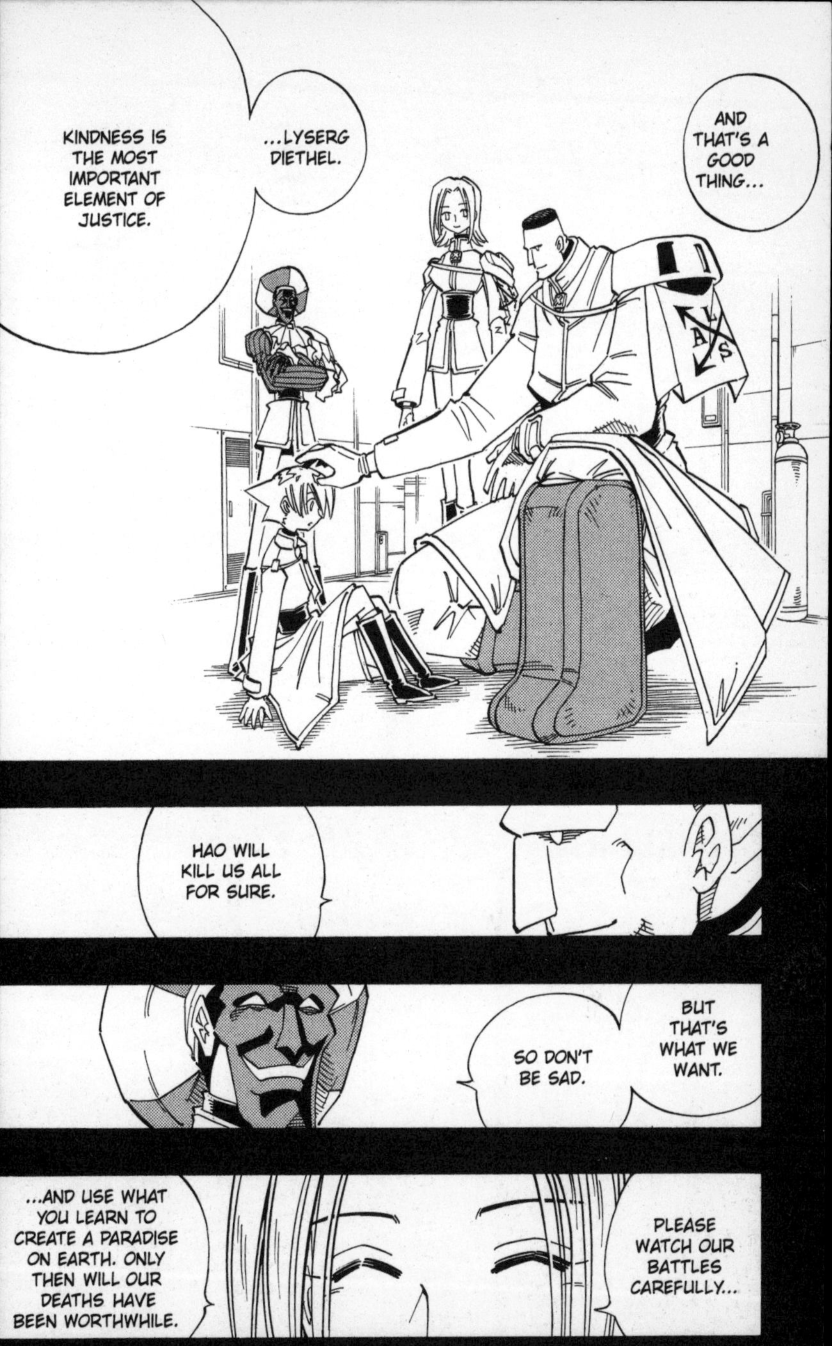
AND THAT'S A GOOD THING...
...LYSERG DIETHEL.
KINDNESS IS THE MOST IMPORTANT ELEMENT OF JUSTICE.
HAO WILL KILL US ALL FOR SURE.
BUT THAT'S WHAT WE WANT.
SO DON'T BE SAD.
PLEASE WATCH OUR BATTLES CAREFULLY...
...AND USE WHAT YOU LEARN TO CREATE A PARADISE ON EARTH. ONLY THEN WILL OUR DEATHS HAVE BEEN WORTHWHILE.

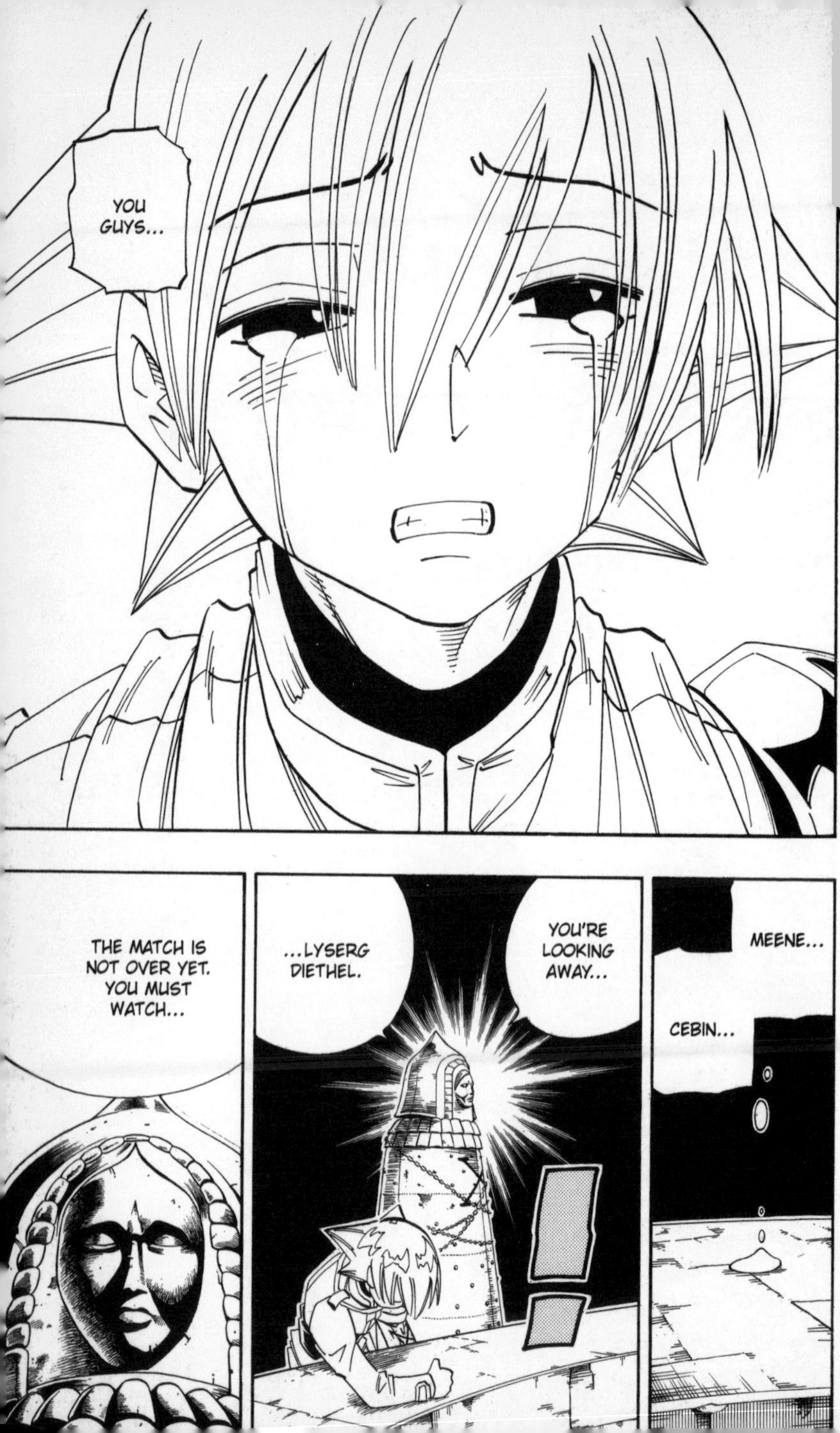
YOU GUYS...
MEENE...
CEBIN...
YOU'RE LOOKING AWAY...
...LYSERG DIETHEL.
THE MATCH IS NOT OVER YET. YOU MUST WATCH...

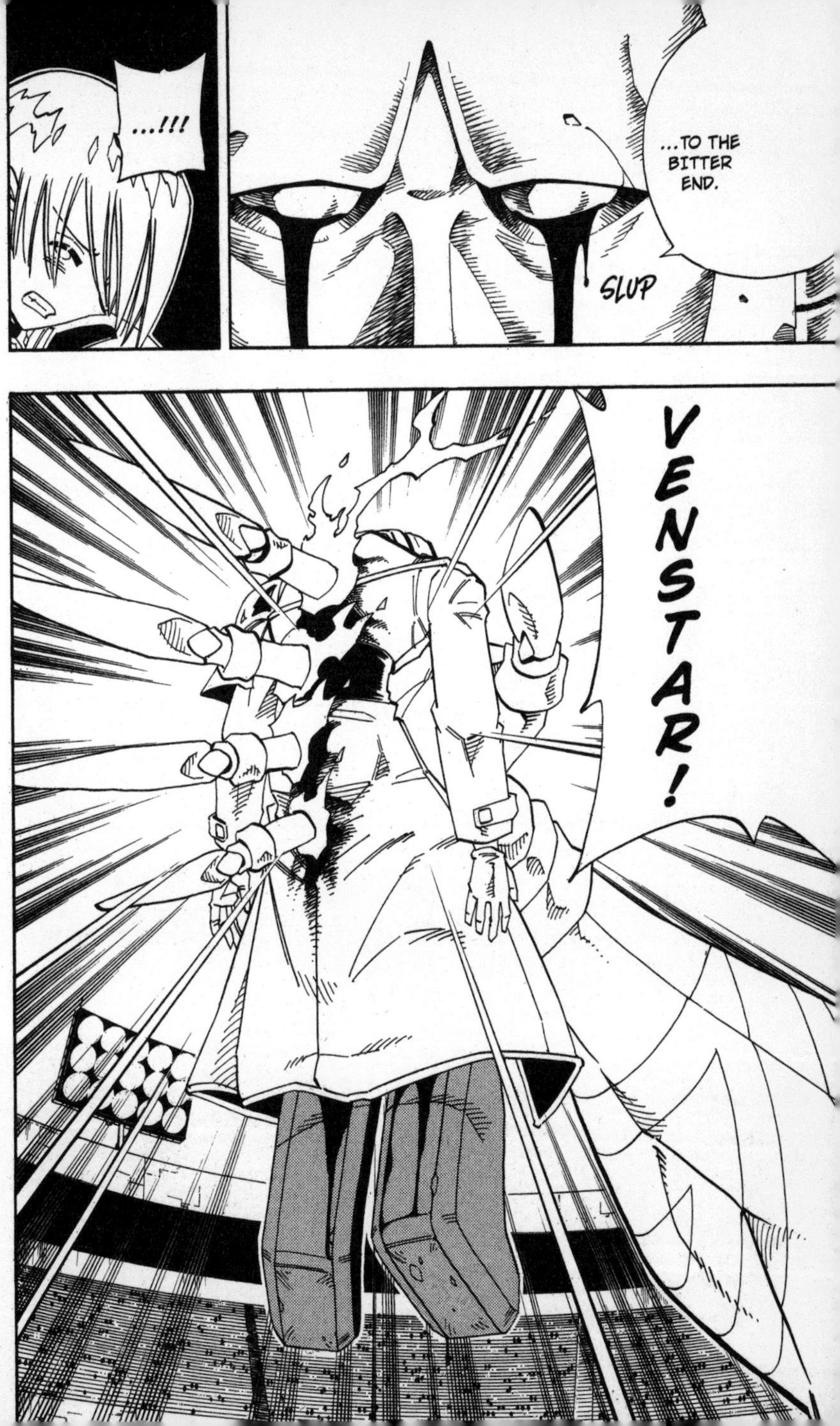
...TO THE BITTER END.
SLUP
...!!!
VENSTAR!

Shaman King

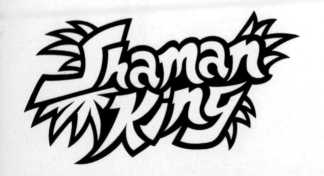

SHAMAN KING CHARACTER FILE No.81

ケビン

CEBIN

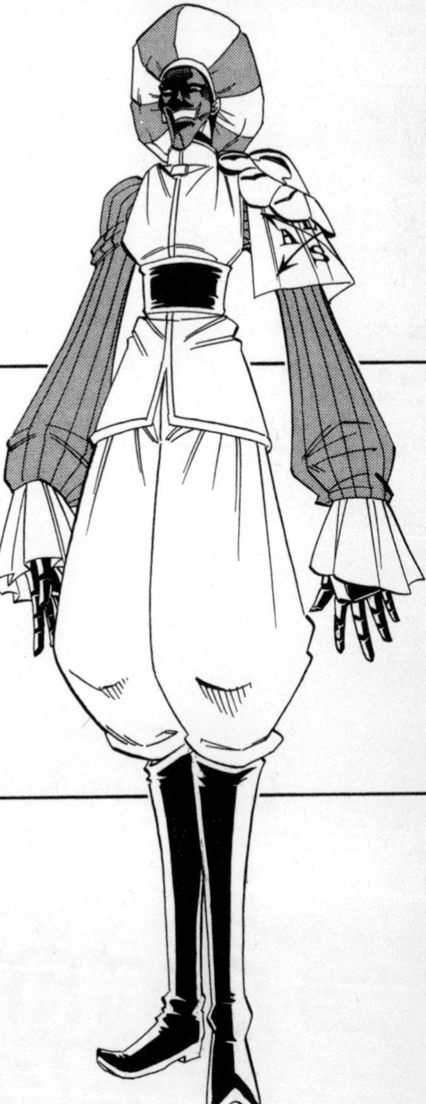

2001
(JAN)

BIRTHDAY: SEPT. 18, 1971
ASTROLOGICAL SIGN: VIRGO
BLOOD TYPE: AB
30 YEARS OLD AT DEATH

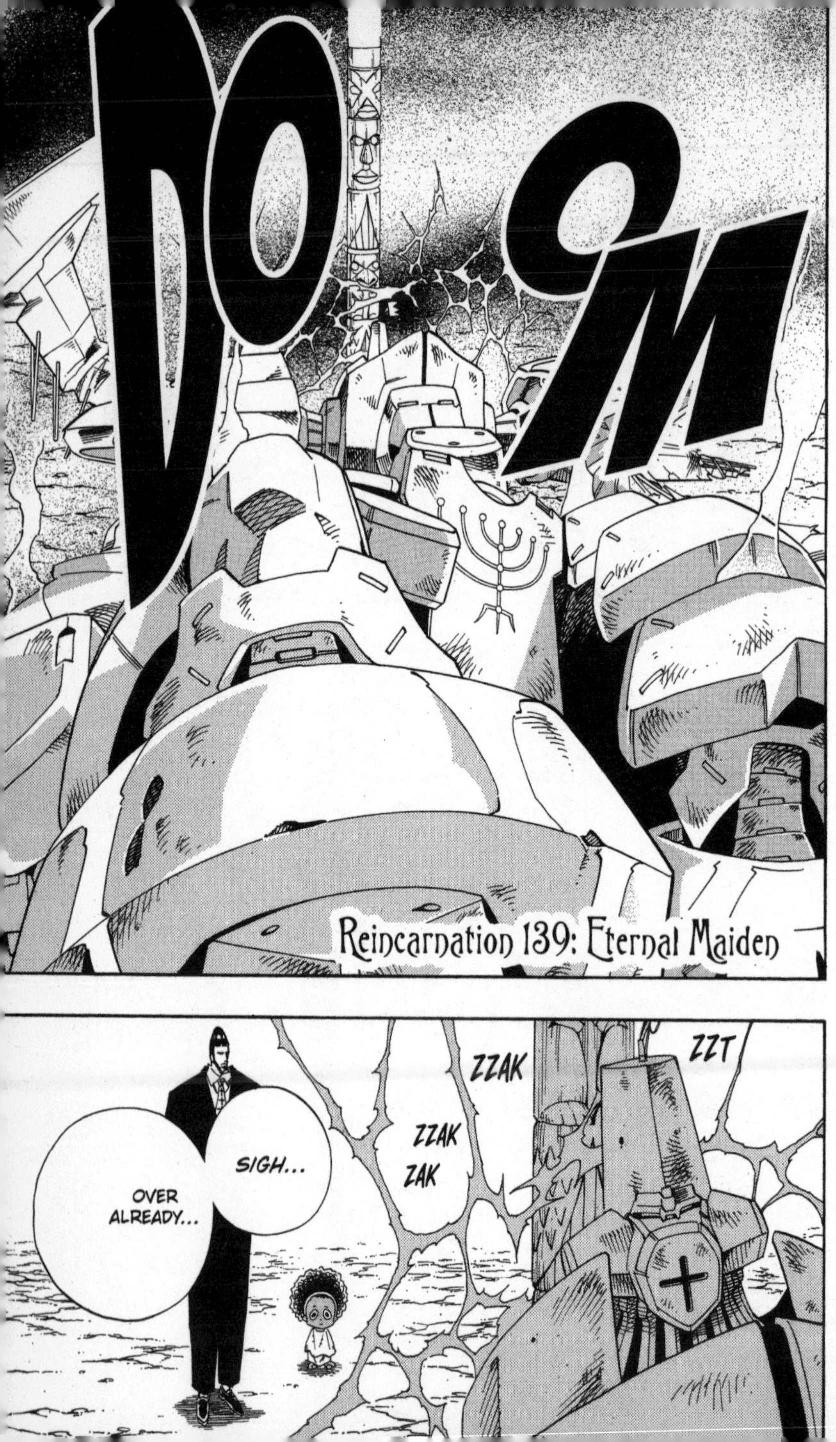
DOOM
Reincarnation 139: Eternal Maiden
ZZT
ZZAK
ZZAK
ZAK
SIGH...
OVER ALREADY...

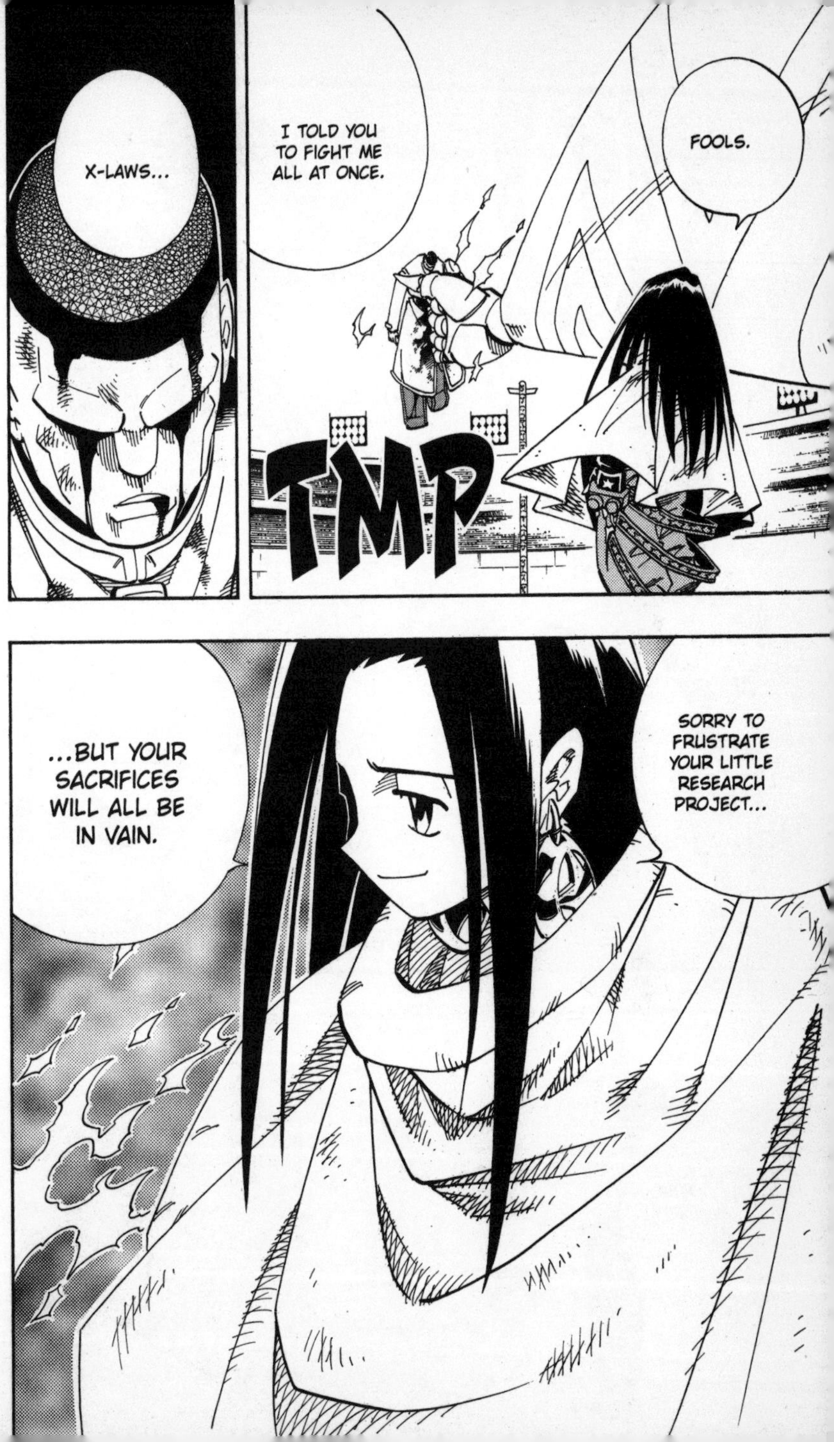
FOOLS.
I TOLD YOU TO FIGHT ME ALL AT ONCE.
TMP
X-LAWS...
SORRY TO FRUSTRATE YOUR LITTLE RESEARCH PROJECT...
...BUT YOUR SACRIFICES WILL ALL BE IN VAIN.

Reincarnation 139:
Eternal Maiden

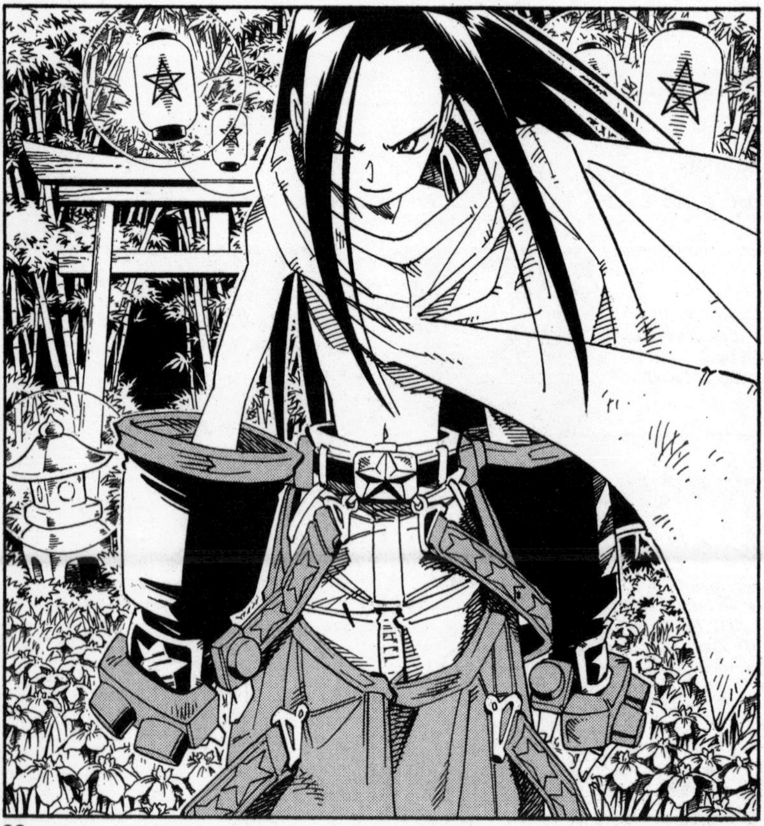

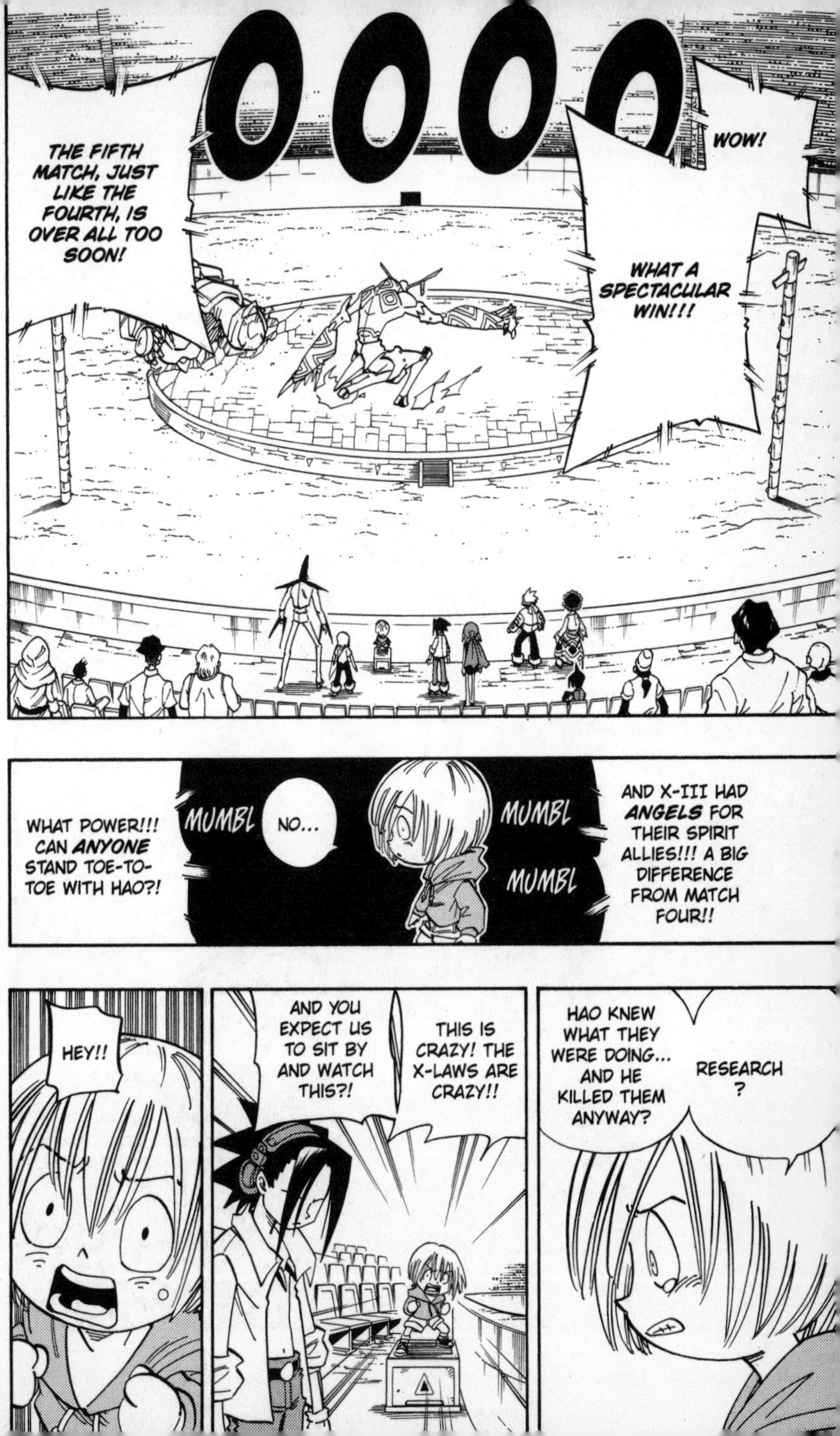
WOW!
WHAT A SPECTACULAR WIN!!!
OOOO
THE FIFTH MATCH, JUST LIKE THE FOURTH, IS OVER ALL TOO SOON!
AND X-III HAD ANGELS FOR THEIR SPIRIT ALLIES!!! A BIG DIFFERENCE FROM MATCH FOUR!!
MUMBL
MUMBL
NO...
MUMBL
WHAT POWER!!! CAN ANYONE STAND TOE-TO-TOE WITH HAO?!
RESEARCH ?
HAO KNEW WHAT THEY WERE DOING... AND HE KILLED THEM ANYWAY?
THIS IS CRAZY! THE X-LAWS ARE CRAZY!!
AND YOU EXPECT US TO SIT BY AND WATCH THIS?!
HEY!!

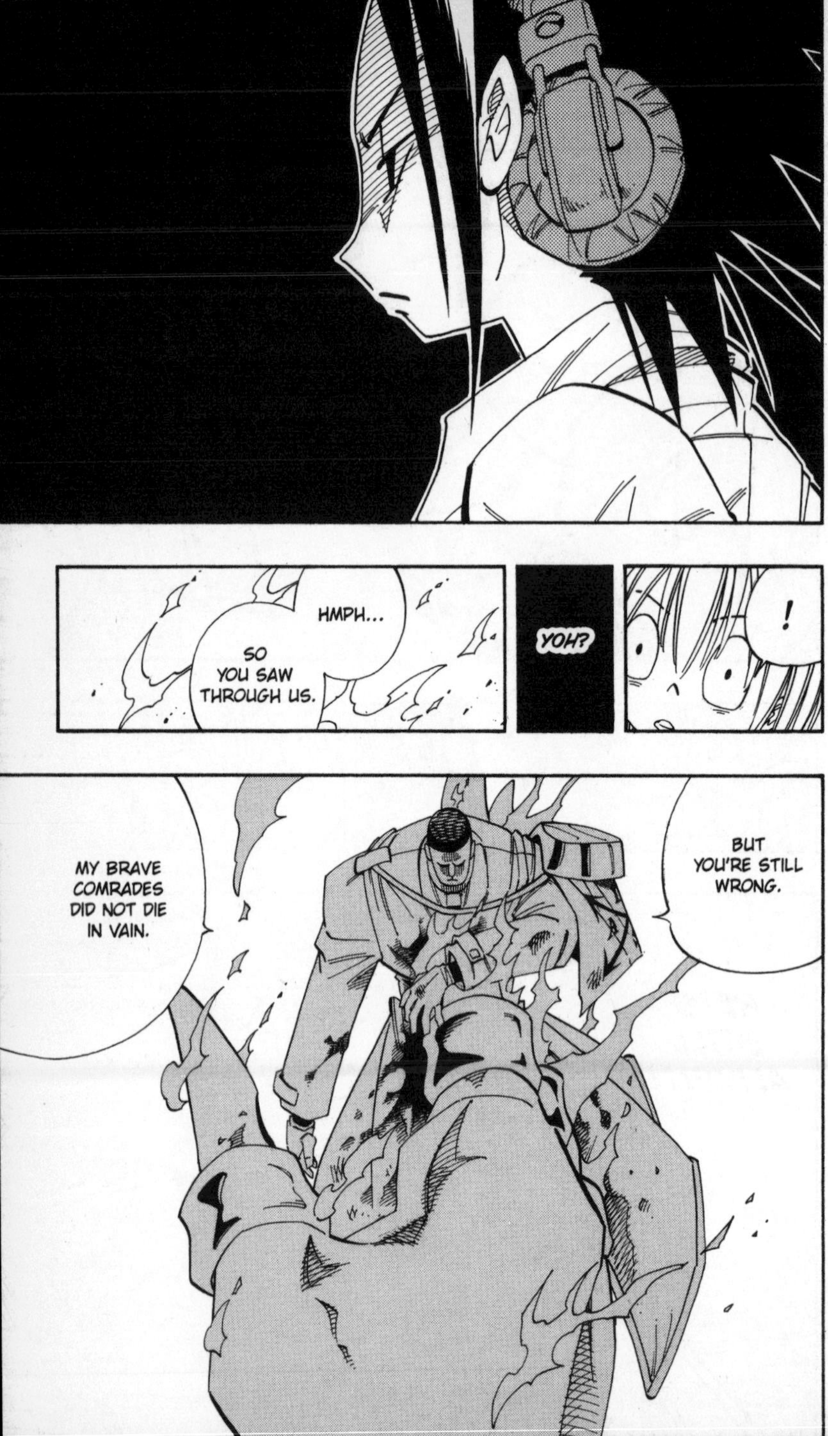
!
YOH?
HMPH...
SO YOU SAW THROUGH US.
BUT YOU'RE STILL WRONG.
MY BRAVE COMRADES DID NOT DIE IN VAIN.

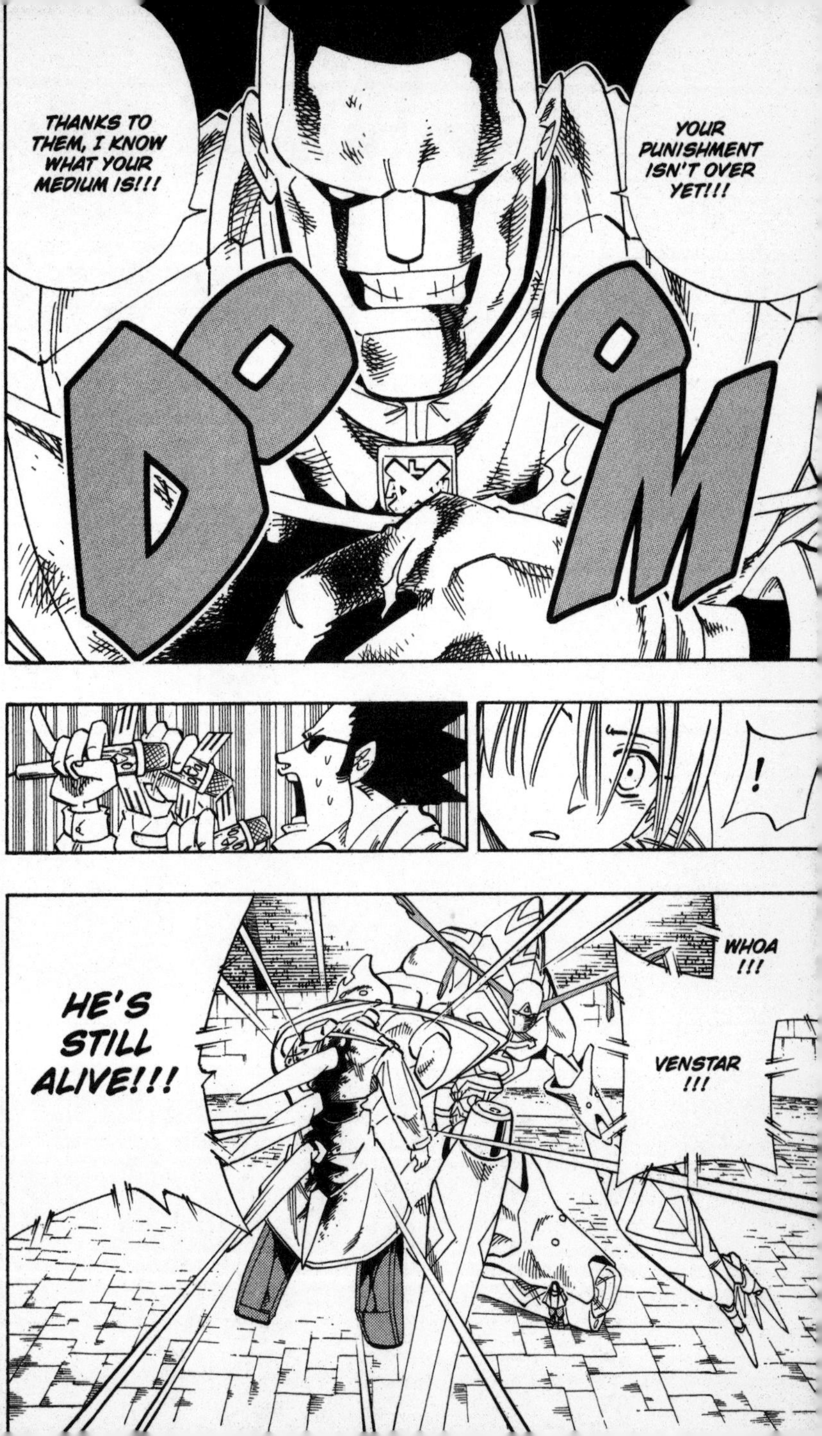
YOUR PUNISHMENT ISN'T OVER YET!!!
THANKS TO THEM, I KNOW WHAT YOUR MEDIUM IS!!!
DOOM
!
WHOA !!!
VENSTAR !!!
HE'S STILL ALIVE!!!

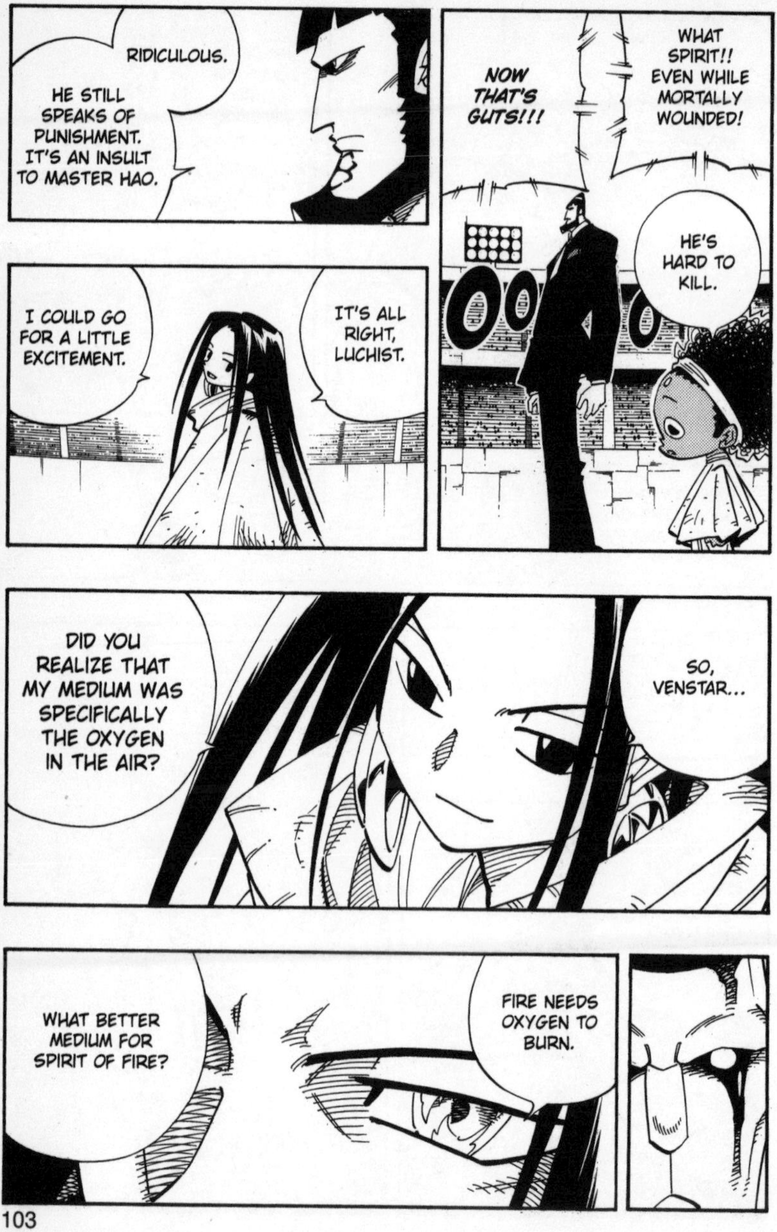
WHAT SPIRIT!! EVEN WHILE MORTALLY WOUNDED!
NOW THAT'S GUTS!!!
HE'S HARD TO KILL.
RIDICULOUS.
HE STILL SPEAKS OF PUNISHMENT. IT'S AN INSULT TO MASTER HAO.
IT'S ALL RIGHT, LUCHIST.
I COULD GO FOR A LITTLE EXCITEMENT.
SO, VENSTAR...
DID YOU REALIZE THAT MY MEDIUM WAS SPECIFICALLY THE OXYGEN IN THE AIR?
FIRE NEEDS OXYGEN TO BURN.
WHAT BETTER MEDIUM FOR SPIRIT OF FIRE?

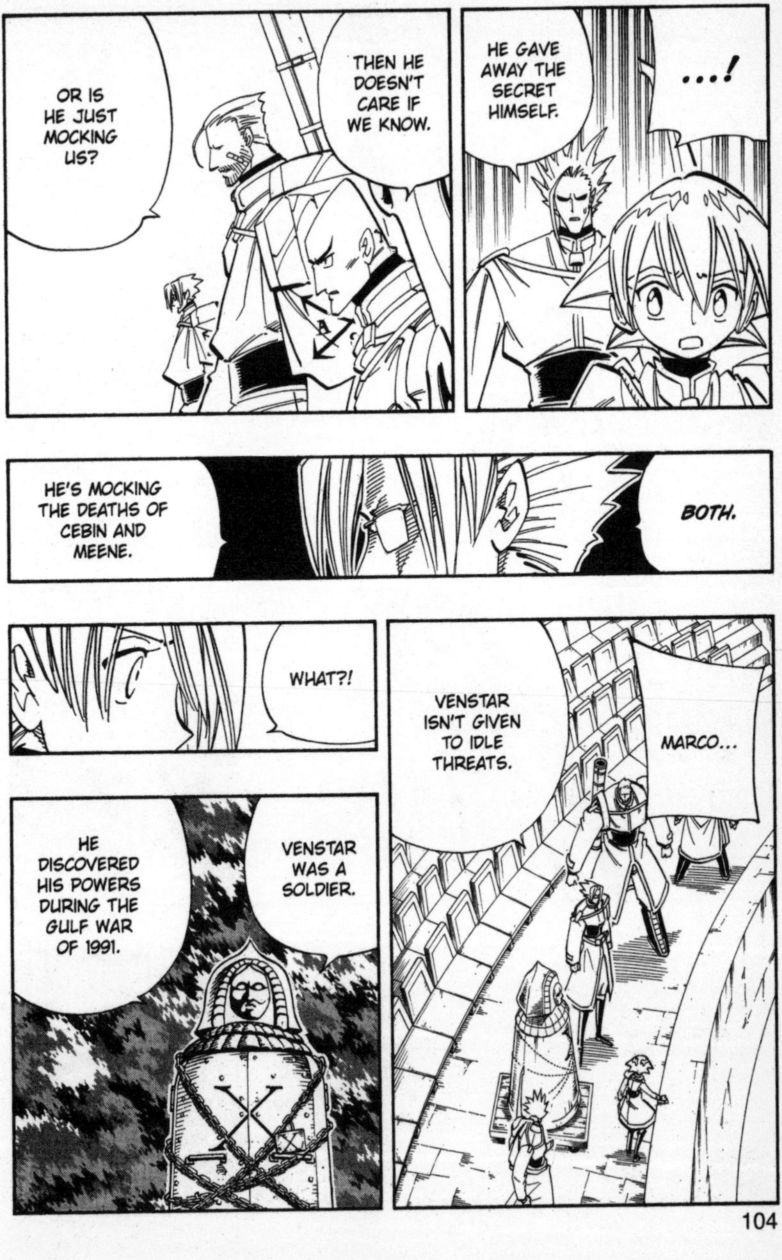
...!
HE GAVE AWAY THE SECRET HIMSELF.
THEN HE DOESN'T CARE IF WE KNOW.
OR IS HE JUST MOCKING US?
BOTH.
HE'S MOCKING THE DEATHS OF CEBIN AND MEENE.
MARCO...
VENSTAR ISN'T GIVEN TO IDLE THREATS.
WHAT?!
VENSTAR WAS A SOLDIER.
HE DISCOVERED HIS POWERS DURING THE GULF WAR OF 1991.

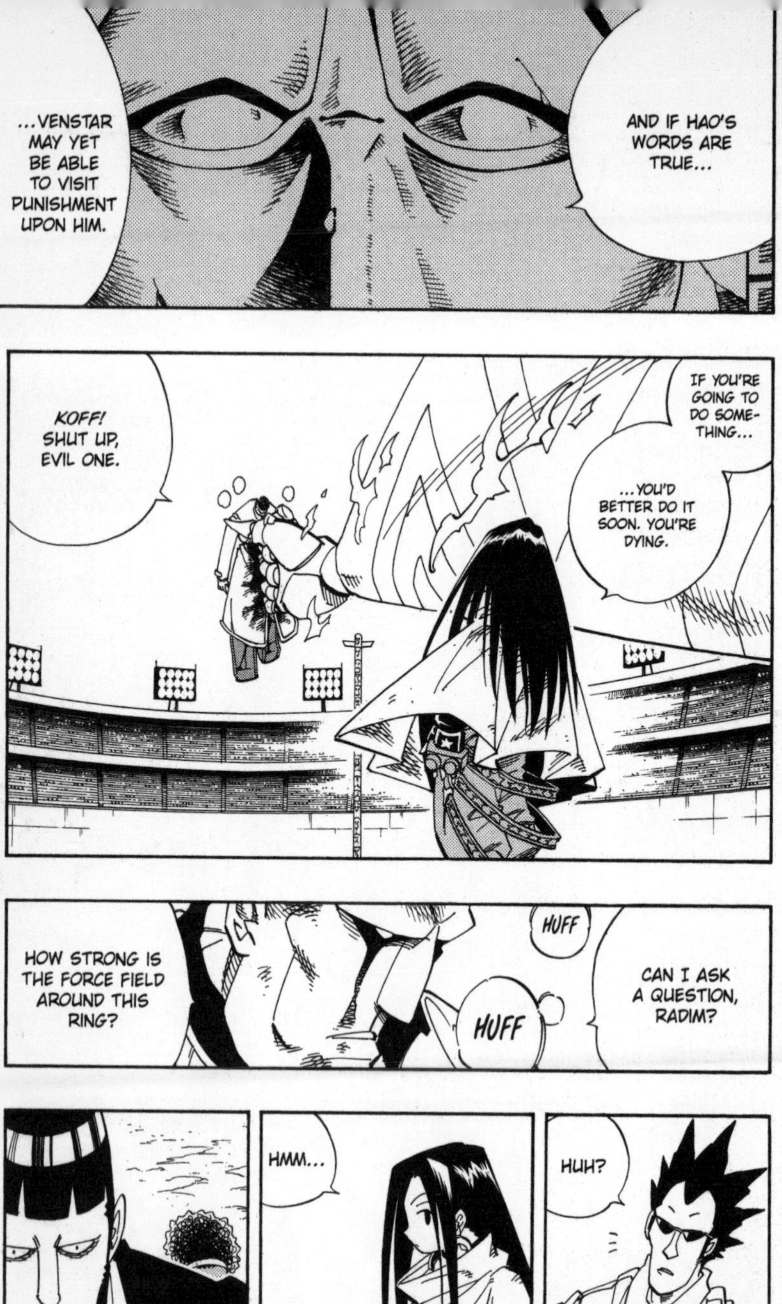
AND IF HAO'S WORDS ARE TRUE...
...VENSTAR MAY YET BE ABLE TO VISIT PUNISHMENT UPON HIM.
IF YOU'RE GOING TO DO SOME-THING...
...YOU'D BETTER DO IT SOON. YOU'RE DYING.
KOFF! SHUT UP, EVIL ONE.
HUFF
CAN I ASK A QUESTION, RADIM?
HUFF
HOW STRONG IS THE FORCE FIELD AROUND THIS RING?
HUH?
HMM...

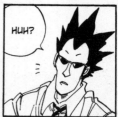

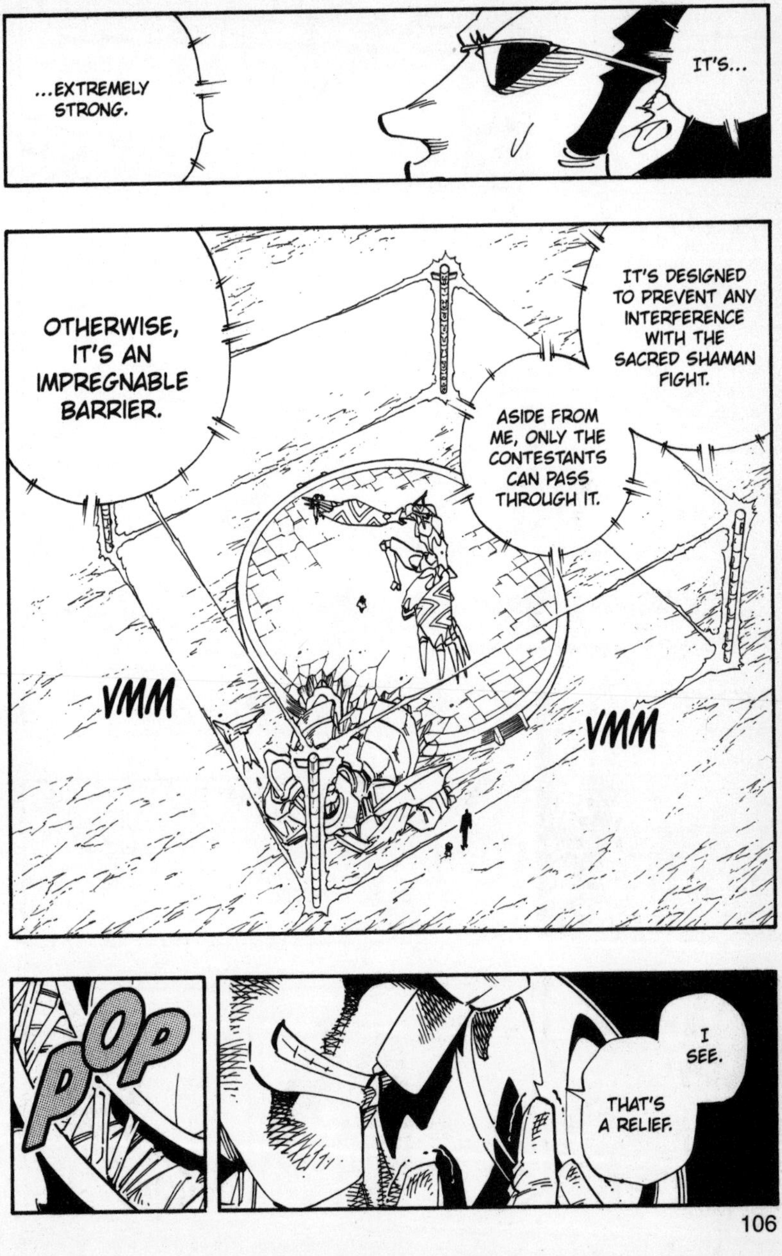
IT'S...
...EXTREMELY STRONG.
IT'S DESIGNED TO PREVENT ANY INTERFERENCE WITH THE SACRED SHAMAN FIGHT.
ASIDE FROM ME, ONLY THE CONTESTANTS CAN PASS THROUGH IT.
OTHERWISE, IT'S AN IMPREGNABLE BARRIER.
VMM
VMM
I SEE.
THAT'S A RELIEF.
POP

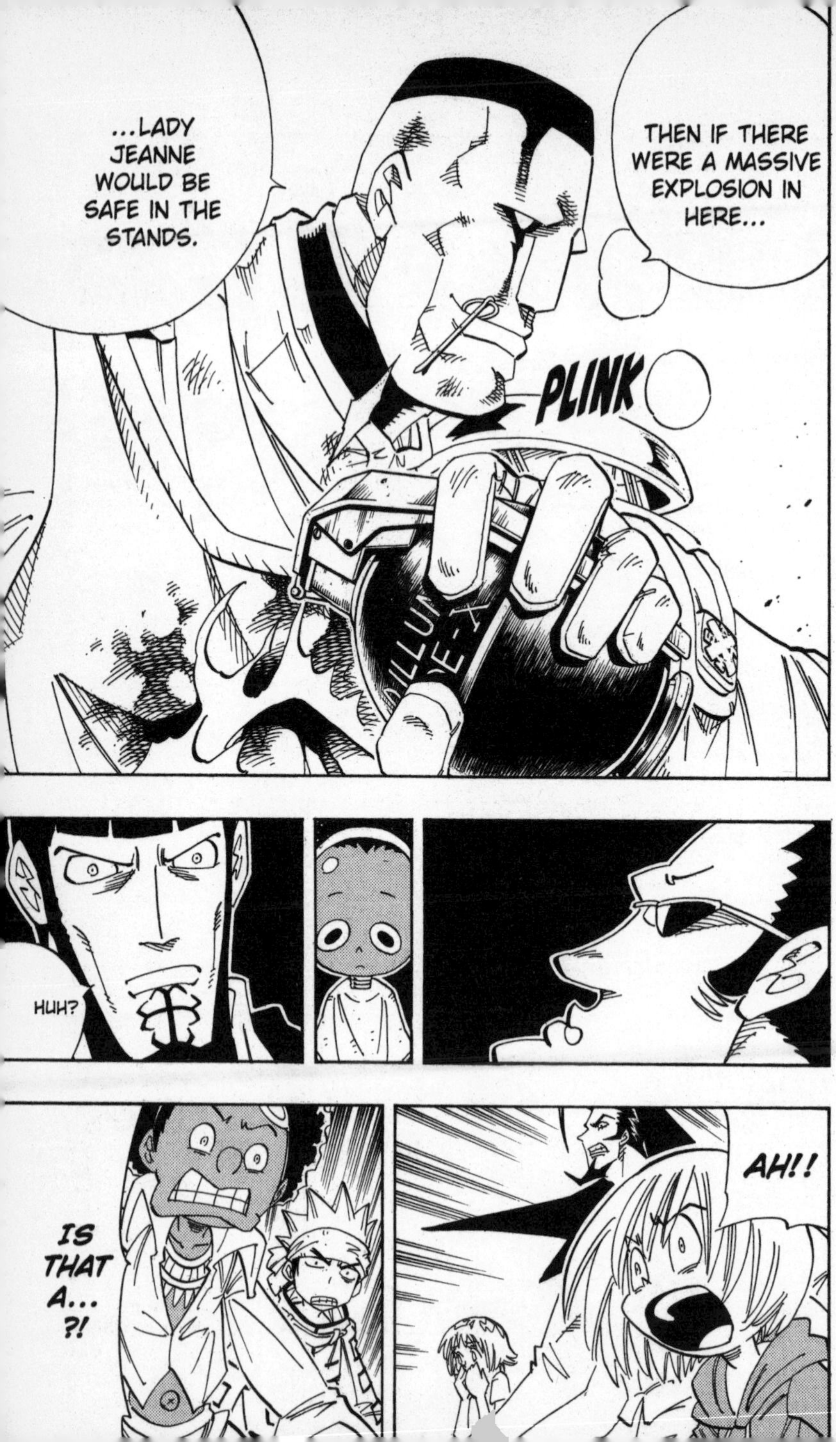
THEN IF THERE WERE A MASSIVE EXPLOSION IN HERE...
...LADY JEANNE WOULD BE SAFE IN THE STANDS.
PLINK
HUH?
AH!!
IS THAT A...?!

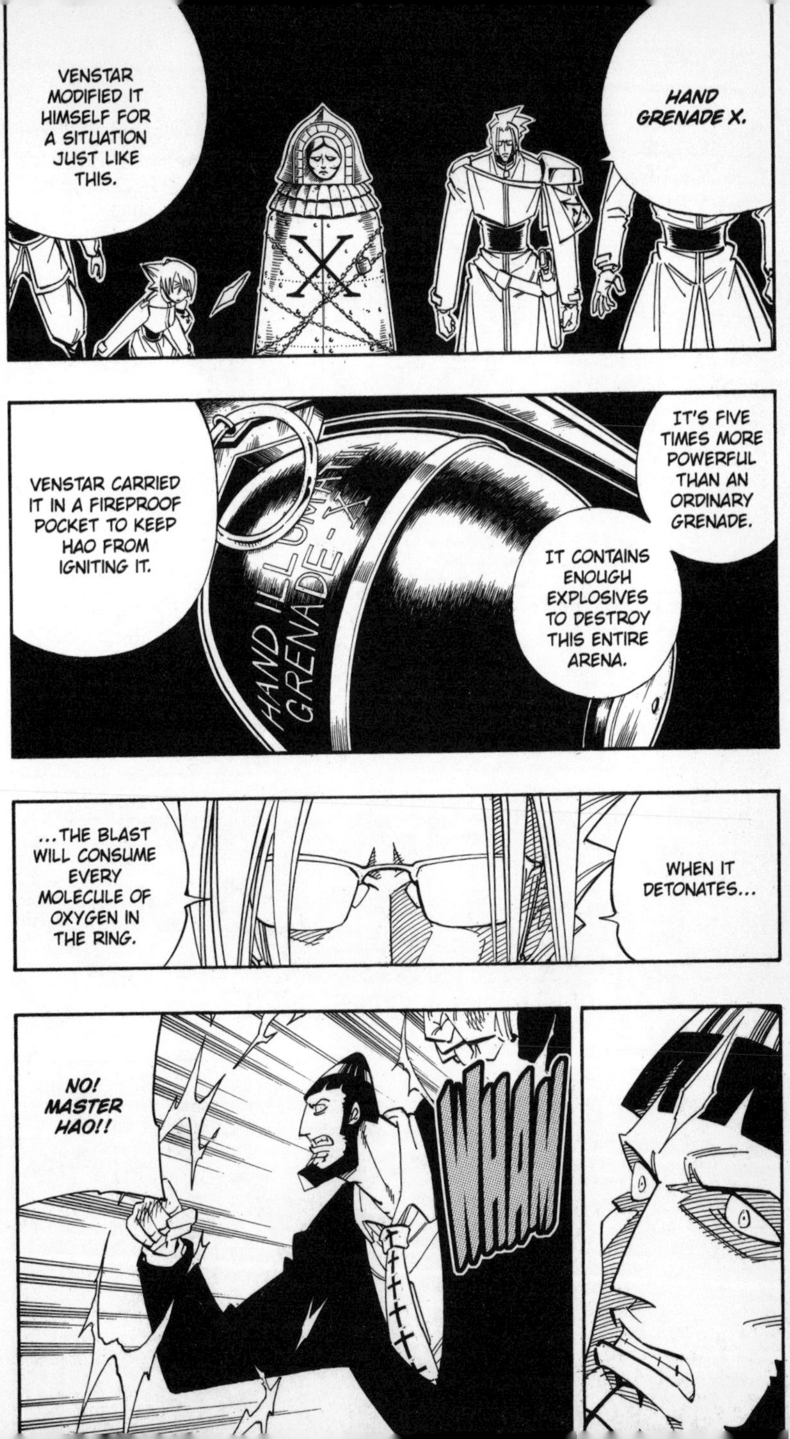
HAND GRENADE X.
VENSTAR MODIFIED IT HIMSELF FOR A SITUATION JUST LIKE THIS.
IT'S FIVE TIMES MORE POWERFUL THAN AN ORDINARY GRENADE.
IT CONTAINS ENOUGH EXPLOSIVES TO DESTROY THIS ENTIRE ARENA.
VENSTAR CARRIED IT IN A FIREPROOF POCKET TO KEEP HAO FROM IGNITING IT.
WHEN IT DETONATES...
...THE BLAST WILL CONSUME EVERY MOLECULE OF OXYGEN IN THE RING.
NO! MASTER HAO!!

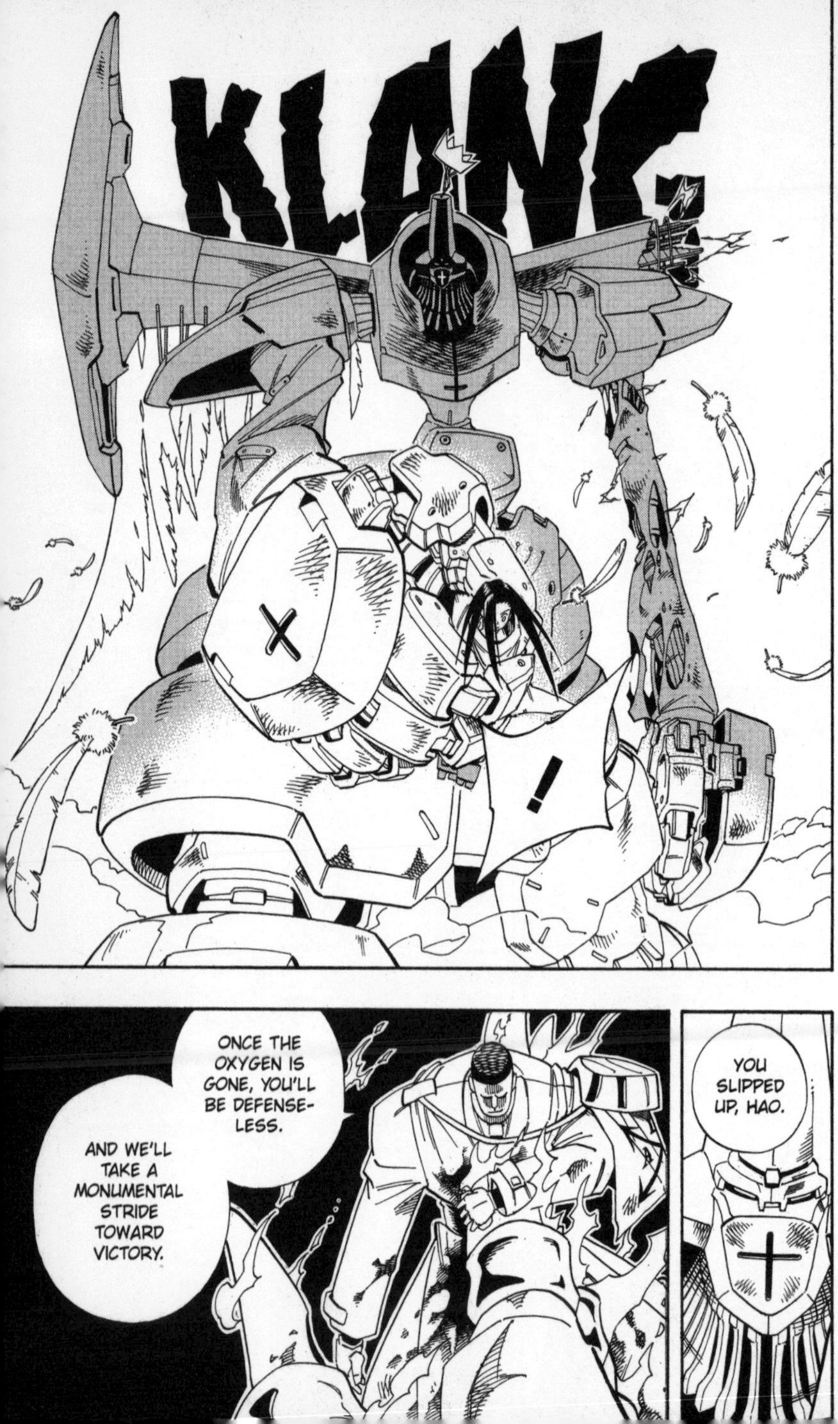
KLANG
!
YOU SLIPPED UP, HAO.
ONCE THE OXYGEN IS GONE, YOU'LL BE DEFENSE-LESS.
AND WE'LL TAKE A MONUMENTAL STRIDE TOWARD VICTORY.

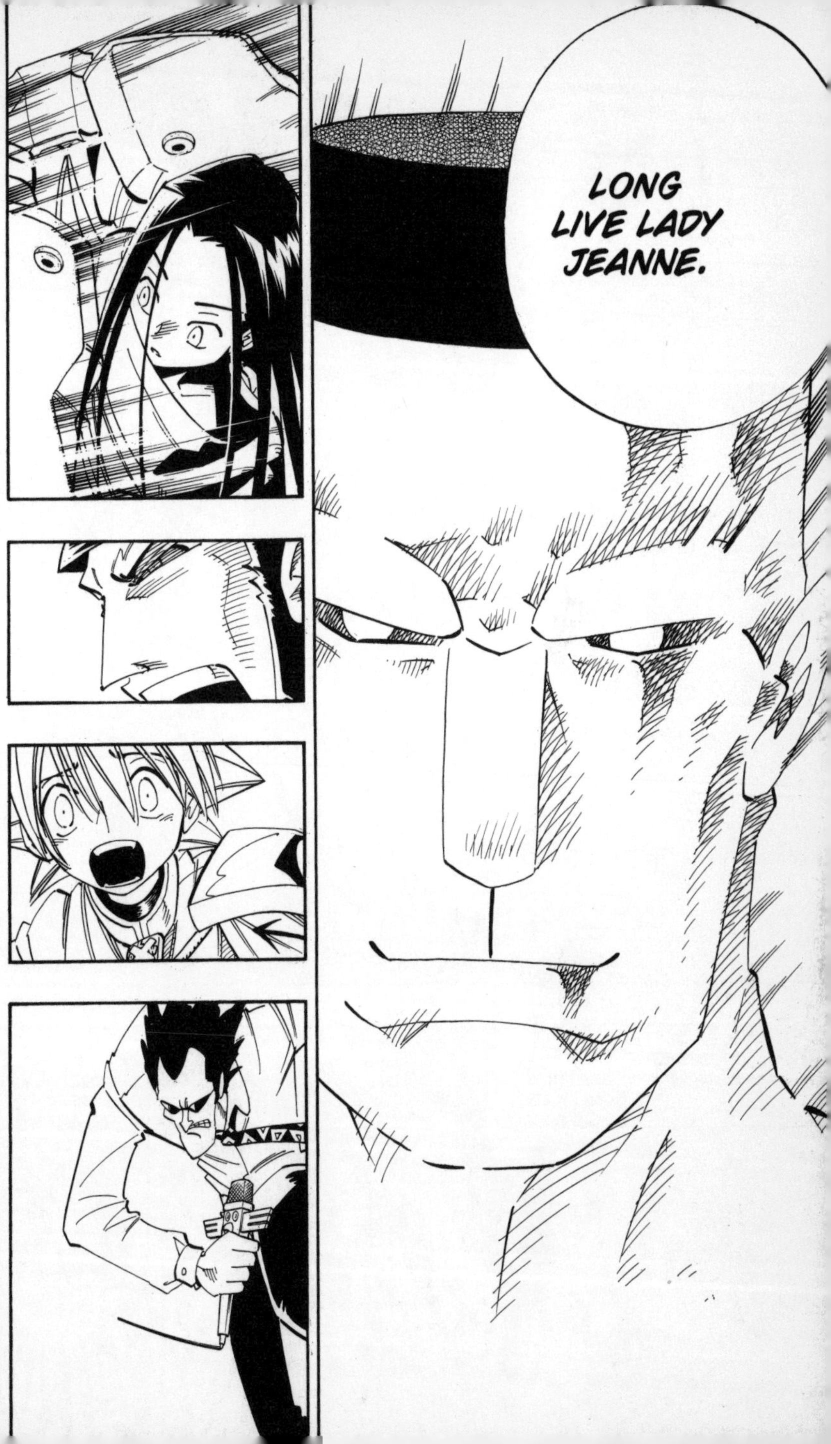
LONG LIVE LADY JEANNE.

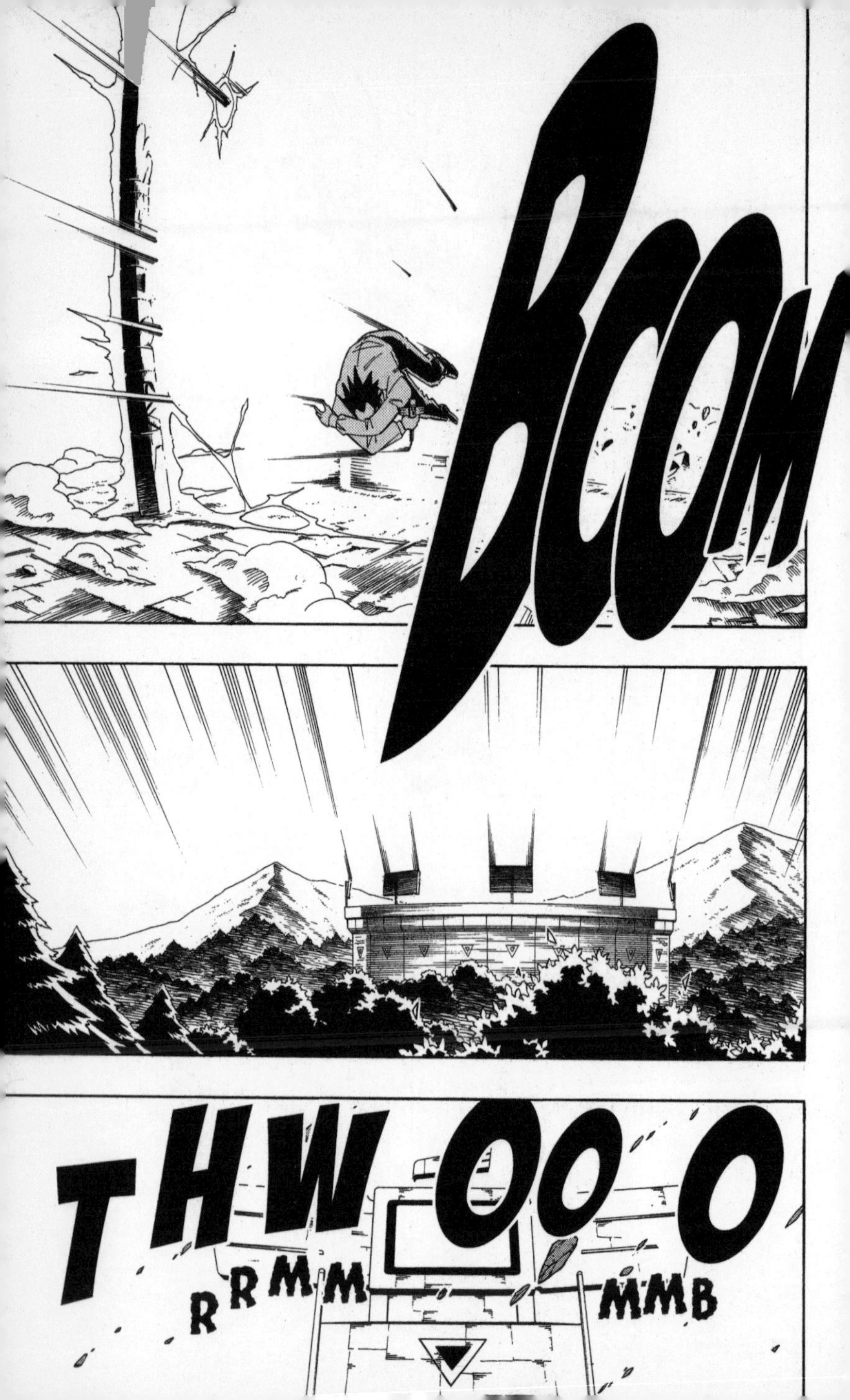
BOOM
THWOOO
RRMMMMMMB

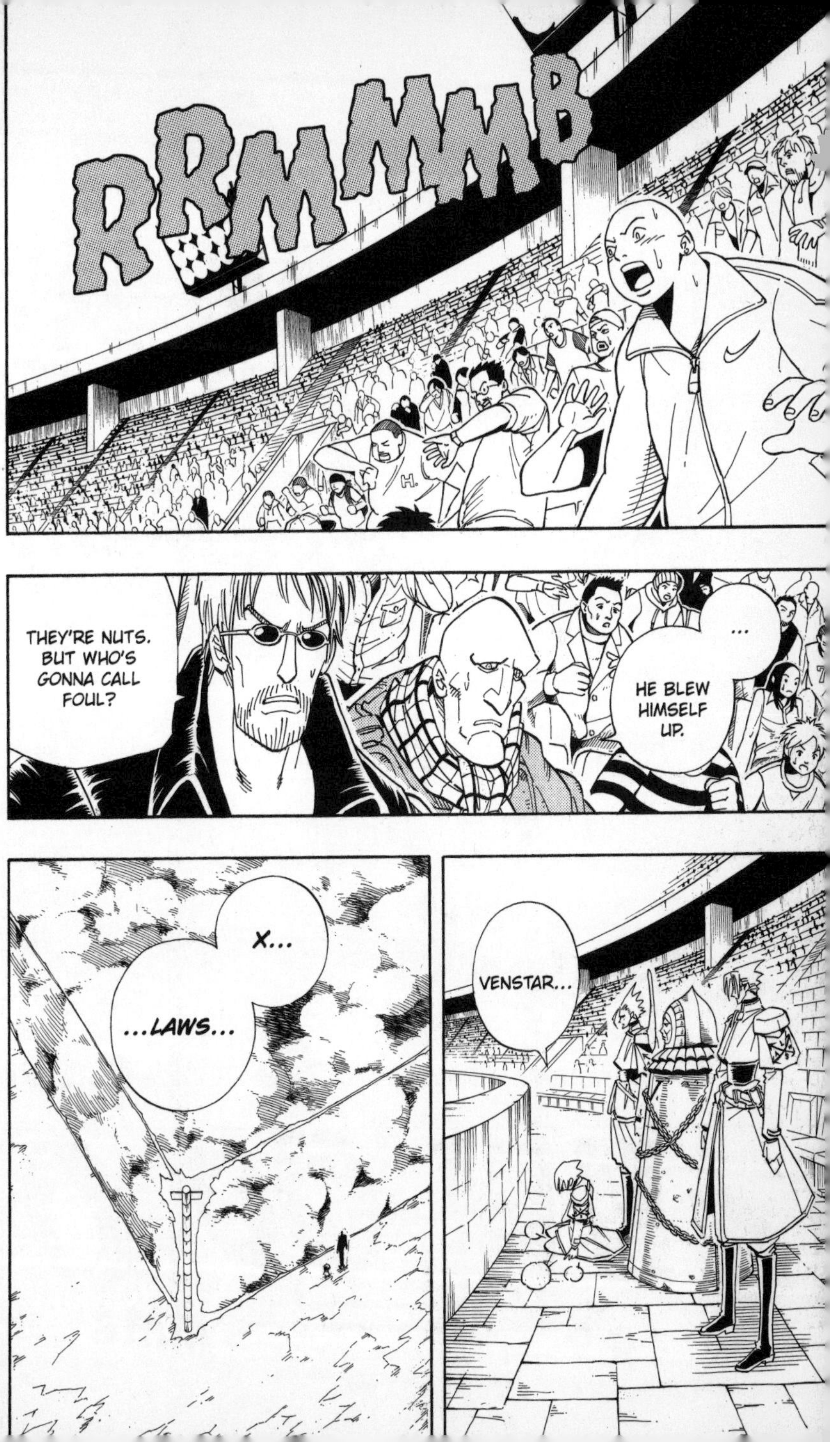
RRMMMB
...
HE BLEW HIMSELF UP.
THEY'RE NUTS. BUT WHO'S GONNA CALL FOUL?
VENSTAR...
X...
...LAWS...

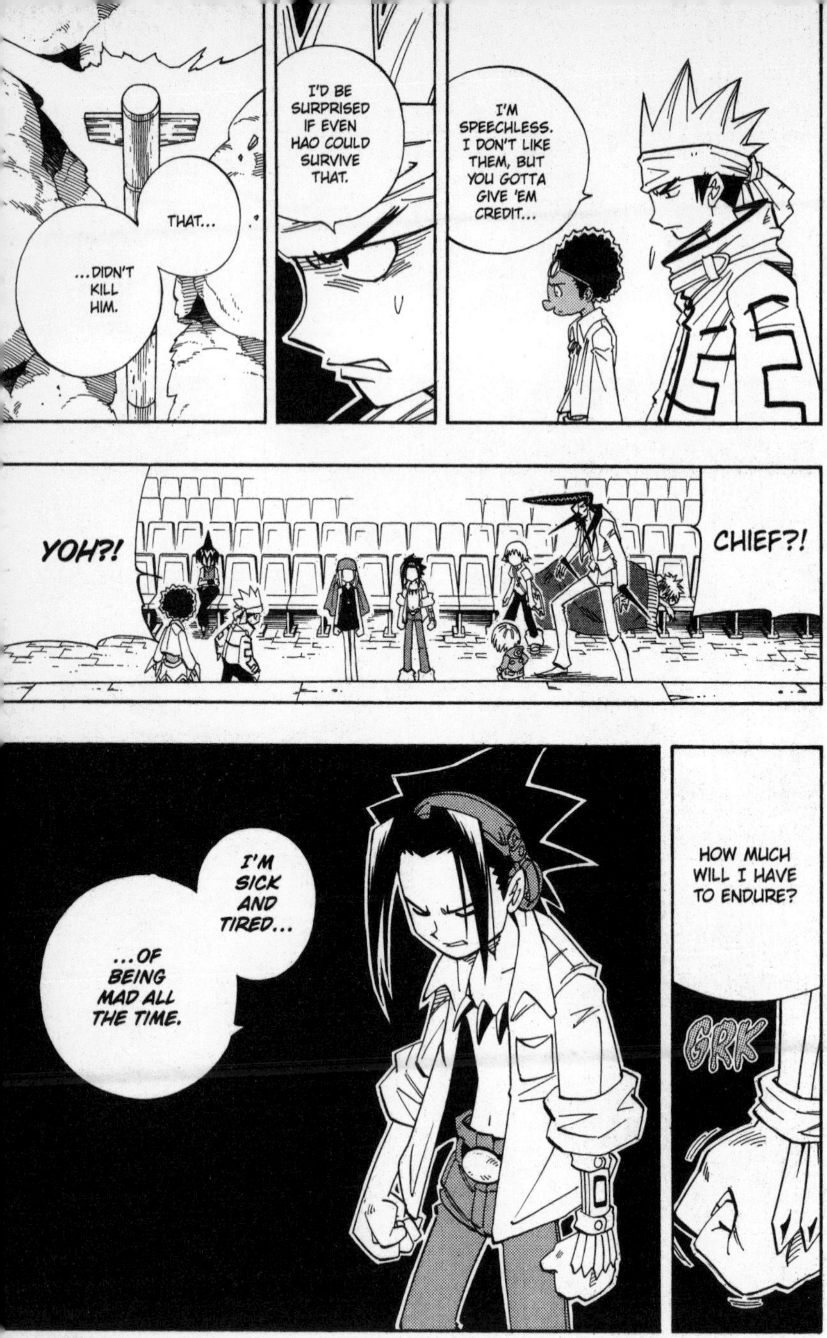
I'M SPEECHLESS. I DON'T LIKE THEM, BUT YOU GOTTA GIVE 'EM CREDIT...
I'D BE SURPRISED IF EVEN HAO COULD SURVIVE THAT.
THAT...
...DIDN'T KILL HIM.
CHIEF?!
YOH?!
HOW MUCH WILL I HAVE TO ENDURE?
GRK
I'M SICK AND TIRED...
...OF BEING MAD ALL THE TIME.

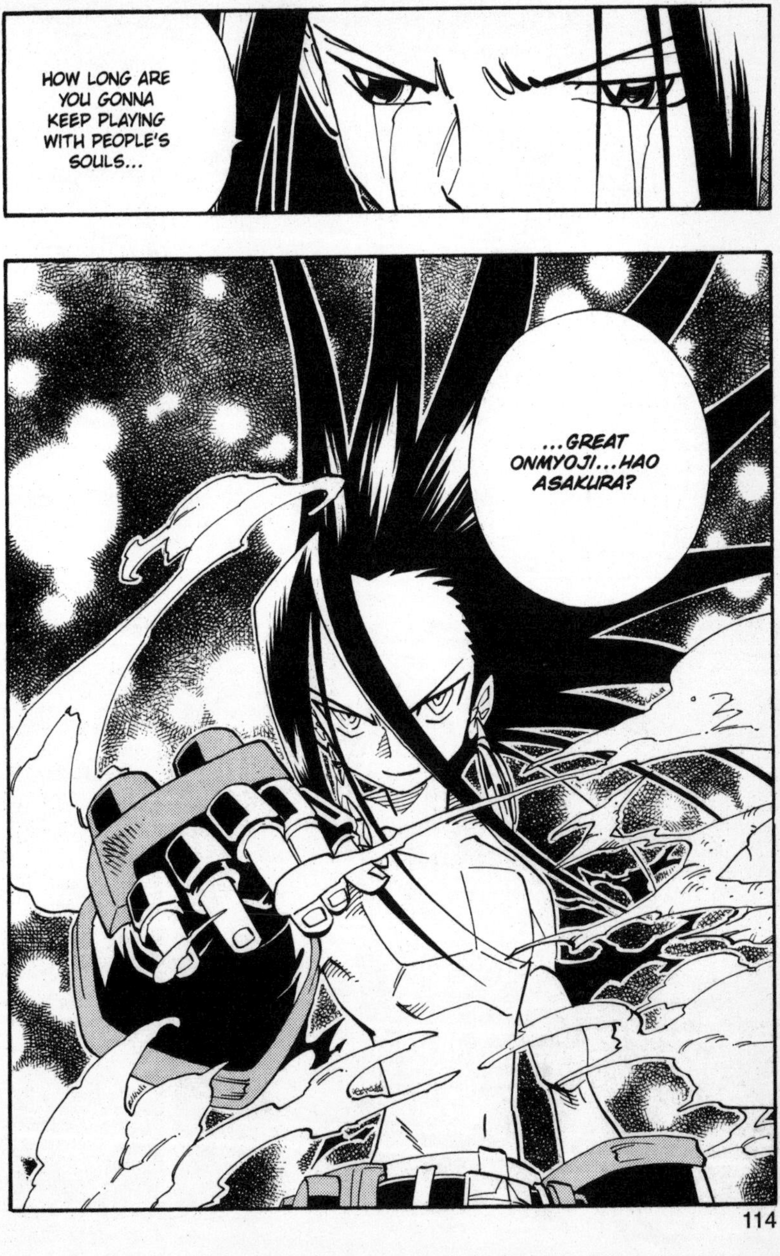
HOW LONG ARE YOU GONNA KEEP PLAYING WITH PEOPLE'S SOULS...
...GREAT ONMYOJI...HAO ASAKURA?

Shaman King

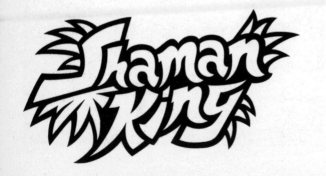

SHAMAN KING CHARACTER FILE No.82

ブンスター

VENSTAR

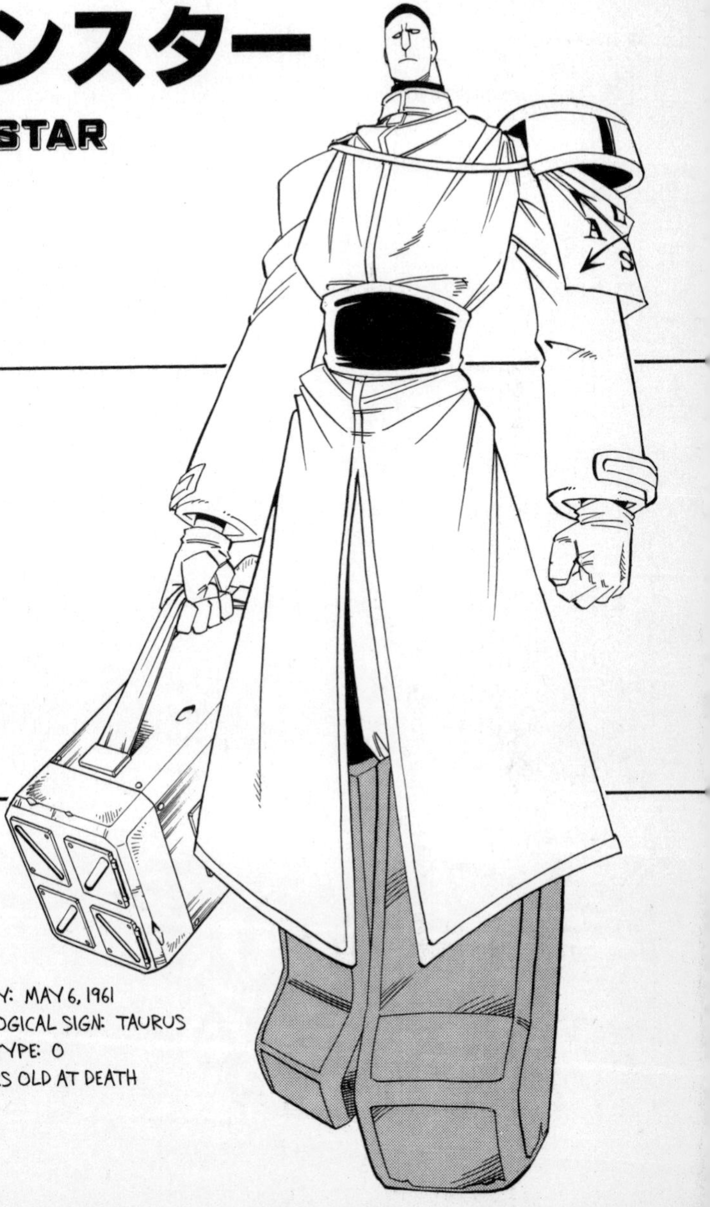

2001
(JAN)

BIRTHDAY: MAY 6, 1961
ASTROLOGICAL SIGN: TAURUS
BLOOD TYPE: O
40 YEARS OLD AT DEATH

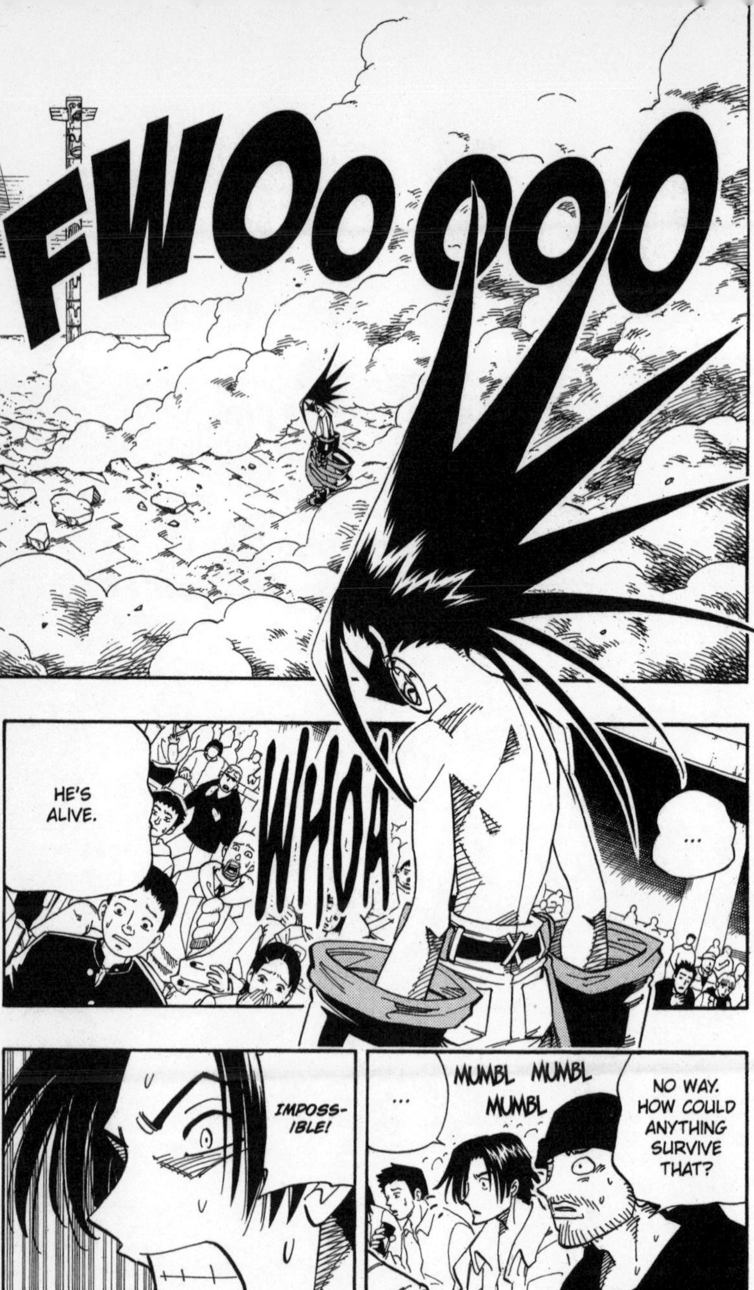
FWOOOOO
...
WHOA
HE'S ALIVE.
NO WAY. HOW COULD ANYTHING SURVIVE THAT?
MUMBL MUMBL MUMBL
...
IMPOSS-IBLE!

Reincarnation 140: Logic

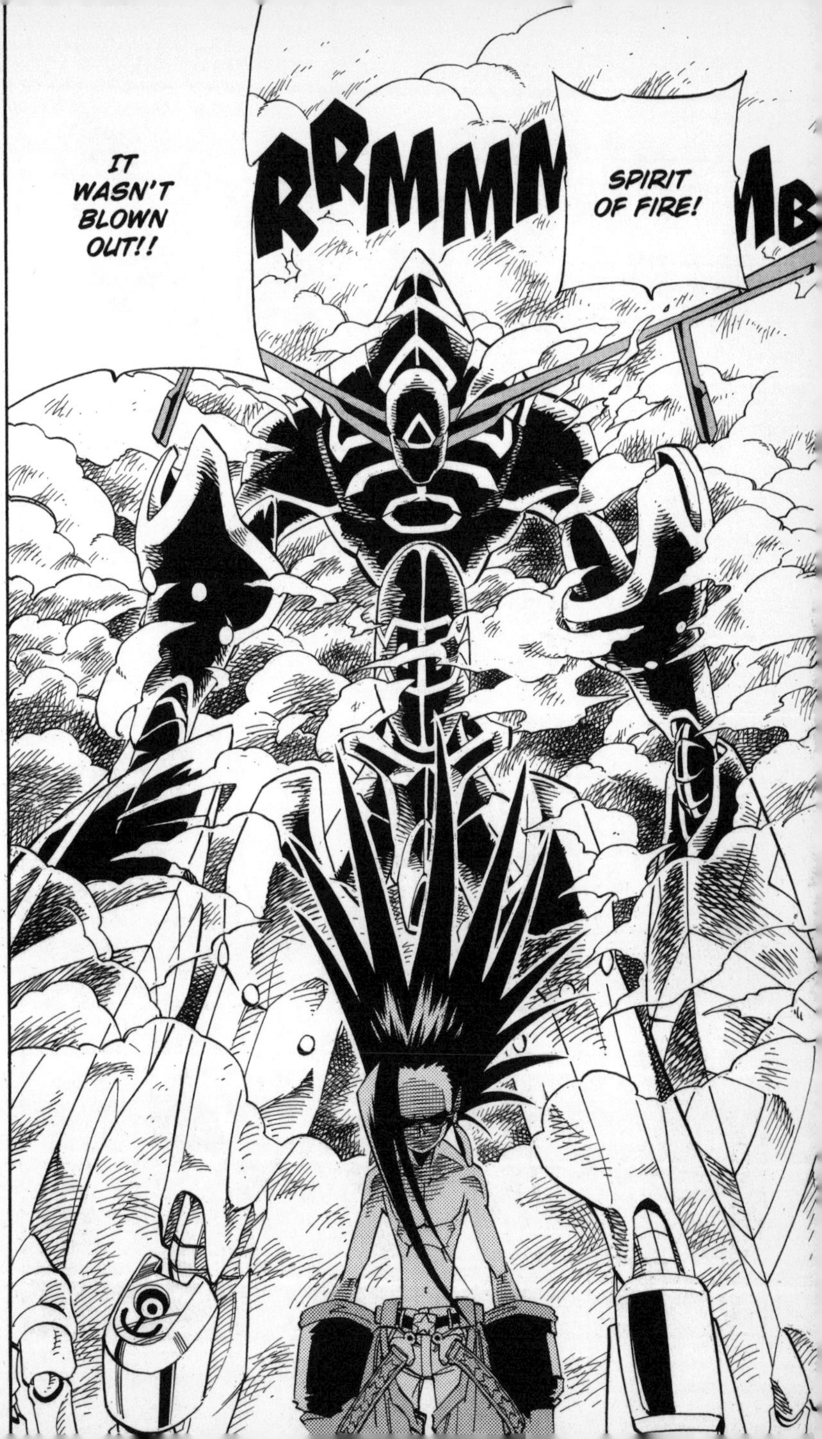
SPIRIT OF FIRE!
RRMMMM MB
IT WASN'T BLOWN OUT!!

Reincarnation 140: Logic

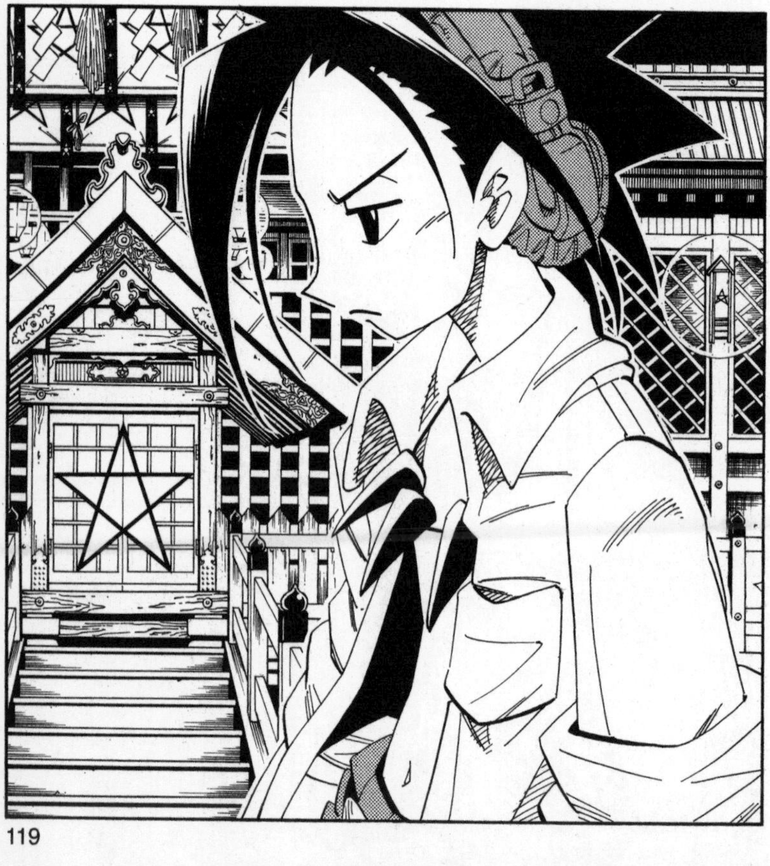

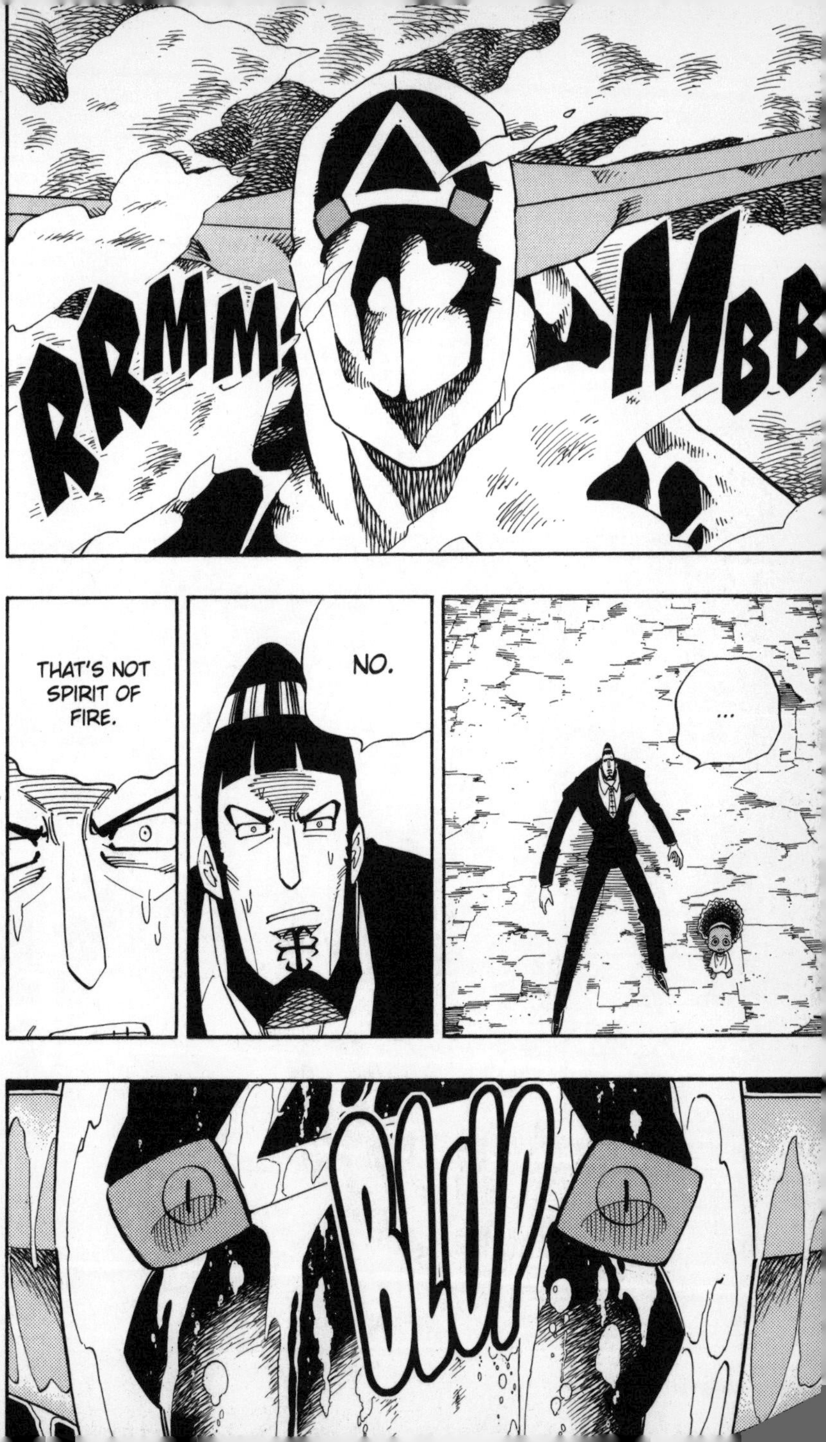
RRMMM
MBB
...
NO.
THAT'S NOT SPIRIT OF FIRE.
BLUP

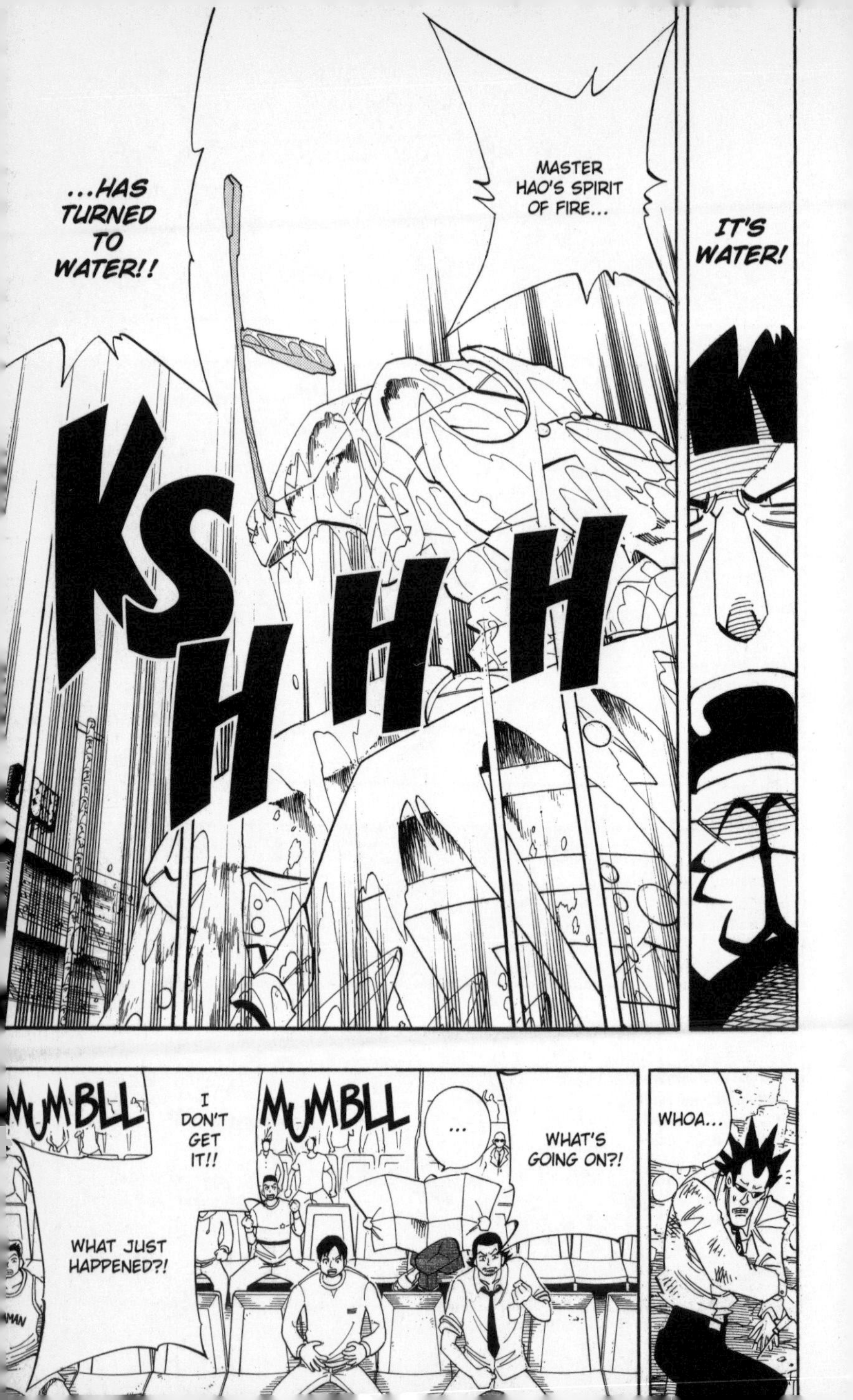
IT'S WATER!
MASTER HAO'S SPIRIT OF FIRE...
...HAS TURNED TO WATER!!
KSHHHH
WHOA...
WHAT'S GOING ON?!
...
MUMBLL
I DON'T GET IT!!
MUMBLL
WHAT JUST HAPPENED?!

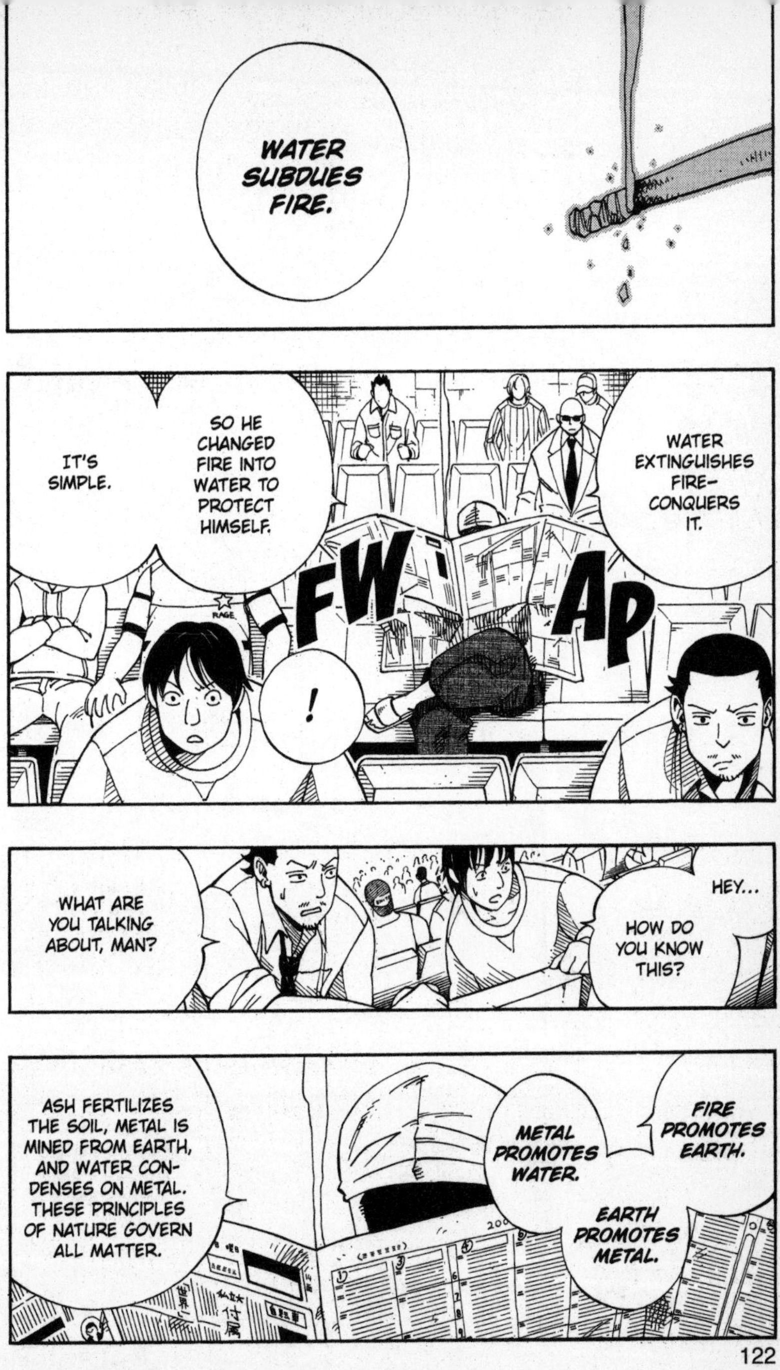
WATER SUBDUES FIRE.
WATER EXTINGUISHES FIRE— CONQUERS IT.
FWAP
!
RAGE
SO HE CHANGED FIRE INTO WATER TO PROTECT HIMSELF.
IT'S SIMPLE.
HEY...
HOW DO YOU KNOW THIS?
WHAT ARE YOU TALKING ABOUT, MAN?
FIRE PROMOTES EARTH.
EARTH PROMOTES METAL.
METAL PROMOTES WATER.
ASH FERTILIZES THE SOIL, METAL IS MINED FROM EARTH, AND WATER CONDENSES ON METAL. THESE PRINCIPLES OF NATURE GOVERN ALL MATTER.

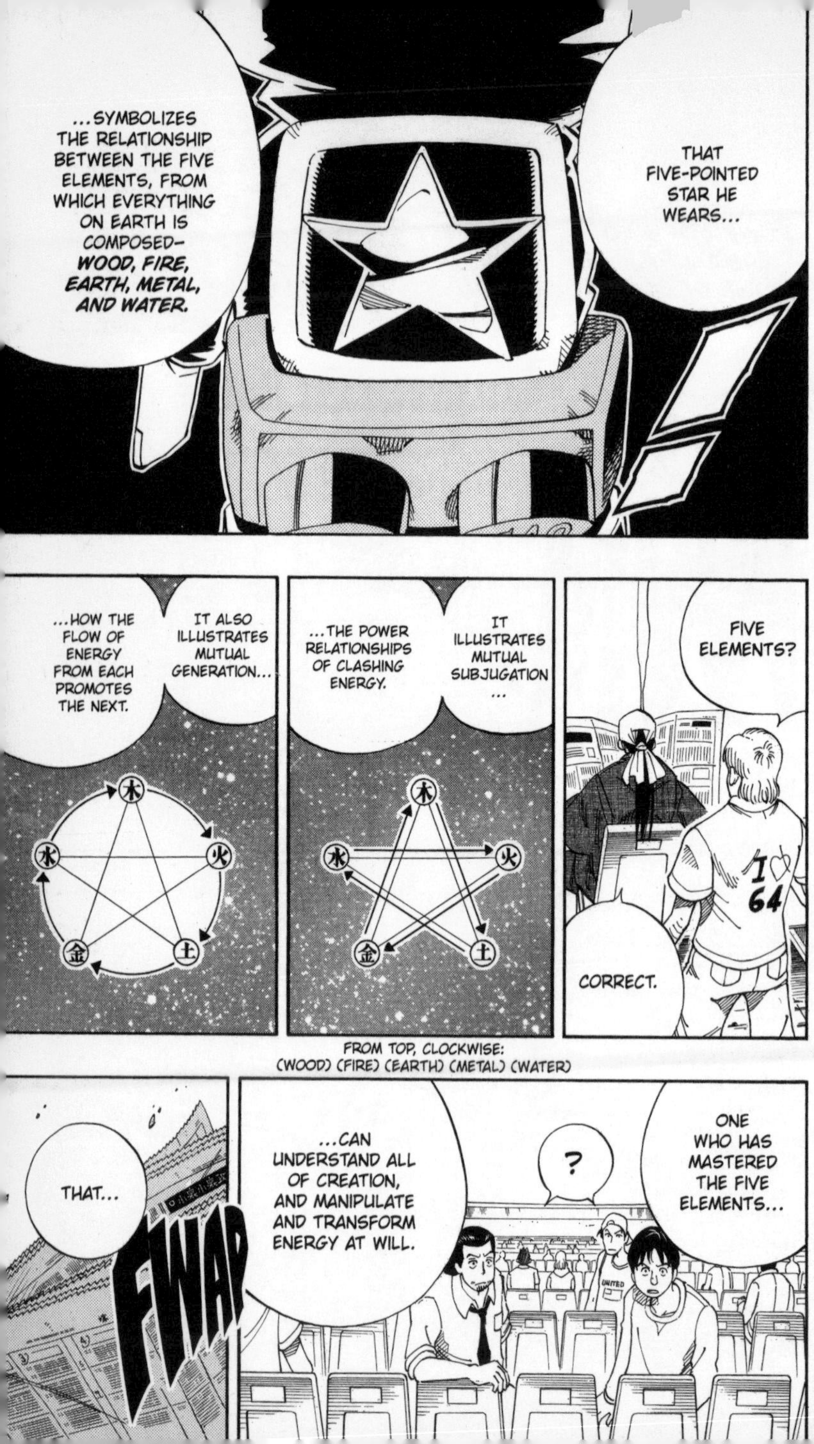
THAT FIVE-POINTED STAR HE WEARS...
...SYMBOLIZES THE RELATIONSHIP BETWEEN THE FIVE ELEMENTS, FROM WHICH EVERYTHING ON EARTH IS COMPOSED— WOOD, FIRE, EARTH, METAL, AND WATER.
FIVE ELEMENTS?
CORRECT.
IT ILLUSTRATES MUTUAL SUBJUGATION...
...THE POWER RELATIONSHIPS OF CLASHING ENERGY.
木 火 土 金 水
IT ALSO ILLUSTRATES MUTUAL GENERATION...
...HOW THE FLOW OF ENERGY FROM EACH PROMOTES THE NEXT.
木 火 土 金 水
FROM TOP, CLOCKWISE: (WOOD) (FIRE) (EARTH) (METAL) (WATER)
ONE WHO HAS MASTERED THE FIVE ELEMENTS...
?
...CAN UNDERSTAND ALL OF CREATION, AND MANIPULATE AND TRANSFORM ENERGY AT WILL.
THAT...
FWAP

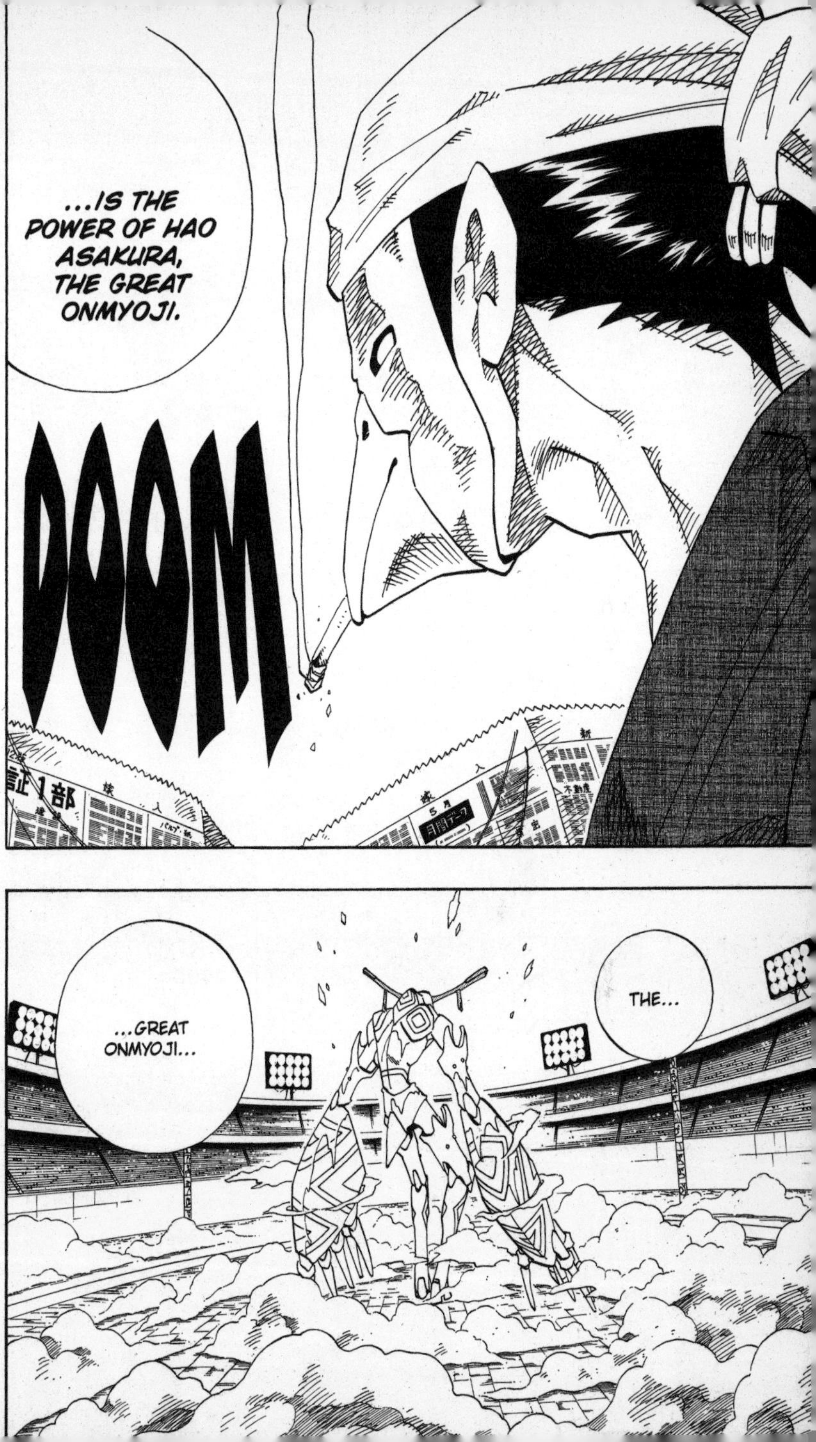
...IS THE POWER OF HAO ASAKURA, THE GREAT ONMYOJI.
DOOM
THE...
...GREAT ONMYOJI...

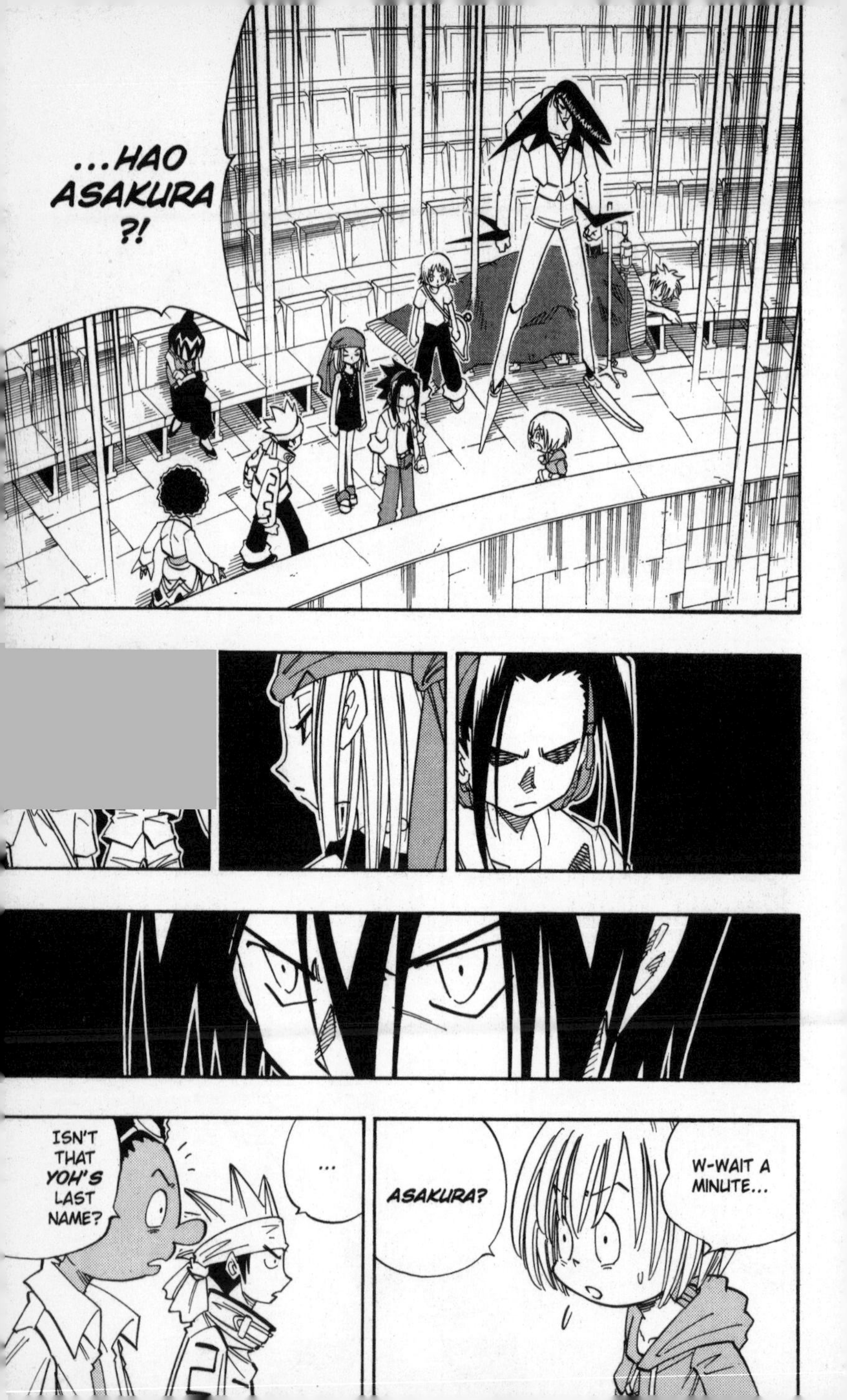
...HAO ASAKURA ?!
W-WAIT A MINUTE...
ASAKURA?
...
ISN'T THAT YOH'S LAST NAME?

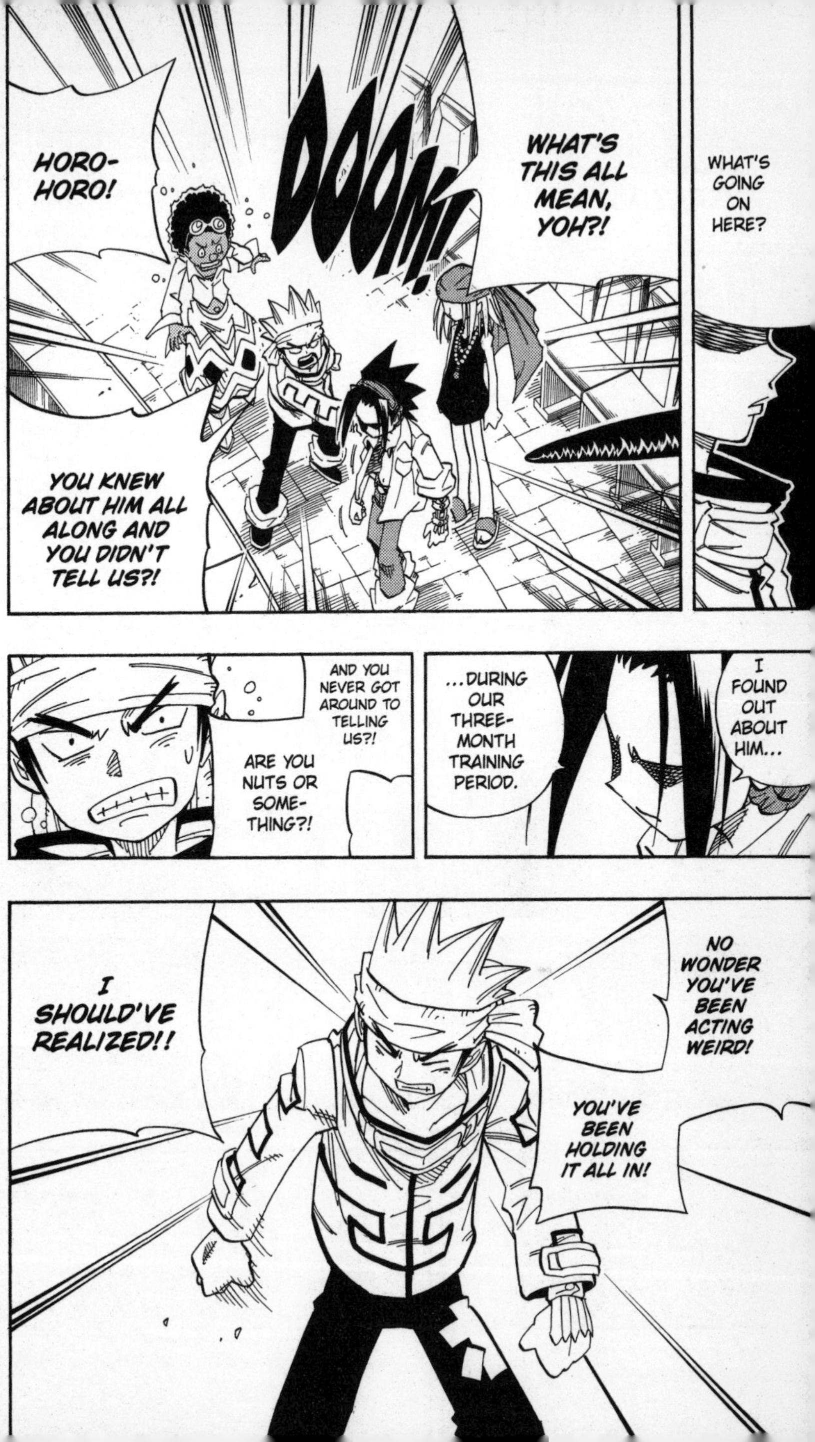
WHAT'S GOING ON HERE?
WHAT'S THIS ALL MEAN, YOH?!
DOOM!!
HORO-HORO!
YOU KNEW ABOUT HIM ALL ALONG AND YOU DIDN'T TELL US?!
I FOUND OUT ABOUT HIM...
...DURING OUR THREE-MONTH TRAINING PERIOD.
AND YOU NEVER GOT AROUND TO TELLING US?!
ARE YOU NUTS OR SOME-THING?!
NO WONDER YOU'VE BEEN ACTING WEIRD!
YOU'VE BEEN HOLDING IT ALL IN!
I SHOULD'VE REALIZED!!

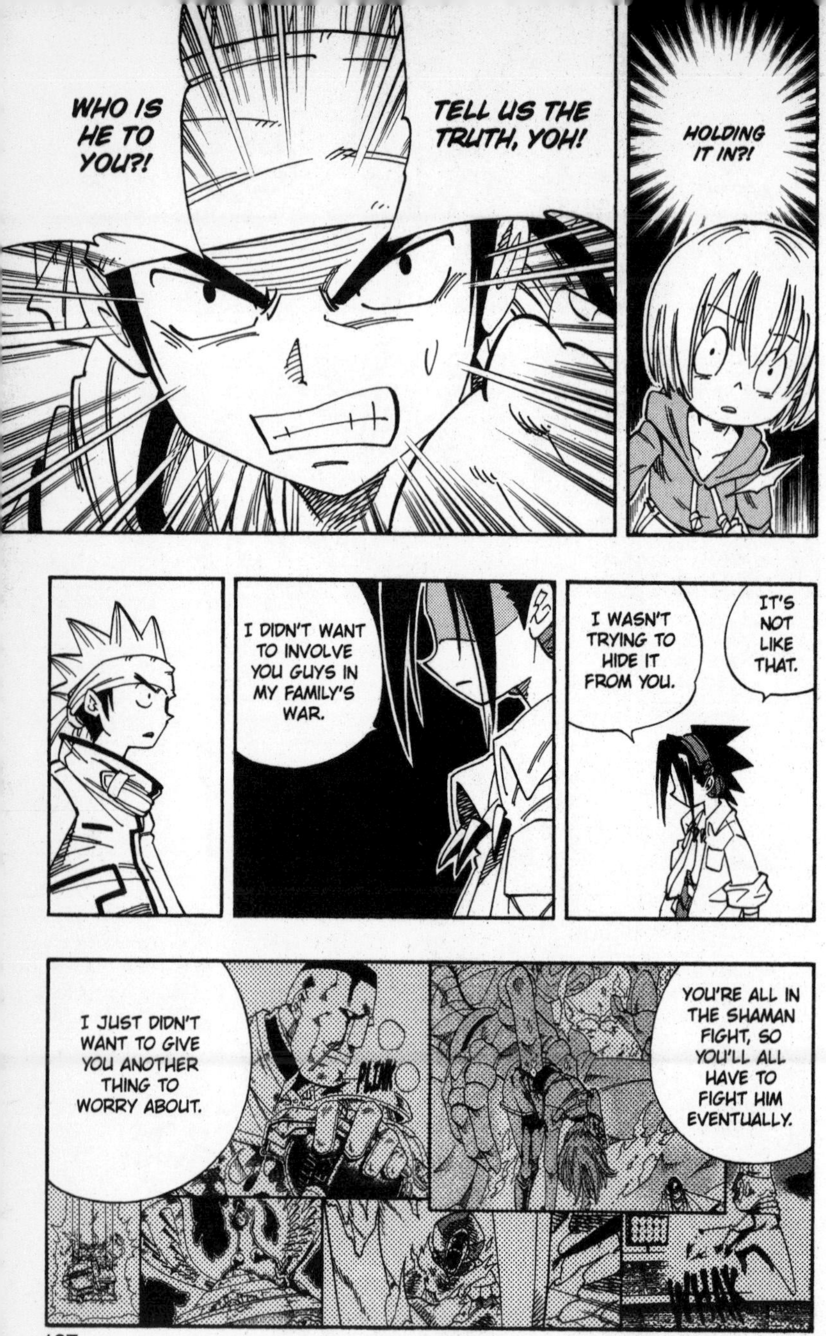
HOLDING IT IN?!
TELL US THE TRUTH, YOH!
WHO IS HE TO YOU?!
IT'S NOT LIKE THAT.
I WASN'T TRYING TO HIDE IT FROM YOU.
I DIDN'T WANT TO INVOLVE YOU GUYS IN MY FAMILY'S WAR.
YOU'RE ALL IN THE SHAMAN FIGHT, SO YOU'LL ALL HAVE TO FIGHT HIM EVENTUALLY.
I JUST DIDN'T WANT TO GIVE YOU ANOTHER THING TO WORRY ABOUT.
PLINK
WHAK

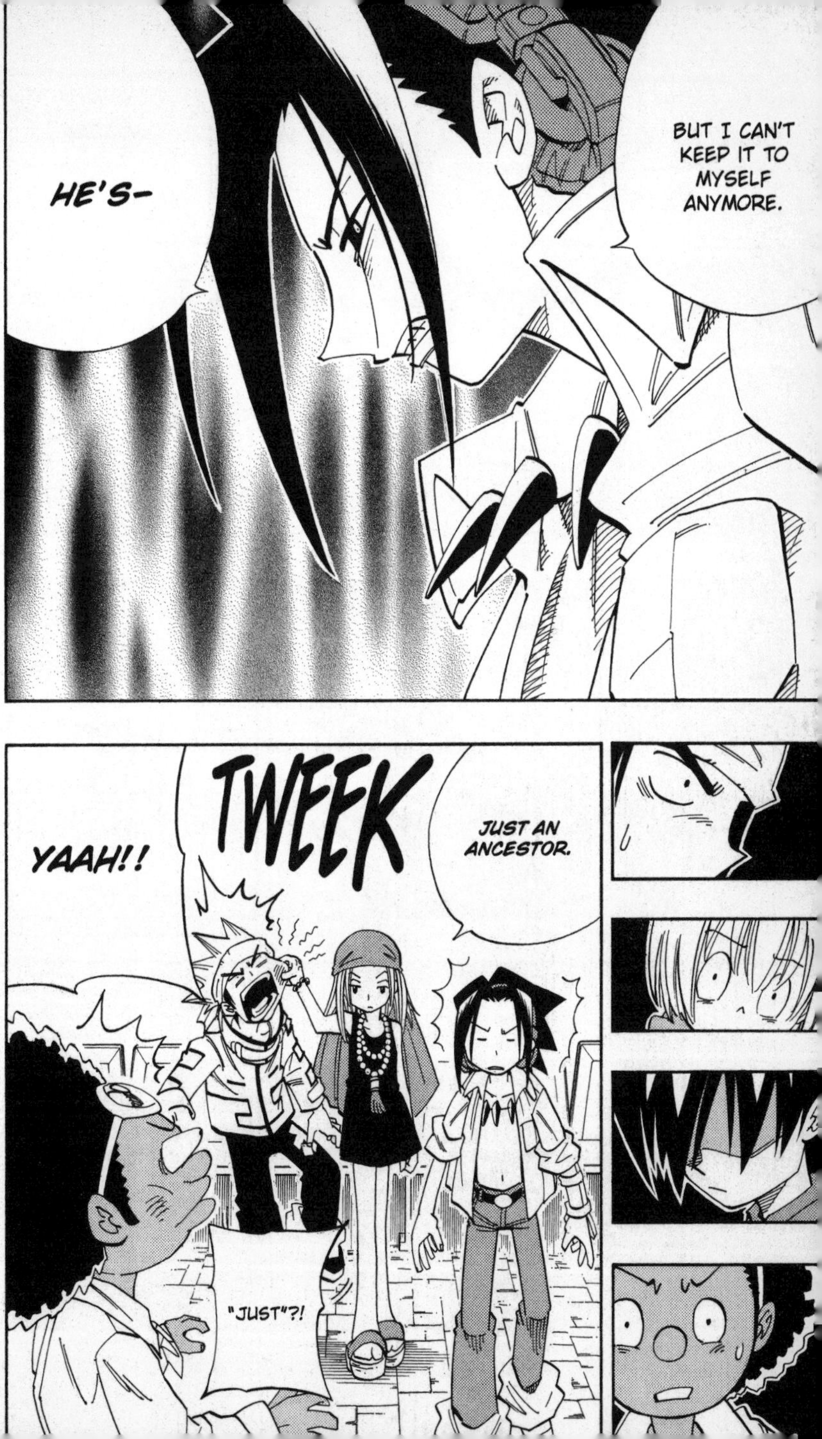
BUT I CAN'T KEEP IT TO MYSELF ANYMORE.
HE'S-
JUST AN ANCESTOR.
TWEEK
YAAH!!
"JUST"?!

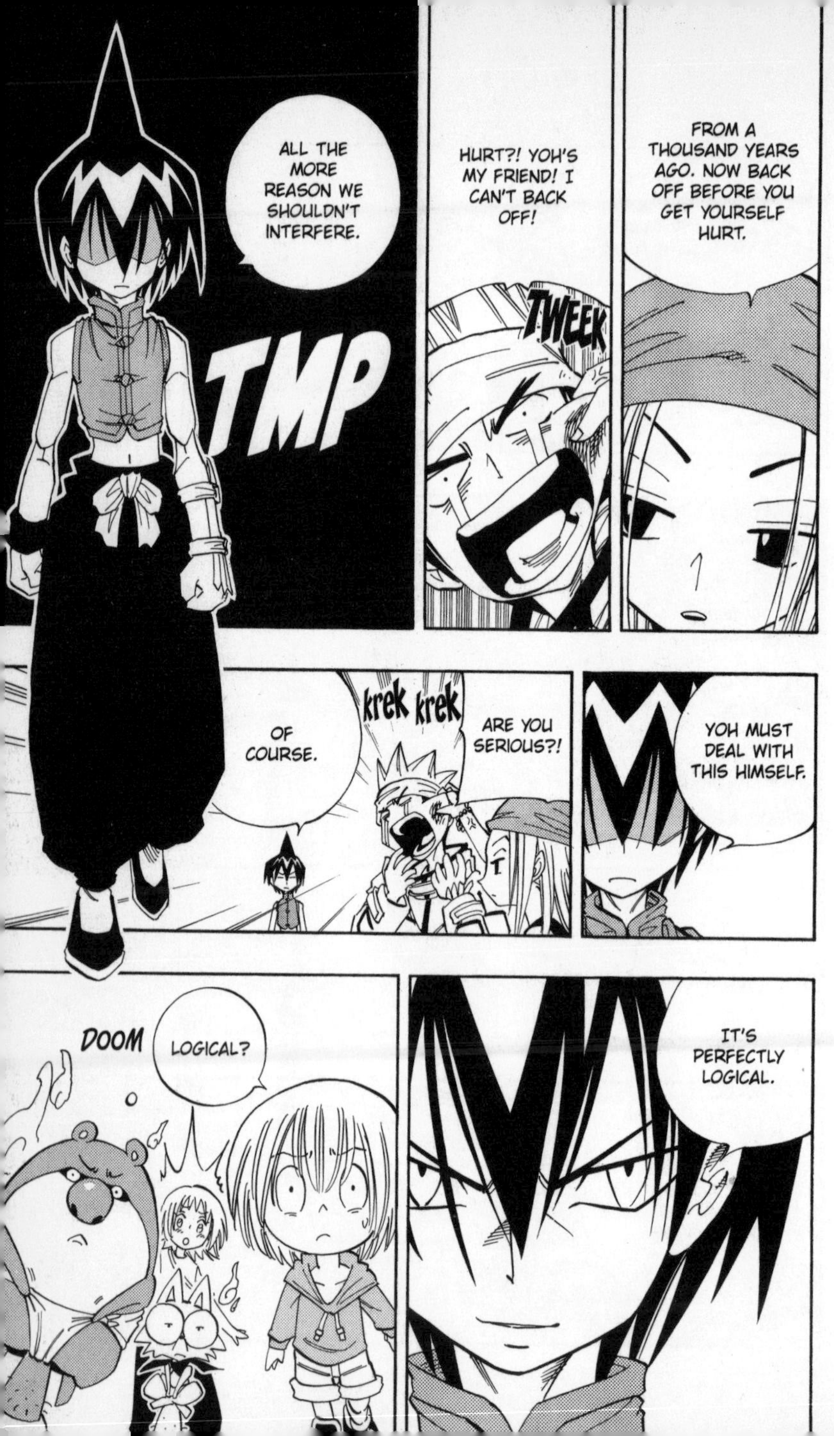
FROM A THOUSAND YEARS AGO. NOW BACK OFF BEFORE YOU GET YOURSELF HURT.
HURT?! YOH'S MY FRIEND! I CAN'T BACK OFF!
TWEEK
ALL THE MORE REASON WE SHOULDN'T INTERFERE.
TMP
YOH MUST DEAL WITH THIS HIMSELF.
ARE YOU SERIOUS?!
krek krek
OF COURSE.
IT'S PERFECTLY LOGICAL.
LOGICAL?
DOOM

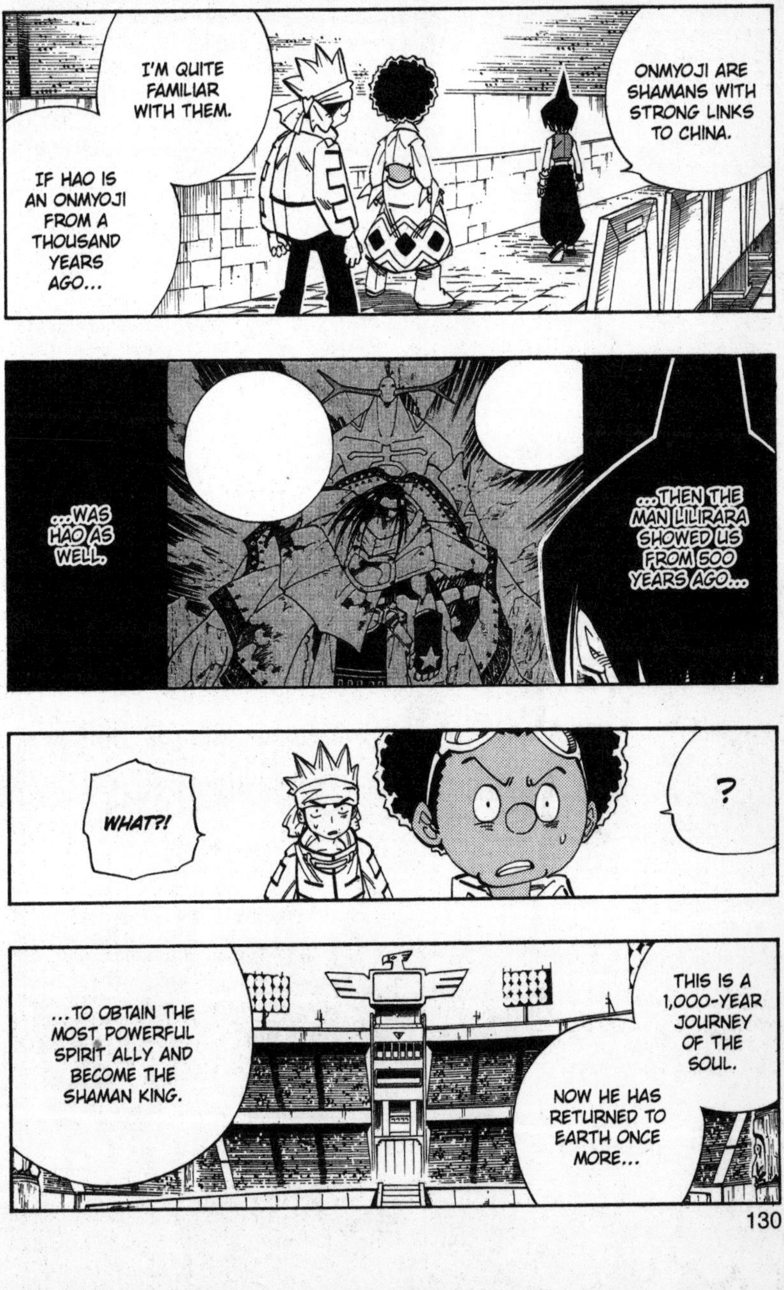
ONMYOJI ARE SHAMANS WITH STRONG LINKS TO CHINA.
I'M QUITE FAMILIAR WITH THEM.
IF HAO IS AN ONMYOJI FROM A THOUSAND YEARS AGO...
...THEN THE MAN LILIRARA SHOWED US FROM 500 YEARS AGO...
...WAS HAO AS WELL.
?
WHAT?!
THIS IS A 1,000-YEAR JOURNEY OF THE SOUL.
NOW HE HAS RETURNED TO EARTH ONCE MORE...
...TO OBTAIN THE MOST POWERFUL SPIRIT ALLY AND BECOME THE SHAMAN KING.

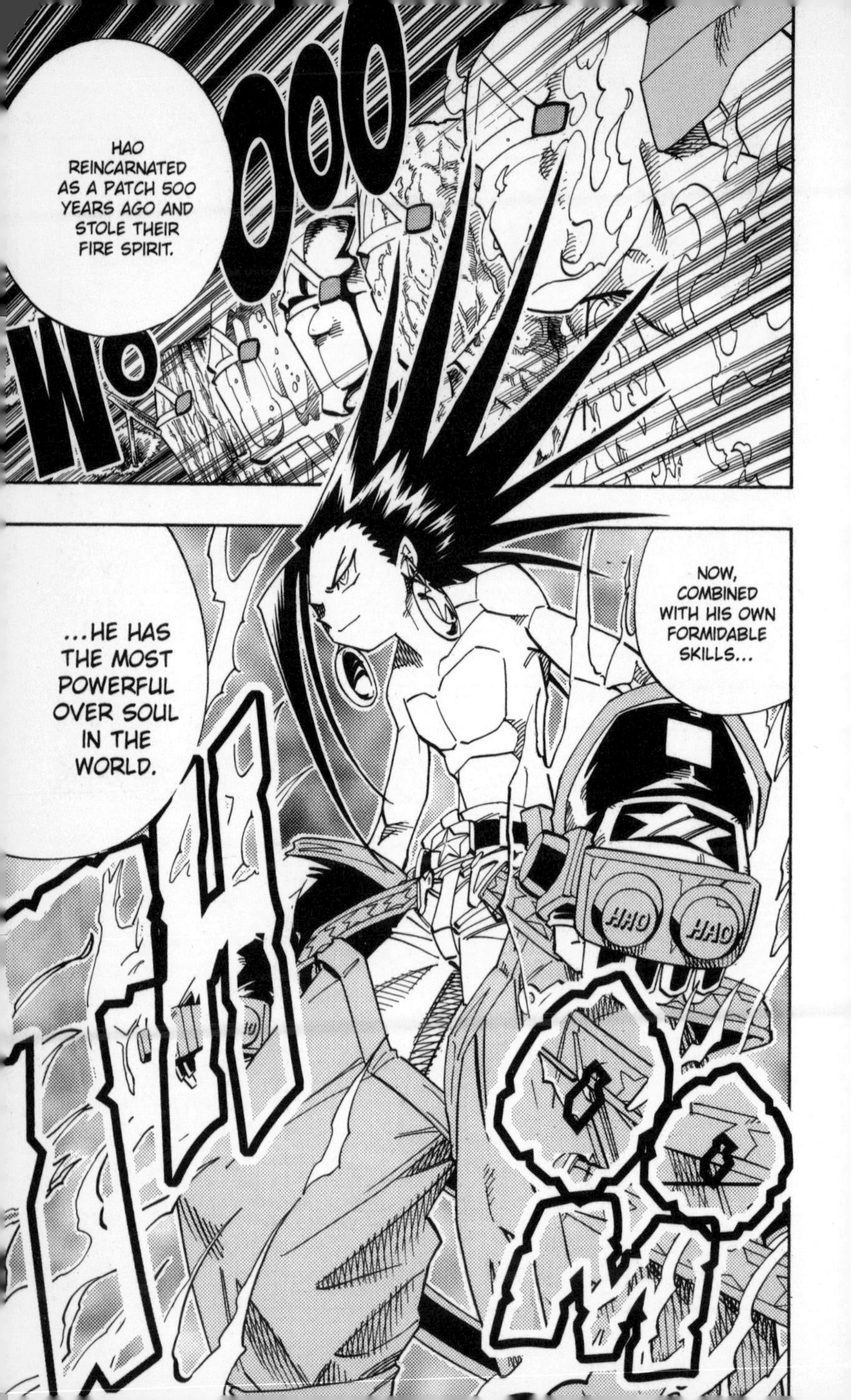
HAO REINCARNATED AS A PATCH 500 YEARS AGO AND STOLE THEIR FIRE SPIRIT.
NOW, COMBINED WITH HIS OWN FORMIDABLE SKILLS...
...HE HAS THE MOST POWERFUL OVER SOUL IN THE WORLD.

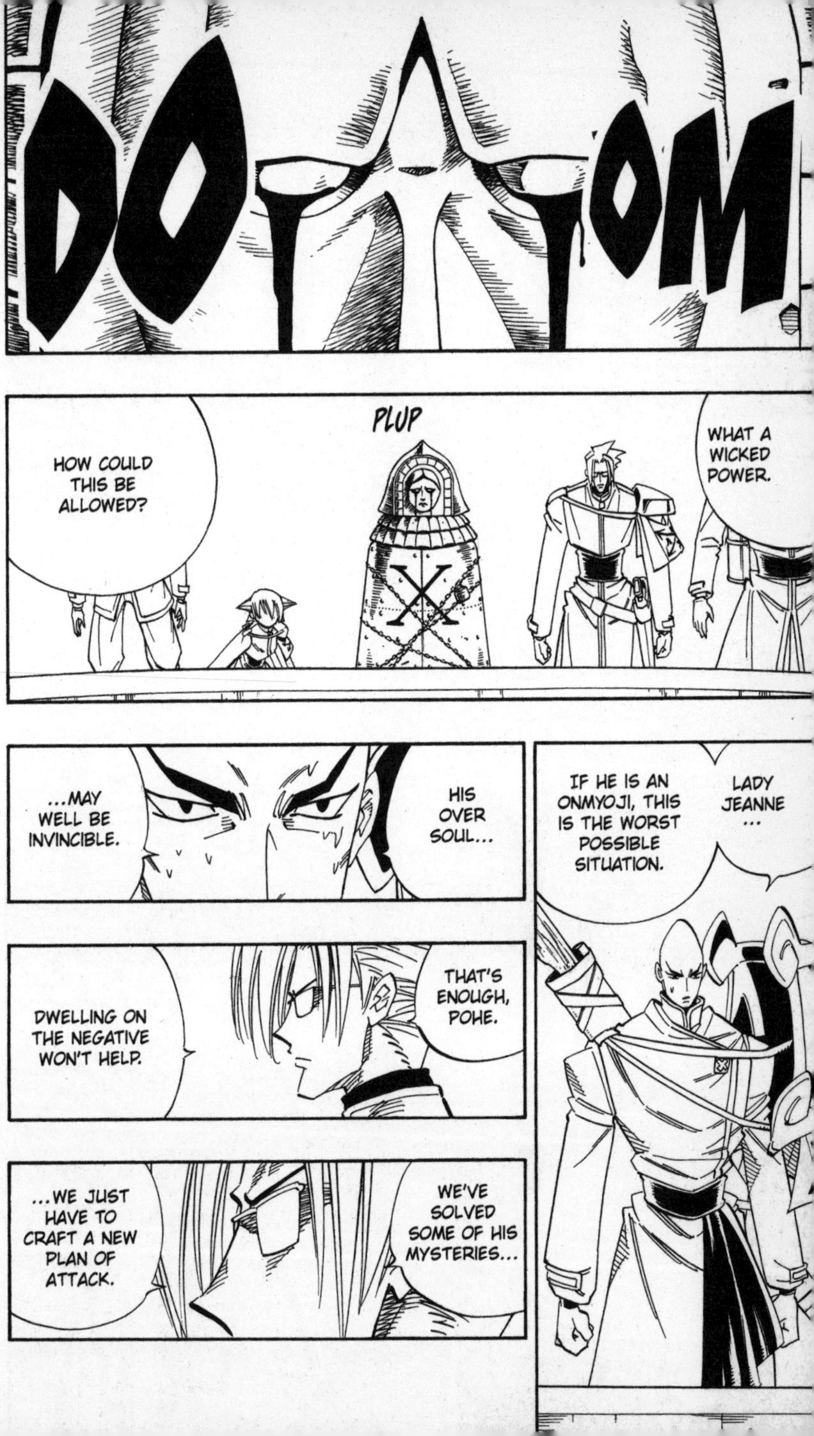
DO OM
WHAT A WICKED POWER.
PLUP
HOW COULD THIS BE ALLOWED?
LADY JEANNE...
IF HE IS AN ONMYOJI, THIS IS THE WORST POSSIBLE SITUATION.
HIS OVER SOUL...
...MAY WELL BE INVINCIBLE.
THAT'S ENOUGH, POHE.
DWELLING ON THE NEGATIVE WON'T HELP.
WE'VE SOLVED SOME OF HIS MYSTERIES...
...WE JUST HAVE TO CRAFT A NEW PLAN OF ATTACK.

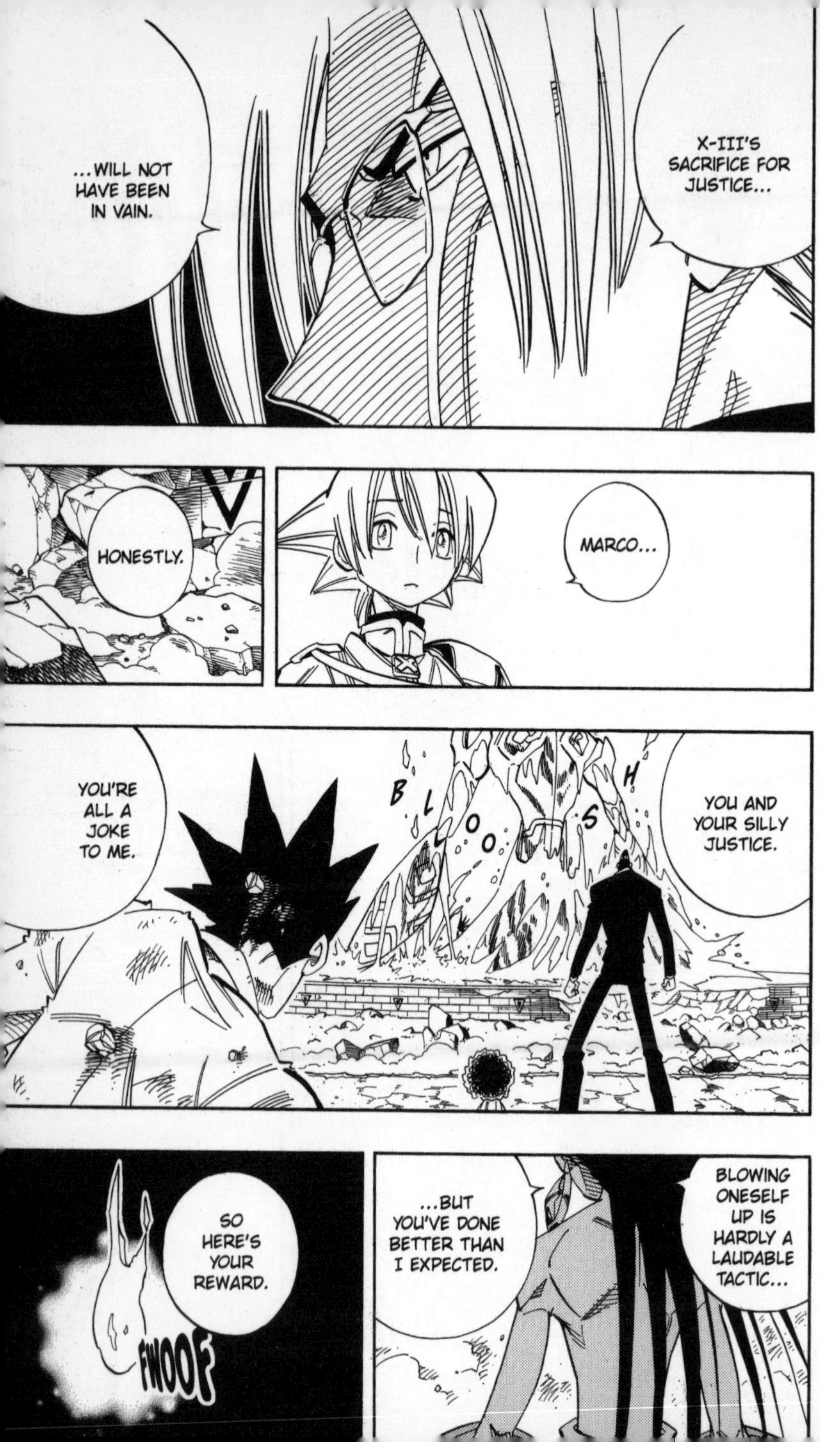
X-III'S SACRIFICE FOR JUSTICE...
...WILL NOT HAVE BEEN IN VAIN.
MARCO...
HONESTLY.
YOU AND YOUR SILLY JUSTICE.
BLOOSH
YOU'RE ALL A JOKE TO ME.
BLOWING ONESELF UP IS HARDLY A LAUDABLE TACTIC...
...BUT YOU'VE DONE BETTER THAN I EXPECTED.
SO HERE'S YOUR REWARD.
FWOOF

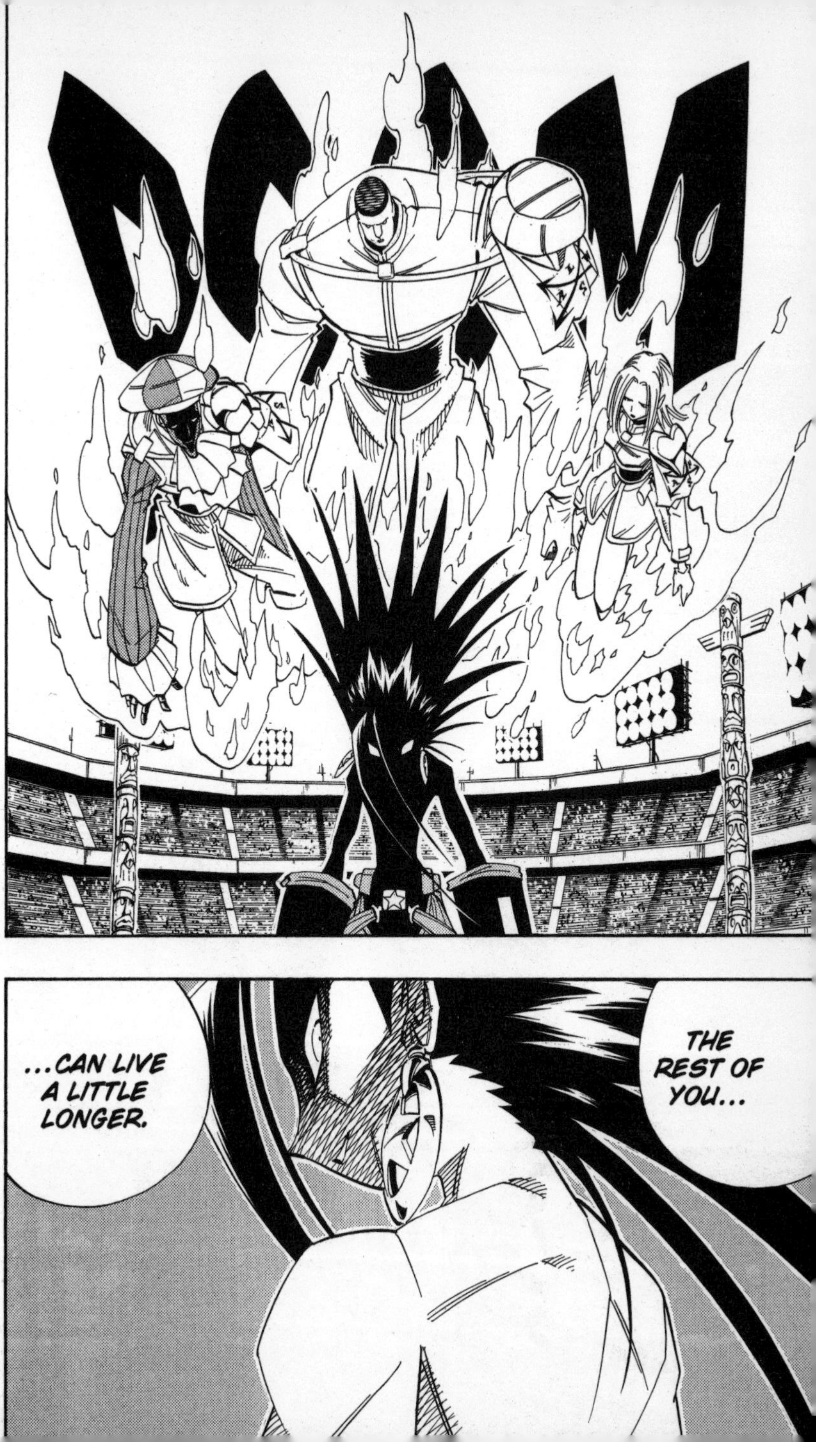
DOM
THE REST OF YOU...
...CAN LIVE A LITTLE LONGER.

Shaman King

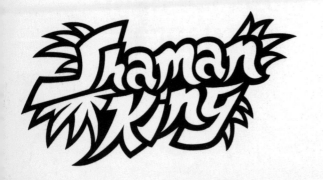

SHAMAN KING ITEM FILE No.48

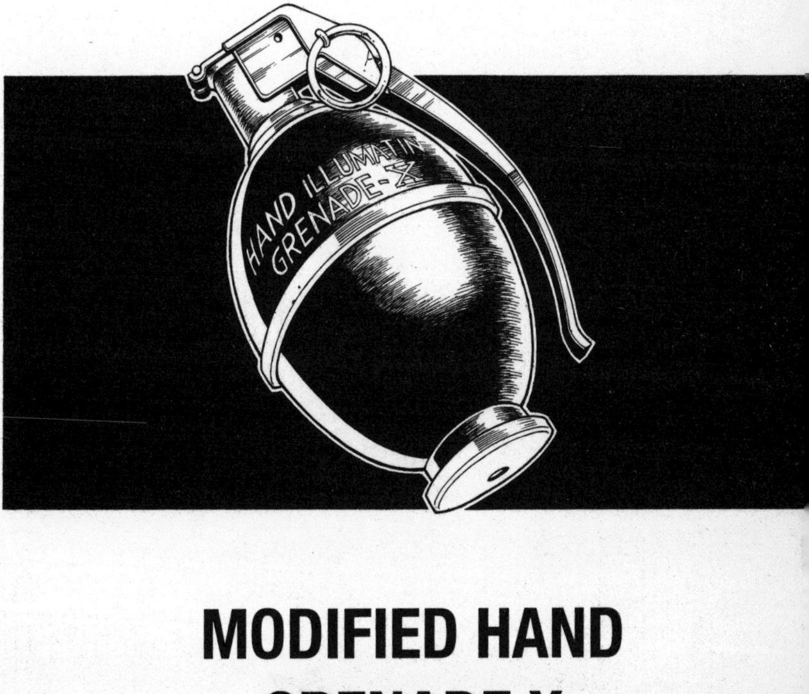
HAND ILLUMATIN
GRENADE-X

MODIFIED HAND GRENADE X

Reincarnation 141: He's My...

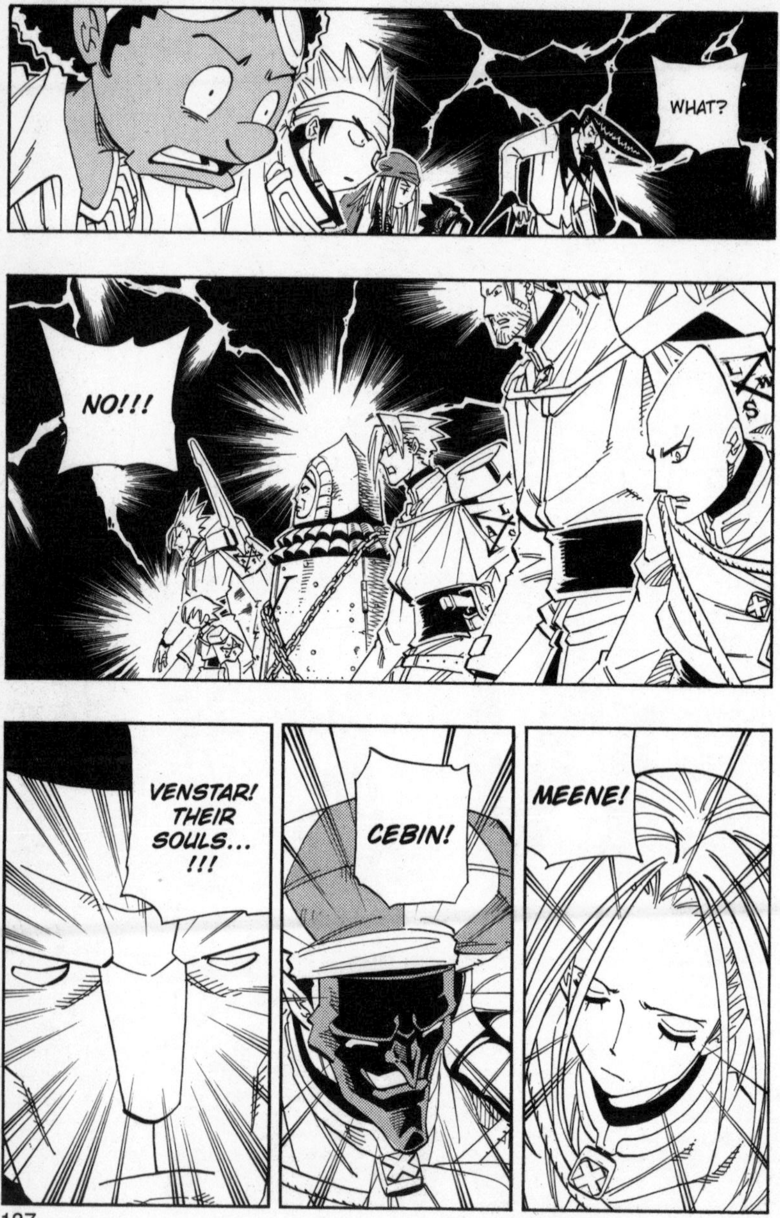
WHAT?
NO!!!
MEENE!
CEBIN!
VENSTAR! THEIR SOULS... !!!

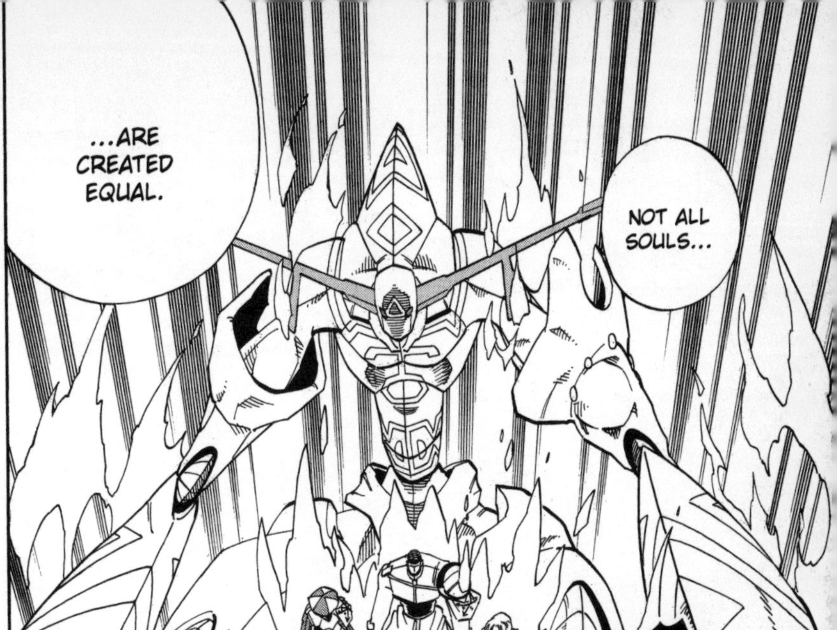
NOT ALL SOULS...
...ARE CREATED EQUAL.
FO OM

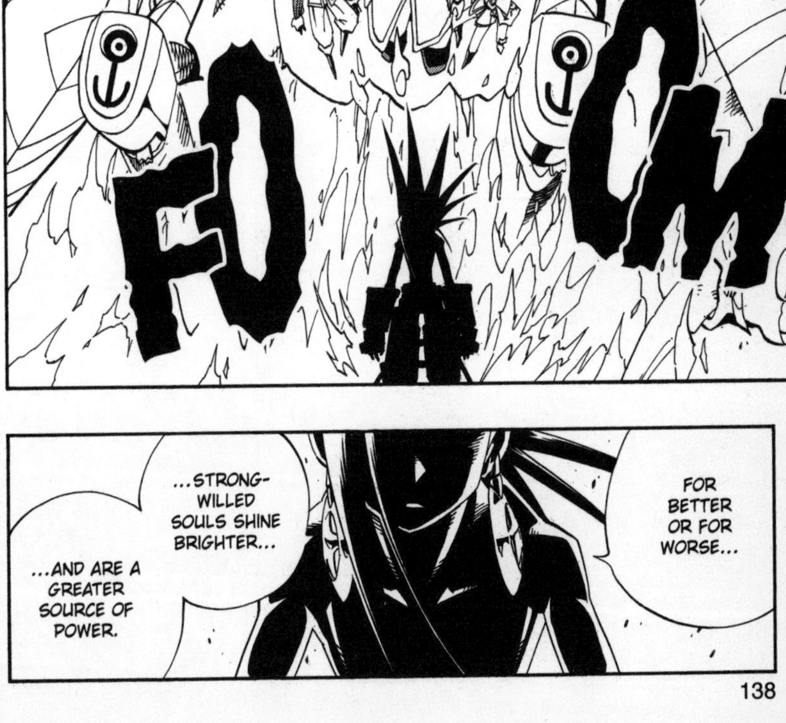
FOR BETTER OR FOR WORSE...
...STRONG-WILLED SOULS SHINE BRIGHTER...
...AND ARE A GREATER SOURCE OF POWER.

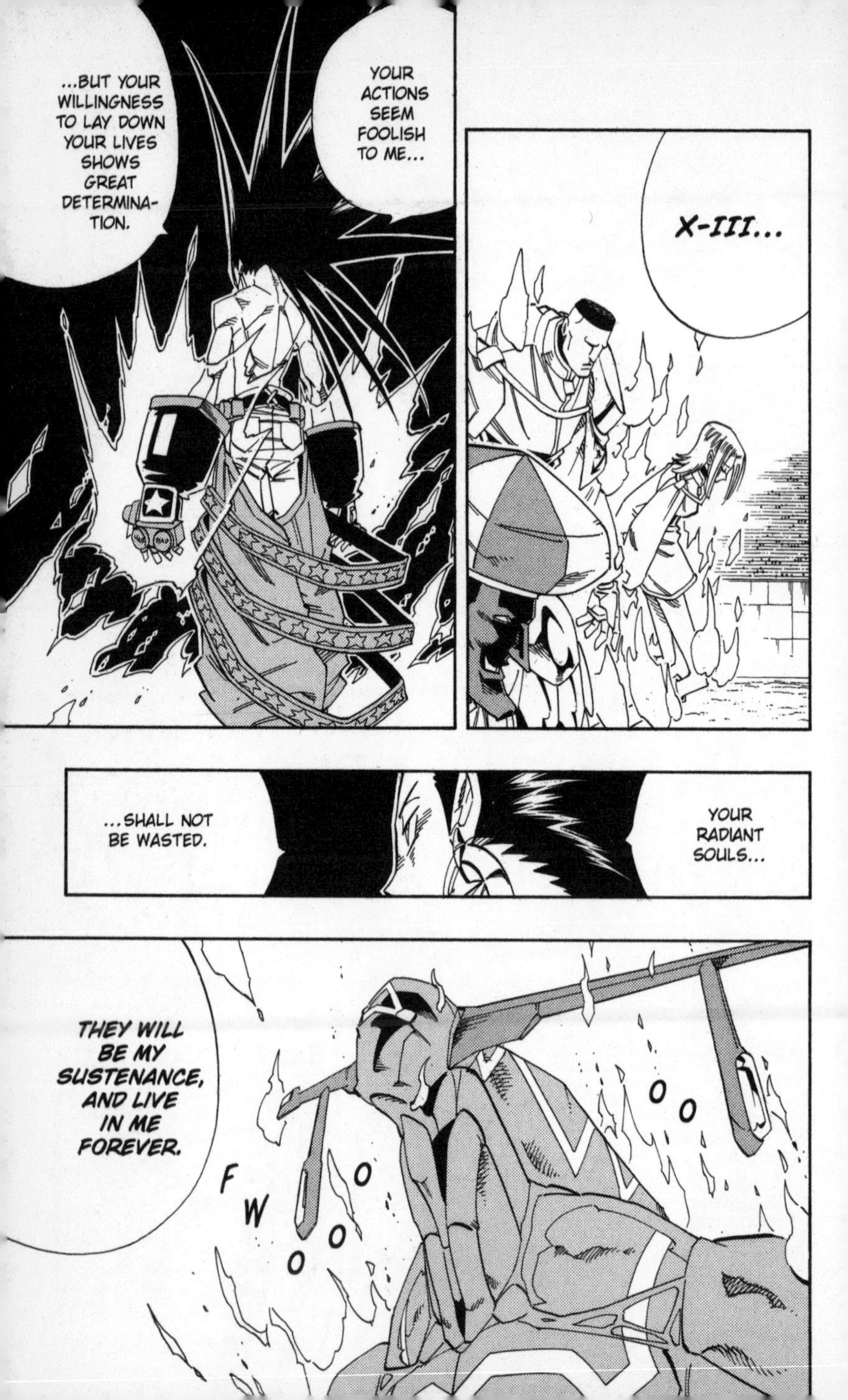

YOUR ACTIONS SEEM FOOLISH TO ME...
...BUT YOUR WILLINGNESS TO LAY DOWN YOUR LIVES SHOWS GREAT DETERMINATION.
X-III...
YOUR RADIANT SOULS...
...SHALL NOT BE WASTED.
THEY WILL BE MY SUSTENANCE, AND LIVE IN ME FOREVER.
FWOOOOOO

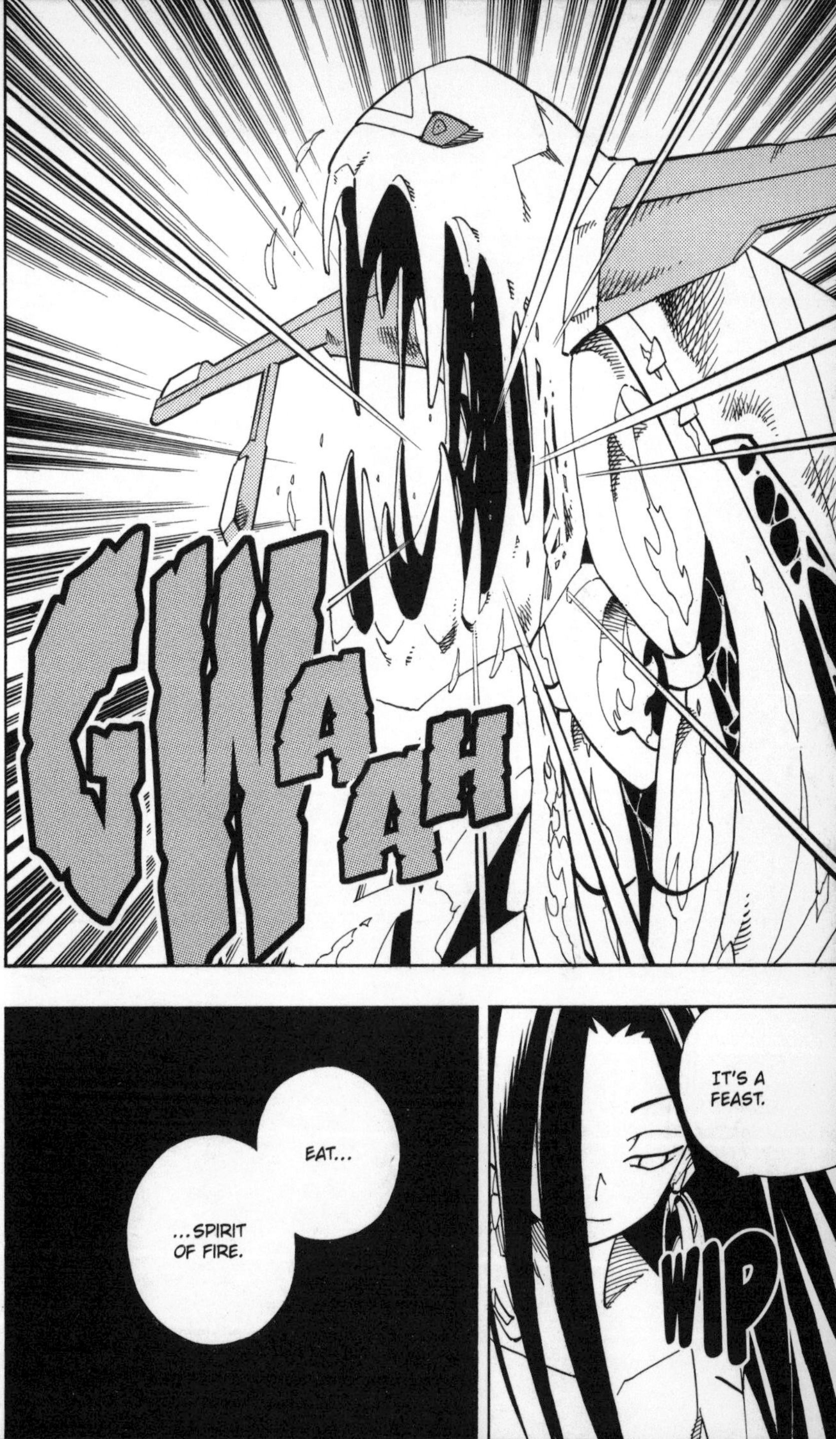
GWAAH
IT'S A FEAST.
WIP
EAT...
...SPIRIT OF FIRE.

Reincarnation 141: He's My...

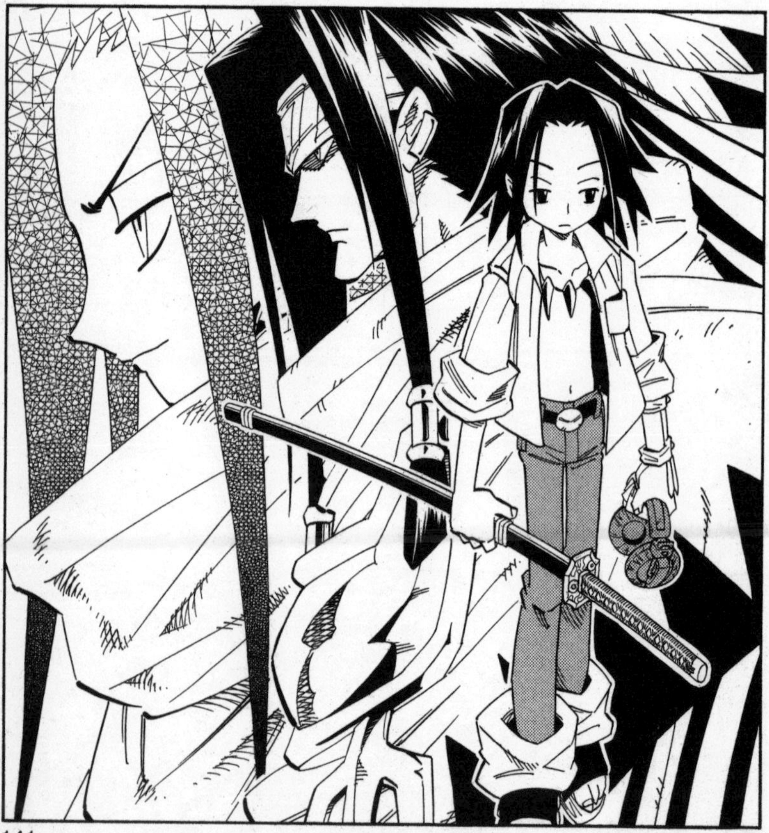

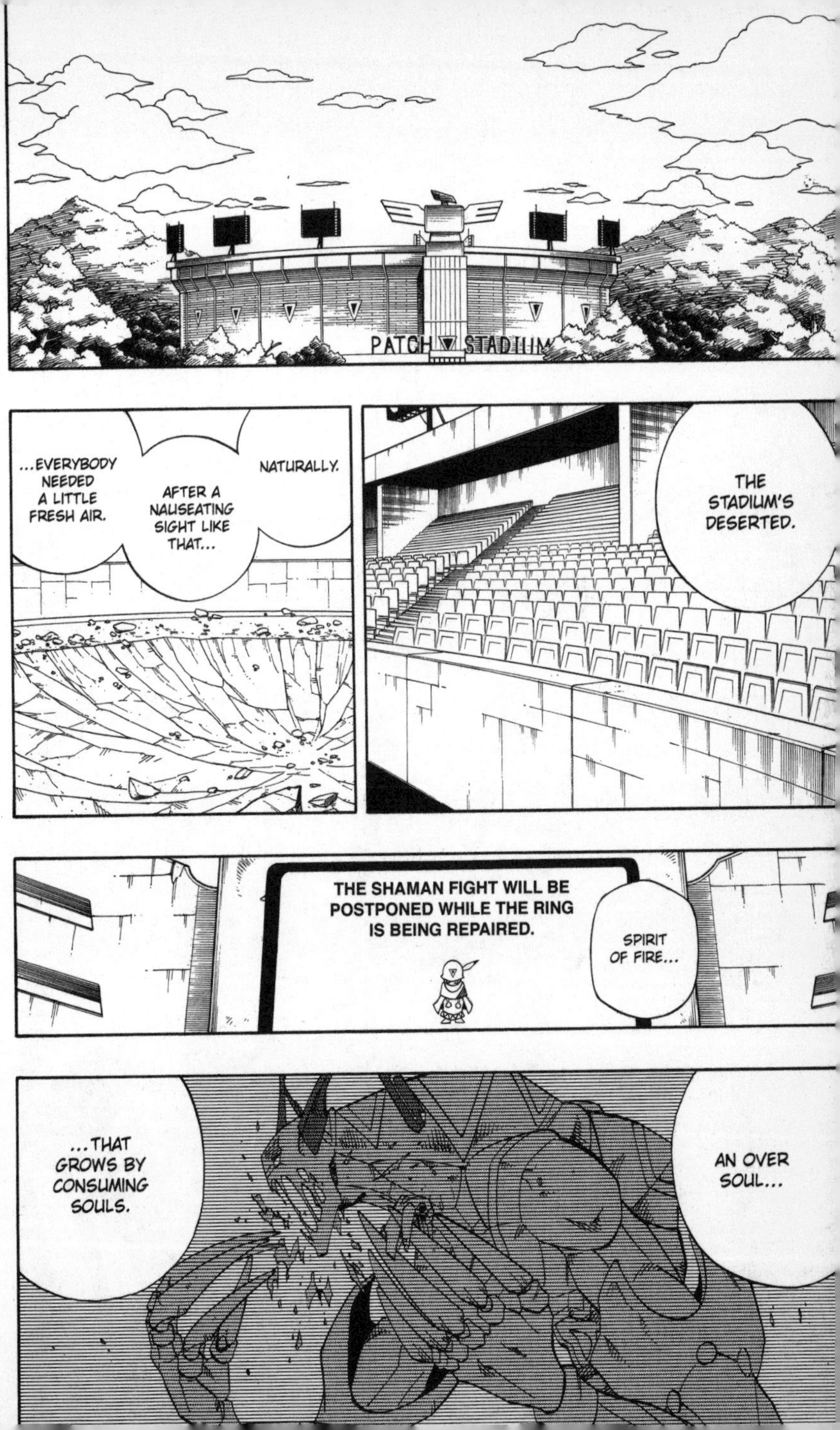
PATCH ▼ STADIUM
THE STADIUM'S DESERTED.
NATURALLY.
AFTER A NAUSEATING SIGHT LIKE THAT...
...EVERYBODY NEEDED A LITTLE FRESH AIR.
THE SHAMAN FIGHT WILL BE POSTPONED WHILE THE RING IS BEING REPAIRED.
SPIRIT OF FIRE...
AN OVER SOUL...
...THAT GROWS BY CONSUMING SOULS.

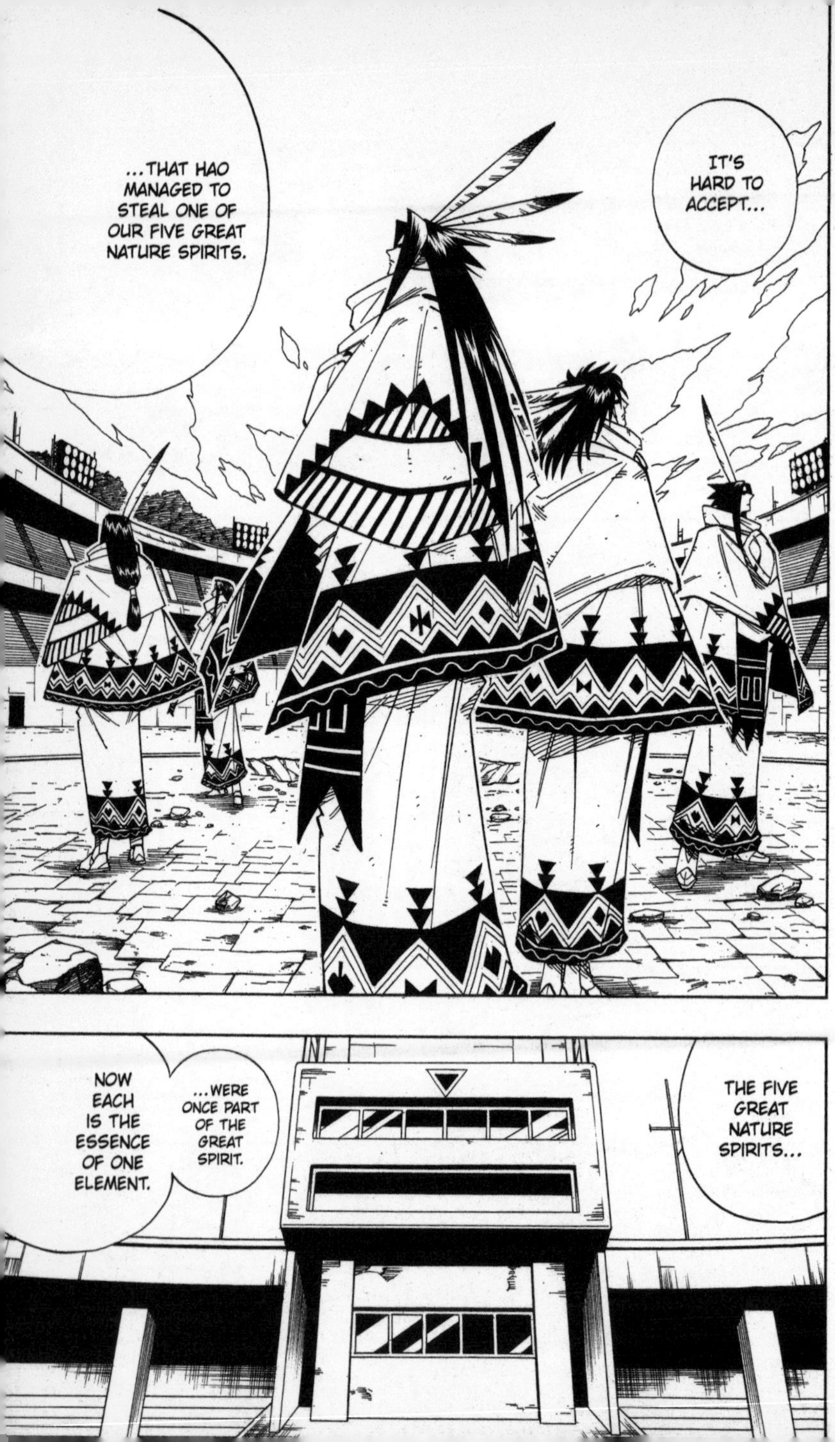
IT'S HARD TO ACCEPT...
...THAT HAO MANAGED TO STEAL ONE OF OUR FIVE GREAT NATURE SPIRITS.
THE FIVE GREAT NATURE SPIRITS...
...WERE ONCE PART OF THE GREAT SPIRIT.
NOW EACH IS THE ESSENCE OF ONE ELEMENT.

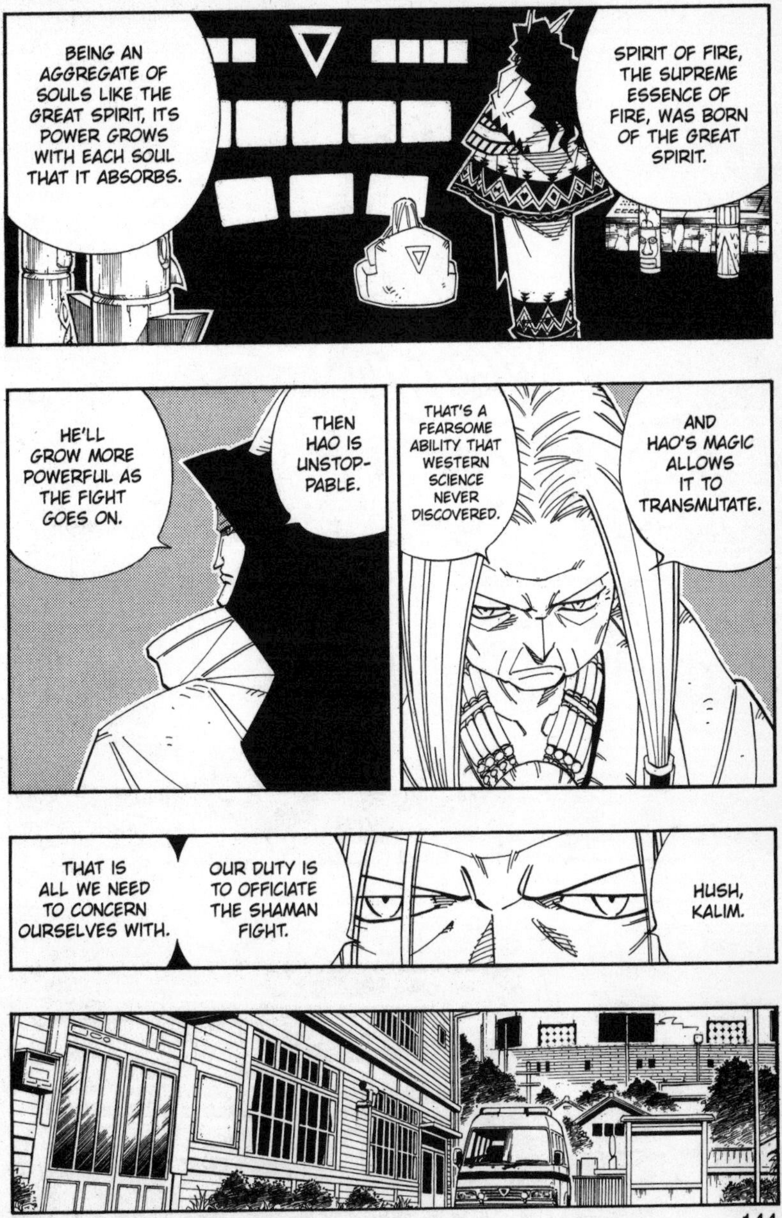
SPIRIT OF FIRE, THE SUPREME ESSENCE OF FIRE, WAS BORN OF THE GREAT SPIRIT.
BEING AN AGGREGATE OF SOULS LIKE THE GREAT SPIRIT, ITS POWER GROWS WITH EACH SOUL THAT IT ABSORBS.
AND HAO'S MAGIC ALLOWS IT TO TRANSMUTATE.
THAT'S A FEARSOME ABILITY THAT WESTERN SCIENCE NEVER DISCOVERED.
THEN HAO IS UNSTOP-PABLE.
HE'LL GROW MORE POWERFUL AS THE FIGHT GOES ON.
HUSH, KALIM.
OUR DUTY IS TO OFFICIATE THE SHAMAN FIGHT.
THAT IS ALL WE NEED TO CONCERN OURSELVES WITH.

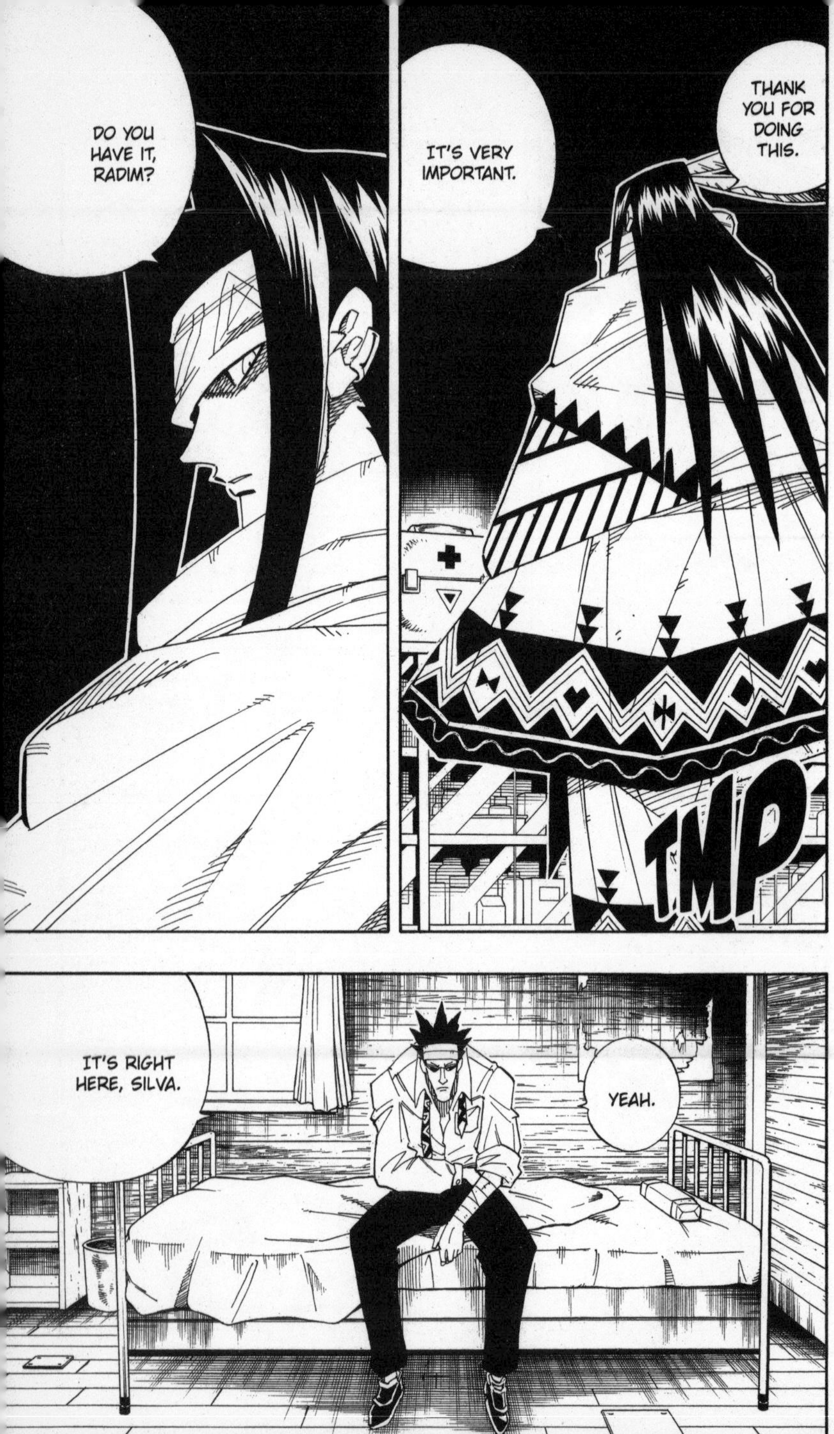
THANK YOU FOR DOING THIS.
IT'S VERY IMPORTANT.
TMP
DO YOU HAVE IT, RADIM?
YEAH.
IT'S RIGHT HERE, SILVA.

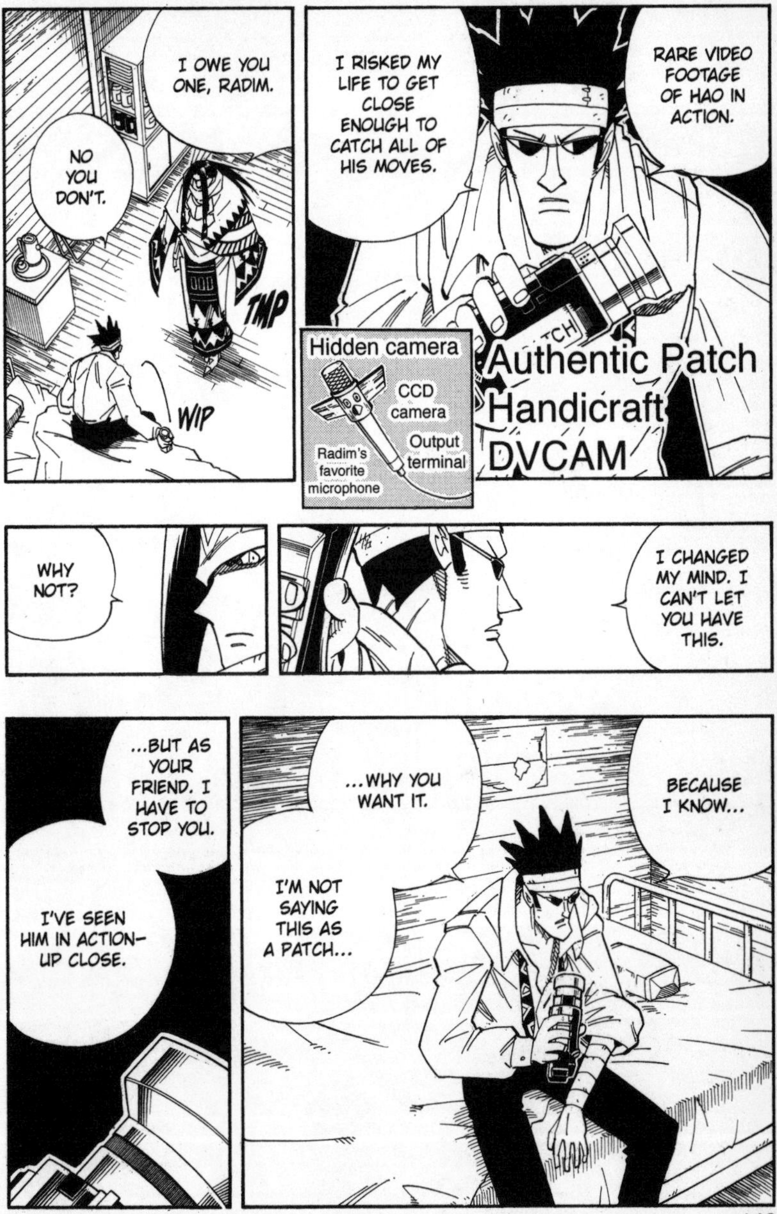
RARE VIDEO FOOTAGE OF HAO IN ACTION.
I RISKED MY LIFE TO GET CLOSE ENOUGH TO CATCH ALL OF HIS MOVES.
Authentic Patch Handicraft DVCAM
Hidden camera
CCD camera
Output terminal
Radim's favorite microphone
I OWE YOU ONE, RADIM.
NO YOU DON'T.
TMP
WIP
I CHANGED MY MIND. I CAN'T LET YOU HAVE THIS.
WHY NOT?
BECAUSE I KNOW...
...WHY YOU WANT IT.
I'M NOT SAYING THIS AS A PATCH...
...BUT AS YOUR FRIEND. I HAVE TO STOP YOU.
I'VE SEEN HIM IN ACTION—UP CLOSE.

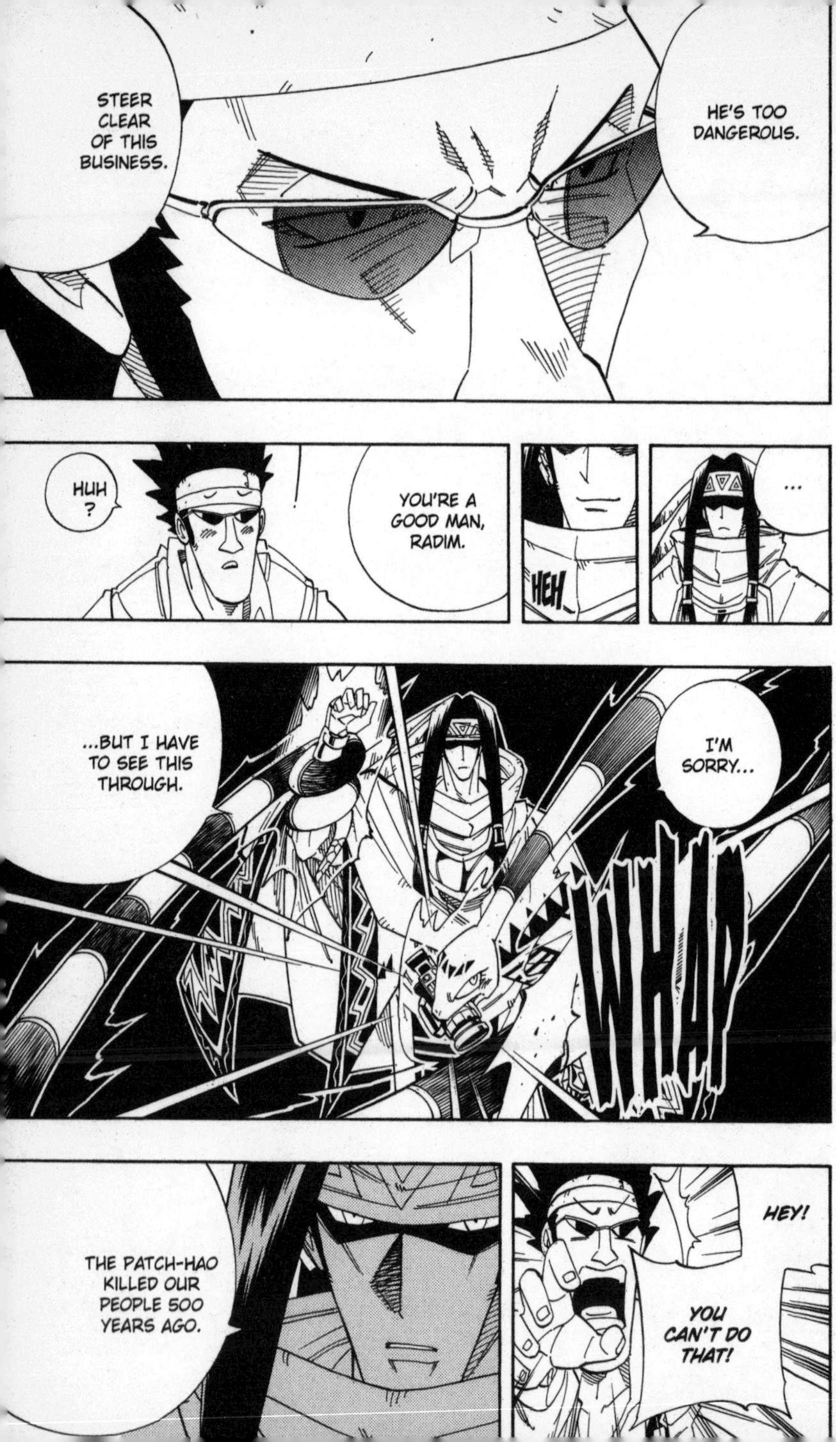
HE'S TOO DANGEROUS.
STEER CLEAR OF THIS BUSINESS.
...
HEH
YOU'RE A GOOD MAN, RADIM.
HUH?
I'M SORRY...
...BUT I HAVE TO SEE THIS THROUGH.
WHAP
HEY!
YOU CAN'T DO THAT!
THE PATCH-HAO KILLED OUR PEOPLE 500 YEARS AGO.

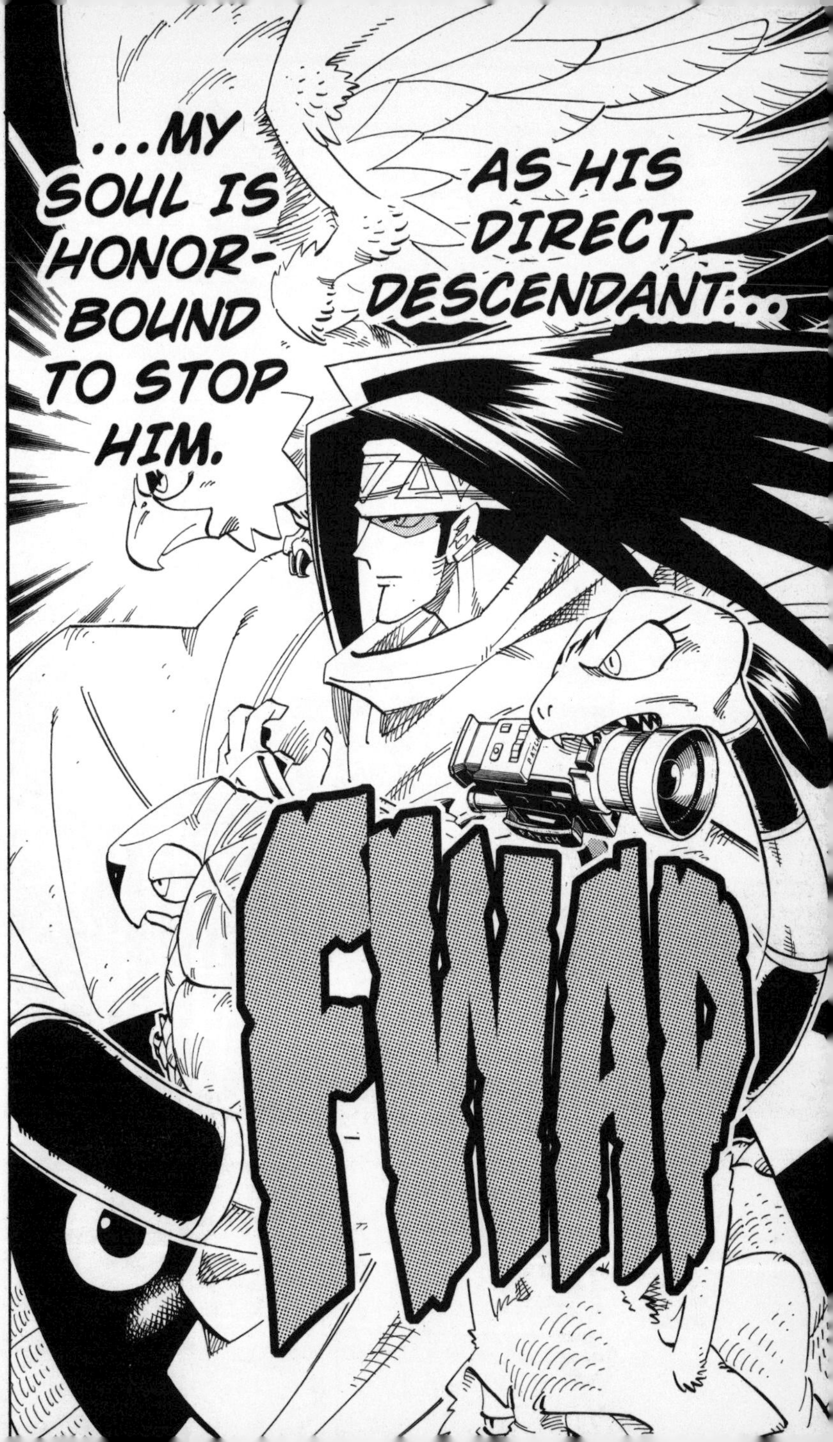
AS HIS DIRECT DESCENDANT...
...MY SOUL IS HONOR-BOUND TO STOP HIM.
FWAP

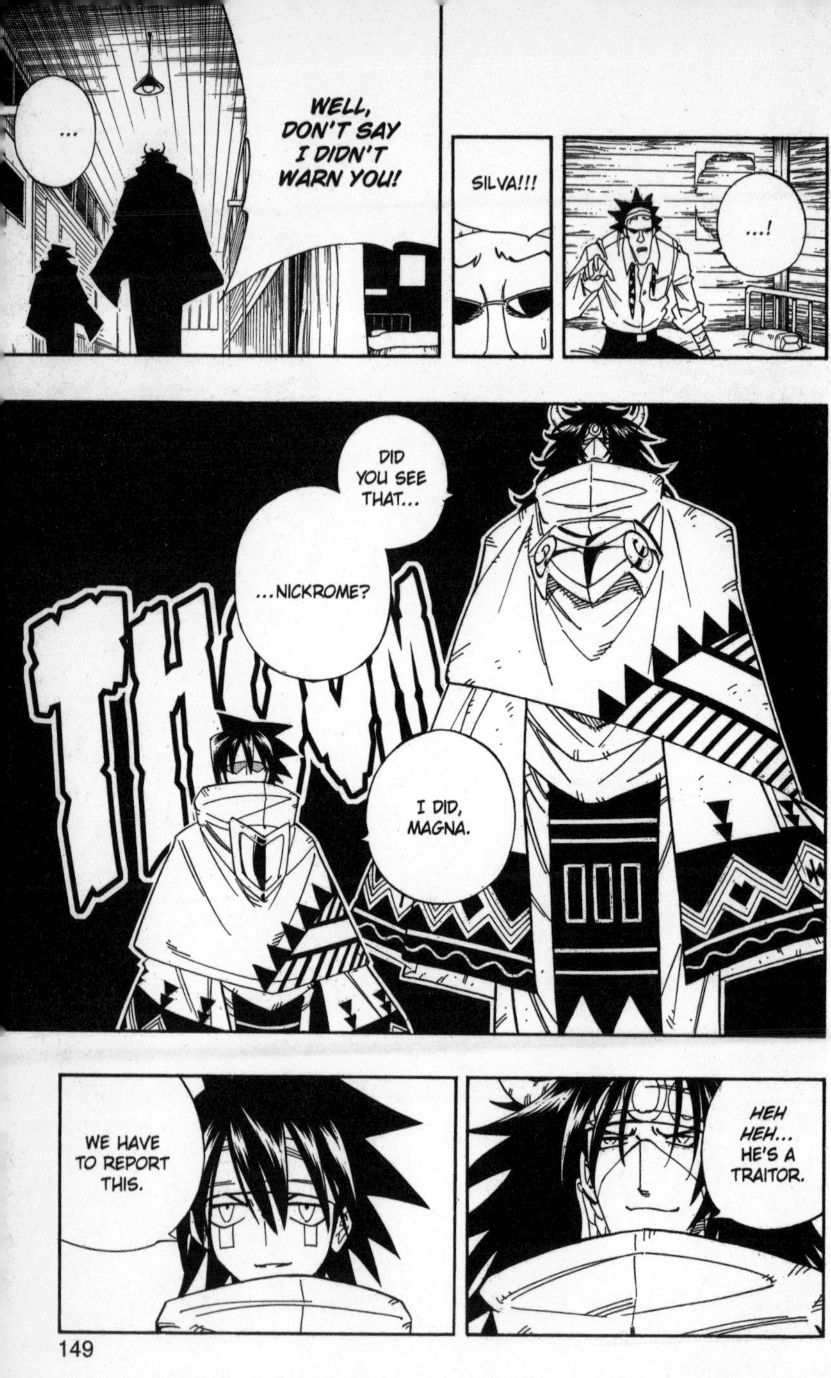
...!
SILVA!!!
WELL, DON'T SAY I DIDN'T WARN YOU!
...
DID YOU SEE THAT...
...NICKROME?
I DID, MAGNA.
HEH HEH... HE'S A TRAITOR.
WE HAVE TO REPORT THIS.

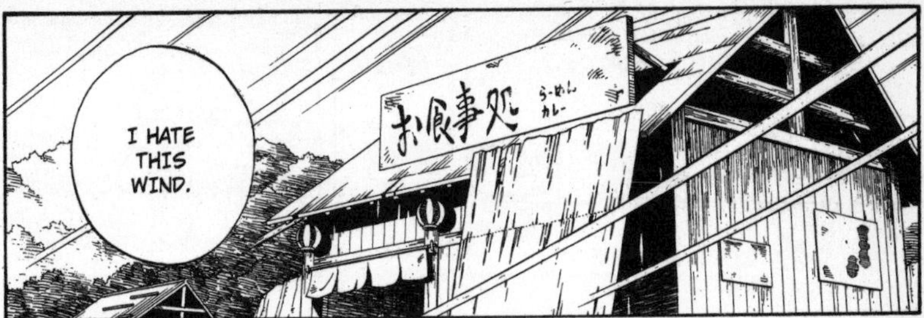
I HATE THIS WIND.
お食事処
らーめん
カレー

SIGN: GRUB RAMEN CURRY RICE

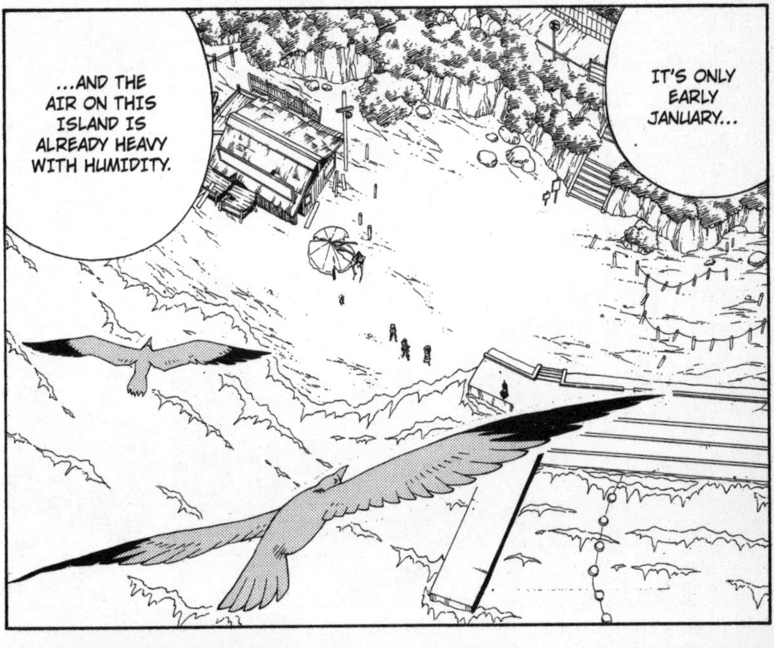
IT'S ONLY EARLY JANUARY...
...AND THE AIR ON THIS ISLAND IS ALREADY HEAVY WITH HUMIDITY.

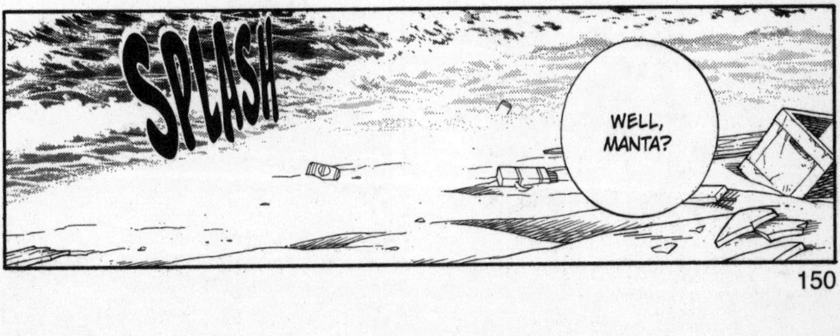
WELL, MANTA?
SPLASH

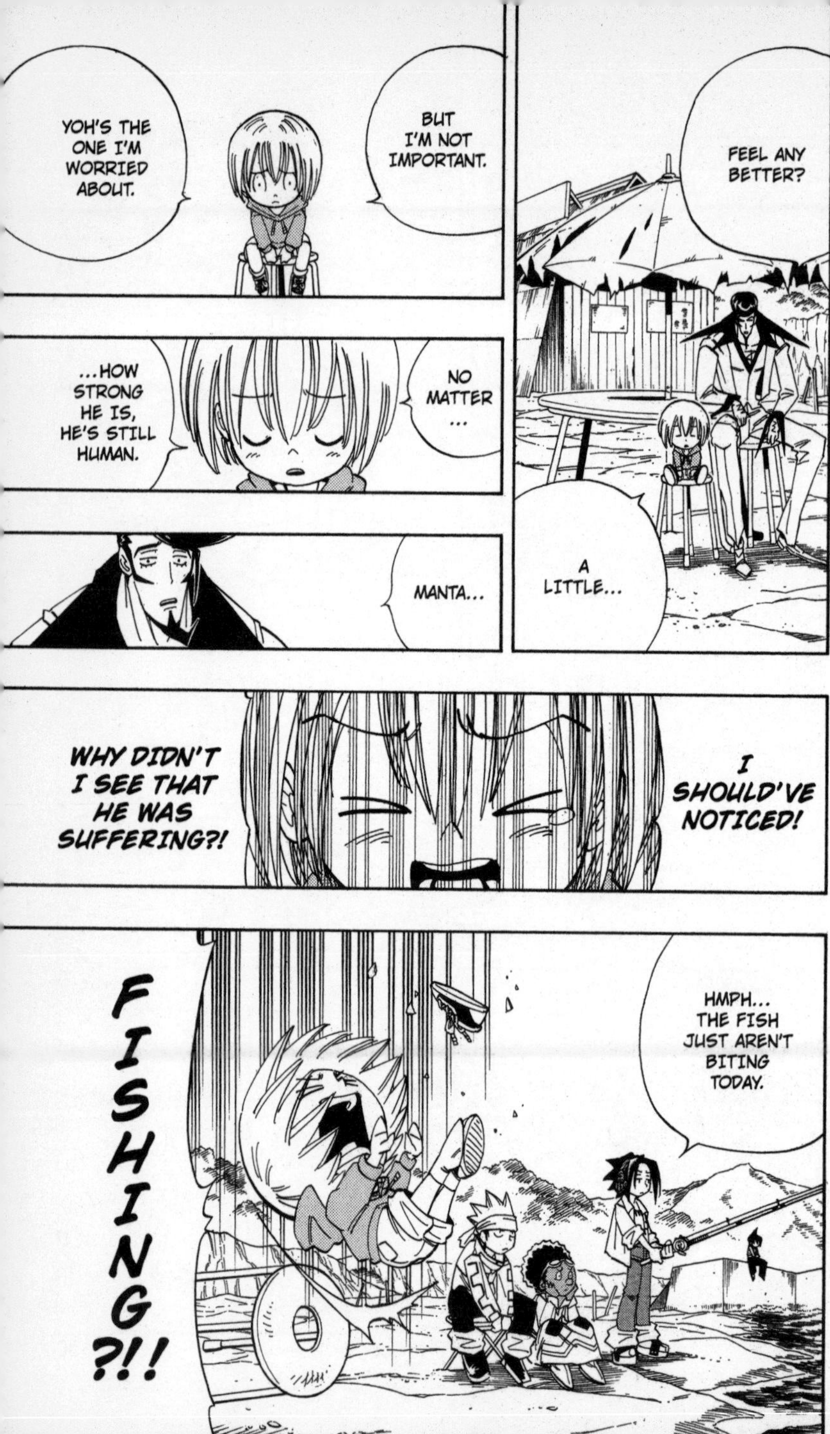
FEEL ANY BETTER?
A LITTLE...
BUT I'M NOT IMPORTANT.
YOH'S THE ONE I'M WORRIED ABOUT.
NO MATTER...
...HOW STRONG HE IS, HE'S STILL HUMAN.
MANTA...
I SHOULD'VE NOTICED!
WHY DIDN'T I SEE THAT HE WAS SUFFERING?!
HMPH... THE FISH JUST AREN'T BITING TODAY.
FISHING?!!

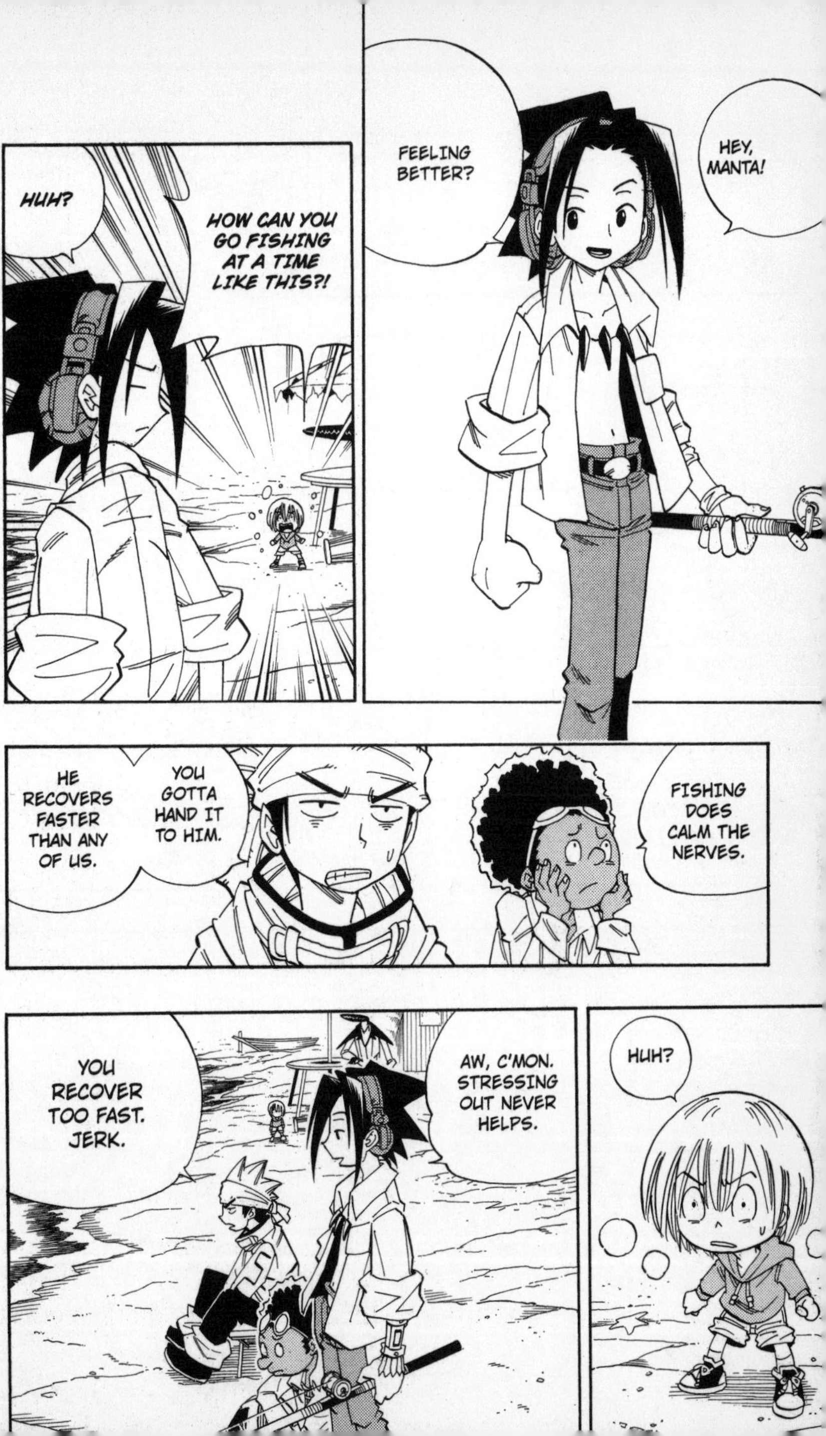
HEY, MANTA!
FEELING BETTER?
HOW CAN YOU GO FISHING AT A TIME LIKE THIS?!
HUH?
FISHING DOES CALM THE NERVES.
YOU GOTTA HAND IT TO HIM.
HE RECOVERS FASTER THAN ANY OF US.
HUH?
AW, C'MON. STRESSING OUT NEVER HELPS.
YOU RECOVER TOO FAST. JERK.

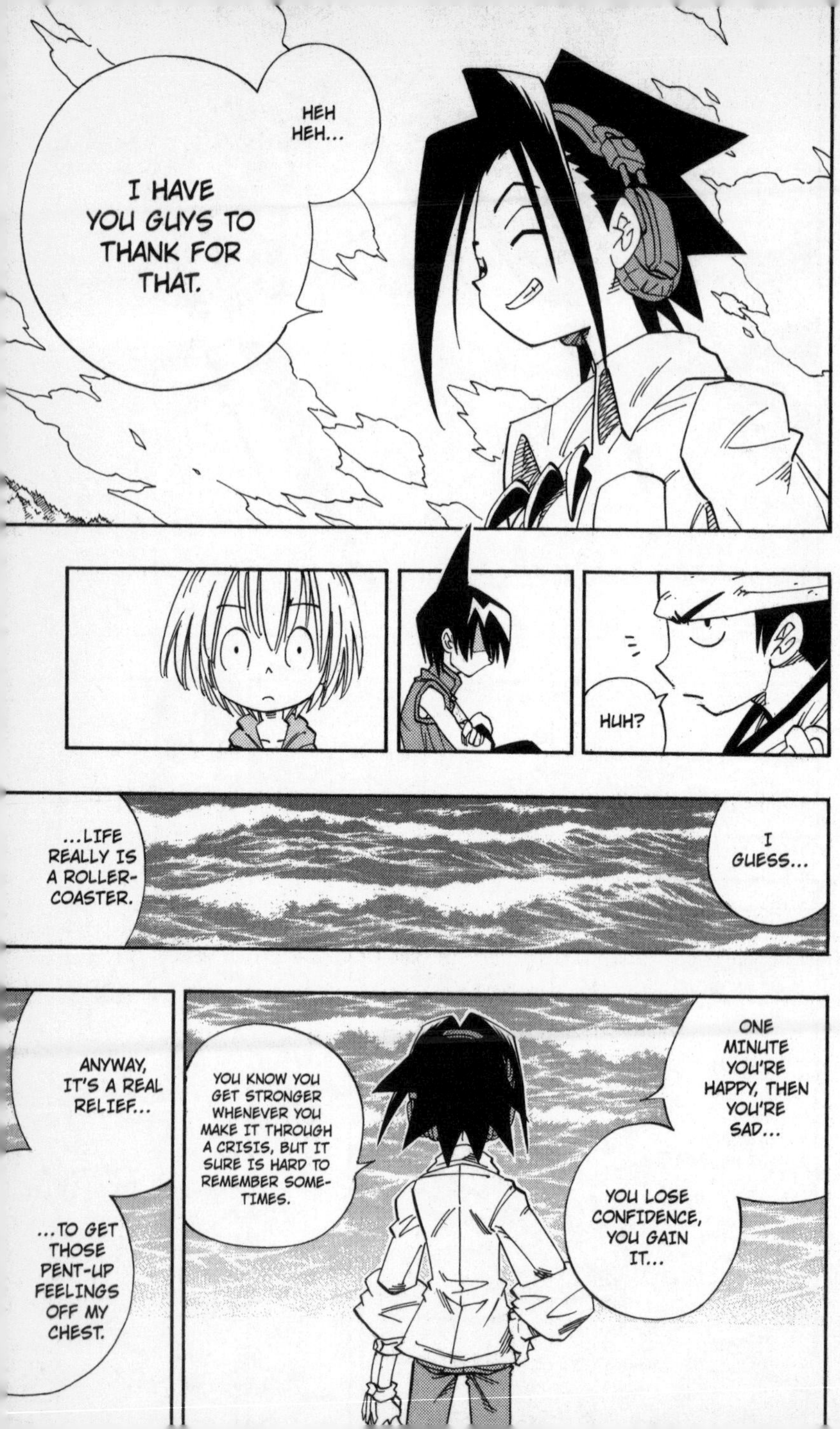
HEH HEH...
I HAVE YOU GUYS TO THANK FOR THAT.
HUH?
I GUESS...
...LIFE REALLY IS A ROLLER-COASTER.
ONE MINUTE YOU'RE HAPPY, THEN YOU'RE SAD...
YOU LOSE CONFIDENCE, YOU GAIN IT...
YOU KNOW YOU GET STRONGER WHENEVER YOU MAKE IT THROUGH A CRISIS, BUT IT SURE IS HARD TO REMEMBER SOME-TIMES.
ANYWAY, IT'S A REAL RELIEF...
...TO GET THOSE PENT-UP FEELINGS OFF MY CHEST.

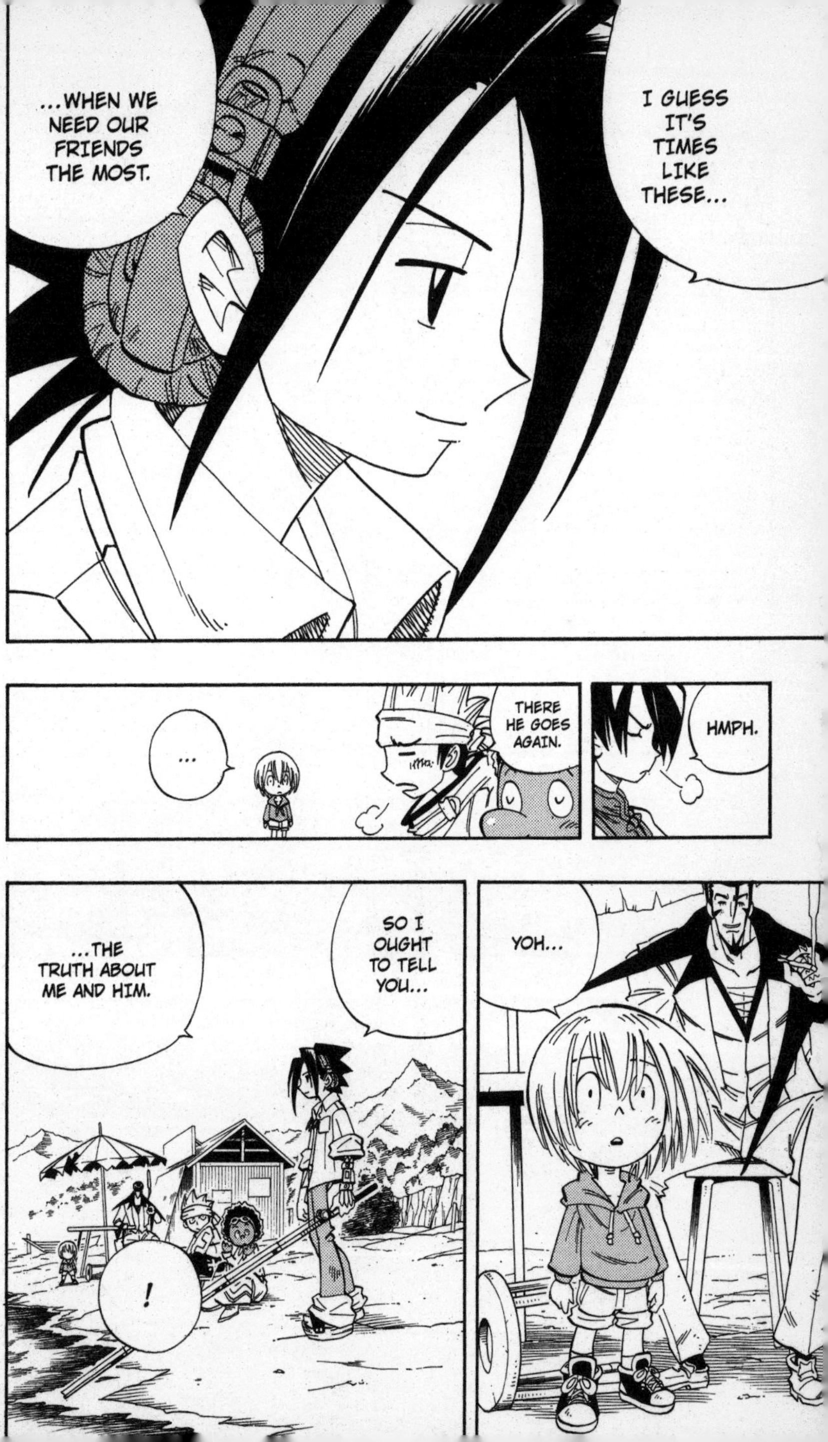
I GUESS IT'S TIMES LIKE THESE...
...WHEN WE NEED OUR FRIENDS THE MOST.
HMPH.
THERE HE GOES AGAIN.
...
YOH...
SO I OUGHT TO TELL YOU...
...THE TRUTH ABOUT ME AND HIM.
!

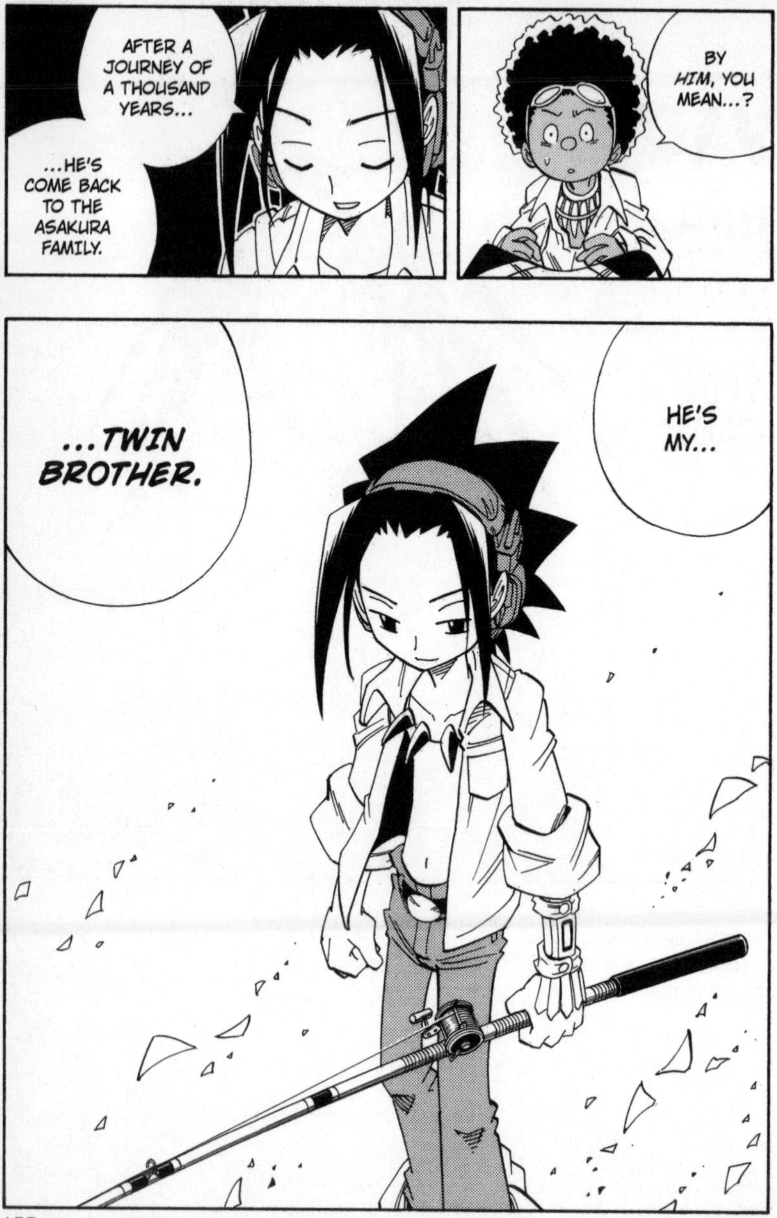
BY HIM, YOU MEAN...?
AFTER A JOURNEY OF A THOUSAND YEARS...
...HE'S COME BACK TO THE ASAKURA FAMILY.
HE'S MY...
...TWIN BROTHER.

SHAMAN KING CHARACTER FILE No.83

ハオ

HAO

2001
(JAN)

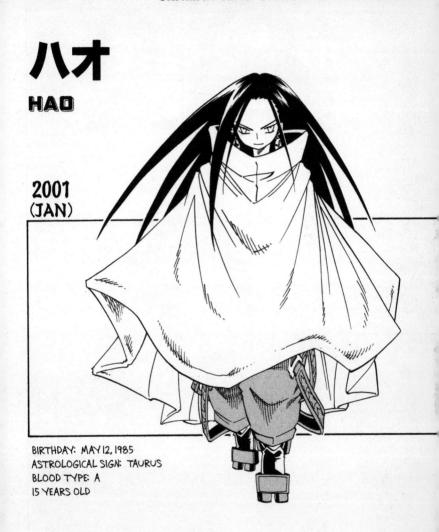

BIRTHDAY: MAY 12, 1985
ASTROLOGICAL SIGN: TAURUS
BLOOD TYPE: A
15 YEARS OLD

Reincarnation 142: Oh, Brother!!

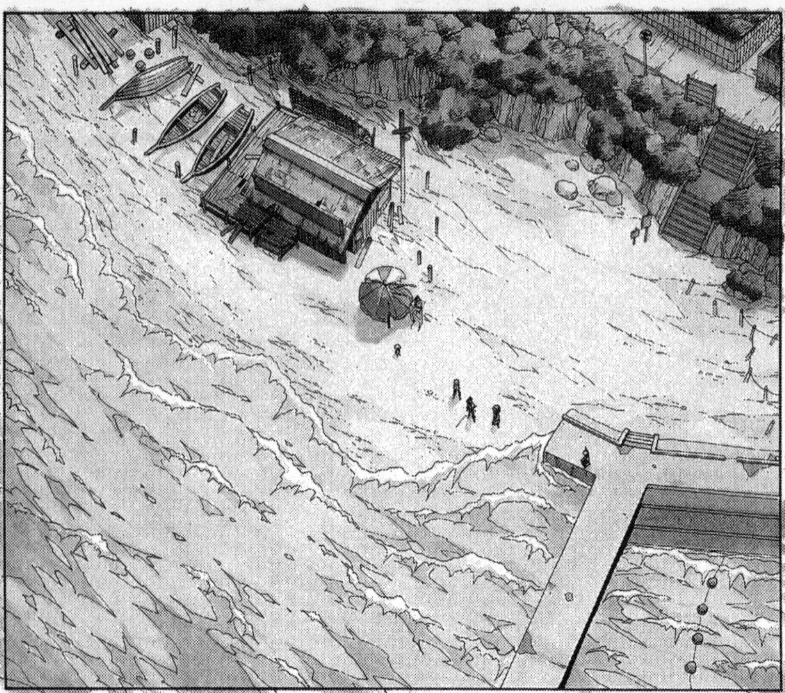

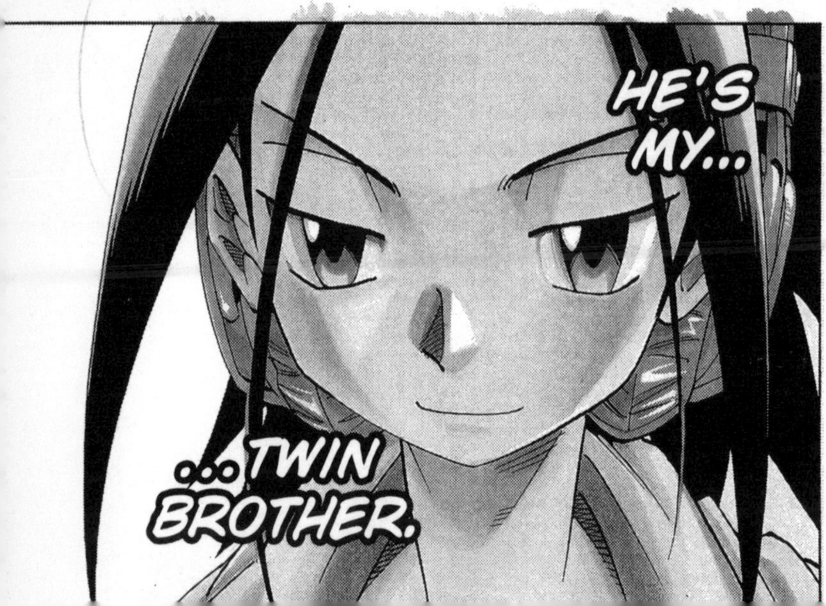
HE'S MY...
...TWIN BROTHER.

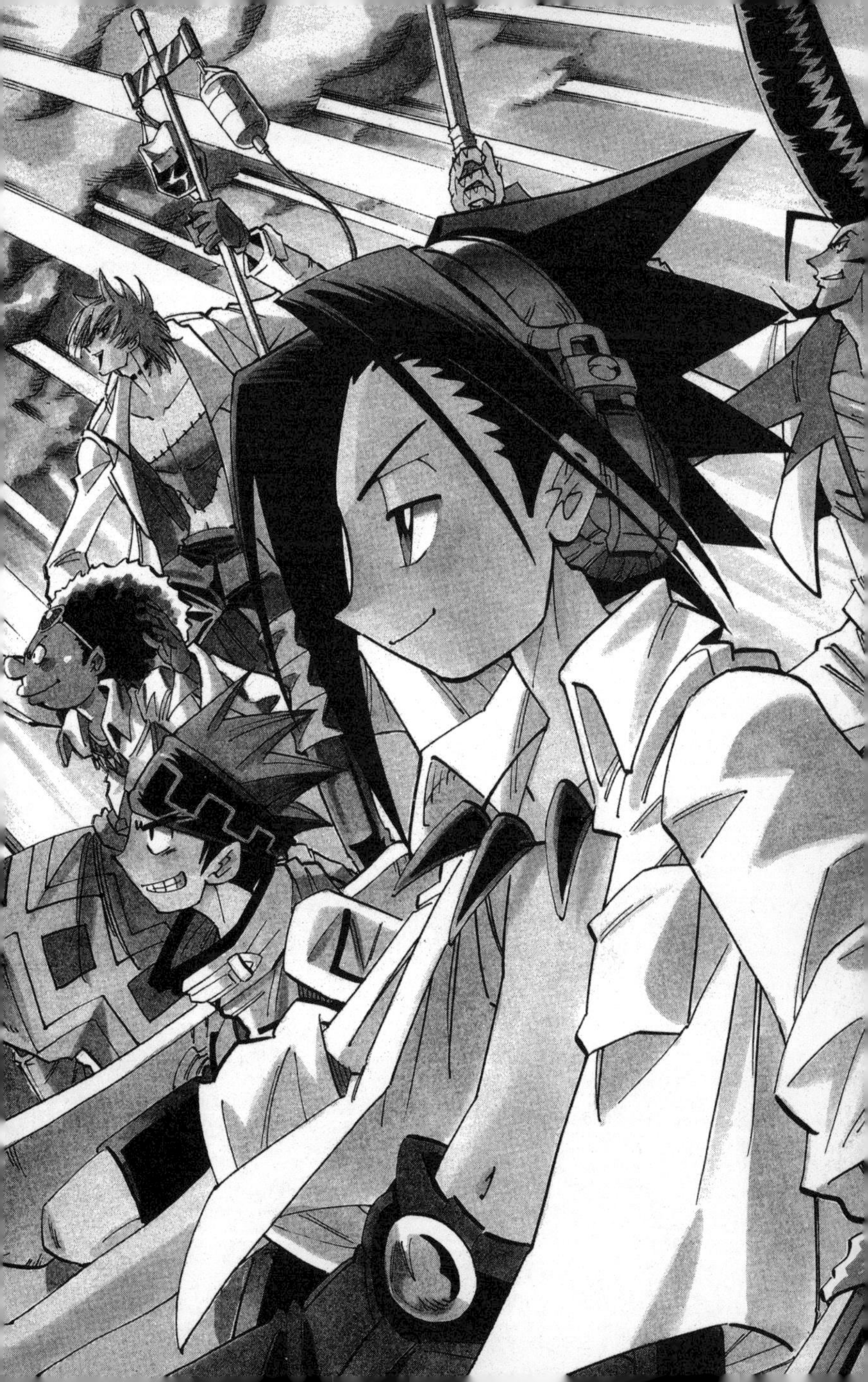

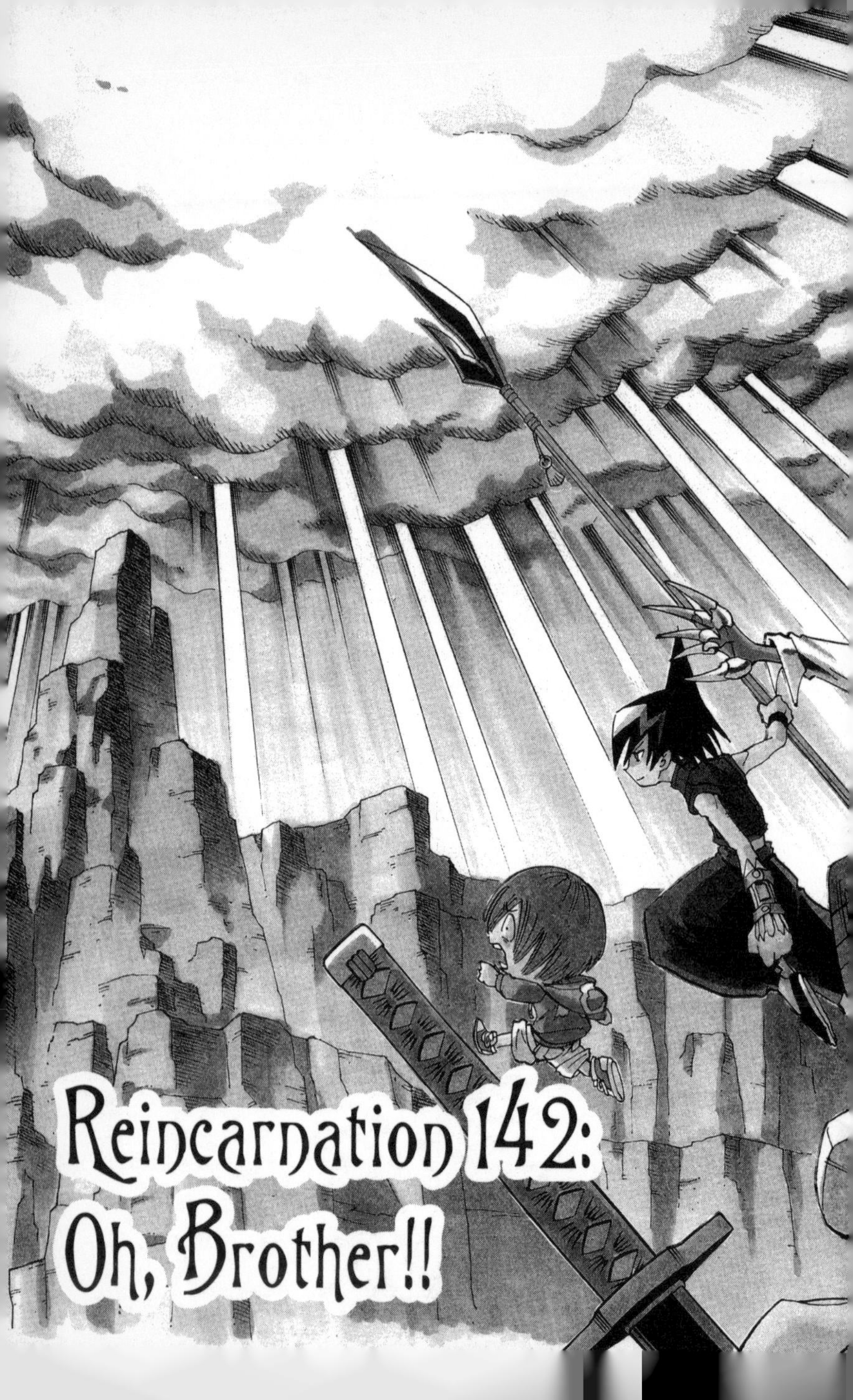
Reincarnation 142:
Oh, Brother!!

Shaman King

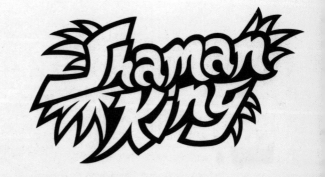

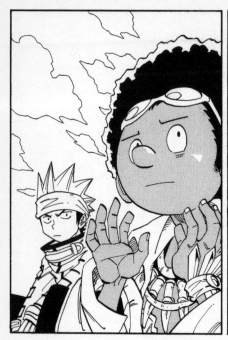

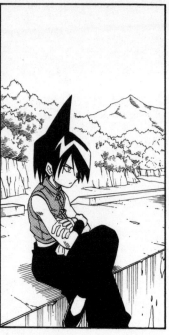

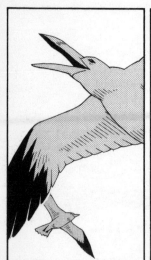

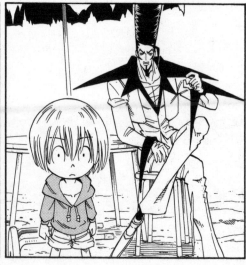

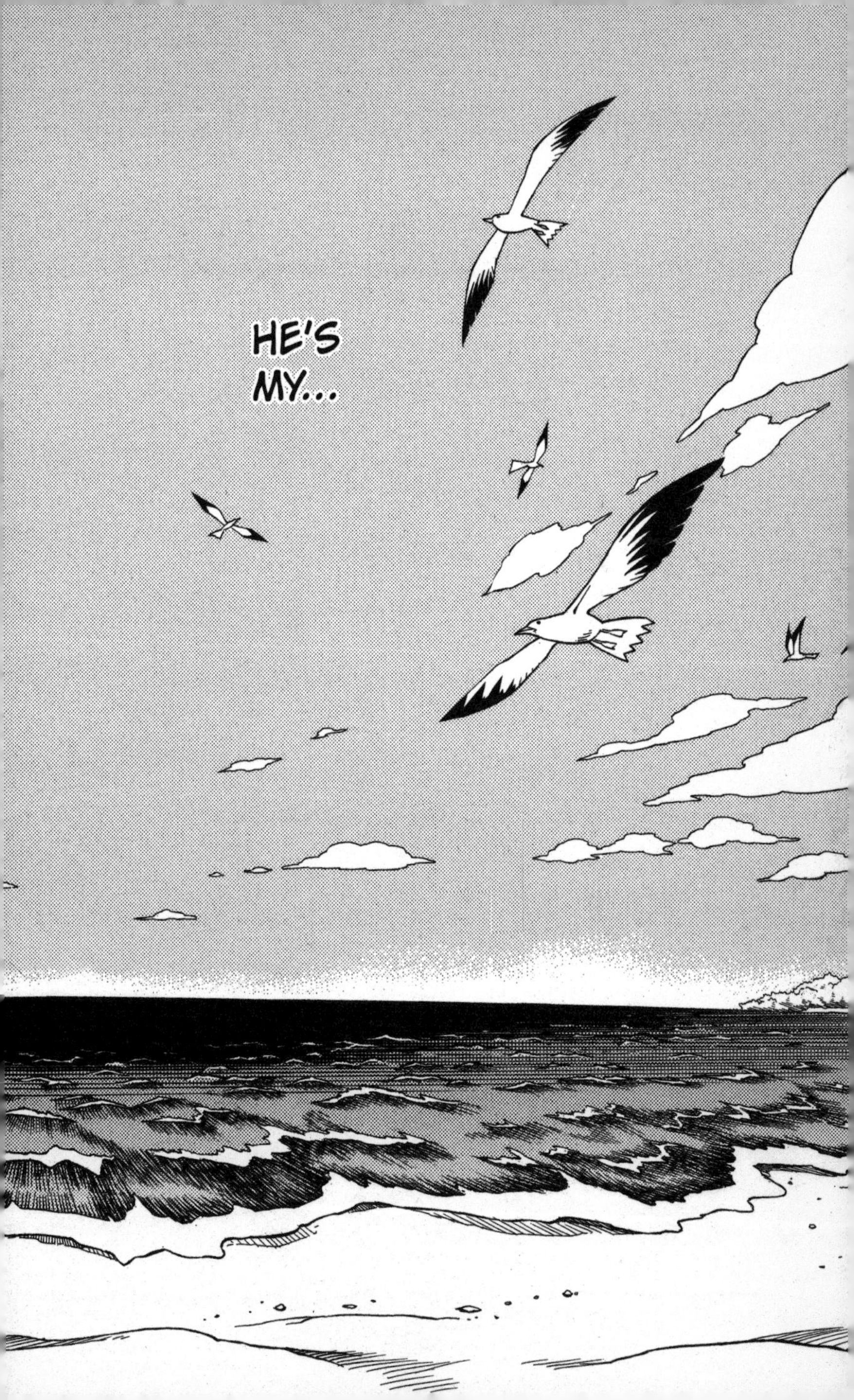
HE'S MY...

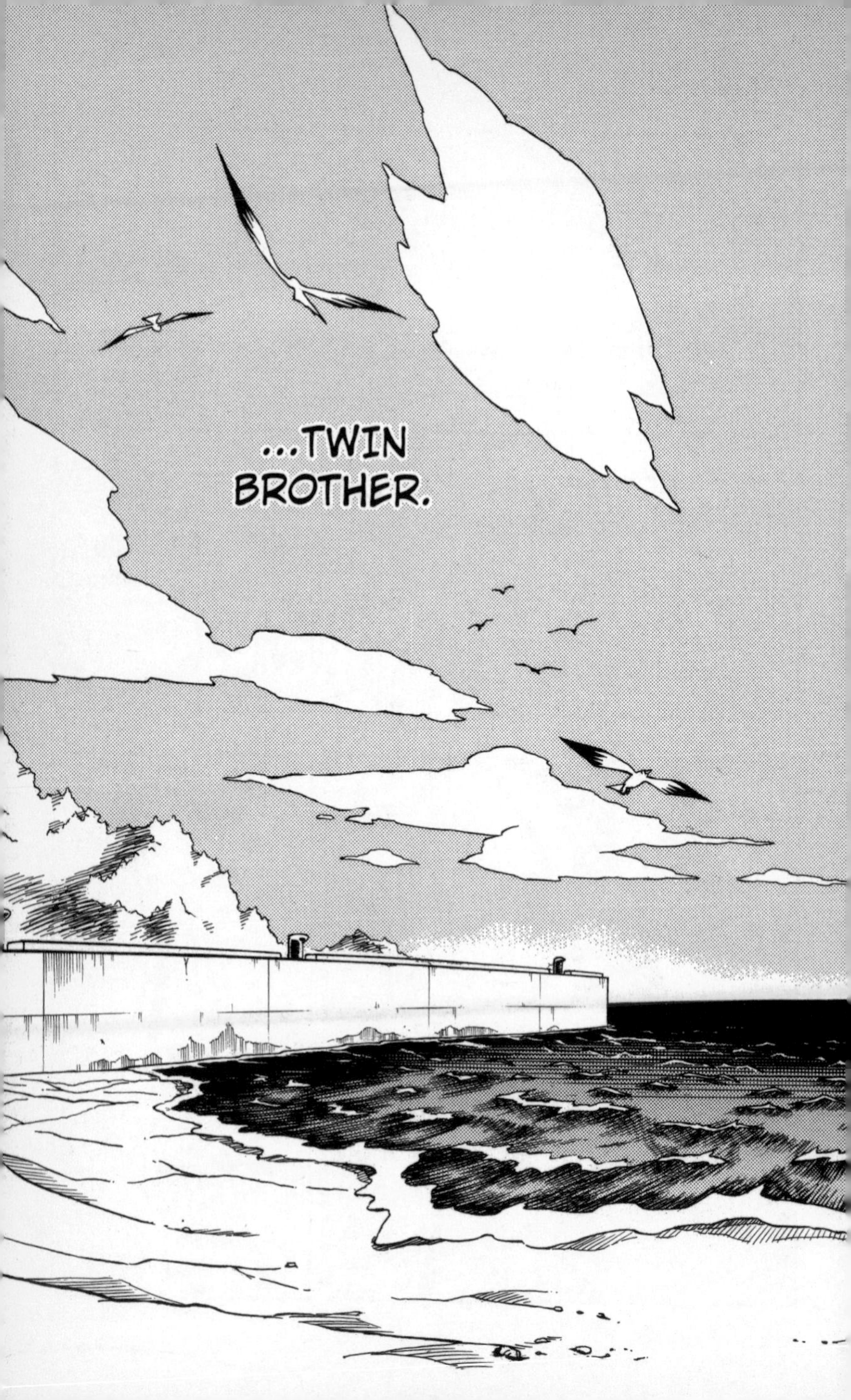
...TWIN
BROTHER.

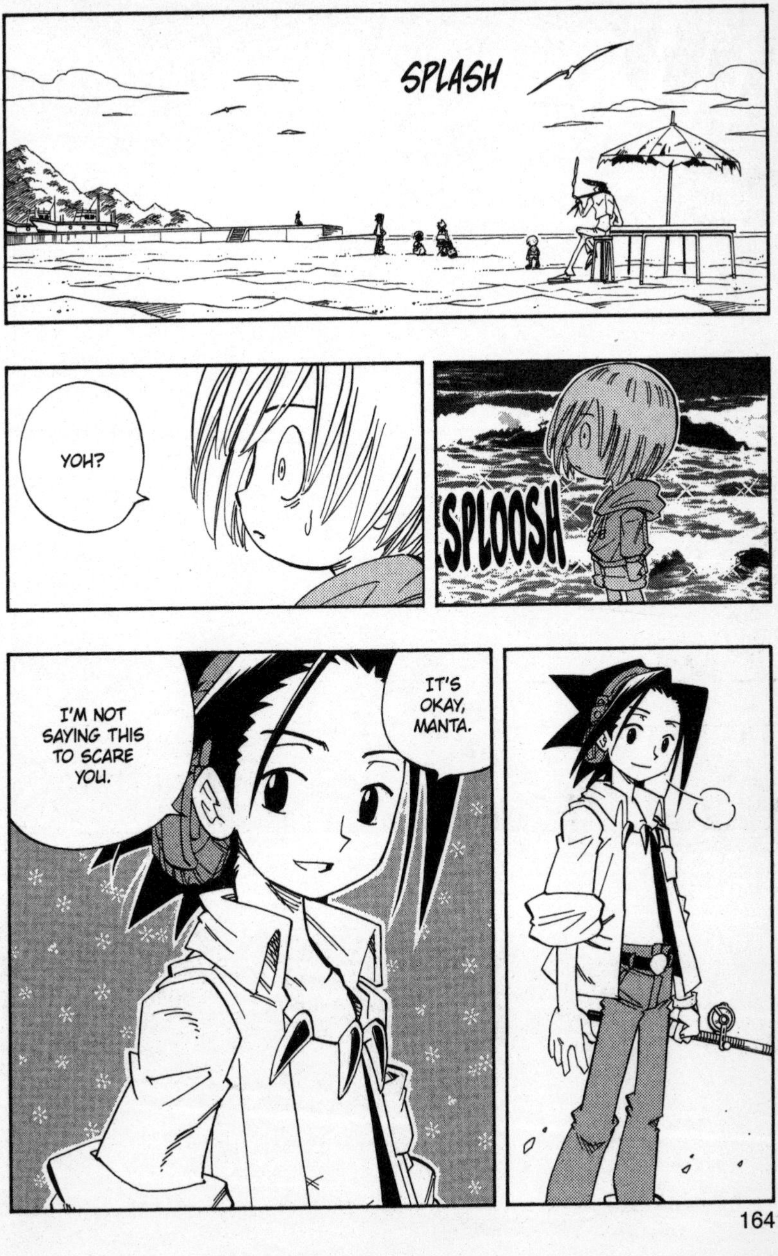
SPLASH
SPLOOSH
YOH?
IT'S OKAY, MANTA.
I'M NOT SAYING THIS TO SCARE YOU.

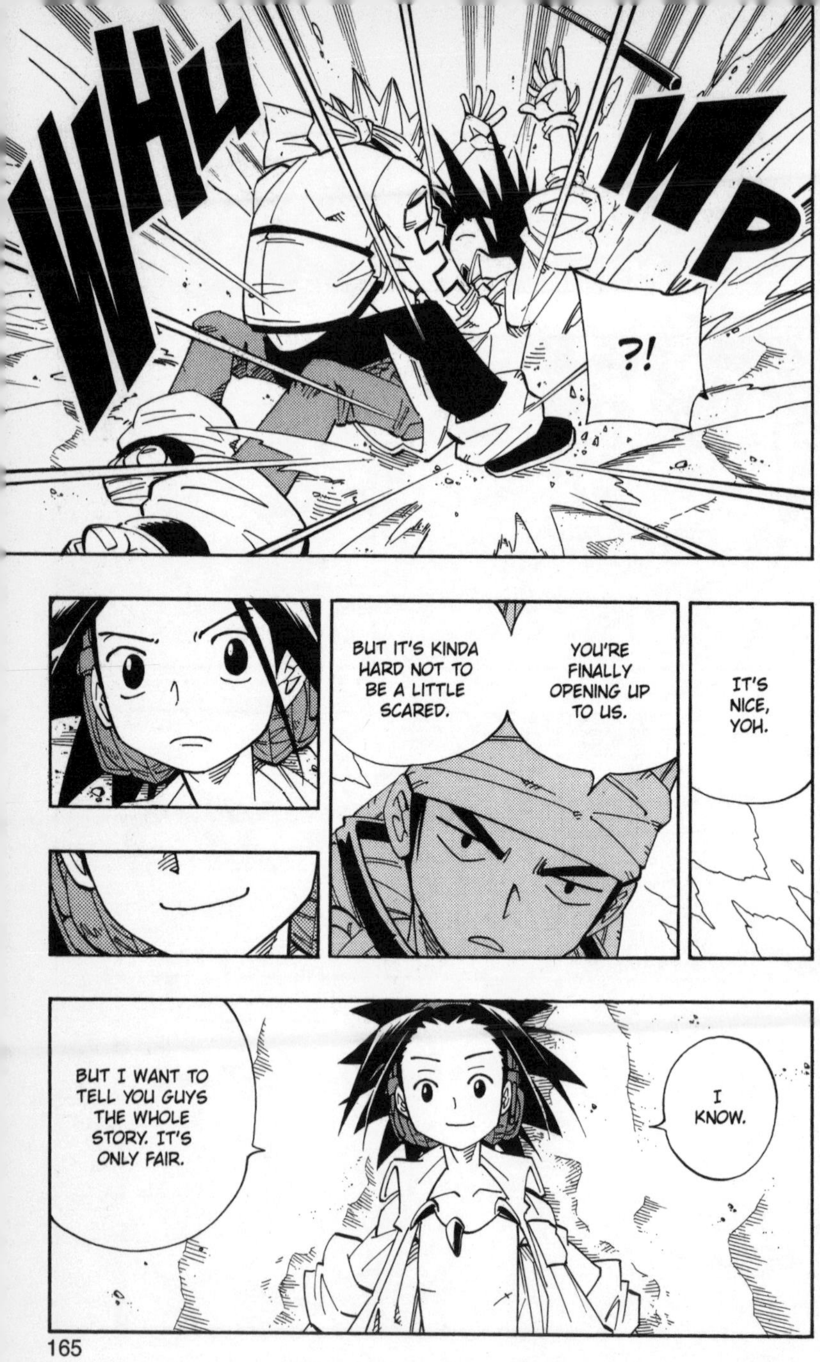
WHUMP
?!
IT'S NICE, YOH.
YOU'RE FINALLY OPENING UP TO US.
BUT IT'S KINDA HARD NOT TO BE A LITTLE SCARED.
I KNOW.
BUT I WANT TO TELL YOU GUYS THE WHOLE STORY. IT'S ONLY FAIR.

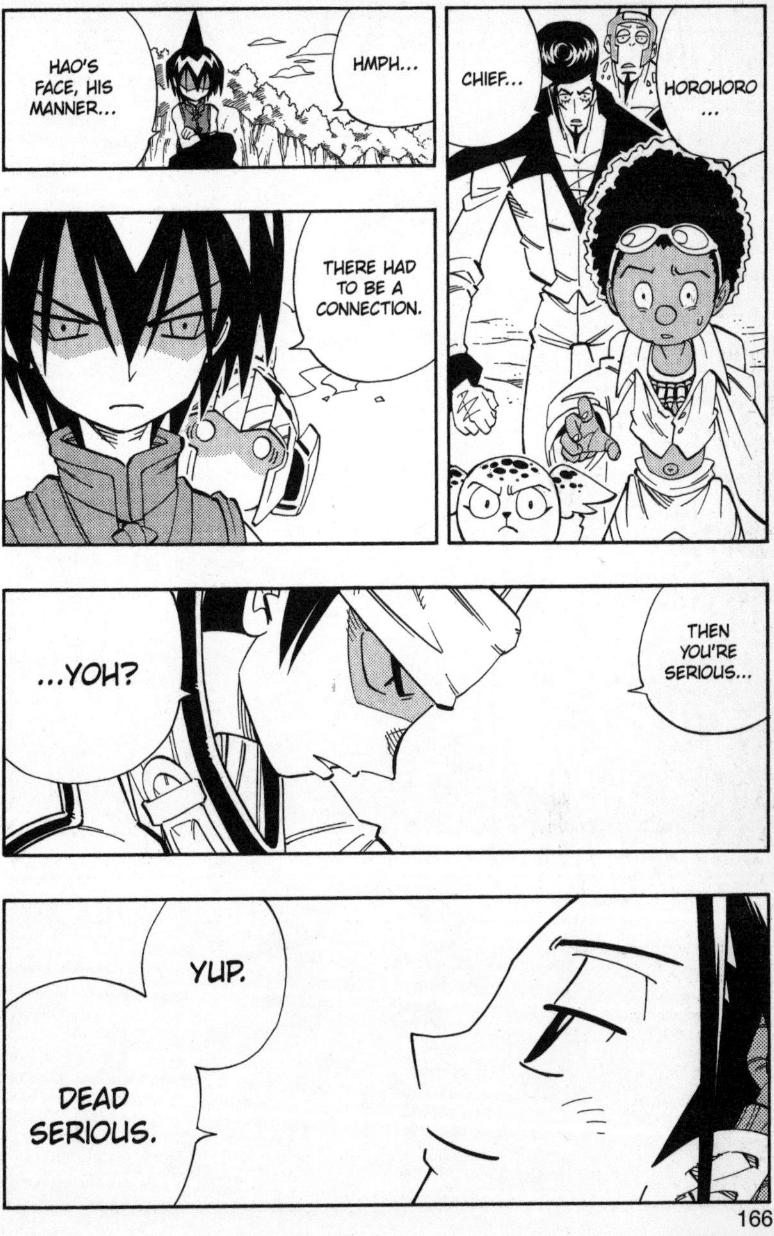
HOROHORO ...
CHIEF...
HMPH...
HAO'S FACE, HIS MANNER...
THERE HAD TO BE A CONNECTION.
THEN YOU'RE SERIOUS...
...YOH?
YUP.
DEAD SERIOUS.

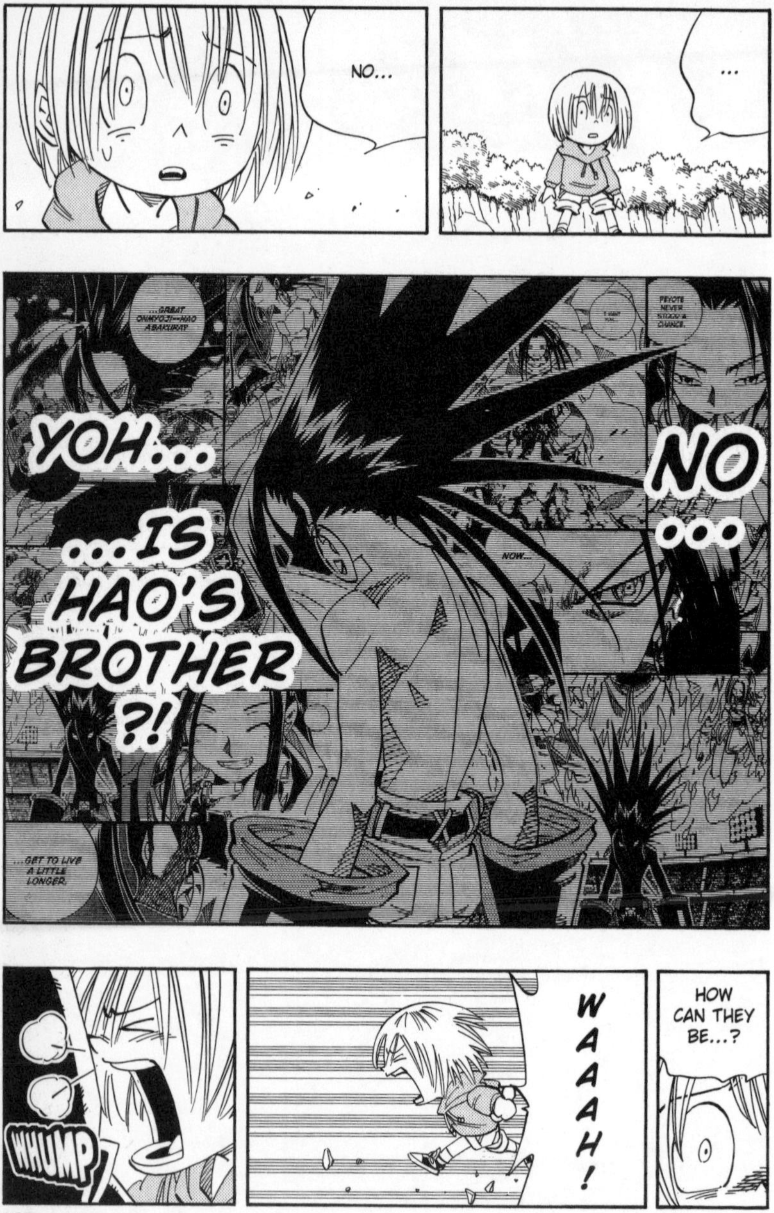
...
NO...
PEYOTE NEVER STOOD A CHANCE.
NO...
NOW...
YOH...
...IS HAO'S BROTHER ?!
...GREAT ONMYOJI—HAO ASAKURA?
...GET TO LIVE A LITTLE LONGER.
HOW CAN THEY BE...?
WAAAAH!
WHUMP

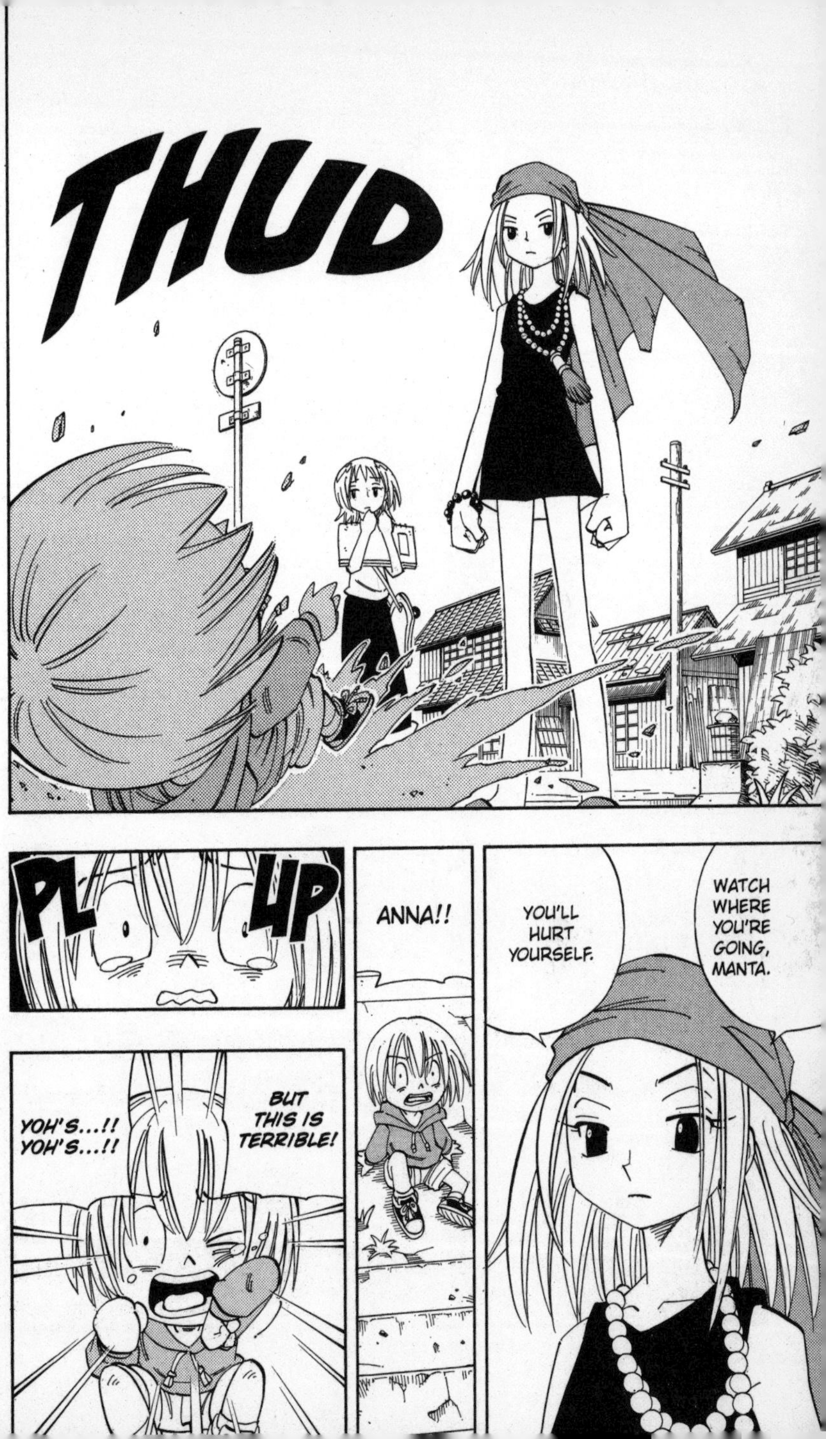
THUD
WATCH WHERE YOU'RE GOING, MANTA.
YOU'LL HURT YOURSELF.
ANNA!!
PL UP
BUT THIS IS TERRIBLE!
YOH'S...!! YOH'S...!!

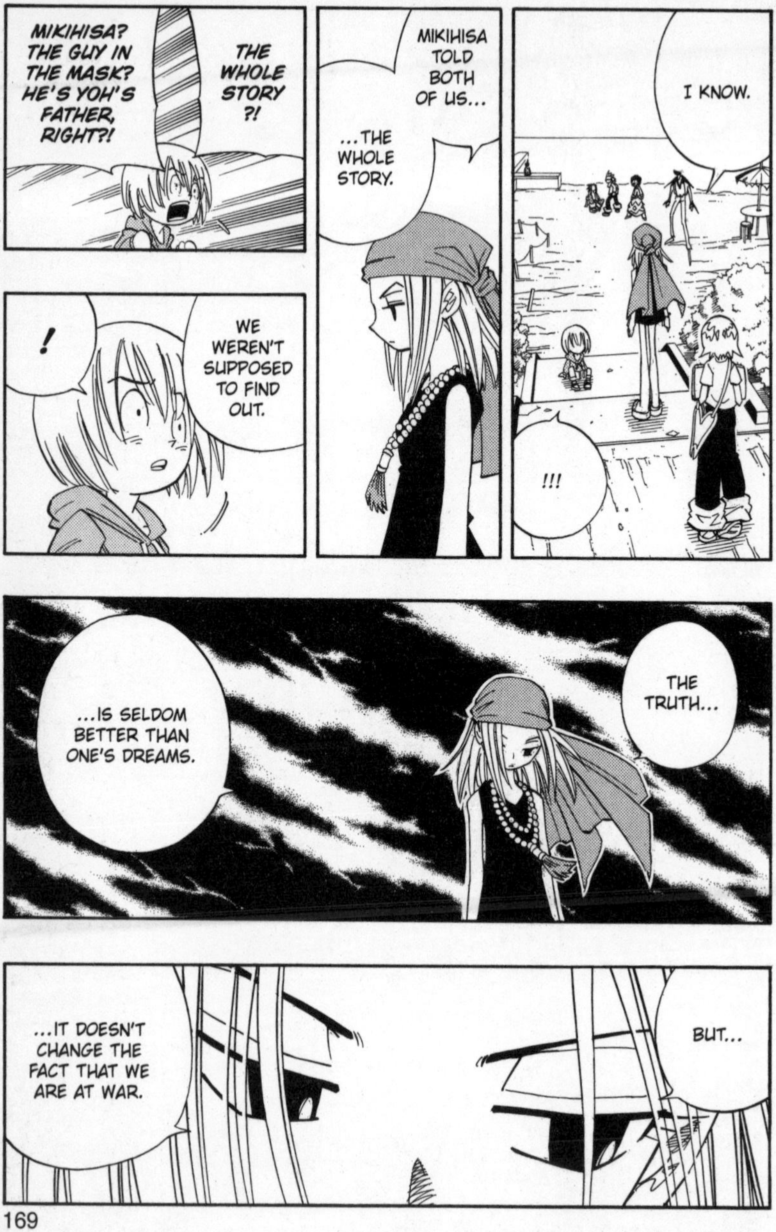
I KNOW.
!!!
MIKIHISA TOLD BOTH OF US...
...THE WHOLE STORY.
THE WHOLE STORY ?!
MIKIHISA? THE GUY IN THE MASK? HE'S YOH'S FATHER, RIGHT?!
WE WEREN'T SUPPOSED TO FIND OUT.
!
THE TRUTH...
...IS SELDOM BETTER THAN ONE'S DREAMS.
BUT...
...IT DOESN'T CHANGE THE FACT THAT WE ARE AT WAR.

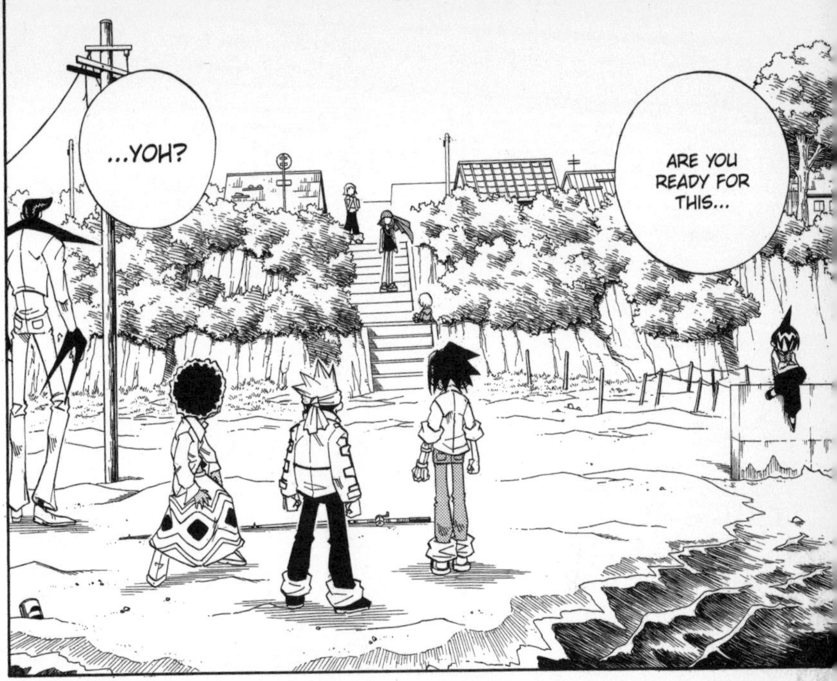
ARE YOU READY FOR THIS...
...YOH?
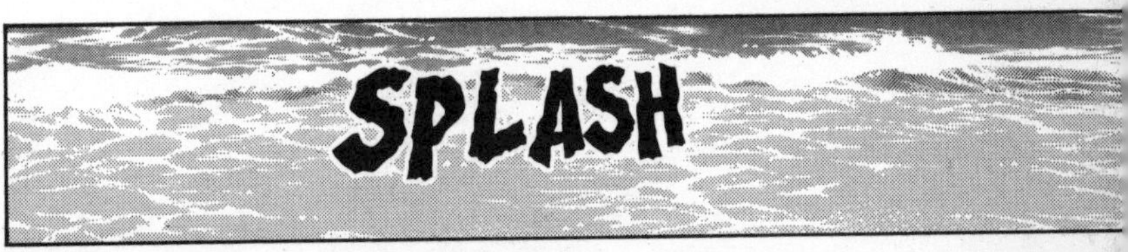
SPLASH
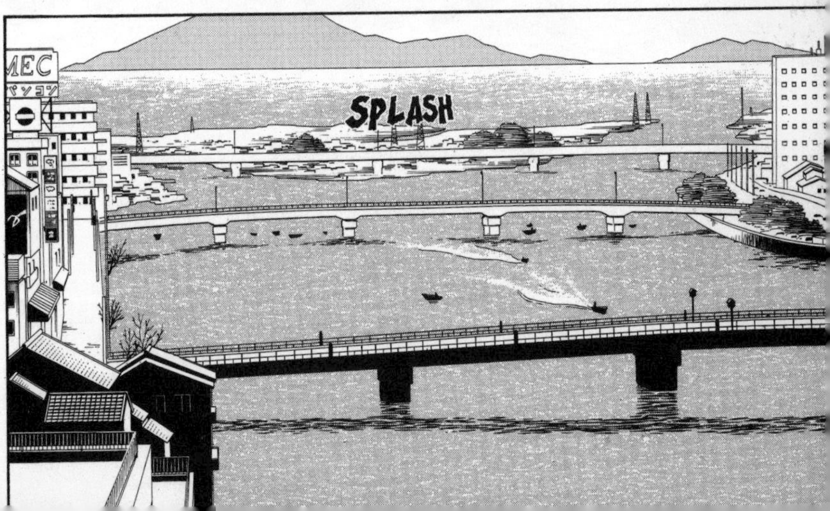
SPLASH
MEC

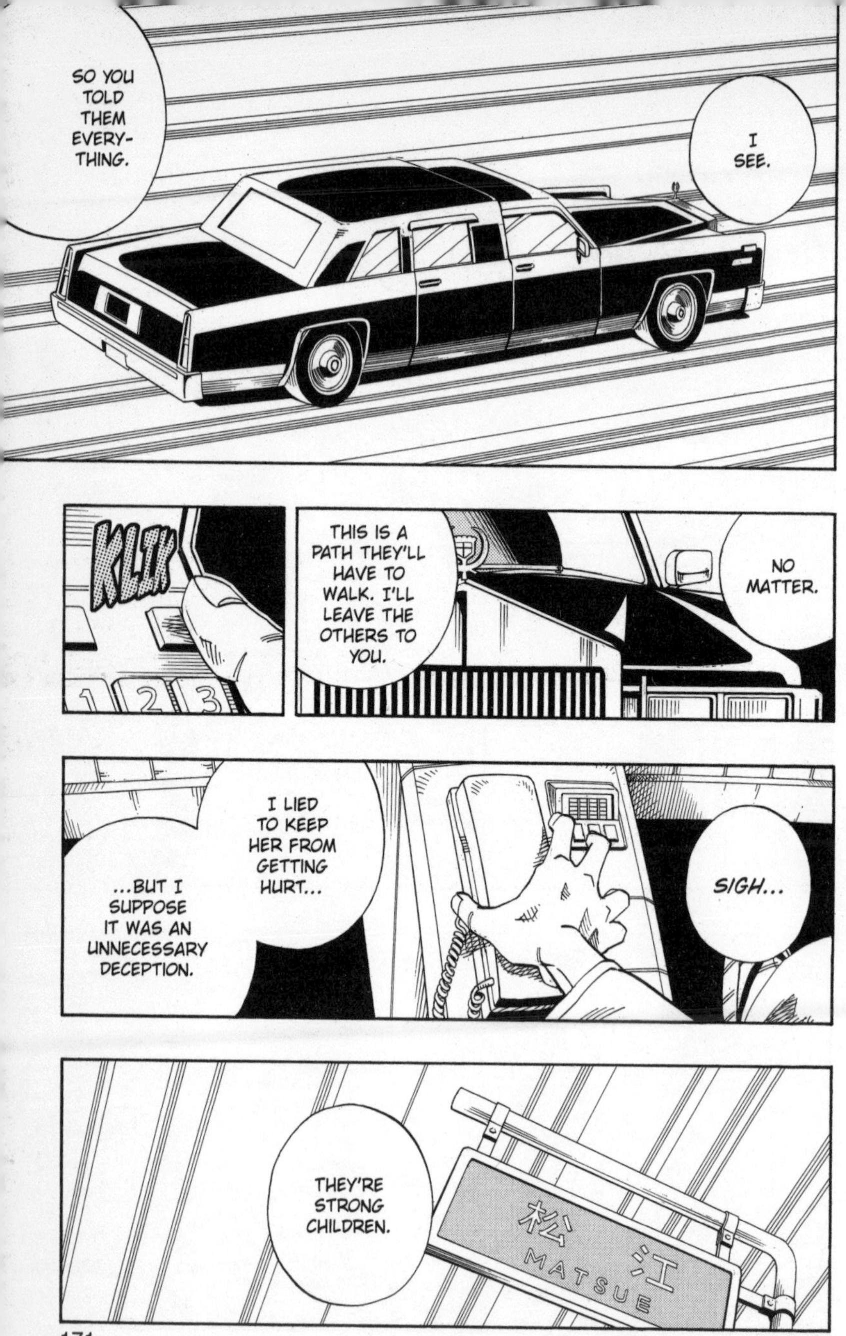
I SEE.
SO YOU TOLD THEM EVERYTHING.
NO MATTER.
THIS IS A PATH THEY'LL HAVE TO WALK. I'LL LEAVE THE OTHERS TO YOU.
KLIK
1 2 3
SIGH...
I LIED TO KEEP HER FROM GETTING HURT...
...BUT I SUPPOSE IT WAS AN UNNECESSARY DECEPTION.
THEY'RE STRONG CHILDREN.
松江
MATSUE

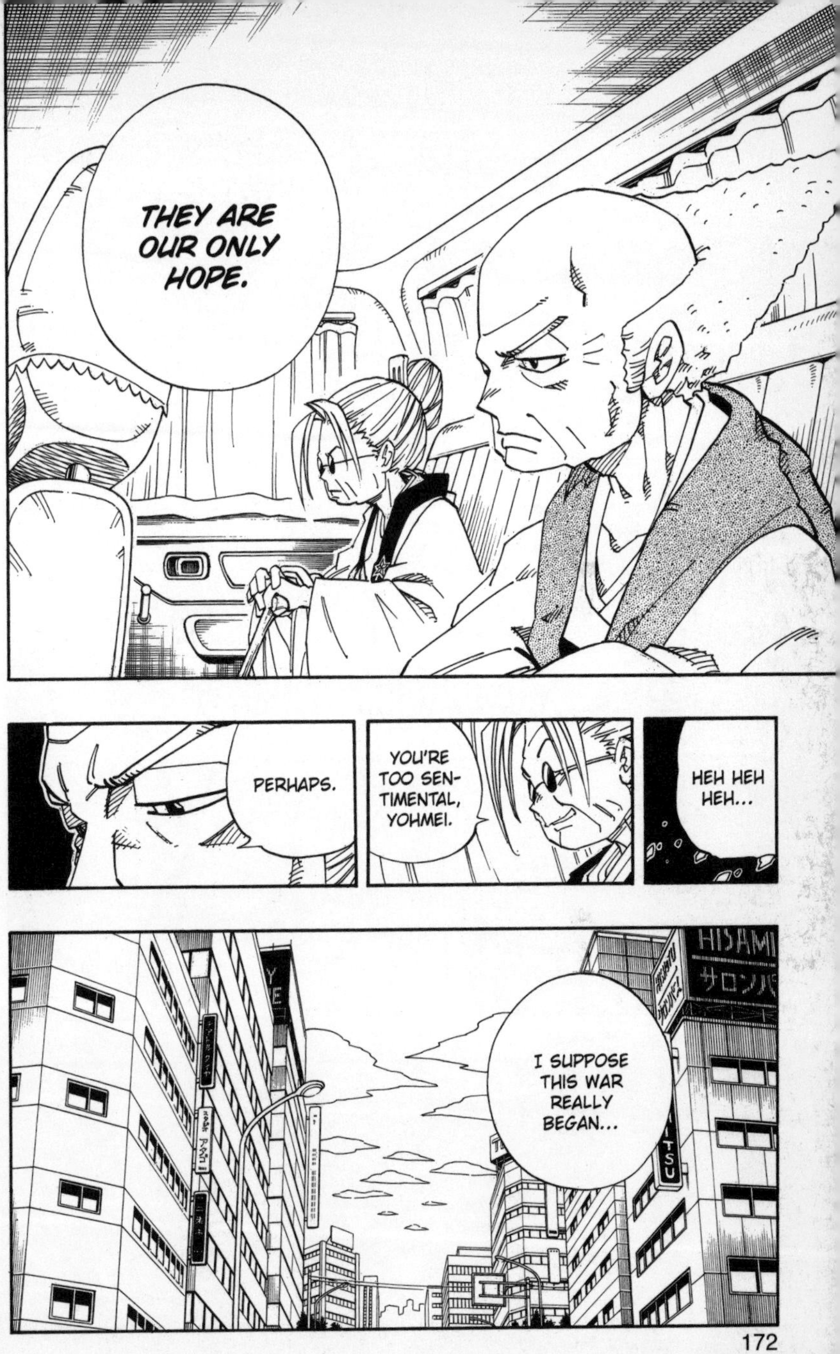
THEY ARE OUR ONLY HOPE.
HEH HEH HEH...
YOU'RE TOO SEN-TIMENTAL, YOHMEI.
PERHAPS.
I SUPPOSE THIS WAR REALLY BEGAN...

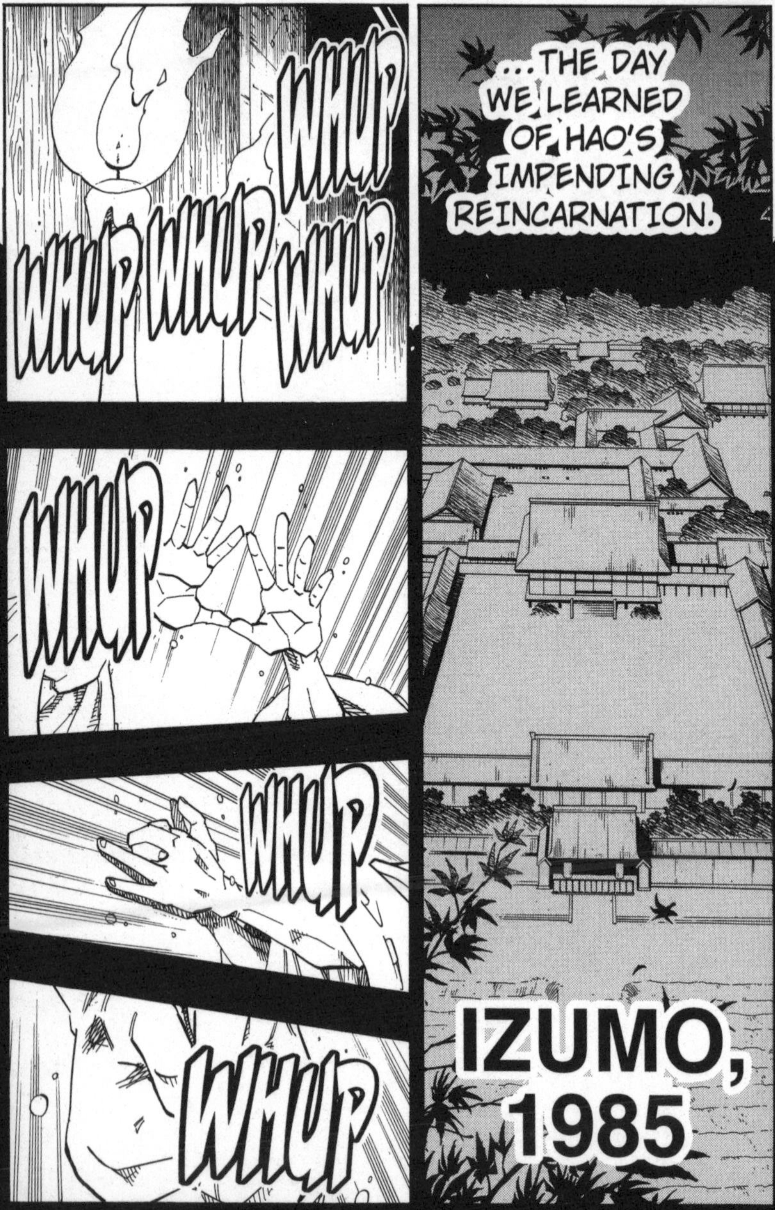
...THE DAY WE LEARNED OF HAO'S IMPENDING REINCARNATION.
IZUMO, 1985
WHUP
WHUP
WHUP
WHUP
WHUP
WHUP
WHUP

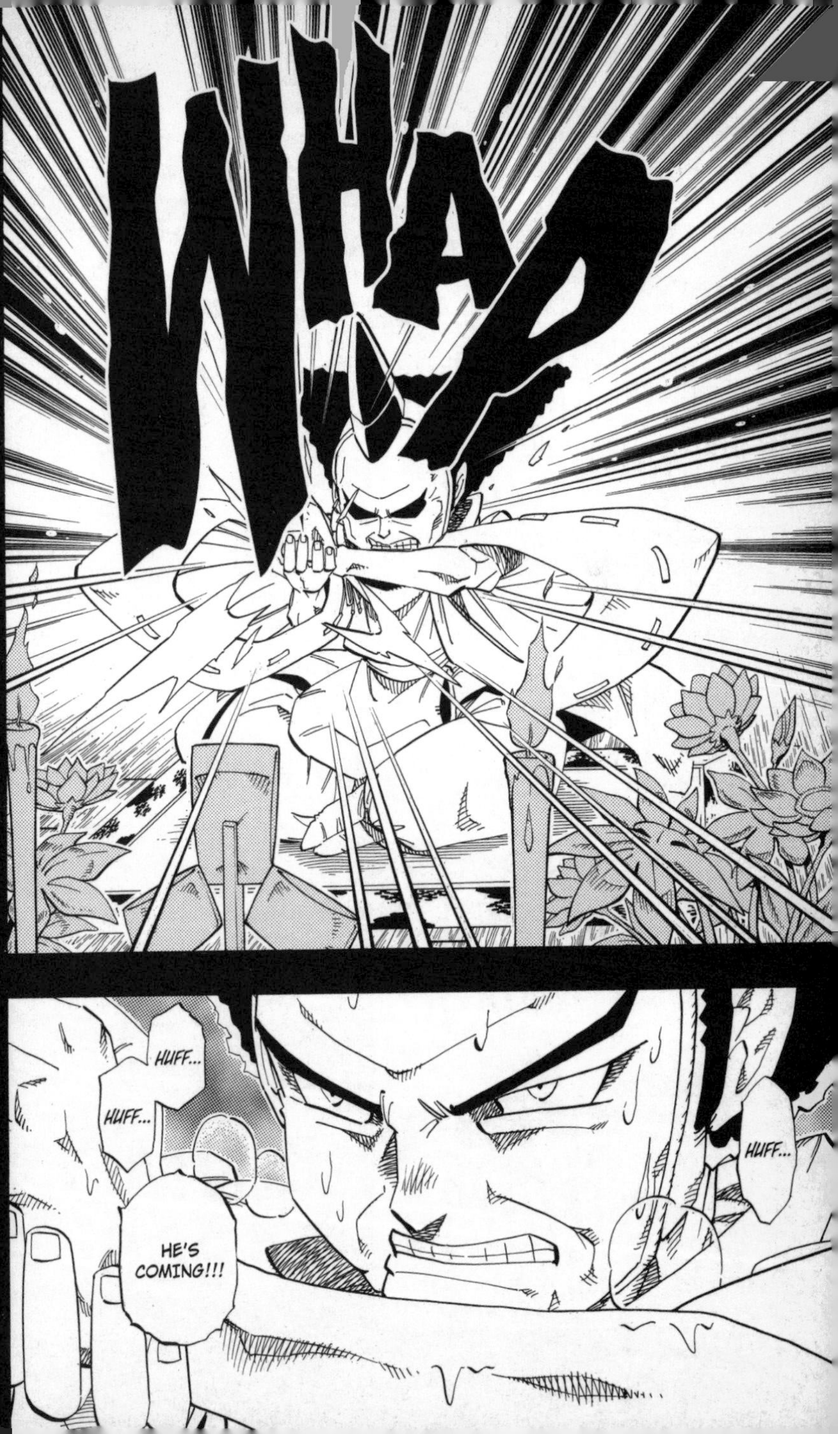
WHAP
HUFF...
HUFF...
HUFF...
HE'S COMING!!!

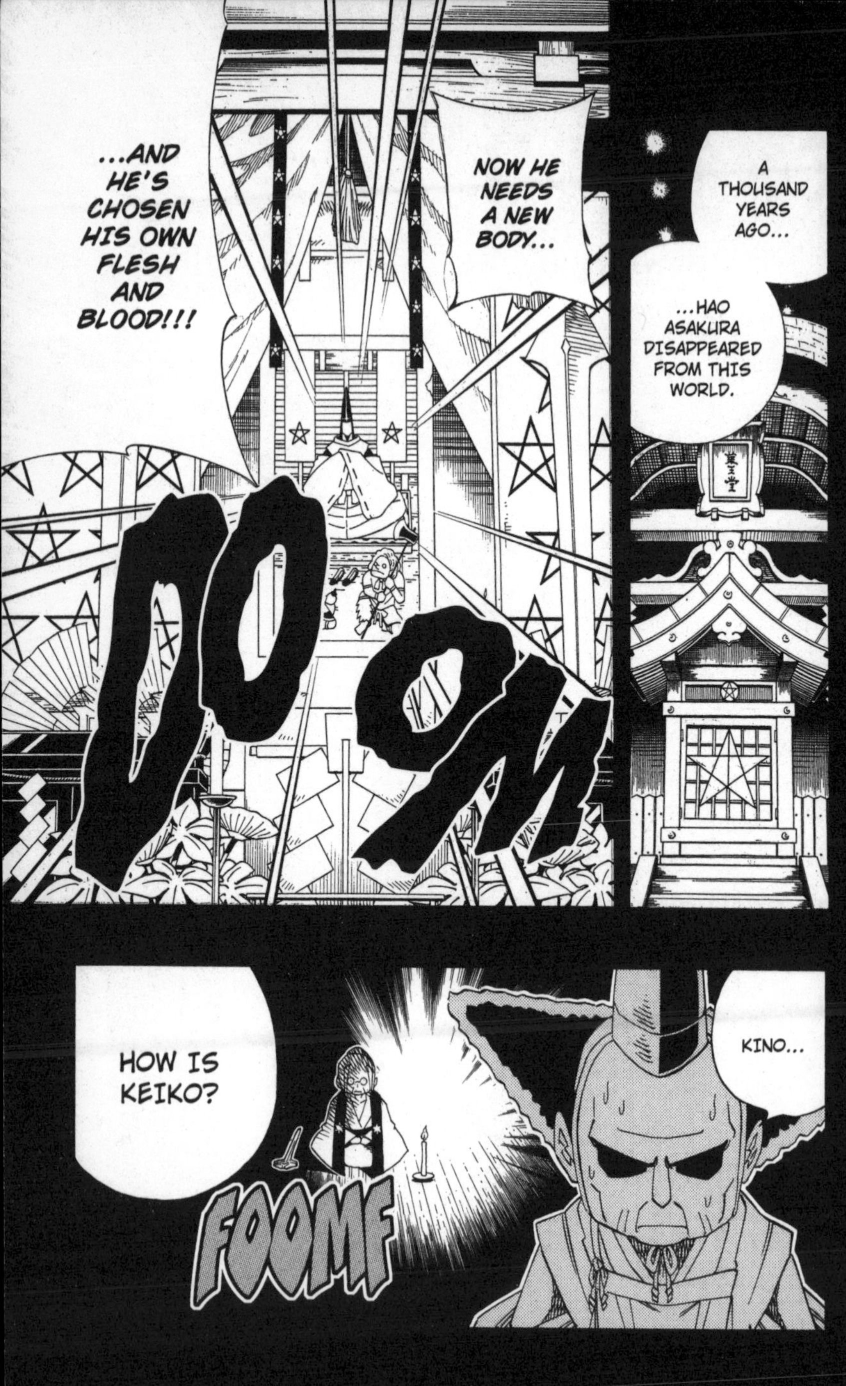
A THOUSAND YEARS AGO...
...HAO ASAKURA DISAPPEARED FROM THIS WORLD.
NOW HE NEEDS A NEW BODY...
...AND HE'S CHOSEN HIS OWN FLESH AND BLOOD!!!
DOOM
KINO...
HOW IS KEIKO?
FOOMF

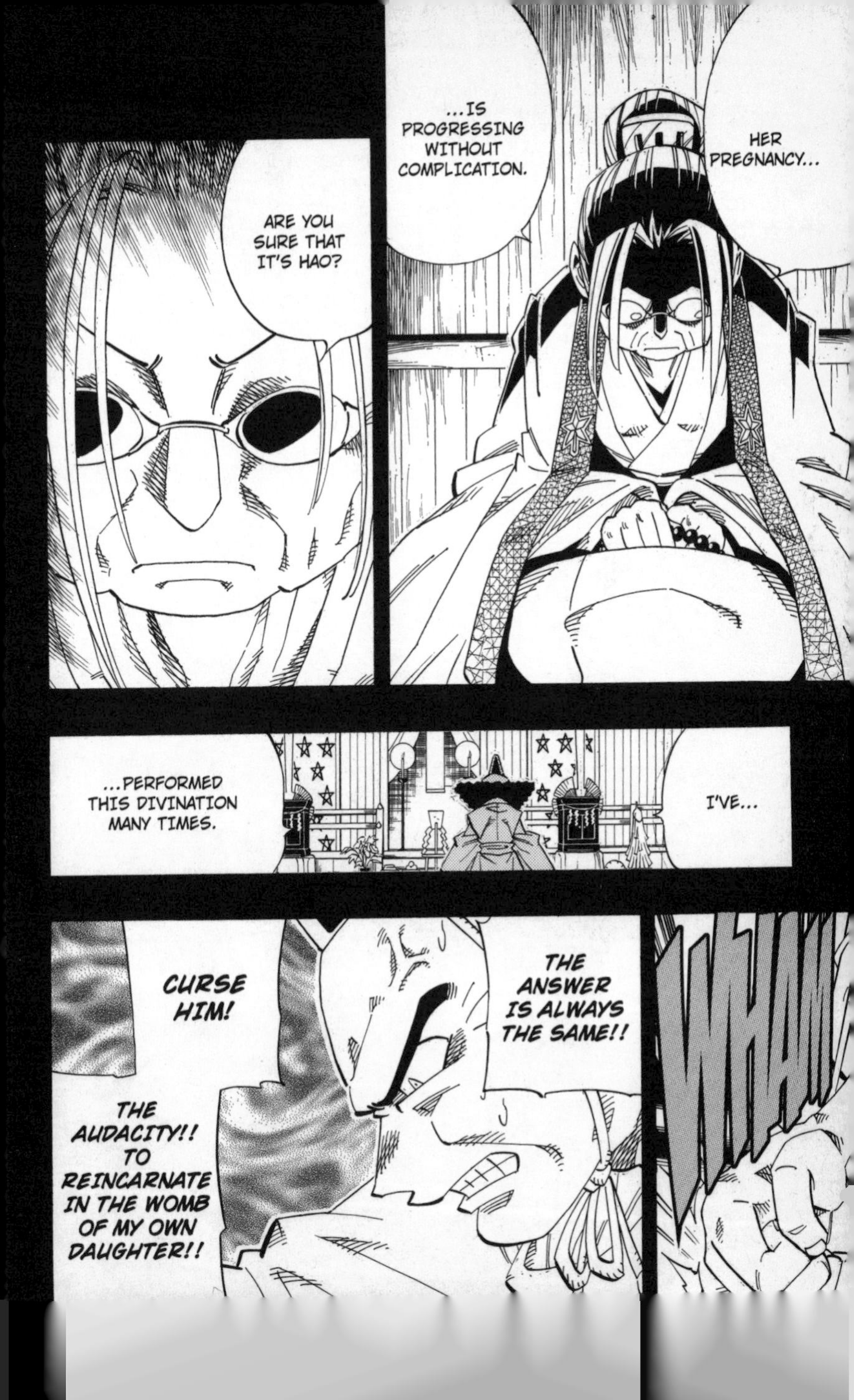
HER PREGNANCY...
...IS PROGRESSING WITHOUT COMPLICATION.
ARE YOU SURE THAT IT'S HAO?
I'VE...
...PERFORMED THIS DIVINATION MANY TIMES.
WHAM
THE ANSWER IS ALWAYS THE SAME!!
CURSE HIM!
THE AUDACITY!! TO REINCARNATE IN THE WOMB OF MY OWN DAUGHTER!!

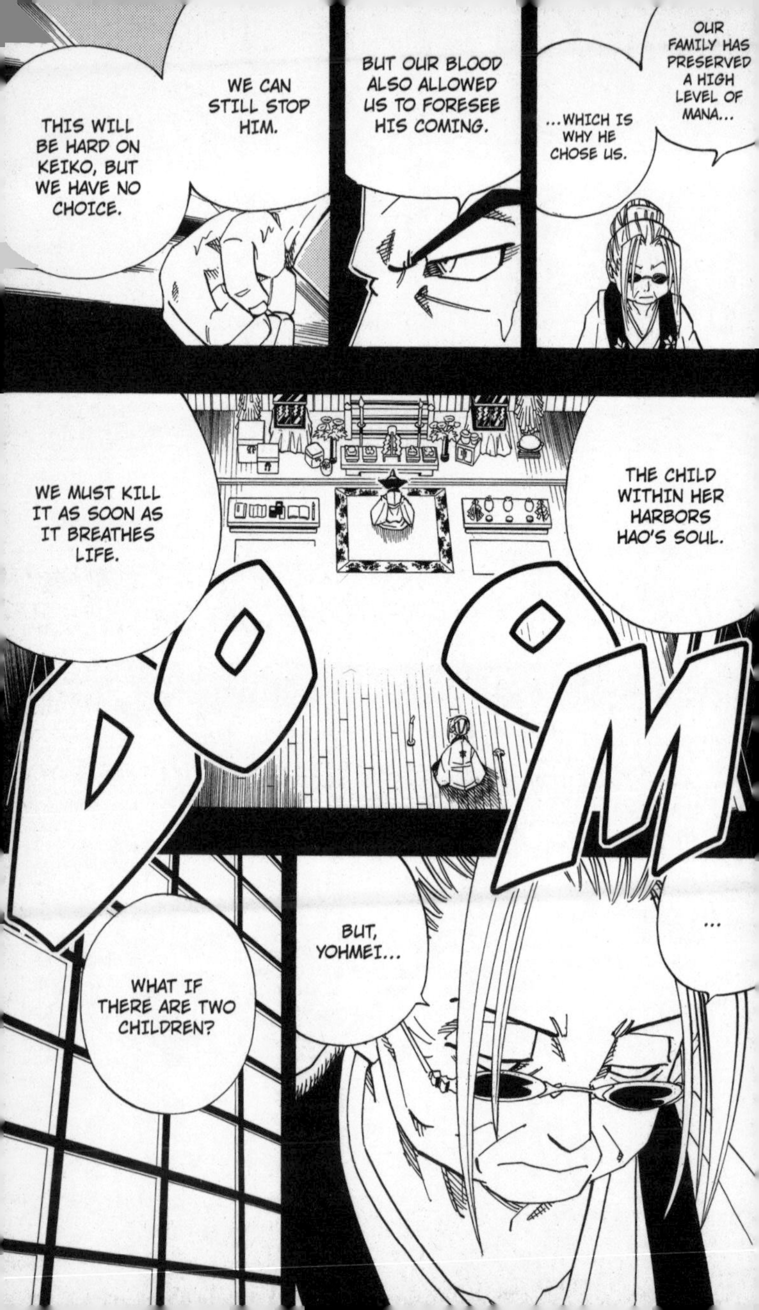
OUR FAMILY HAS PRESERVED A HIGH LEVEL OF MANA...
...WHICH IS WHY HE CHOSE US.
BUT OUR BLOOD ALSO ALLOWED US TO FORESEE HIS COMING.
WE CAN STILL STOP HIM.
THIS WILL BE HARD ON KEIKO, BUT WE HAVE NO CHOICE.
THE CHILD WITHIN HER HARBORS HAO'S SOUL.
WE MUST KILL IT AS SOON AS IT BREATHES LIFE.
DOOM
...
BUT, YOHMEI...
WHAT IF THERE ARE TWO CHILDREN?

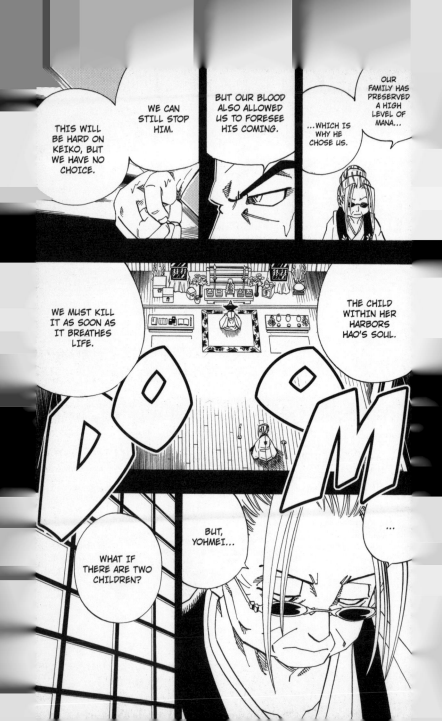

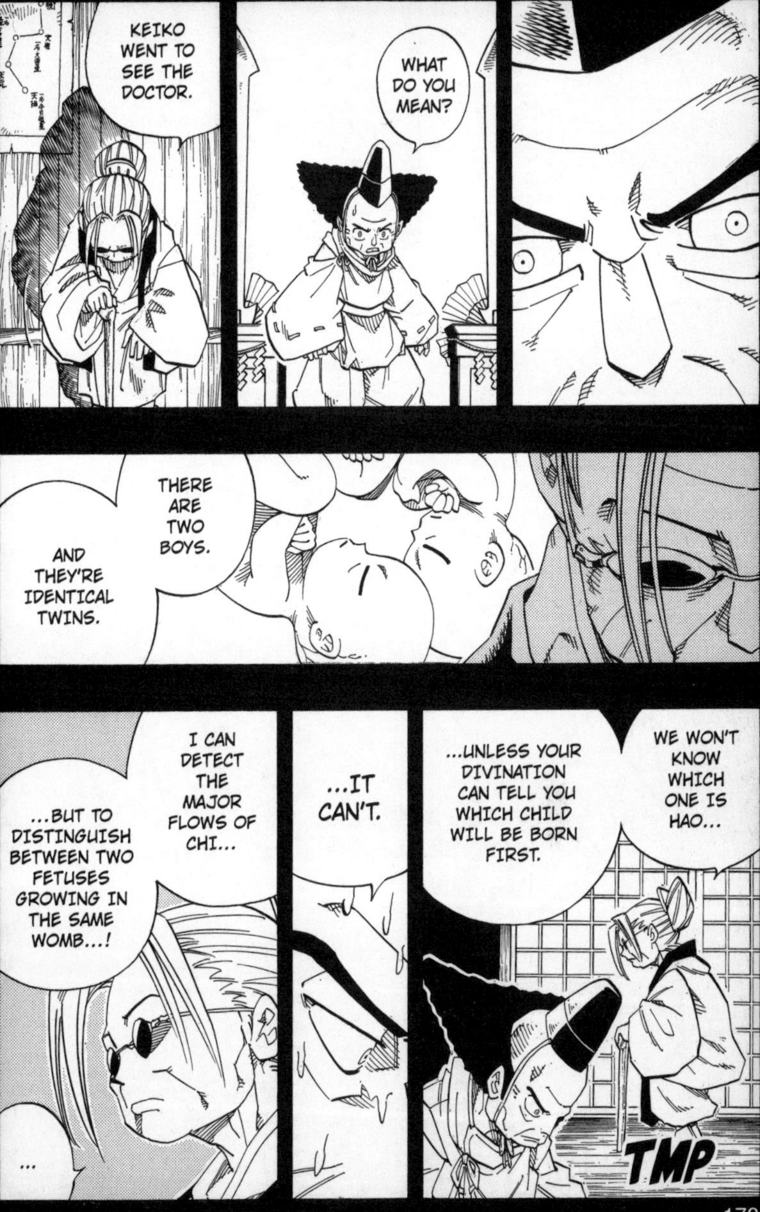
WHAT DO YOU MEAN?
KEIKO WENT TO SEE THE DOCTOR.
THERE ARE TWO BOYS.
AND THEY'RE IDENTICAL TWINS.
WE WON'T KNOW WHICH ONE IS HAO...
...UNLESS YOUR DIVINATION CAN TELL YOU WHICH CHILD WILL BE BORN FIRST.
TMP
...IT CAN'T.
I CAN DETECT THE MAJOR FLOWS OF CHI...
...BUT TO DISTINGUISH BETWEEN TWO FETUSES GROWING IN THE SAME WOMB...!
...

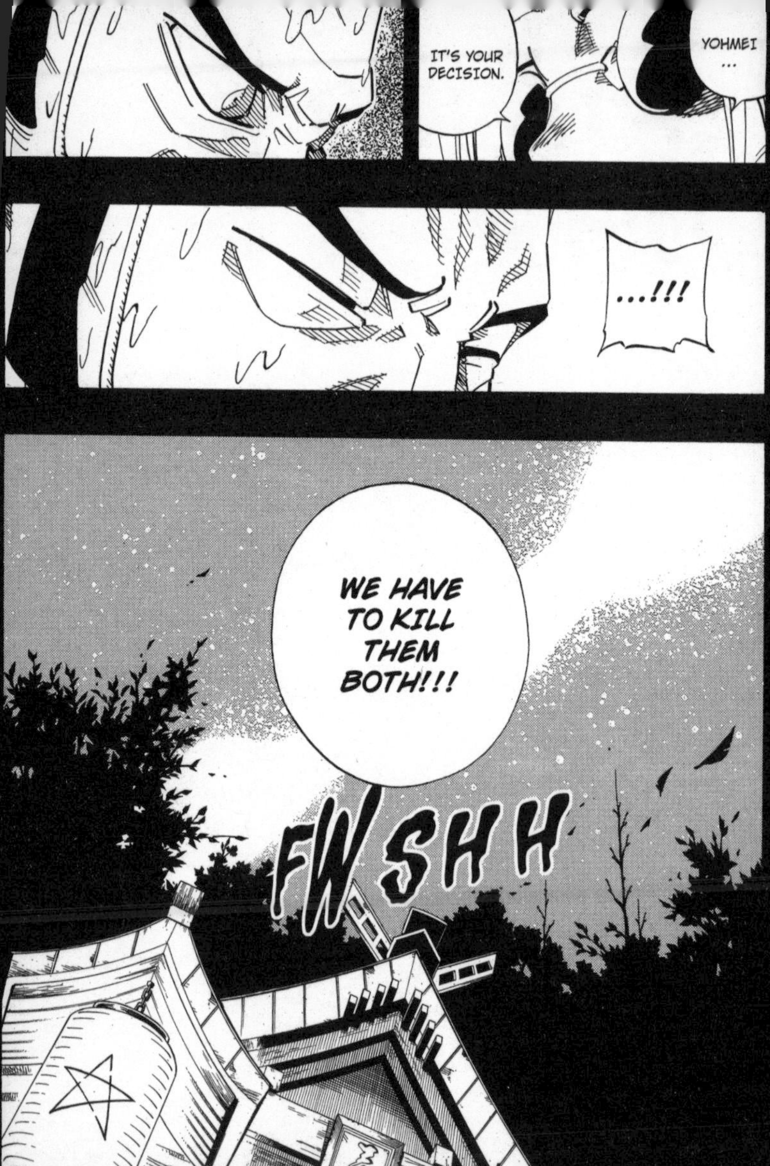
YOHMEI ...
IT'S YOUR DECISION.
...!!!
WE HAVE TO KILL THEM BOTH!!!
FWSHH

SHAMAN KING CHARACTER FILE No.84

スピリット・オブ・ファイア

1985
(MAY)

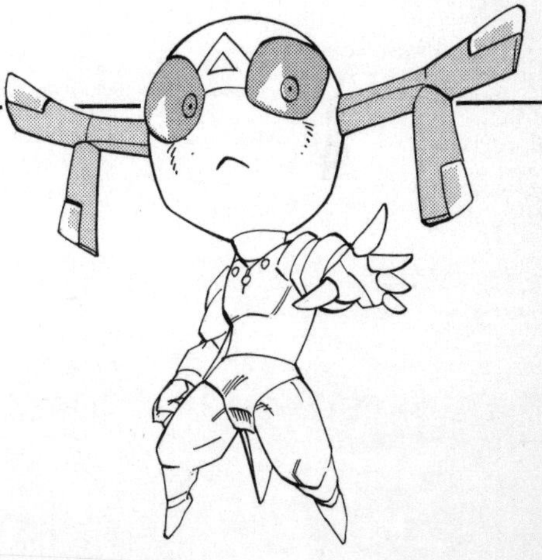

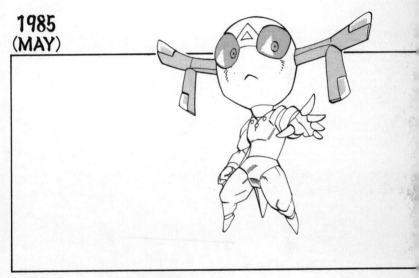

SPIRIT OF FIRE

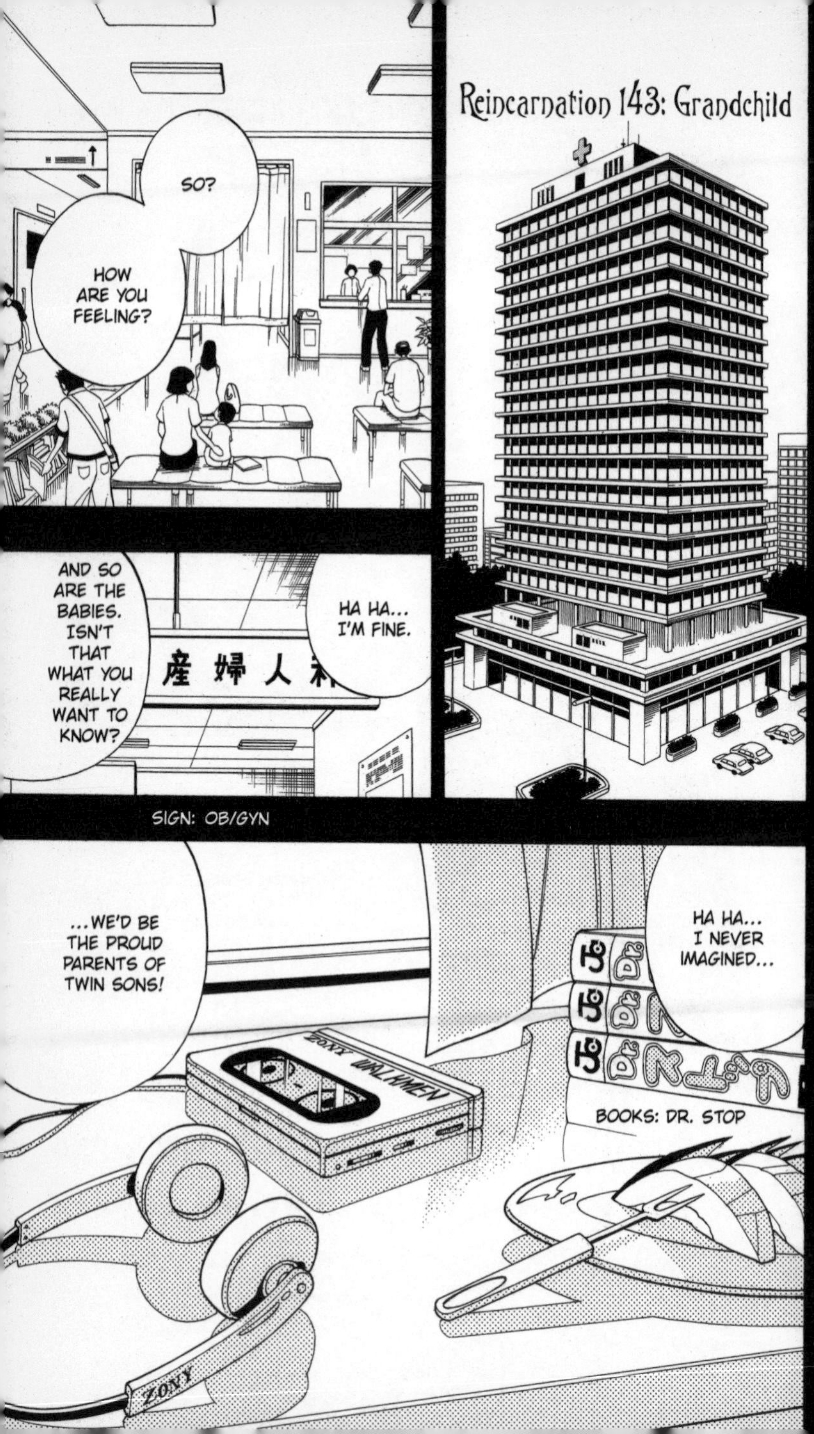
Reincarnation 143: Grandchild
SO?
HOW ARE YOU FEELING?
HA HA... I'M FINE.
AND SO ARE THE BABIES. ISN'T THAT WHAT YOU REALLY WANT TO KNOW?
SIGN: OB/GYN
HA HA... I NEVER IMAGINED...
...WE'D BE THE PROUD PARENTS OF TWIN SONS!
BOOKS: DR. STOP
ZONY WALKMEN
ZONY

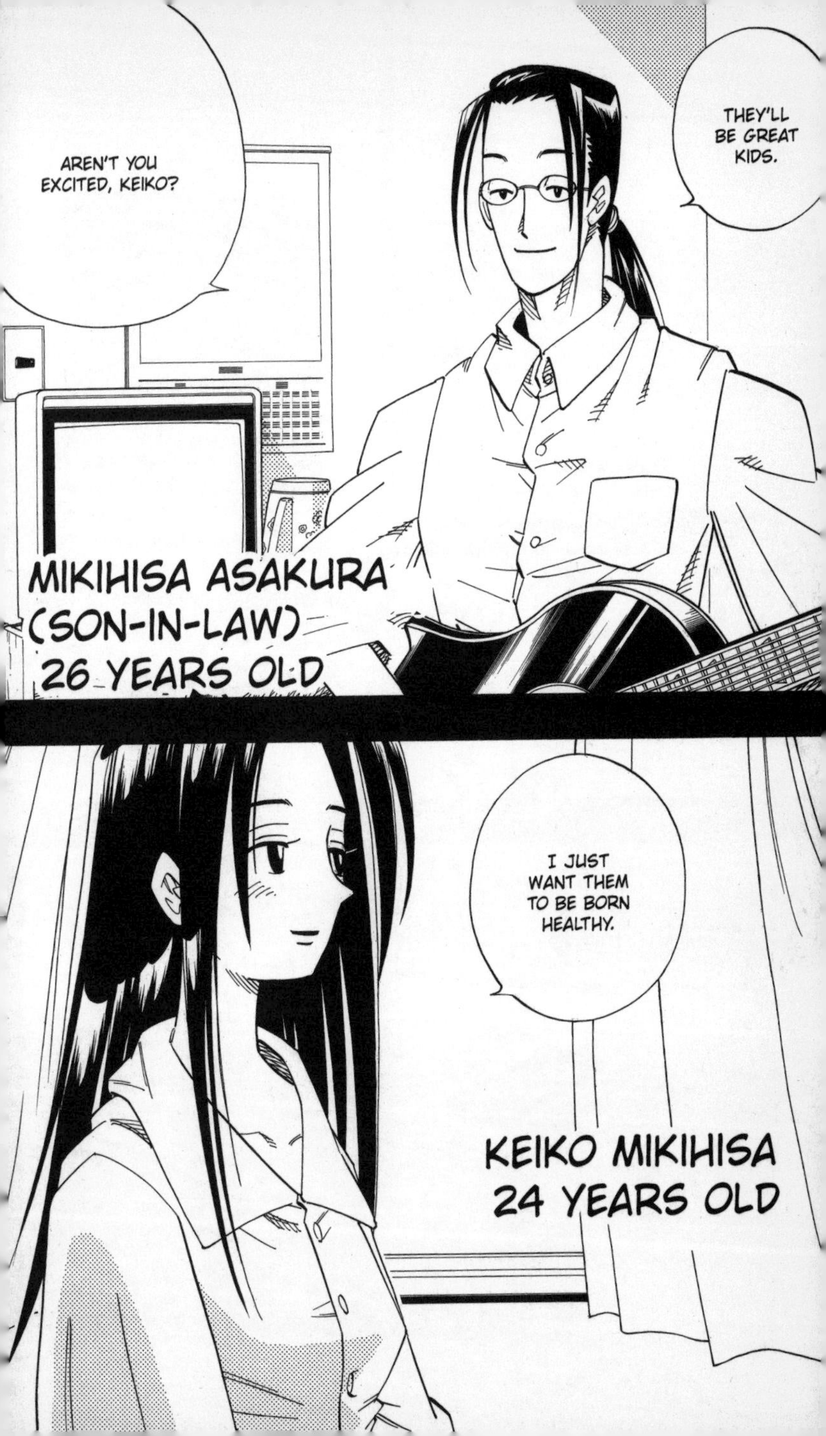
THEY'LL BE GREAT KIDS.
AREN'T YOU EXCITED, KEIKO?
MIKIHISA ASAKURA (SON-IN-LAW) 26 YEARS OLD
I JUST WANT THEM TO BE BORN HEALTHY.
KEIKO MIKIHISA 24 YEARS OLD

Reincarnation 143: Grandchild

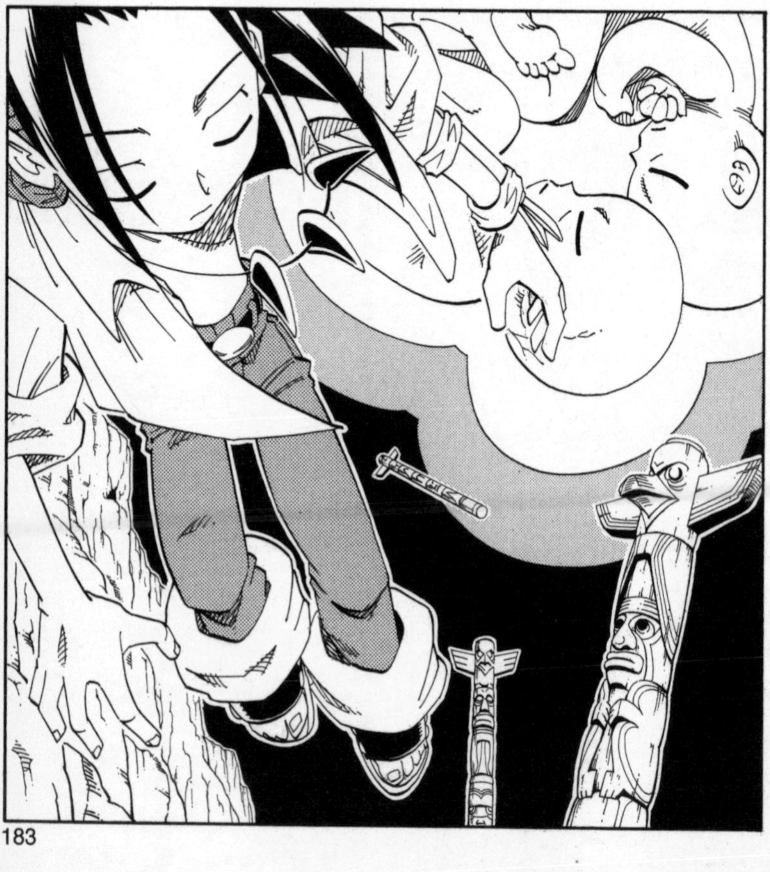

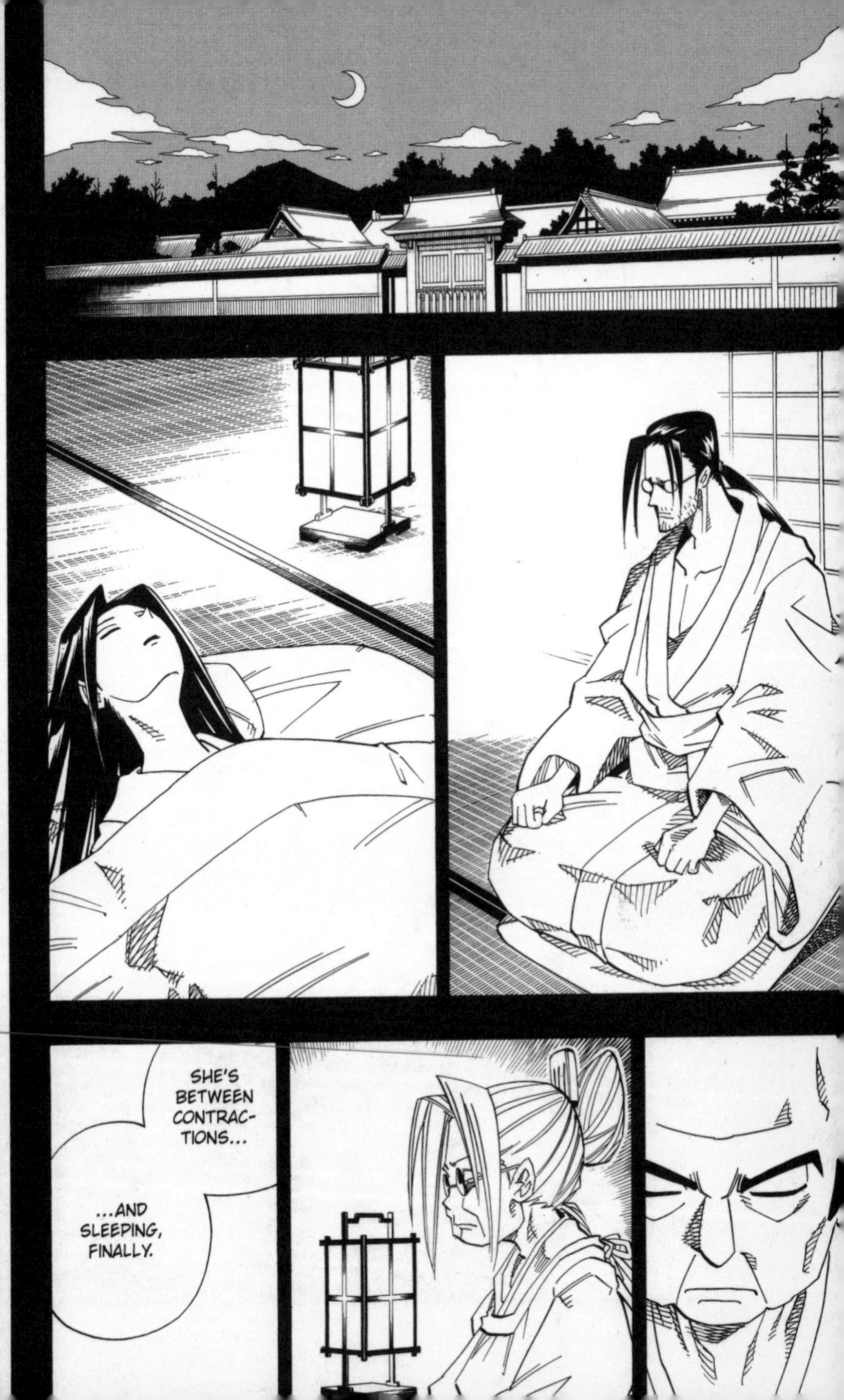
SHE'S BETWEEN CONTRAC-TIONS...
...AND SLEEPING, FINALLY.

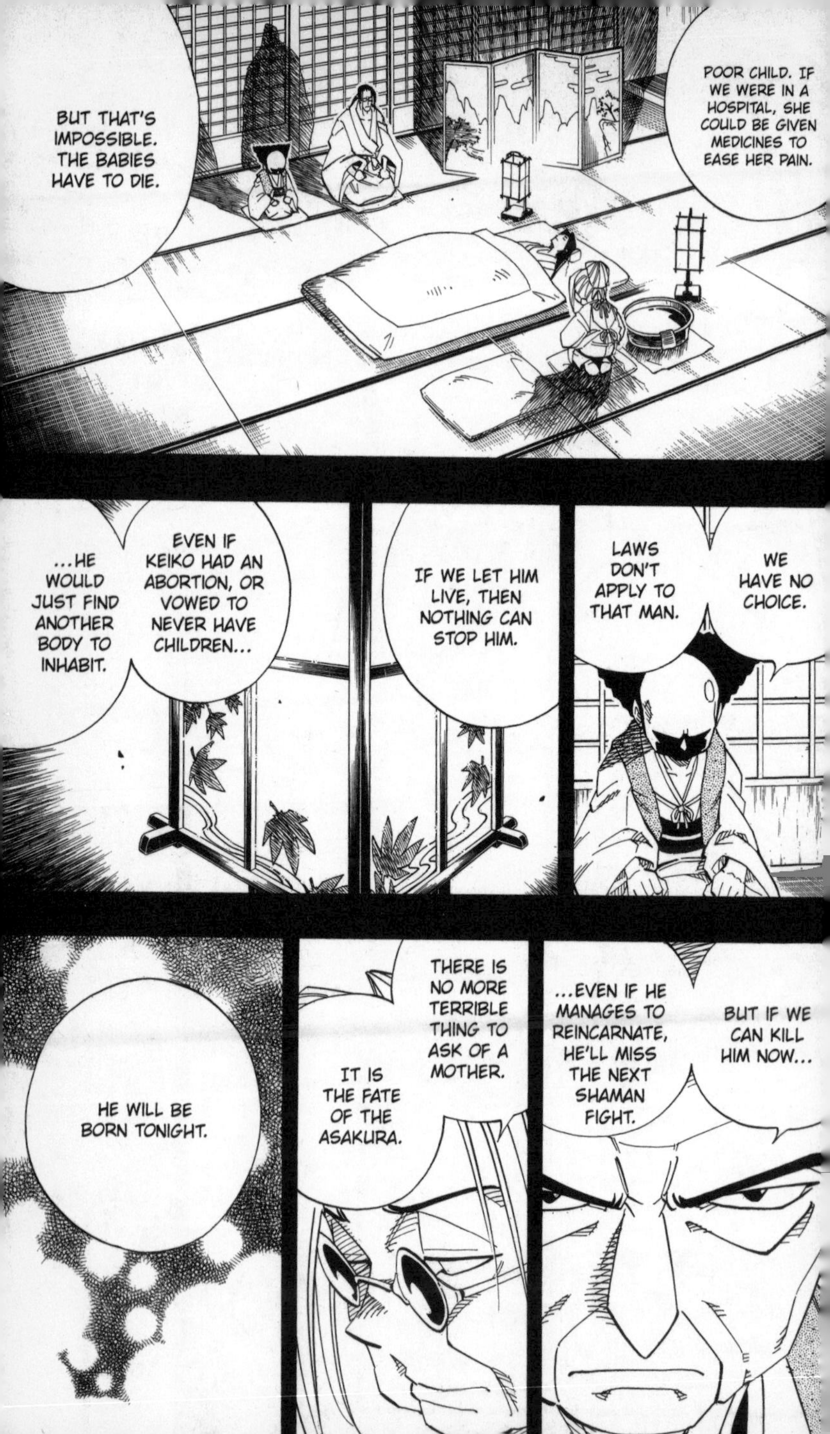
POOR CHILD. IF WE WERE IN A HOSPITAL, SHE COULD BE GIVEN MEDICINES TO EASE HER PAIN.
BUT THAT'S IMPOSSIBLE. THE BABIES HAVE TO DIE.
WE HAVE NO CHOICE.
LAWS DON'T APPLY TO THAT MAN.
IF WE LET HIM LIVE, THEN NOTHING CAN STOP HIM.
EVEN IF KEIKO HAD AN ABORTION, OR VOWED TO NEVER HAVE CHILDREN...
...HE WOULD JUST FIND ANOTHER BODY TO INHABIT.
BUT IF WE CAN KILL HIM NOW...
...EVEN IF HE MANAGES TO REINCARNATE, HE'LL MISS THE NEXT SHAMAN FIGHT.
THERE IS NO MORE TERRIBLE THING TO ASK OF A MOTHER.
IT IS THE FATE OF THE ASAKURA.
HE WILL BE BORN TONIGHT.

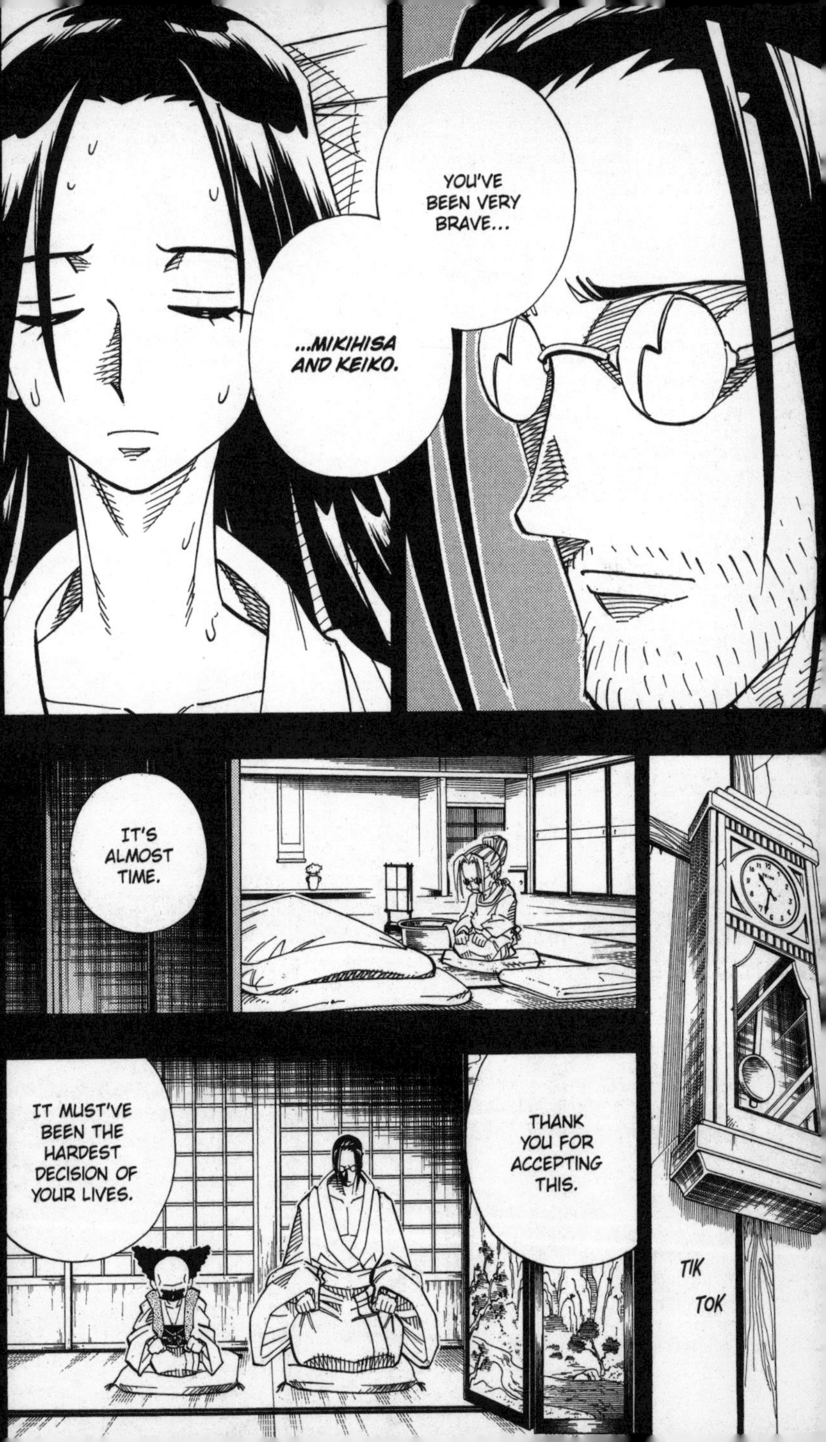
YOU'VE BEEN VERY BRAVE...
...MIKIHISA AND KEIKO.
TIK
TOK
IT'S ALMOST TIME.
THANK YOU FOR ACCEPTING THIS.
IT MUST'VE BEEN THE HARDEST DECISION OF YOUR LIVES.

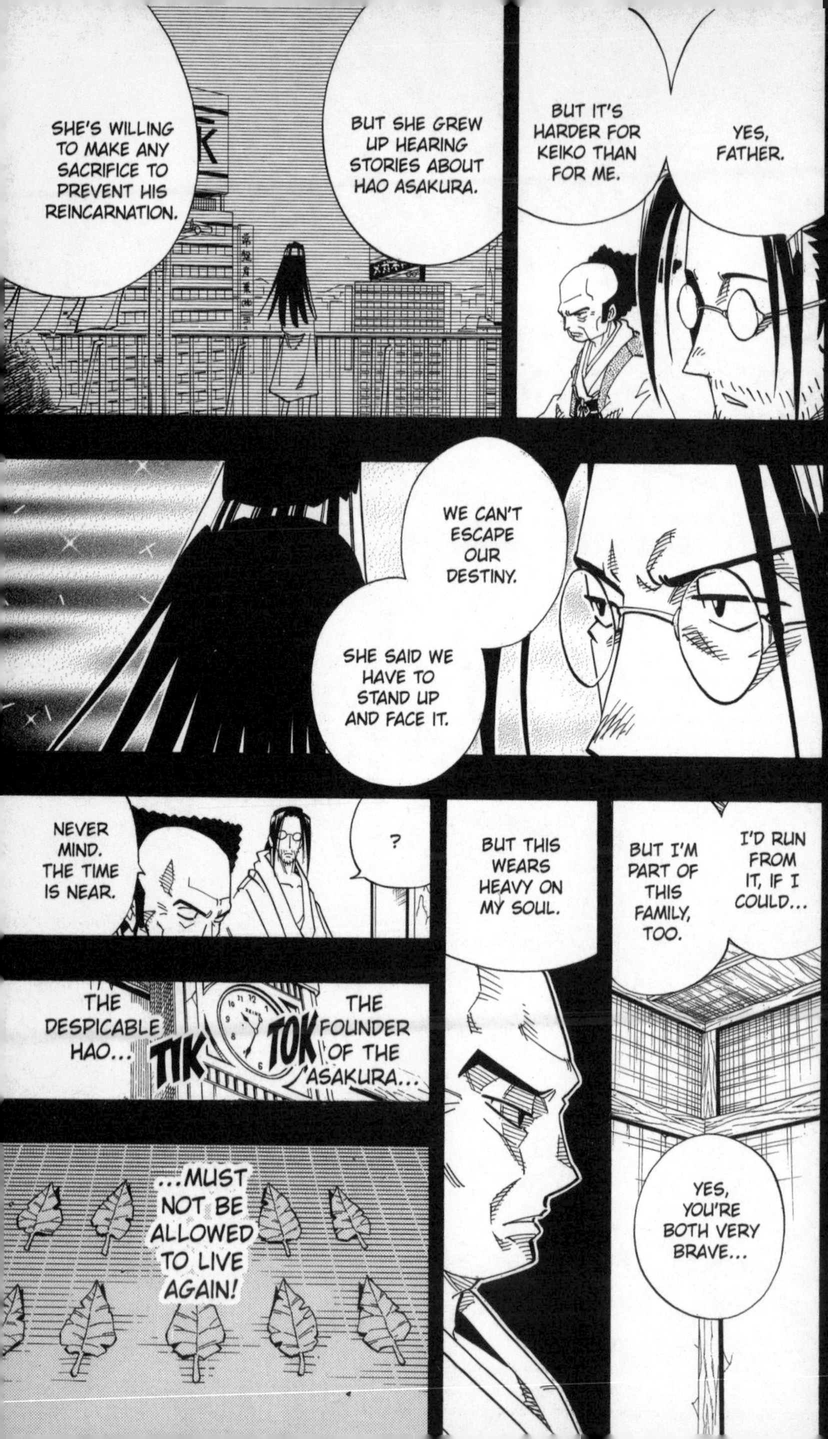
YES, FATHER.
BUT IT'S HARDER FOR KEIKO THAN FOR ME.
BUT SHE GREW UP HEARING STORIES ABOUT HAO ASAKURA.
SHE'S WILLING TO MAKE ANY SACRIFICE TO PREVENT HIS REINCARNATION.
WE CAN'T ESCAPE OUR DESTINY.
SHE SAID WE HAVE TO STAND UP AND FACE IT.
I'D RUN FROM IT, IF I COULD...
BUT I'M PART OF THIS FAMILY, TOO.
YES, YOU'RE BOTH VERY BRAVE...
BUT THIS WEARS HEAVY ON MY SOUL.
?
NEVER MIND. THE TIME IS NEAR.
THE FOUNDER OF THE ASAKURA...
TOK
TIK
THE DESPICABLE HAO...
...MUST NOT BE ALLOWED TO LIVE AGAIN!

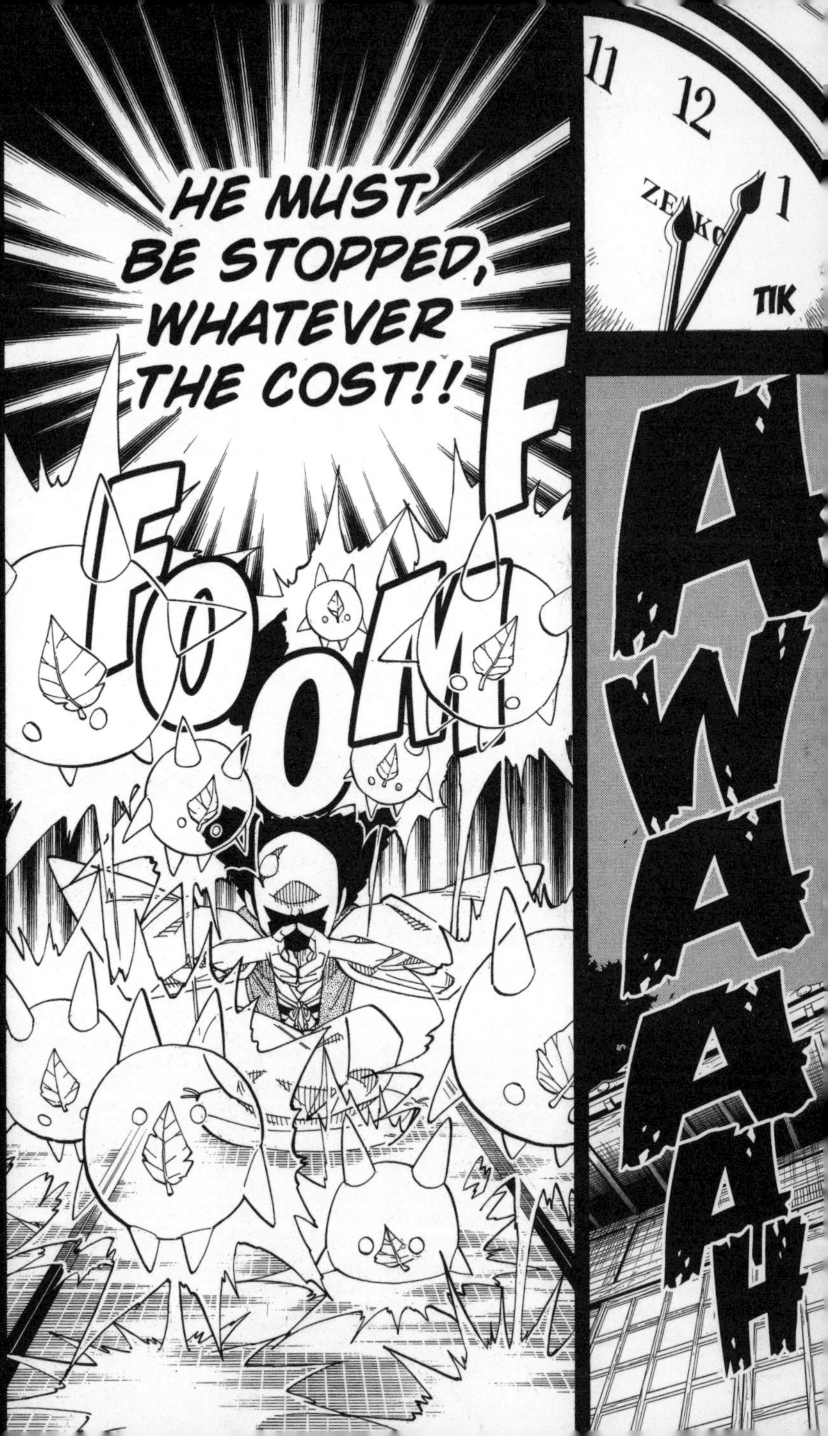
TIK
AWAAAH
HE MUST BE STOPPED, WHATEVER THE COST!!
FOOM

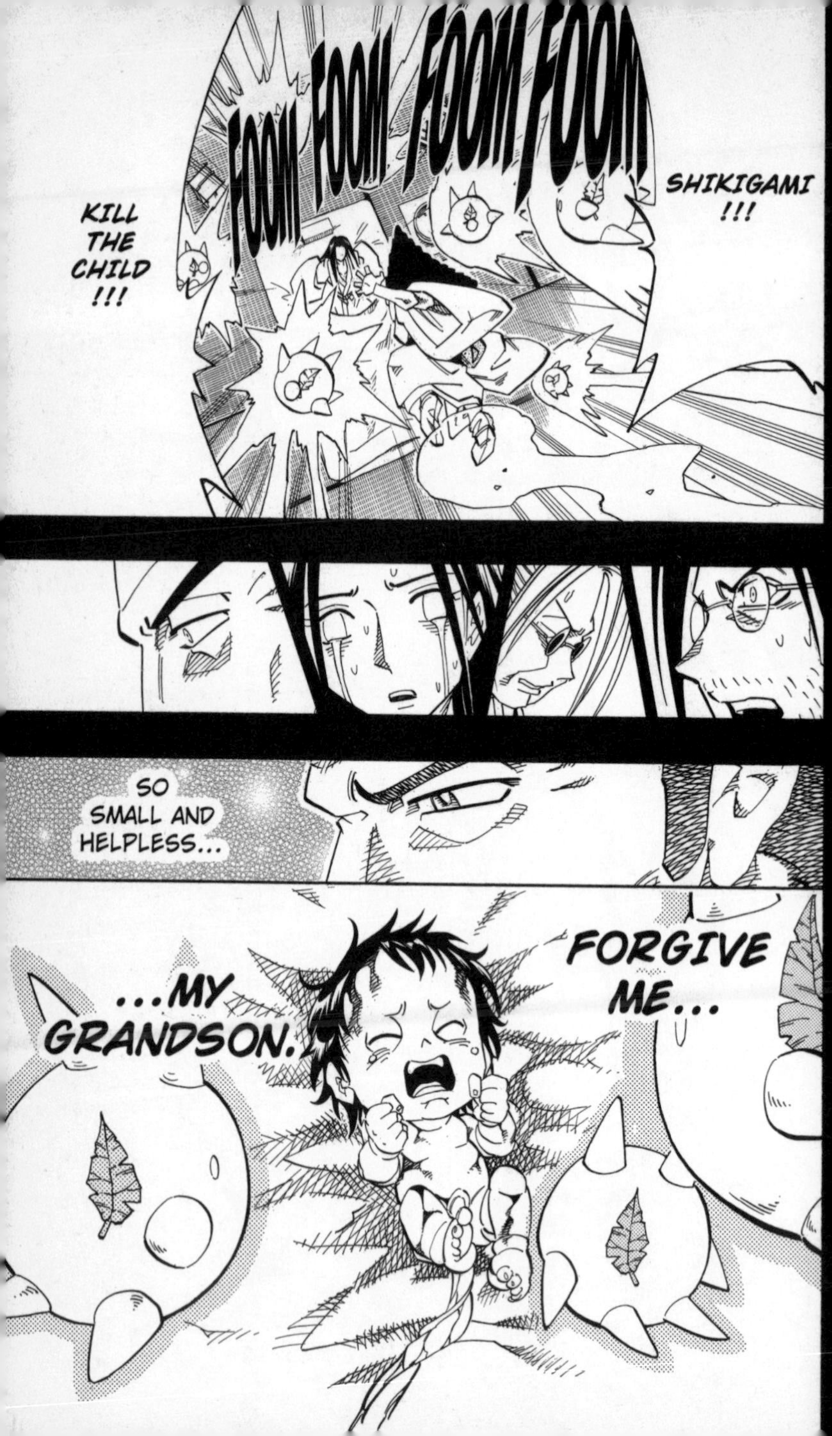
SHIKIGAMI !!!
FOOM FOOM FOOM FOOM
KILL THE CHILD !!!
SO SMALL AND HELPLESS...
FORGIVE ME...
...MY GRANDSON.

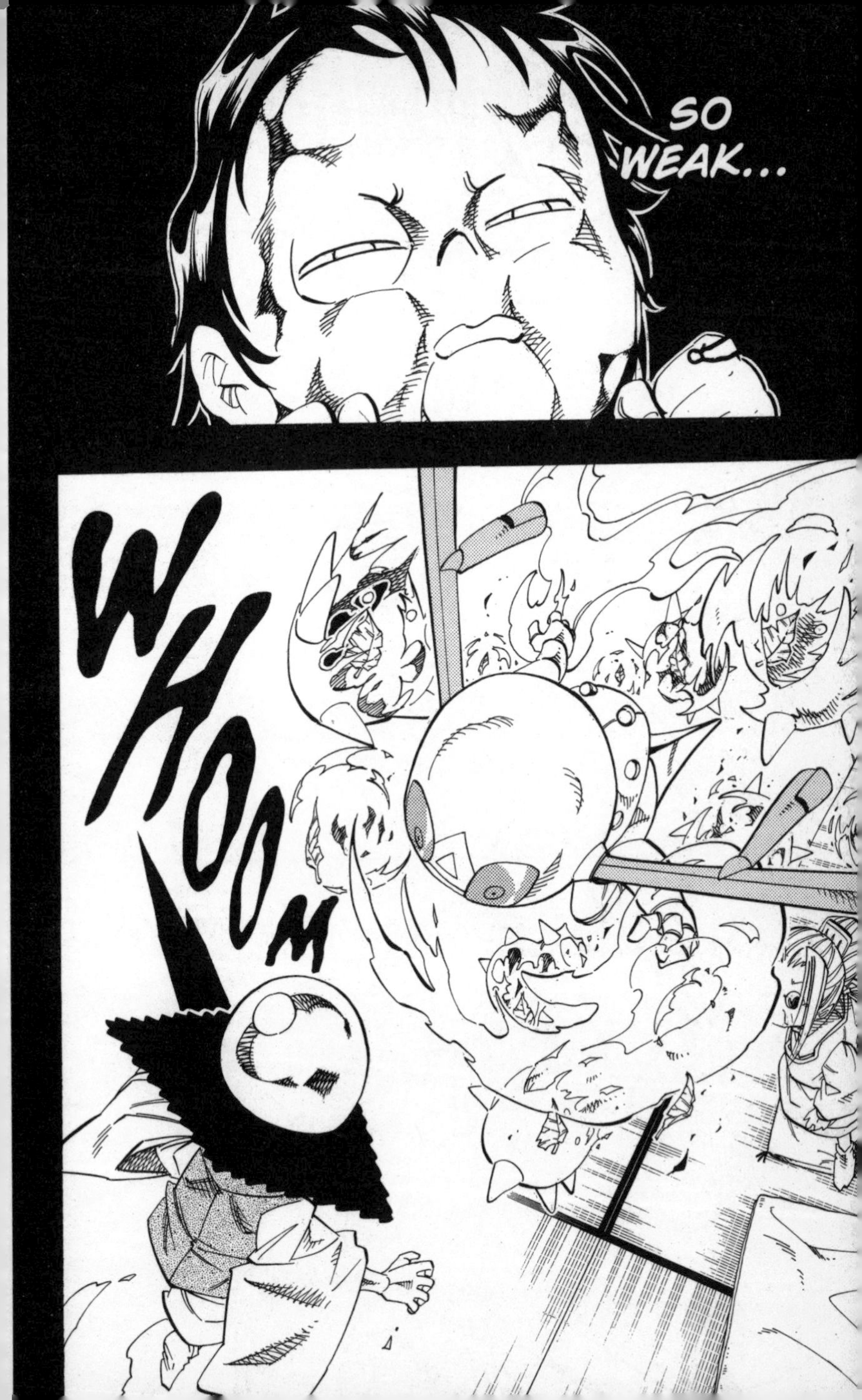
SO WEAK...
WHOOM

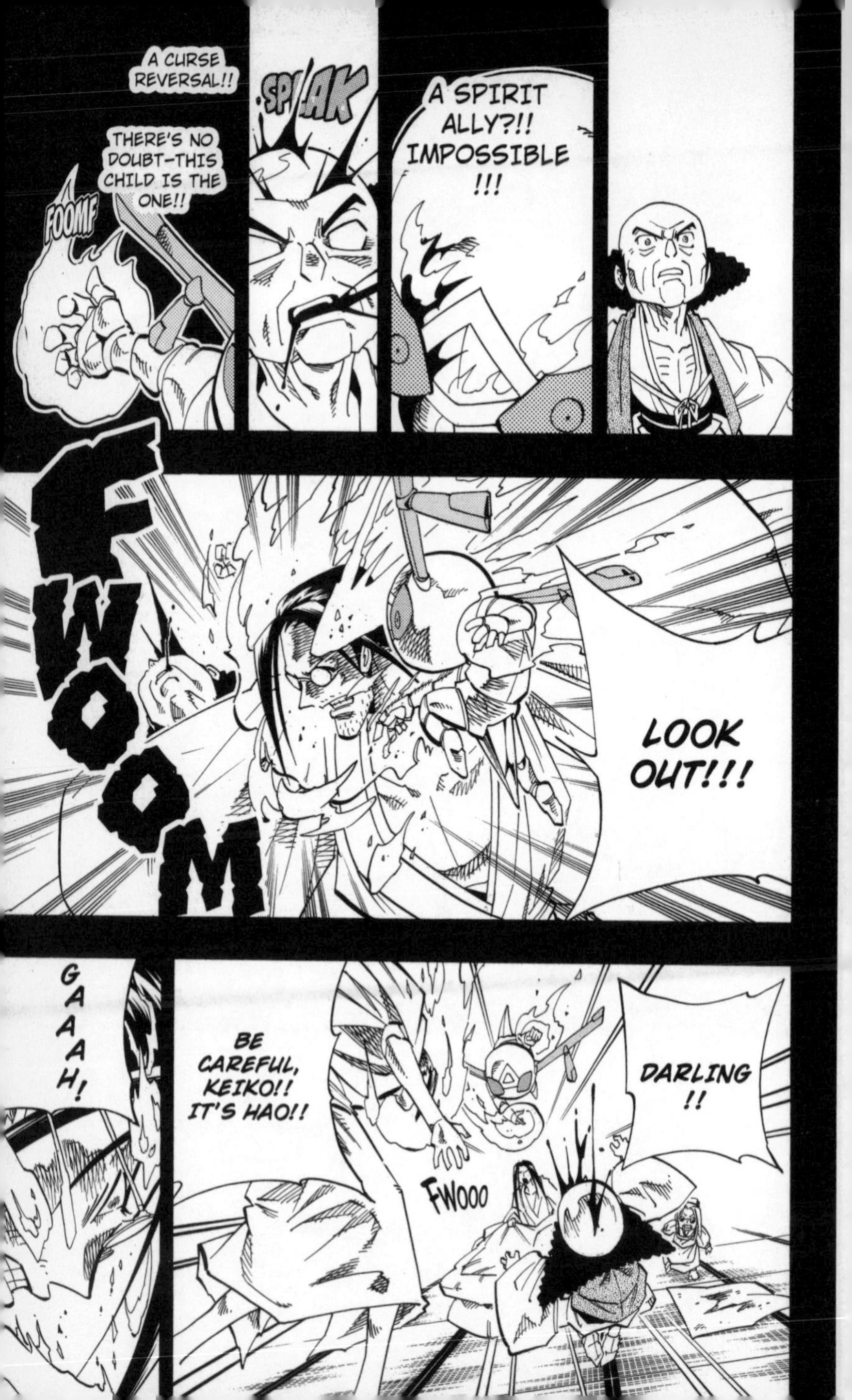
A SPIRIT ALLY?!! IMPOSSIBLE !!!
SPLAK
A CURSE REVERSAL!!
THERE'S NO DOUBT—THIS CHILD IS THE ONE!!
FOOMF
LOOK OUT!!!
FWOOM
DARLING !!
FWOOO
BE CAREFUL, KEIKO!! IT'S HAO!!
GAAAH!

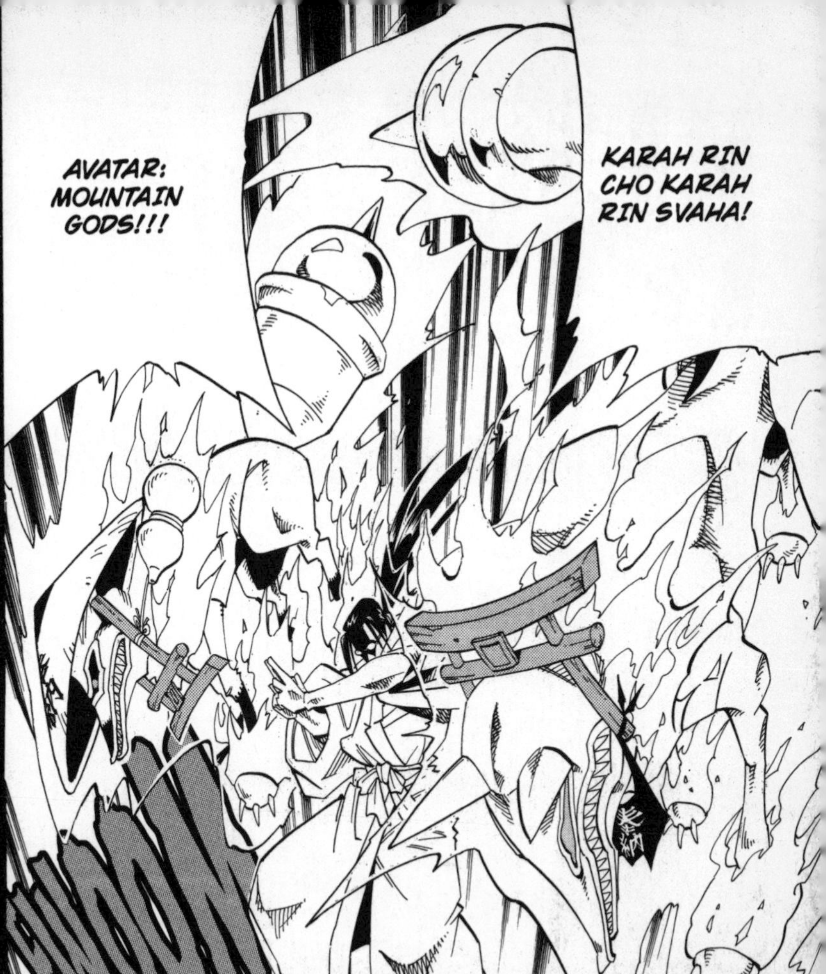
KARAH RIN CHO KARAH RIN SVAHA!
AVATAR: MOUNTAIN GODS!!!
WHOOM
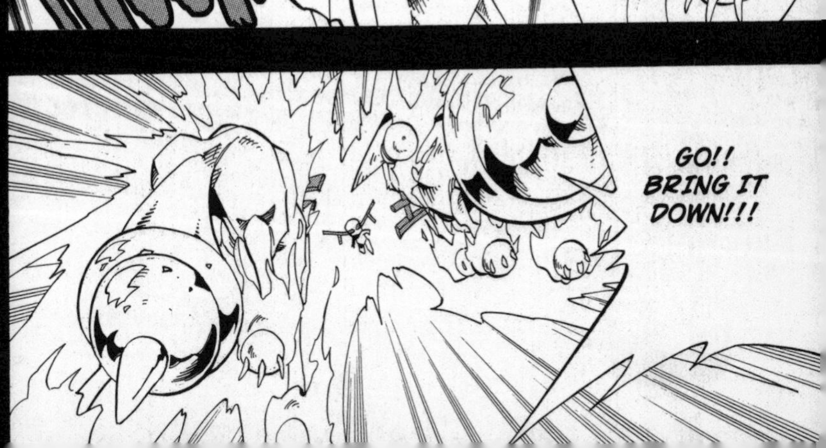
GO!! BRING IT DOWN!!!

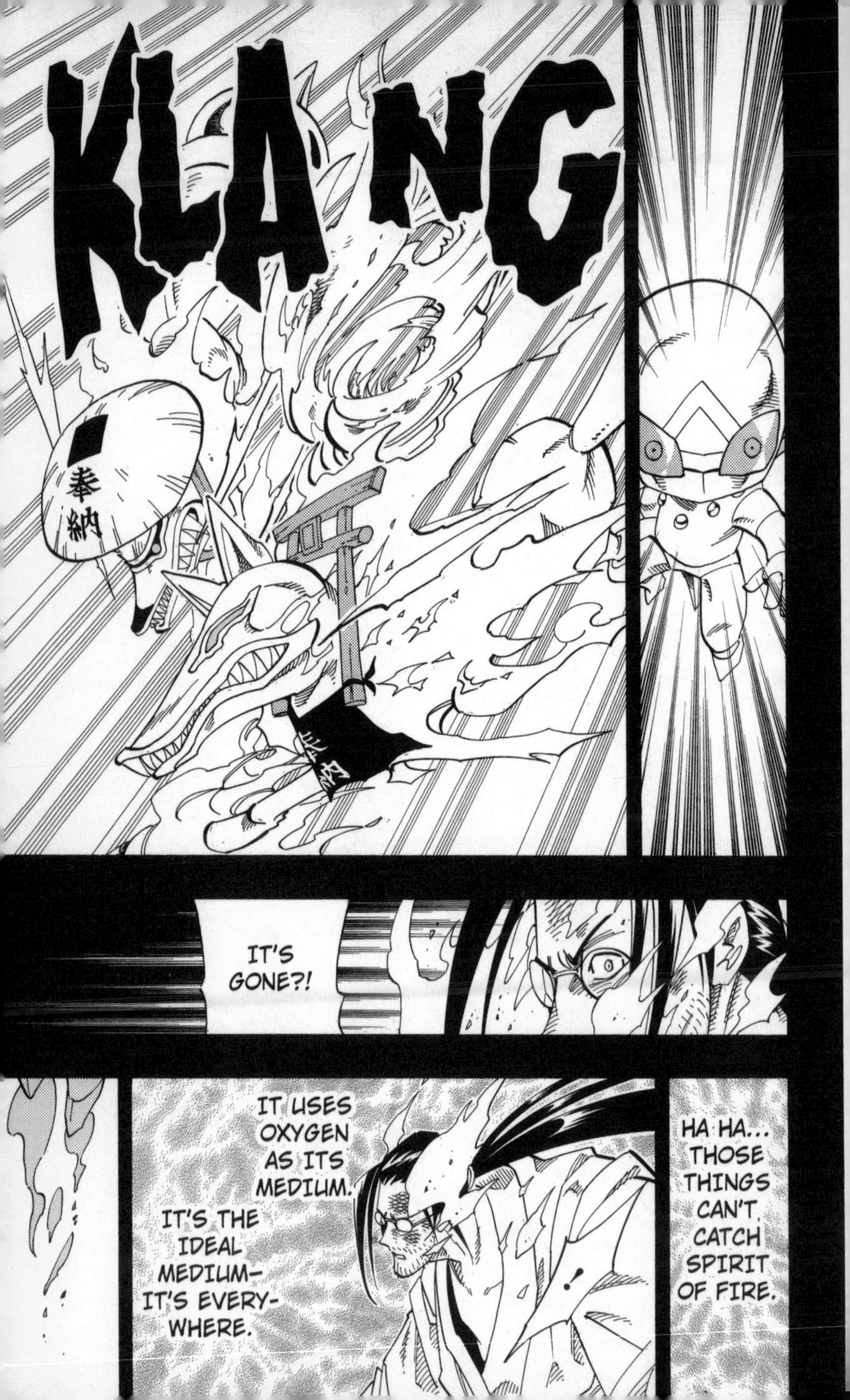
KLANG
奉納
IT'S GONE?!
HA HA... THOSE THINGS CAN'T CATCH SPIRIT OF FIRE.
IT USES OXYGEN AS ITS MEDIUM.
IT'S THE IDEAL MEDIUM— IT'S EVERY-WHERE.

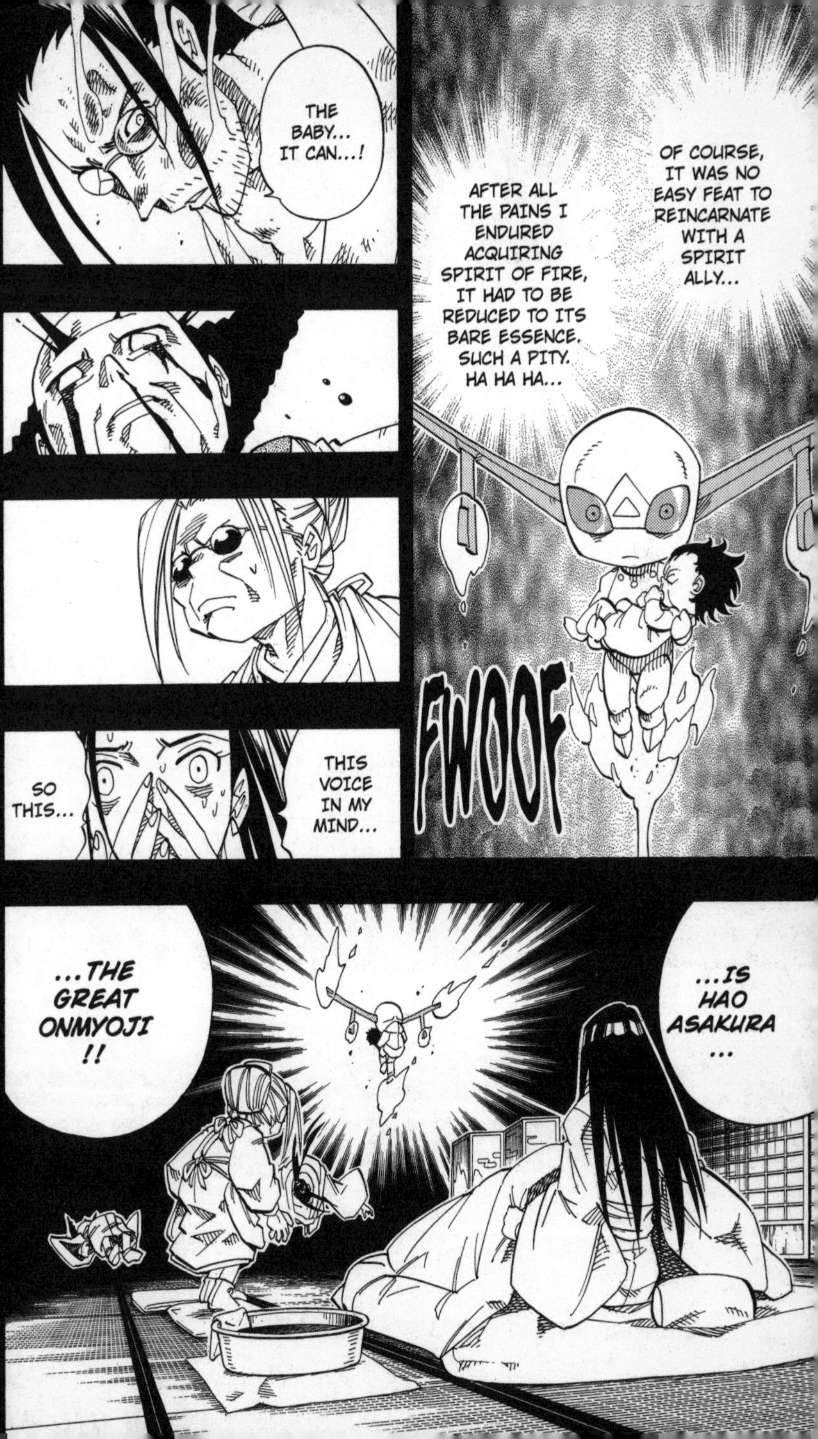
OF COURSE, IT WAS NO EASY FEAT TO REINCARNATE WITH A SPIRIT ALLY...
AFTER ALL THE PAINS I ENDURED ACQUIRING SPIRIT OF FIRE, IT HAD TO BE REDUCED TO ITS BARE ESSENCE. SUCH A PITY. HA HA HA...
FWOOF
THE BABY... IT CAN...!
THIS VOICE IN MY MIND...
SO THIS...
...IS HAO ASAKURA...
...THE GREAT ONMYOJI!!

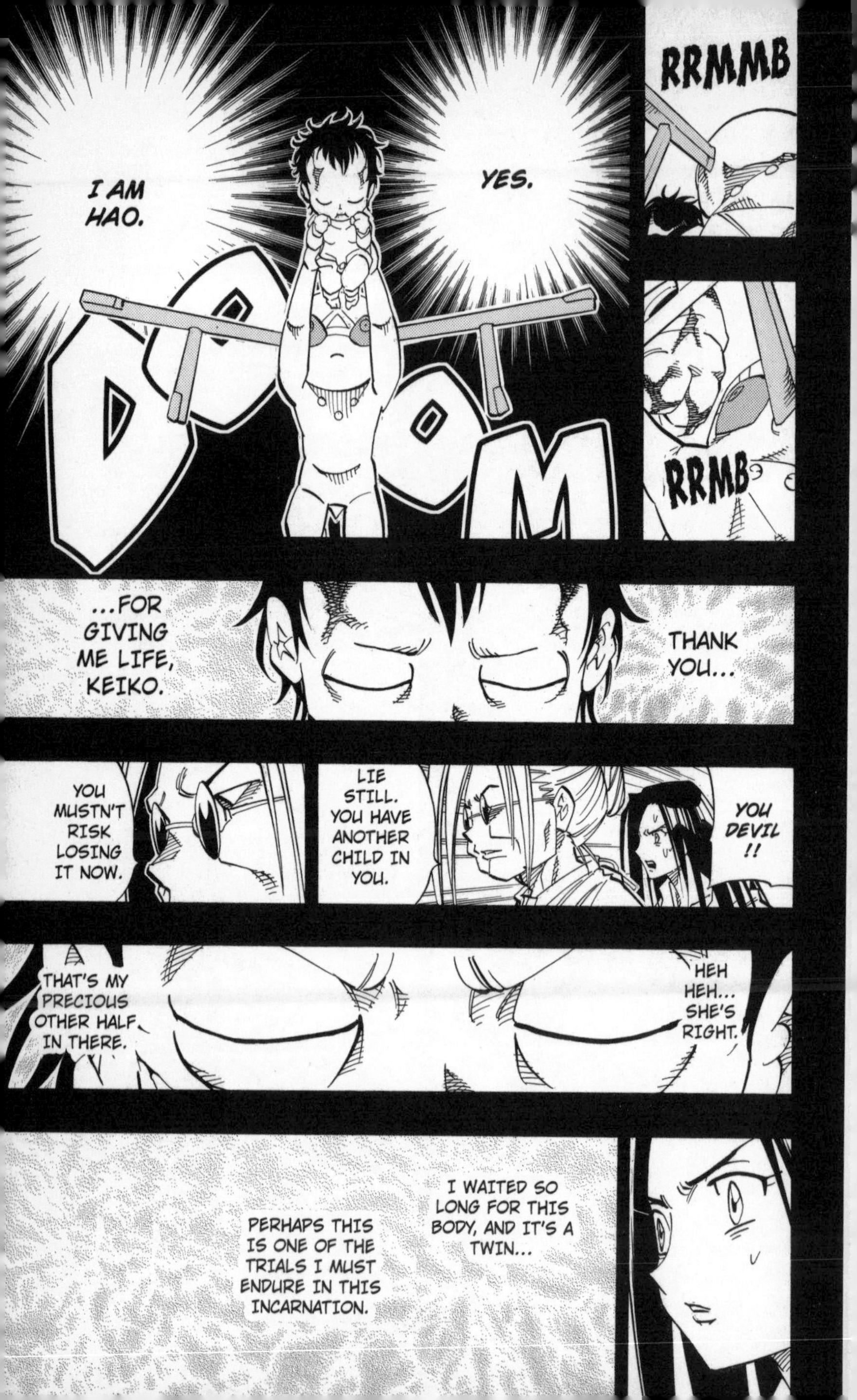
RRMMB
RRMB
YES.
I AM HAO.
DOOM
THANK YOU...
...FOR GIVING ME LIFE, KEIKO.
YOU DEVIL!!
LIE STILL. YOU HAVE ANOTHER CHILD IN YOU.
YOU MUSTN'T RISK LOSING IT NOW.
HEH HEH... SHE'S RIGHT.
THAT'S MY PRECIOUS OTHER HALF IN THERE.
I WAITED SO LONG FOR THIS BODY, AND IT'S A TWIN...
PERHAPS THIS IS ONE OF THE TRIALS I MUST ENDURE IN THIS INCARNATION.

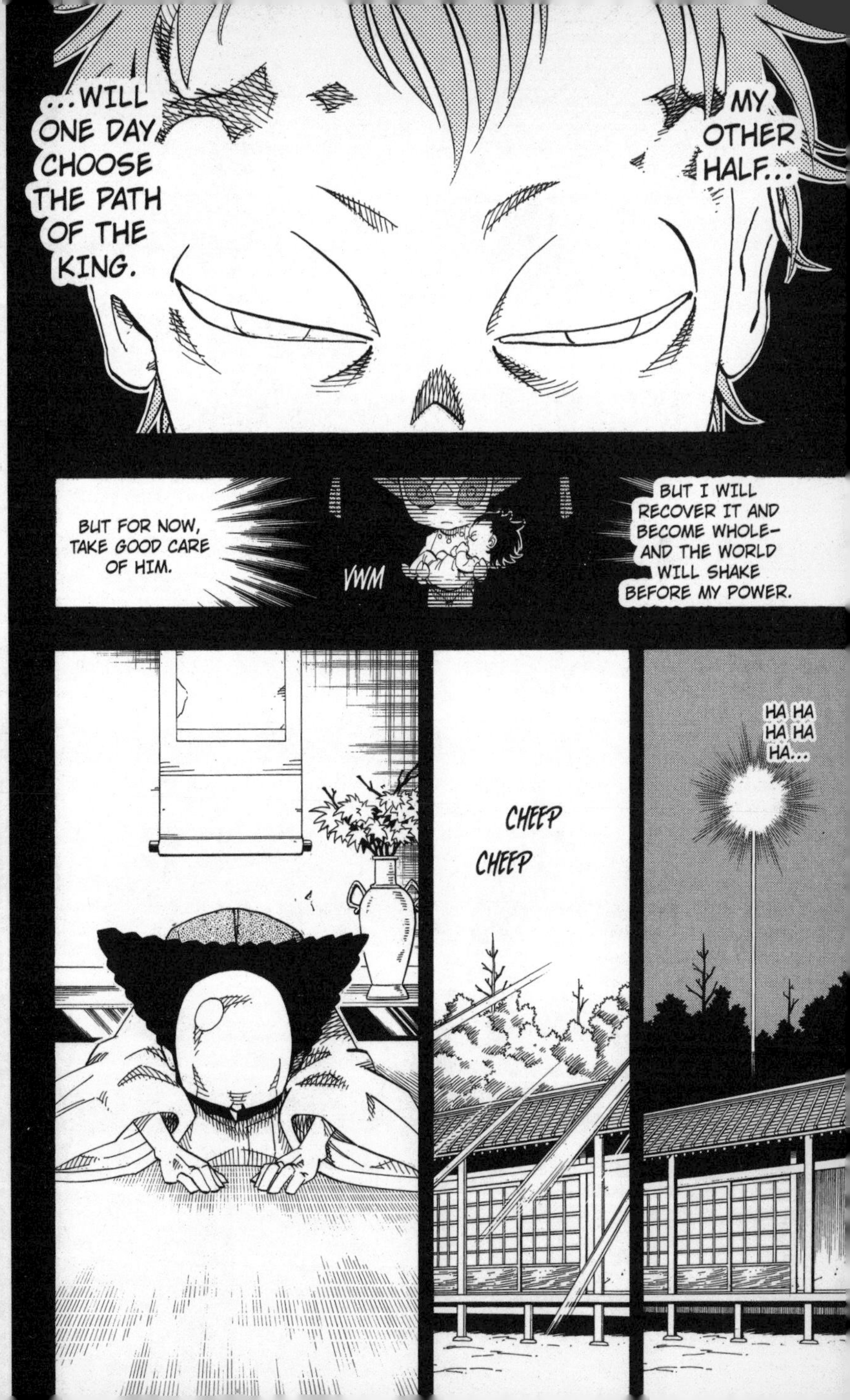
MY OTHER HALF...
...WILL ONE DAY CHOOSE THE PATH OF THE KING.
BUT I WILL RECOVER IT AND BECOME WHOLE- AND THE WORLD WILL SHAKE BEFORE MY POWER.
VWM
BUT FOR NOW, TAKE GOOD CARE OF HIM.
HA HA HA HA HA...
CHEEP
CHEEP

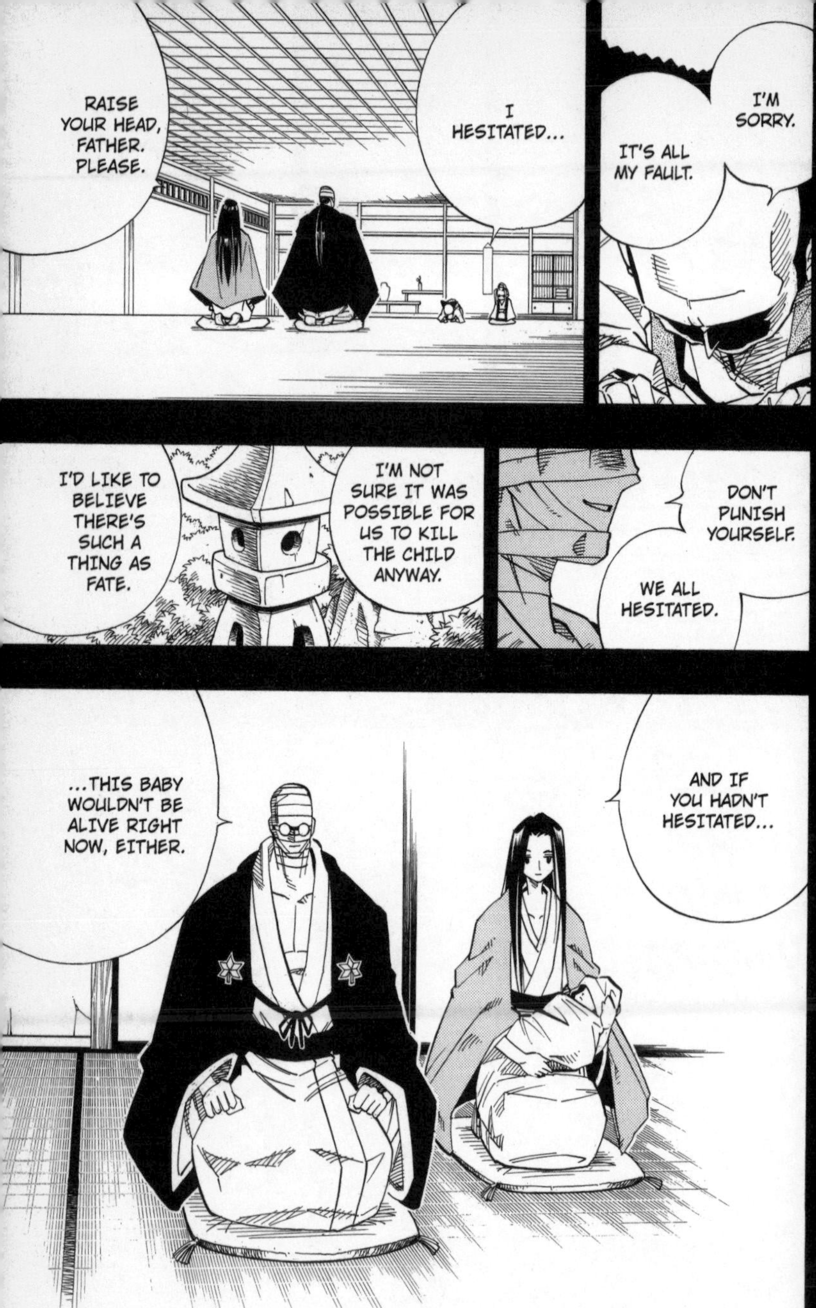
I'M SORRY.
IT'S ALL MY FAULT.
I HESITATED...
RAISE YOUR HEAD, FATHER. PLEASE.
DON'T PUNISH YOURSELF.
WE ALL HESITATED.
I'M NOT SURE IT WAS POSSIBLE FOR US TO KILL THE CHILD ANYWAY.
I'D LIKE TO BELIEVE THERE'S SUCH A THING AS FATE.
AND IF YOU HADN'T HESITATED...
...THIS BABY WOULDN'T BE ALIVE RIGHT NOW, EITHER.

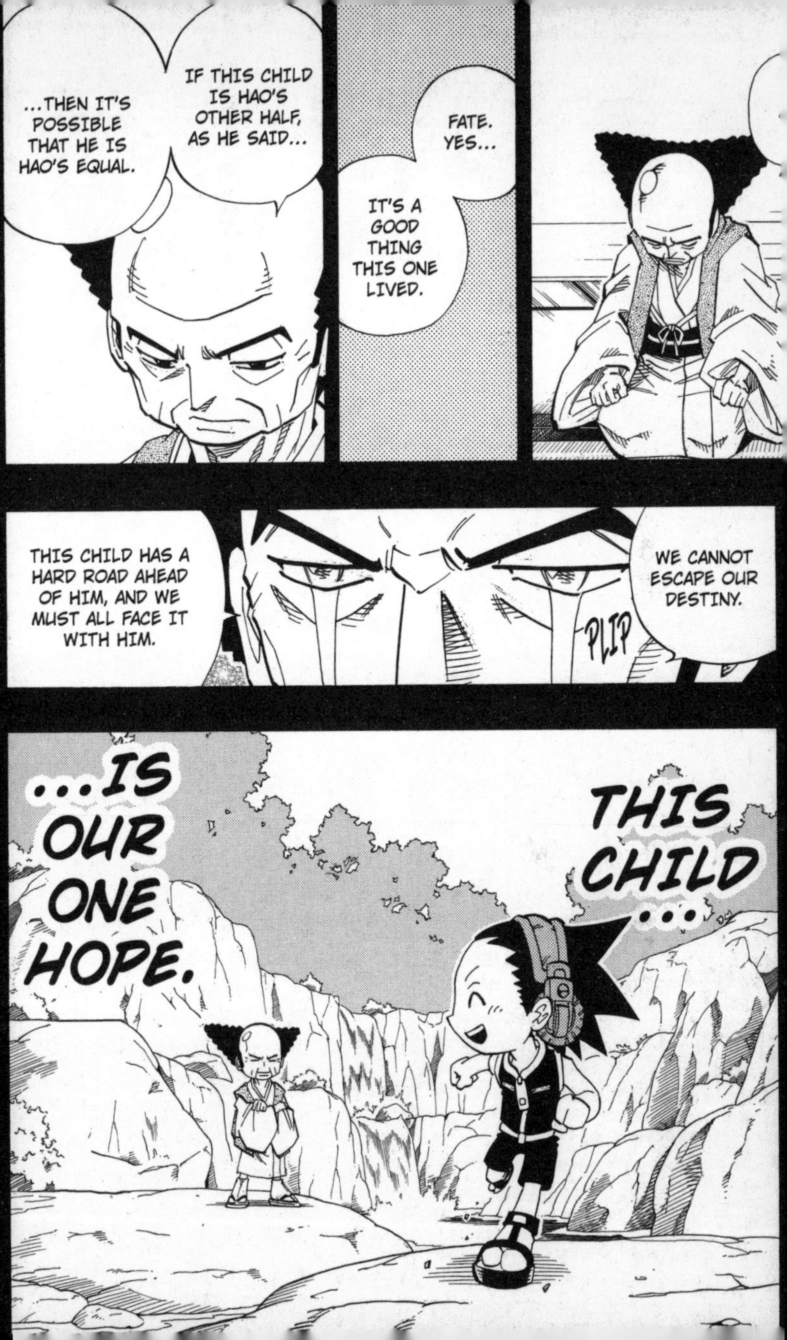
FATE. YES...
IT'S A GOOD THING THIS ONE LIVED.
IF THIS CHILD IS HAO'S OTHER HALF, AS HE SAID...
...THEN IT'S POSSIBLE THAT HE IS HAO'S EQUAL.
WE CANNOT ESCAPE OUR DESTINY.
PLIP
THIS CHILD HAS A HARD ROAD AHEAD OF HIM, AND WE MUST ALL FACE IT WITH HIM.
THIS CHILD...
...IS OUR ONE HOPE.

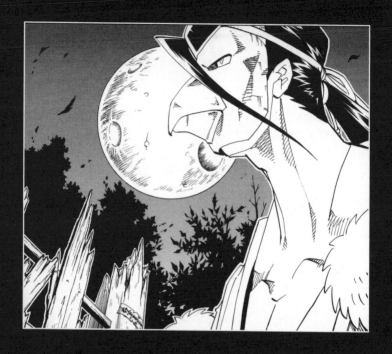

IN THE NEXT VOLUME...

Hao possesses so much mana that it virtually guarantees his victory in the Shaman Fight. So how in the world can Yoh and his friends beat him?! Mikihisa offers to teach Ren the Ultra-Senji Ryakketsu, but is Ren too stubborn to accept his help? If Hao's power doesn't destroy our heroes, perhaps pride will...

AVAILABLE JULY 2008!

SHAMAN KING VOL. 16
The SHONEN JUMP Manga Edition

STORY AND ART BY
HIROYUKI TAKEI

English Adaptation/Lance Caselman
Translation/Lillian Olsen
Touch-up Art & Lettering/John Hunt
Additional Lettering/Josh Simpson
Cover Design/Sean Lee
Interior Design/Nozomi Akashi
Editor/Carol Fox

Editor in Chief, Books/Alvin Lu
Editor in Chief, Magazines/Marc Weidenbaum
VP of Publishing Licensing/Rika Inouye
VP of Sales/Gonzalo Ferreyra
Sr. VP of Marketing/Liza Coppola
Publisher/Hyoe Narita

Printed in the U.S.A.

Published by VIZ Media, LLC
P.O. Box 77010
San Francisco, CA 94107

SHONEN JUMP Manga Edition
10 9 8 7 6 5 4 3 2 1
First printing, May 2008

T 252531

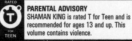

PARENTAL ADVISORY
SHAMAN KING is rated T for Teen and is
recommended for ages 13 and up. This
volume contains violence.
ratings.viz.com

THE WORLD'S
MOST POPULAR MANGA
www.shonenjump.com

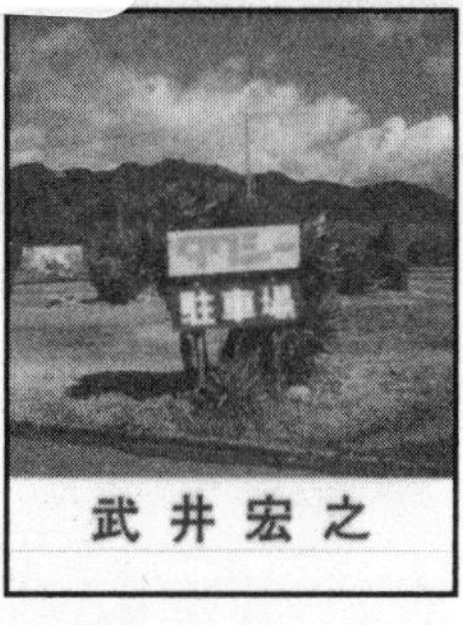
駐車場

武井宏之

I'm changing the cover design starting with this volume. The previous cover was so bright that I just couldn't turn back. It's kind of like inflation that way. I'm sorry I always talk about trivial stuff in this space. Please forgive me.

—Hiroyuki Takei

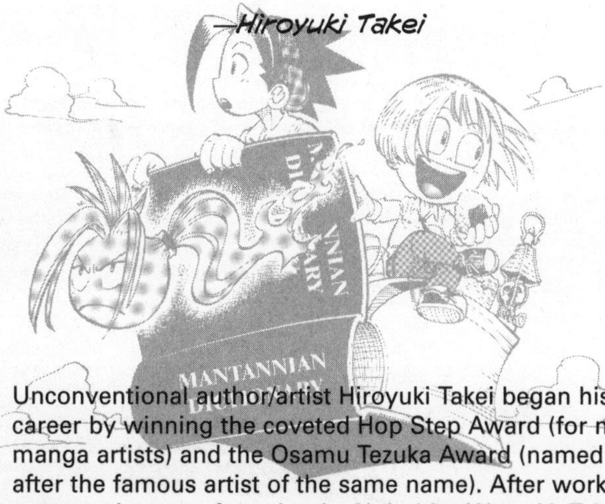
MANTANNIAN

Unconventional author/artist Hiroyuki Takei began his career by winning the coveted Hop Step Award (for new manga artists) and the Osamu Tezuka Award (named after the famous artist of the same name). After working as an assistant to famed artist Nobuhiro Watsuki, Takei debuted in **Weekly Shonen Jump** in 1997 with **Butsu Zone**, an action series based on Buddhist mythology. His multicultural adventure manga **Shaman King**, which debuted in 1998, became a hit and was adapted into an anime TV series. Takei lists Osamu Tezuka, American comics and robot anime among his many influences.